£7.25

EPEN

AF765925

NOT FOR LOAN BEFORE 16 JUL 1975

UNIVERSITY OF BRISTOL
LIBRARY

Staff and Research Students	Other Borrowers
Date Borrowed	Date due back
~~-5 DEC 1975~~	~~20 NOV 1975~~
~~-3. SEP. 1981~~	~~27. NOV. 1975~~

WITHDRAWN
University of Bristol

Public Utilities

Public Utilities: Regulation, Management, and Ownership

Martin T. Farris
Arizona State University

Roy J. Sampson
University of Oregon

Houghton Mifflin Company · Boston
Atlanta   Dallas   Geneva, Illinois   Hopewell, New Jersey   Palo Alto

Photo Credits

Part I M. Massachi. Stock, Boston
Part II Bonnie I. Hammer
Part III T. A. Rothschild. Stock, Boston
Part IV Peter Travers
Part V W. B. Finch

UNIVERSITY OF BRISTOL LIBRARY
W.M.L.
WITHDRAWN
University of Bristol

Copyright © 1973 by Houghton Mifflin Company. All rights reserved. No part of this work may be reproduced or transmitted in any form or by any means, electronic, or mechanical, including photocopying and recording, or by any information storage or retrieval system, without permission in writing from the publisher.

Printed in the U.S.A.

Library of Congress Catalog Card Number: 72-85908

ISBN: 0-395-13884-1

Preface

A number of excellent books in past years have dealt with the application of economic theory to public utility problems. Some have emphasized, almost to the exclusion of all else, practices and problems of utility regulation or public ownership. Some texts have combined these approaches. We feel, however, despite their scholarly qualities, that none of these past treatments are completely satisfactory for an introductory course for present-day business administration or economics students, and perhaps they are even less satisfactory for students in other disciplines (engineering, law, arts and sciences, etc.) who eventually may be employed by a privately or publicly owned utility, or by a regulatory agency.

Many students have not advanced beyond elementary economics when they take a utilities course, and some may lack economics entirely. Too much emphasis on an extremely rigorous level of theoretical analysis, therefore, may discourage some capable students. Further, regulation and public ownership, while they are important, are not the only topics worthy of consideration in a utilities course.

Although most large and medium-sized universities and colleges, and many smaller institutions, offer at least one utilities course, recent enrollments have not kept pace with increases in many other economics and business subjects. Our observations and conversations with students and other instructors lead us to believe that the lack of popularity of public utilities courses during recent years may be partially attributable to the lack of suitable textbooks—without which even excellent instructors are hampered and excellent students are frustrated.

Certainly the public utility industry itself is not declining in importance. Instead, as we reach higher and higher levels of production and standards of living, electrical and gas energy, communications, water supplies, and efficient local transport assume even greater importance, and supplying these services at the lowest possible economic, ecological, and sociological costs provides even greater challenges. By any economic criteria—investment, output, employment—the provision of utility services is expanding, with corresponding opportunities for young people with almost every type of background and interest.

With these considerations in mind, we undertook this textbook. Although most university students currently taking utilities courses are business or economics majors, we have attempted to make our treatment suitable for instructing college students of all majors. Also, we hope the book will be useful to present employees in the utilities industries or regulatory agencies, either for self-study or in more formal training programs.

We have not diluted quality, but we have recognized that many beginners in utility courses or employment actually have only a rudimentary knowledge of business and a smattering of economics. We hope that the presentation of public utilities instruction in this format will make it more attractive to students and practitioners of all backgrounds. In addition, we hope that this approach may promote an understanding of private and governmental problems and policies in one of our most important and controversial areas of economic endeavor, and that it may lead some into further study of these matters.

Part One of this textbook establishes the nature, background, and significance of public utilities in our economy. Part Two continues with a discussion of public regulation of the private utilities sector. This includes the legal basis for and restrictions upon, federal, state, and local regulatory authorities, as well as the historical development and present status of the most important regulatory areas and techniques.

Several general and specific management problems and policies of privately owned utilities are discussed in Part Three. We consider some knowledge of the management area, as affected by the peculiar institutional environment within which private utilities function, to be particularly desirable for those considering utility employment or any other business or governmental position. Most previous introductory utility texts for university students have ignored this area or have treated it only incidentally.

Part Four considers the extent, policies, and problems of public ownership of utilities at the federal, state and local levels. Finally, Part Five includes some observations on utility problems and the prospects for future utility growth and change in our environment-conscious and service-oriented world.

Each chapter is followed by a very specific bibliography, and documentation is designed for actual use. While our references are not exhaustive and vary in nature depending upon the topics being treated, they have been selected carefully for both suitability and availability. We believe that our documentation and bibliographical method is useful to students, and that it provides considerable flexibility for instructors to make outside assignments. Ideally, it may even encourage that dream of all instructors, non-assigned outside reading by students!

In conclusion, this book is an equal and joint endeavor in conception and execution. There is no junior or senior author. Our text has grown out of many conversations and much correspondence over a long period of time. It is based upon material and teaching approaches developed in our own classes over a combined total of almost forty teaching years. Each of us has added, deleted, revised, and experimented as our individual and joint experiences dictated. We do wish, however, to acknowledge our indebtedness to many present and past scholars, authors, teachers, regulators, and management practitioners in both private and publicly owned utilities, as well as our gratitude to our former students who have been guinea pigs for the evolution of this text. We particularly thank Professors James R. Nelson, Amherst College, and Harry M. Trebing, Michigan State University, for their helpful comments. The errors of omission or commission, of course, are ours.

Martin T. Farris
Department of Economics
Arizona State University

Roy J. Sampson
College of Business Administration
University of Oregon

Contents

Part One

Introduction

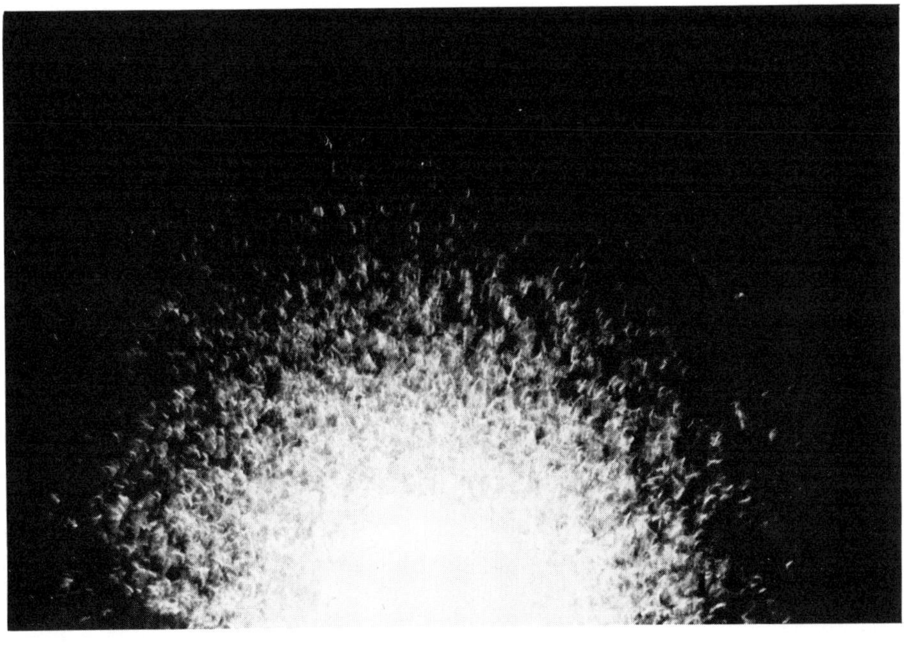

1

The Role of Utilities in the American Economy

Before exploring the legal basis for utility regulation, it is desirable to consider the role of the utility industries in the total American economy. Since this is a very broad subject, three aspects of the role of utilities will be selected for consideration here. These are (1) the economic role of utilities in the United States, (2) the social function of public utilities, and (3) the historical evolution of public utilities. The last aspect emphasizes the relation between utility services and economic development as well as the evolutionary nature of utilities through time.

THE ECONOMIC ROLE OF UTILITIES

The economic role of public utilities in American capitalism is a very distinctive one. Every business has a function in the economy, but utilities are especially important from at least three viewpoints.

ESSENTIAL NATURE OF UTILITY SERVICES

First, the services provided by public utilities are essential for economic growth and development. No economy can progress very far without what has been referred to by economic growth theorists as "social overhead capital."[1] This factor is pivotal.

Basically, the three types of social overhead capital necessary for economic growth which are of interest to us are (1) effective transportation, (2) good communication, and (3) flexible and reliable power sources. All of these may be considered utilities in the broad sense, and the last two are utilities in the narrower sense of the term. These three types of social overhead capital are necessary for economic growth regardless of the type of economic system: utility services are just as pivotal under socialism as under capitalism. They are mandatory for a developed nation, an underdeveloped nation, or an emerging nation; and they are equally essential for a geographic region, a state, or a city.

Transportation is needed to assemble the means of production and to bring the raw materials or semifinished products to the site of the production or manufacturing process. The more efficiently this is performed, the more the productive process can become profitable and grow. An effective transportation system allows producers a wider choice of suppliers, more reliable sources of supply, and more specialization of labor. Similarly, effective transportation is required to distribute the goods produced. Mass production must be accompanied by mass distribution and consumption. Transportation is equally important as an agent of distribution and as an agent of assembly.[2]

In today's business world rapid communication is essential. Orders must be placed, contracts processed, sales made, capital sought, and the like. Good communication facilities, generally telephone or telegraph, are the life lines of the rapid, modern business scene. If an economy possesses a slow or ineffective communications system, the pace of business slows and economic growth is difficult. Generally, several communications systems exist in a complex economy. Newspapers, magazines, mail, telephone, telegraph, teletype, microwave, radio, and television are the types used in our own economy. While all of these are not considered "traditional" utilities, they all possess many of the characteristics of utilities, and they add to the effectiveness of communication in a modern economy.

A flexible and reliable source of power is a third factor mandatory for economic growth and development. Production depends on reliable power. Unless this is available it is impossible to plan and execute production and marketing processes. Flexibility of power sources is also necessary. When energy can be added or subtracted as needed, it is possible to change the productive process in response to market forces. And flexibility of power may also be used to free production from a fixed location (such as the early water-power mills of New England). Flexibility permits industry to follow market demands, to utilize competing sources of supply, and to be free of constraining location factors. In all economies the three factors of transportation, good communication, and reliable and flexible sources of power are the foundation of economic growth and development.

DEPENDENCE UPON UTILITY SERVICES

A second distinctive economic role of utilities stems from the complete dependence of a modern complex society upon utility services. Electricity, telephone, natural gas, and water services are now so much a part of our modern way of life that to do without them has become unthinkable. While one may argue as to what is "essential" to life, modern society is without doubt dependent on utility services.

This dependence is forcefully brought to our attention when services are interrupted. Chaos prevailed without electricity in the famous "Northeast Blackout" a few years ago. Elevators stopped, vehicular traffic became hopelessly snarled without traffic lights, airports could not operate without landing aids, furnaces were cold, dinners remained uncooked, and radio and television stations were dead. The indispensability of electric power in our society was thus dramatically demonstrated to a large segment of the American public.

Weather occurrences such as storms and hurricanes sometimes knock down telephone lines, interrupt natural gas service, and occasionally affect water service. Fortunately, these occurrences are rare, but they do remind us how difficult modern life would be without power, telephones, gas, and water.

Yet these utilities are generally available, and in unlimited quantities. They are provided by many economic organizations, both private and public, in an unspectacular way which does not encourage appreciation of their role. It is only when deprived of the services of utilities that we realize how utterly dependent on them we have become.

ECONOMIC IMPACT OF UTILITIES

The third distinctive economic role of utilities is as large users of economic resources. The capital invested in utility services in the United States is enormous. It has been estimated that 20 per cent of all business assets, exclusive of banking, are invested in utilities. During a recent year one report indicated that the value of the capital invested in privately owned power companies was $46 billion, with an additional $31 billion invested in communications plants, and another $20 billion in the gas and pipeline industry.[3]

In addition, utilities are large users of new capital. During another recent year the United States Department of Commerce reported that public utilities accounted for more than $6.9 billion of the $24 billion in new securities issued. This was approximately 30 per cent of all new securities issued by corporations.[4] Most of this new capital was used for new plant and equipment. Other sources of capital (mainly retained earnings) were also used for the same purpose. While all industries were spending $61 billion for new plant, public utilities spent almost $16 billion, or 26 per cent of the total.

The utilities are not large users of labor. However, the same Department of Commerce report stated that some 4.3 million workers were employed by utilities and transportation organizations and that wages and salaries in utilities were higher than overall industrial averages.

For the services provided, utilities collect revenues. In the late 1960's the annual operating revenues of utilities amounted to around $40 billion. Of this, the electric power industry had operating revenues of more than $17 billion, telephone utilities more than $13 billion, and natural gas utilities more than $8 billion. Or considered from another viewpoint, around 4 per cent of Gross National Product is attributable to utilities.

There are no complete statistics available concerning the role of utilities as customers. However, it is known that a substantial amount of the copper and aluminum produced in the United States, a considerable share of the steel pipe, most of the poles, much of the cement, and much of the electrical equipment is used by utilities.

Finally, utilities pay very large amounts in taxes to all levels of government. During a recent year, it appears, utilities paid federal, state, and local taxes of around $8 billion.[5]

An alert reader can no doubt think of other distinctive economic roles of the public utility industries. However, an appreciation of the utilities' role in economic growth and development, of the dependence of modern life on utility services, and of the utilities' role as large users of economic resources, especially capital, sets a framework for consideration of the social function of public utilities.

THE SOCIAL FUNCTION OF PUBLIC UTILITIES

Economic functions under capitalism are predominantly provided by privately owned businesses. This is the way the American system has been constructed and the way in which it developed. Most of these economic undertakings exist with a minimum of social control. Indeed, the proper role of society, acting through its democratically constituted government, is a subject of constant concern.

Preference traditionally has been for as little government interference as possible and as great a reliance as possible on the forces of the impersonal marketplace. The philosophy of this approach has been characterized by the term *laissez faire*, or "allow to do." Many people mean the same thing when they speak of the free enterprise economy. ("Free" here refers both to freedom of choice by participants in the system and to the freedom of the group or society from government controls).

THE GOVERNMENT'S ROLE IN THE ECONOMY

It is generally recognized, however, that society, through government, does have a part to play in the economy. The role of government varies according to the particular situation and the economic function involved. Generally, it is agreed that where the common benefit is dominant, where the whole of society is involved, economic functions will be performed by society itself. Further, where the common interest requires interference with private functions, government will intervene. In this case, the responsibility of government may be limited to enforcement of the "rules" of the economy (for example, police protection against theft, laws against fraud and misrepresentation). But the degree of government involvement may be considerably greater: government may control the entry of new firms, set the rules under which businesses operate, and even control business prices and earnings.

In summary, then, the degree of economic control exercised by society through government action lies on a range of social control, with some functions provided by society entirely, at the one end, and at the other, society merely enforcing the basic "rules of the game." Between these two extremes lie varying degrees of social action. It is in this "between" area that public utilities fall.

THE RANGE OF SOCIAL CONTROL

Actually, one may think of this range in terms of public, or common, interest and private, or individual, interest. Practically all undertakings or economic functions include some of each of these interests. But the particular degree of common interest and individual interest varies considerably along the range. Hence, in some functions, the social, common, or public interest is dominant; in some, the private or individual interest is dominant; and in some, both interests will be important. It is in this last category that public utilities are found.

Market institutions also vary along this same range, mainly in terms of the pricing of the service or product and the characteristics of entry of the economic units. At one extreme, where society provides the service and the public interest is dominant, entry of new economic units is completely closed and pricing comes from taxation (or involuntary contribution of all units of society to the service of the whole). At the other extreme, where private interest is dominant, entry and pricing are free from social control. This is the familiar free enterprise economy. Between these two extremes are varying degrees of entry and pricing constraints.

When public utilities are placed within this framework (degree of interest of public and private sectors, types of pricing, and characteristics of entry), it is clear that they perform a distinctive social function that other businesses do not. An understanding of this social function is necessary to appreciate the role of public utilities in American capitalism and to understand why society treats them differently than many other businesses.

Table 1-1, ranging from government to free enterprise functions, shows the place of public utilities in relation to other kinds of economic organizations in our system.

Government Function

Where the public interest predominates, we generally find government, or some agency of society as a whole, performing the economic function. Generally, entry is

Table 1-1 The Range of Social Control

Function	Degree of Interest	Type of Pricing	Entry Characteristic
Government	Public interest predominates	Taxes	Closed entry
Transitional zone I	Public interest predominates, private interest secondary	Fees, assessments, subsidy	Relatively closed entry
Public Utility	Both public and private interest	Enforced rates and rule-making	Controlled entry
Transitional zone II	Private interest predominates, public interest secondary	Free pricing but social rule-making	Relatively free entry
Free enterprise	Private interest predominates	Free pricing	Free entry

closed, because the function is not provided on a profit-making basis. Society as a whole pays for the provision of this function by taxation: everyone contributes regardless of his use of the function, to benefit the entire society. Some examples of such functions are police protection, the armed forces, basic education, and fire protection.[6]

Transitional Zone I

A bit further along the range is a transitional zone. Here the public interest continues to predominate, but private interest also exists. Functions here still are provided by government but are supported by a special charge, fee, or assessment of some type. Society as a whole is not expected to stand all the costs of the function. In a very rough sense, charges are related to use of the function. Entry is difficult, but sometimes privately owned enterprises provide the same function at a fee or charge. Some examples of these functions are sewer districts, special water and irrigation districts, higher education, and airports.

These functions differ from purely government functions in two ways. A fee, assessment, or special charge, rather than a tax, is levied to support their services, and private enterprise may supply the same function. Government is predominant, but entry is not completely closed, and both public and private enterprises may exist side by side.

Public Utility Function

Public utilities and similarly regulated industries are a "halfway house" between completely government functions and free enterprise functions.[7] Here both the common interest and individual interests are found. Some of the functions may be provided by government and some may be privately provided. (The matter of public ownership is discussed in greater detail in Part Four.)

In this category prices are strictly controlled, although privately owned organizations follow the profit motive in providing their services. The rules under which services are provided are also strictly regulated. Generally, society recognizes that a monopolistic organization of the market serves it best—but it controls the monopoly. Entry is restricted in order to preserve the beneficial results of a monopoly, with public regulation limiting the exercise of monopoly power. Examples of businesses in this category are electric power, natural gas, communications, and transit firms—that is, the traditional public utilities.

Transitional Zone II

Further along the range is a group of functions that resemble both the public utility and the free enterprise functions. Generally, private interest predominates here, but the public interest remains a strong if secondary factor. Usually pricing is free, but rules are specified in various ways to reflect the common interest. Entry is often relatively free.

Examples of economic enterprises in this transitional zone are insurance companies, banks, broadcasting stations, and milk and coal producers. Entry is relatively easy and pricing usually is free. Yet the social role is important, and government rule-making exceeds that of the free enterprise area (yet it is less than in public utilities). For example, insurance companies and banks are required to maintain various reserves and are limited in their financial dealings. Health and safety standards are closely policed in milk and coal production. Entry (but not pricing) is controlled in broadcasting, and several other restrictions are applied.

In summary, transitional zone II possesses more of the characteristics of free enterprise than of social enterprise. Even so, some types of social control and rules like those for public utilities prevail.

Free Enterprise Function

At the final section of the range we find the free enterprise function. Here private interests predominate and the public interest is at a minimum. The role of society is mainly to provide an arena where competitive forces can work themselves out and to lay down a few basic "rules of the game" under which competition can operate. Entry and pricing are relatively free from controls.

It should be noted that the majority of businesses in our economy and most of the economic functions of our society are found in this last category. This follows the ideals of *laissez faire* and free enterprise that characterize the general philosophy of our nation.

SUMMARY

The social function of public utilities in American capitalism is that of a "halfway house." They are not provided wholly by government nor by private enterprises. They are not free to set their own prices, but they are expected to be profit seekers. They are permitted to be somewhat monopolistic because of the benefits arising from such a structure, but entry is strictly controlled and service standards are established.

Thinking of public utilities in terms of the "halfway house" concept explains many of the regulatory rules under which they operate. In effect, society uses this concept in an attempt to reach two somewhat contradictory goals. One, it attempts to obtain efficiency by reducing duplication and allowing semi-monopolistic firms to exist. Two, it tries to protect the public from the adverse actions to be expected from the monopolistic elements which it has created or permitted.

THE HISTORICAL EVOLUTION OF PUBLIC UTILITIES

There have been several phases or steps in the evolution of public utilities in the American economy. Also, society has looked at the various industries which comprise the public utilities differently at different periods. Since the various industries did not all begin at the same time, because of technology and historical accident, it is possible to find different views of the various positions of utilities at a given time. In other words, each utility (as a firm or as an industry) has passed through several stages of evolution. Some of these stages have different historical dates, but essentially they are similar in developmental patterns.

Essentially, most utilities have passed through four stages and are presently in a fifth stage of development. Firms of more recent origin may have by-passed one of the earlier stages, but in general there is a well-defined path of progression through which most utilities in our society have passed. These stages, in order, are the promotional, the competitive, the monopolistic, the regional, and the cooperative.

It should be pointed out, however, that it is difficult to identify the beginning and ending of a given stage of growth and development of an industry or a firm. One stage blends into another, and some characteristics of an earlier stage may remain well into the next phase. Thus, an overlapping of stages or phases is easily found in the development of utilities (or any other industry).

Also, three factors can be isolated in each stage of the historical development of utilities. These are the public image of the utility, the degree of social control, and the sophistication of service. "Public image" as used here refers to how society in general views the role of utilities and utility firms; "social control" concerns the rules and regulations applied by society as a reflection of the public image; "sophistication of service" refers to the technological and managerial state of the industry and its firms.

THE PROMOTIONAL STAGE

Since utilities are so necessary for economic growth and development, originally they were highly sought. Indeed, society was so anxious to have utilities as social overhead capital that they were actively promoted by government.

In our economy this stage is well represented by the public promotion of the basic means of transportation (a utility-like business) during the nineteenth century. During the early "Canal Era," for instance, cheap basic transportation was encouraged by various states in the form of state investment in canal facilities. The same phenomenon occurred in the case of early turnpikes. The adaptation of the joint stock company, the forerunner of the modern corporation, as a device to raise capital and promote turnpikes is an example of this stage. When railroads proved to be a superior type of overland transportation, they were vigorously promoted in the form of both public and private investment as well as by a minimum of social control. Individuals, cities, counties, and states invested in railroads. Tax advantages, gifts, and subsidies were provided to help create rail services. At the federal level, grants of land and subsidies were provided. At a later period similar aids were supplied for highway, water, and air transportation. In these last modes of transportation the promotional stage occurred in the twentieth century, and in some instances it is still going on.

In the area of the traditional utilities (power, gas, water, communication, and transit) a promotional stage can also be discerned. Public subsidies were often provided in the early days of these utilities. These subsidies took the form of outright grants of money to assist in the tremendous capital investment necessary, relief from taxes, grants of land, guarantees of bonds, and the creation of a favorable climate for development. This last point, a favorable climate, involved minimum social control or regulation and a willingness to look the other way when abuses occurred. Society was so anxious to have utilities that for a time, during their initial development, they could do no wrong.

During this stage firms typically were small and struggling. Technology was crude. Many modern utility conveniences were unknown. Service was often erratic and limited. As an example, it was not unusual in the electric power industry to find early plants operating on a limited schedule—simply being shut down after 9 or 10 P.M. Plant breakdowns were frequent, and the reliability of utility service as we know it today was nonexistent.

Management and pricing techniques also were very primitive. In practically all utilities there was little precedent upon which to base operations. Pricing was often on a fixed base per month. Sophisticated pricing forms had to be developed as the utilities developed. Similarly, no source of experienced management existed and internal management techniques had to be developed as the utilities grew. For some utilities, such as natural gas, which arrived on the scene at a later period, the lessons of early utility management and regulation were available, so that early conditions were not quite so crude.

Water utilities, being the most essential of all, typically come very early in development. Even the smallest amount of urbanization calls for a water utility. Because of the early need for water utilities in the United States, and because of the many alternative uses of capital in a developing economy, much of the water utility service was furnished by the public rather than by private sources. The overall social benefits for sanitation and fire protection also tended to make water a publicly provided utility. Yet where water has been supplied by private sources, a definite promotional era is discernible, with public subsidies, lack of social control, and slowly increasing sophistication of service.

Transit and manufactured gas utilities and communications also experienced early stages of promotion during which they were greatly sought after, subsidized, and encouraged. Again, little or no social control existed, and firms were small, isolated, and offered crude service. Natural gas and electric power utilities, coming at a somewhat later date, had shorter promotional eras. However, in all utilities there is a definitely discernible stage at which social benefits so exceeded social costs that this type of enterprise was promoted.

THE COMPETITIVE STAGE

As the social costs of utilities increased, the promotional stage blended into a succeeding phase—competition. Very often the shift resulted from abuses inherent in the lack of social control and the growing monopolistic form of utility organization.

Again transportation provides an example. The promotion of railroads often encouraged competition. Given a favorable climate of opinion, promoters and developers of railroads built competitive lines. Society was so eager to have this type of transportation that no entry controls existed. Competitive railroads, locked in a life-or-death struggle for survival, often entered into discriminatory practices. Where they possessed a monopoly, they exploited this fact with high charges and poor service. When they were competitive with other railroads, they gave unusually low rates to large shippers and entered into all types of shady dealings to secure traffic. When society sought relief from such practices, the usual proposal was to have more competition.[8]

Because of the abuses which often accompanied the promotional stage, the public image of utilities tended to change from a favorable to a negative one. Too often the public felt that its expectations had not been fulfilled. Perhaps it was impossible for utilities to live up to the public's expectations, and perhaps some utilities did abuse their mandates in the era of good feeling associated with promotion. At any rate, society soon realized that the social costs sometimes exceeded the social benefits of utilities.

The response was to increase social control—more often than not, by sponsoring more competitive firms. Competing franchises for manufactured gas, transit, telephones, and power can be found in the development of each of these utilities. The idea was to protect society by having individual firms struggle against one another. In some utilities competitive firms in a given service area still can be found. Until comparatively recently, for instance, Philadelphia had two telephone companies serving side by side. Many cities had competing transit companies, competing power companies, and competing gas companies. At a later time municipally owned electric power and telephone companies competed with private companies.

The franchise type of control was used during this stage. Cities have always had the right to restrict the use of their streets and alleys. States won the right to exercise a type of entry control over utilities in *Munn v. Illinois* (1877) and to control the prices of services (see Chapter 2). The right of control over "common callings" had been established for many years, and this control of entry was used to sponsor competition.

From the viewpoint of sophistication of service, there was also reason for the public to be disillusioned. While advances in technology were achieved during the promotional period, services remained erratic and relatively primitive. Firms remained small and poorly managed. Although pricing forms became more sophisticated, prices remained high. Management had not learned that economies of scale were possible and that stimulation of use was desirable. Once the competitive era began, service deteriorated further. When firms are engaged in an economic struggle, one of the first places they economize is in the level of service. Hence, expectations of improved service under the spur of competition rarely materialized.

THE MONOPOLISTIC STAGE

Conditions of the competitive era led to the next stage: recognition of the benefits of monopoly. Mergers abounded as competing firms tried to hold down costs, and monopolies developed despite the best efforts of public authorities to stimulate competition. Prevailing public opinion generally favored private ownership. The alternative of publicly owned competing producers was not always popular, even though it was sometimes attempted during the competitive era.

It was only reluctantly that society decided that the monopolistic form of business organization was inevitable in utilities. This had been true in transportation, which once more had set the path. The federal government had decided to regulate transportation in 1887, after state attempts at control had broken down. In the traditional utilities recognition of the benefits of monopoly occurred during the first fifteen years of the present century. By this time, most utilities had either merged naturally into city-wide monopolies, or the authorities had recognized that issuing competitive franchises was wasteful.

The key to maximizing the economic benefits of a monopoly was effective regulation. Hence, in state after state, commissions were established or re-established during the 1900–1915 period. These commissions were given authority to control earnings and prices, levels of service, and discriminatory practices. The idea was to secure the benefits of monopoly but to regulate so that the public was spared most of the abuses of monopoly. The philosophy was that regulation was a "substitute for competition."[9]

Generally, the public image of utilities, once they were regulated, was quite good. Services improved as units of production became larger and economies of scale apparent. Prices usually went down, partly because of regulation and partly because of the economies practiced by monopolistic-type enterprises. City-wide systems generally evolved, and with growing urbanization, utilities became a "growth industry."

In transit this "growth industry" image was found in the interurban transit systems of the early twentieth century. A tremendous increase in interurban systems took place between 1900 and 1920 because of two factors: electricity was applied as motive power and increased urbanization required a more widespread transit system. Interurban stocks were the growth industry of the day, and there was much speculation in this utility. But the coming of the automobile, public roads, and inflationary pressures on costs without corresponding price increases during the 1920's helped force this industry into decline.

The gas industry was also considered a growth industry. Prior to the widespread introduction of natural gas the manufactured gas industry was in great financial trouble because of competition from electric power. However, a firm base of expansion was established in 1918, when Texas discoveries made natural gas a surplus commodity. The only factor needed for an expanding natural gas industry was effective pipeline transportation. Natural gas revived the gas business and laid the foundation for the astounding growth in this utility during recent decades.[10]

To a lesser extent, the same growth image was found in electric power during this era. The opportunities for economies of scale were greatest here. Urbanization, lower prices, and increasing affluence led to constant growth in sales. To some degree, the same was true of the telephone and other communications industries.

Social control through regulatory state commissions had to be worked out. At first, regulation was unevenly applied, with some states regulating more firmly than others. Many of the principles of regulation were still evolving, but, generally, regulation was effective—at least for a time.

During the monopolistic era relatively high levels of sophistication of service and management prevailed. Many of the modern pricing forms were developed under the conditions of monopoly and growth. Systems of utilities tended to grow outside their city boundaries, and centralization through control by large corporations was prevalent.

Management became highly sophisticated. Indeed, many were attracted by the growth aspects of utilities, and public utility holding companies proliferated. Eventually, utilities found effective ways to get around regulation, and financial abuses grew. Too much speculation and too much intercorporate dealing aroused increasing concern by society. In the late 1920's public disillusionment with state regulation set in. Attempts at competition by municipal ownership increased, and there was a movement for "Home Rule." However, utility managements had become quite effective at public relations, and, in general, little significant social control was achieved. While the monopolistic period started with social benefits exceeding social costs because of the benefits of monopoly plus dynamic and effective social control, the period ended in public frustration and doubt.

THE REGIONAL STAGE

The regional stage evolved out of the monopolistic period. Utility organizations expanded to state-wide and even regional systems. Some of this expansion took place by means of holding companies and financial controls. Although transit and water utilities generally did not pass into this stage, a few large companies controlled the electric power and gas systems, and the telephone system was dominated by subsidiaries of one large company. There was talk of super-power systems and a growing recognition that the economies of scale could be pushed even farther.

Yet public opinion of utilities was at its lowest point. Feelings of exploitation, frustration, fear, and distrust were common. State regulation was frustrated by holding companies; congressional investigation revealed the extent of holding company power and malpractices. Customers, stockholders and bondholders, and regulators were unhappy. Utility prices remained high, holding company manipulations continued, and even business failures drained the public purse. A few persons seemed to have taken advantage of the many.

Public control took three forms, starting with investigation and publicity. One of the longest public hearings of all time took place during an investigation of holding companies.[11] Many liberal writers had a field day branding utility monopolies as "bad."

The second form of control was regulation by the federal government, which came during the 1930's. The Federal Power Commission was given control over interstate sale of electric power in 1935, and over natural gas in 1938. The Federal Communications Commission was created in 1934. The Securities and Exchange Commission was created in 1934 and given control over holding companies in 1935. Large regional utilities were controlled by national commissions as well as by state commissions.

The third public response was to provide and finance federal competition. Many large federal multiple-purpose projects were proposed and authorized. These typically produced electric power, much of which was sold in competition with private utilities.

Similarly, the Rural Electrification Administration, established in 1936, offered help to rural electric and telephone cooperatives. Although these federal actions did not establish direct control, their acceptance was evidence of the public disillusionment with utility performance.

This government entry into the utility field led to several decades of bitter political infighting between vested interests on both sides. "Public power" became an issue in presidential and congressional campaigns. Adroit propaganda and public relations programs were launched. Private utilities were bent on defending their way of operation and the "capitalistic system." Public power advocates argued just as fervidly that utilities were monopolistic, abusive, and exploitive. The public image of utilities clearly depended upon who was speaking.

Service continued to improve in quality. Federal holding company regulation, in effect, generally limited electric power systems to state-wide systems or to systems in two adjacent states. However, these grew more efficient. Telephone systems based on one large holding company competing with growing independents also increased in efficiency. Long-distance natural gas transmission facilities grew rapidly, and consumers were frequently offered choices of energy sources. Water utilities continued to grow slowly, and transit continued its decline.

When management was not concerned with philosophical issues, it was concerned with efficiency. Better transmission facilities were built, prices held steady or declined in the face of inflation, and utilities slowly restored their image of dependability, public service, and efficiency. Early in the regional period it was popular to be against utilities; after World War II, a new public image emerged. Much of this resulted from the concentration on efficiency and good engineering, and the diminished concern for philosophical issues.

THE COOPERATION STAGE

The "big three" modern utilities—power, gas, and telephone—have recently passed into a fifth stage, that of cooperation. Since the mid-1950's more and more cooperation has been found among utility firms. The Bell System now explicitly cooperates with independent telephone companies and by so doing provides a better public service for all. Gas utilities cooperate in underground storage, financing, public relations, and other ways.

In the electric power field cooperation has taken several forms. First, although competition still exists and occasional ideological struggles still occur, there has been increasing cooperation between public and private suppliers of power. This cooperation usually takes the form of banding together to build interconnecting lines, creating massive "power pools" of private and public participating members, and accepting the fact that both forms of ownership will be able to survive side by side.

Cooperation is also expressed by national power and energy planning.[12] Inventories of future power and energy needs, surveys of existing facilities and reserves, and long-term plans to meet the needs of the public are increasing. All firms and all forms of ownership cooperate in these. Finally, in communications, the cooperation that was necessary to establish COMSAT is yet another piece of evidence that a new stage has come.

The cooperative stage is only beginning, but there are signs of a different degree of social control. Some question the old holding company type of controls. In an era of cooperation and national planning regulations of the 1930's may be out of date. Service levels are highly sophisticated, pricing forms highly advanced, and management very efficient. It should be stressed that cooperation is most often forced or justified on economic grounds and not on ideological grounds. Differences in ideology continue, but the economies of working together are overcoming these differences. By working together, different firms and various forms of ownership find that they can achieve better economies of scale and better returns while giving more efficient service. Cooperation pays—ideological conflicts do not.

In summary, utilities have developed in an evolutionary fashion through the stages of promotion, competition, monopoly, regionalism, and cooperation. In each stage the public image, the degree of social control, and the sophistication of service have varied. Each stage has blended into the next, and events in one stage seem to have set off the succeeding stage. Finally, while dates are hard to assess for each stage, and the various firms and industries have developed during various time periods, each of the stages of development is discernible in the history of each utility group.

SUMMARY

In this chapter we have discussed the role of utilities in the American economy. We have spoken of their economic role in terms of the pivotal nature of utilities in economic growth, the extreme dependence of modern society upon utility service, and the role of utilities as large users of resources. The social role of utilities as a "halfway house" in American capitalism has been examined. Finally, the historical evolution of public utilities through various discernible stages has been described. Our next step toward understanding the place of utilities in the American economy is to explore the evolution and present status of economic and legal definitions of the public utility concept. This is done in Chapter 2.

NOTES

1. The literature on economic growth is prodigious. A discussion of the importance of social overhead capital is contained in Walt W. Rostow's *The Stages of Economic Growth* (London: Cambridge University Press, 1960).
2. The importance of transportation in economic growth is discussed in Roy J. Sampson and Martin T. Farris, *Domestic Transportation: Practice, Theory and Policy,* 2d ed. (Boston: Houghton Mifflin, 1971), ch. 1.
3. *The Investor-Owned Electric Utility Industry* (New York: Edison Electric Institute, 1963).
4. U. S. Department of Commerce, *Survey of Current Business,* Vol. 48, no. 10 (October 1968).

5. Authors' estimate using data from *Moody's Public Utility Manual.*
6. While it is true that private police and private fire protection companies do exist, these are not common. Typically they exist where the same government function is either inadequate or completely lacking. Private educational facilities also exist, but their use does not exempt the user from an obligation to support public education by taxes.
7. The authors do not claim originality in labeling utilities as a "halfway house." This idea has been stated many times, perhaps most eloquently by the late Professor Martin G. Glaeser.
8. An interesting example of this reasoning is found in the so-called Windom Committee Report of 1874, which proposed national or state-owned railroads in competition with privately owned railroads. It was claimed that such publicly owned lines would "serve as regulators of other lines." *Transportation Routes to the Seaboard,* 43d Congress, 1st Session, Senate Report No. 307 (1874), p. 242.
9. For an interesting discussion of this philosophy, see Ben Lewis, "The Rationale of Regulation," in L. S. Lyon, V. Abramson and associates, *Government and Economic Life* (Washington, D. C.: Brookings Institution, 1940), II, 618–626.
10. See Paul J. Garfield and Wallace F. Lovejoy, *Public Utility Economics* (Englewood Cliffs, N. J.: Prentice-Hall, 1964), pp. 297–299.
11. One Federal Trade Commission investigation of the holding company device lasted for six years and filled more than one hundred volumes with evidence of malpractice.
12. The National Power Surveys are but one example of this type of planning and national cooperation.

ADDITIONAL READINGS

1. Barnes, Irston R., *The Economics of Public Utility Regulation* (New York: F. S. Crofts, 1942), ch. 2, "The Historical Emergence of the Utility Industries," pp. 23–41.
2. Bonbright, James C., and Gardiner C. Means, *The Holding Company: Its Public Significance and Its Regulation* (New York: McGraw-Hill, 1932).
3. Clemens, Eli Winston, *Economics and Public Utilities* (New York: Appleton-Century-Crofts, 1950), ch. 21, "The Problem of the Holding Company," pp. 486–521.
4. Garfield, Paul J., and Wallace F. Lovejoy, *Public Utility Economics* (Englewood Cliffs, N. J.: Prentice-Hall, 1964), ch. 1, "The Public Utility Concept," pp. 1–15.
5. Glaeser, Martin G., *Public Utilities in American Capitalism* (New York: Macmillan, 1957), ch. 1, "The Function of Public Utilities in a National Economy," pp. 3–14; ch. 2, "The Promotional Epoch in the Evolution of Public Utilities," pp. 14–30; ch. 4, "The Competitive Epoch," pp. 40–56; ch. 7, "Public Utilities in the Twentieth Century," pp. 97–111.
6. Phillips, Charles F., Jr., *The Economics of Regulation*, rev. ed. (Homewood, Ill.: Richard D. Irwin, 1969), ch. 1, "The Regulated Industries in the American Economy," pp. 3–16.
7. Ripley, William Z., *Main Street and Wall Street* (Boston: Little, Brown, 1927).

2

Economic and Legal Definitions of the Public Utility Concept

Public utilities are easy to recognize but difficult to describe. Certain kinds of businesses, whether privately or publicly owned, are generally considered to be "affected with a public interest" and customarily are classified as public utilities. Traditionally, such businesses have included those supplying water, artificial and natural gas, telegraph and telephone services, electricity, and street transportation.[1] More recently, newer types of businesses, such as radio and television broadcasting, have been brought at least partially within the public utility orbit.

One might well ask, What is the basis for declaring that certain types of businesses are public utilities and others not? Do public utilities possess characteristics which set them apart from other businesses? If so, what are these characteristics?

ECONOMIC CHARACTERISTICS OF PUBLIC UTILITIES

It is often said that a public utility supplies a necessary or essential service. What is a necessary service, however? One person's necessity may be another's luxury. Striped pants and a top hat may be as indispensable to a diplomat as coveralls to a mechanic. Is gas or electricity more essential than oil or coal? Are telephones more essential than houses, or water more essential than food? Most products and services are necessities to some individuals, and many items are at least as necessary for most of us as are some that we commonly classify as public utilities.

Consumers' demands for the products of the traditional public utilities are usually somewhat inelastic; that is, the quantity purchased is normally not significantly affected by small price changes. A typical family probably will not burn 1 per cent fewer lights or use 1 per cent less water just because the electric or water rate has increased 1 per cent. Nor will it consume 1 per cent more when the rates are decreased by 1 per cent.[2]

The demands of large industrial users for public utility services may be much more elastic than those of household consumers, however. A manufacturing plant may be in a better position to shift to an alternative source of power (as coal for gas or electricity) if its utility rates become too high. Similarly, an individual who has not yet committed himself to a particular type of utility service (one building a new factory or a home, for example) is in a much better bargaining position, and thus has a more elastic demand, than one who already has invested in facilities useful only in consuming a certain type of product. For this reason, it is often possible for a public utility to discriminate between different classes of customers, charging higher rates to small users than to large buyers and giving lower rates to newcomers than to old-timers.

Inelasticity of demand, insofar as it exists, is not unique in the public utility industry, of course. Most of us would probably make little change in buying quantities of salt, shoe laces, automobiles, and many other everyday necessities even if their prices (or our incomes) should change slightly.

It is often pointed out that firms selling a necessity (or enjoying the benefits of an inelastic demand for their product) have a more steady and dependable income than less fortunate establishments. No doubt this is true, and most public utilities do enjoy a relative steadiness of income. It could also be pointed out, however, that many nonutility industries are favored with income stability comparable to that found in those which we classify as public utilities, and that some segments of the traditional public utility industry (street transportation, for example) have not enjoyed income stability during recent years. Further, some of the traditional stability in public utilities must be attributed to the fact that firms classified as public utilities have been given a certain amount of legal protection (monopoly) in their market area; they do not necessarily possess any inherent advantages.

Public utilities, according to the traditional classification, are mainly sellers of services that can neither be stored nor deferred. Light (like time) not used today cannot be used tomorrow. As sellers of services, some utilities, such as electric companies, are in frequent or continuous contact with their customers. Others, however, such as street transportation companies, may have much less buyer-seller contact. Actually, it is difficult to see how services sold by public utility companies differ substantially in this respect from services sold by attorneys, medical doctors, go-go dancers, and other dealers in intangible products.

Government regulation or ownership of public utilities is sometimes defended on the grounds that the utility is a monopoly (which apparently means, in most cases, that only one firm is selling the particular service in a given market area). Economists, lawyers, businessmen, and legislators have been arguing about what a monopoly is and is not for many decades. Some maintain that a true monopoly would exist only if one firm had control of every item for sale throughout the world. Others maintain that a monopoly would exist if Hicksville (population 343) is served by only one natural gas company. For practical purposes, the truth probably is found somewhere between these extremes.

Gas is used for heating. If Hicksville is served by one gas company and has no other source of fuel supply most reasonable persons probably would concede that a monopoly exists. On the other hand, if Hicksville is served also by an electric company, a coal company, and a fuel oil company, or has ready access to fuel wood, sawdust, and various other forms of heating materials, can we dogmatically say that its one gas company has a monopoly? The latter situation is found more often than the former.

Telephone companies compete with the telegraph and the mails. Street railways compete with taxicabs and private automobiles. To some, beer is a suitable substitute for drinking water. Some utility officials would maintain that they actually are competing for the consumers' dollars and that, since some consumers prefer dress shirts and opera tickets to gas-burning water heaters, in reality every type of business may be a direct competitor to the public utility firm!

Insofar as monopoly does exist in the public utility field, it may be attributed either to "natural" or "artificial" causes. A natural monopoly is brought about by inherent factors in an industry or firm, such as economies of large-scale production, which may make it possible for one large firm to supply a market at a much lower cost (and price) than would be possible if several smaller firms undertook to supply an equivalent quantity of service. Natural monopolies also may arise from technical conditions, such as the possession of "know-how" or the control of patents, and from site limitations (for example, sites where power dams can be located or natural gas found are fairly limited in number). The so-called artificial monopolies arise from legal barriers to the entry of competing firms, as by the granting of exclusive franchises, or by aggressive policies of public utility management officials who crush or buy out their competitors.

All in all, whatever our definition of monopoly, it is likely that fewer monopolies exist in the public utility field than is commonly supposed, and it is very doubtful if public utilities are any more monopolized than some of our other large industries.

A large amount of capital equipment (or investment) is typically required to establish and maintain a public utility business. This, together with the nature of its assets and sales, means that the traditional public utility concern usually has a low rate of turnover of its investment and a high fixed (or overhead) cost. In addition, utilities have to build plant capacity sufficient to take care of peak loads or demands for services, although this peak demand is not uniform over time. Electric lights are turned on at night so that father can read his newspaper at the same time that mother is preparing dinner on her electric range and the children are watching television. The electric company must have facilities to supply this heavy demand, but these facilities may not be utilized fully during twenty or more hours out of twenty-four. Also, since utilities are expected to provide services sufficient for their entire marketing area, in growing communities they may be forced to build additional capacity a little ahead of actual needs so that the growing demand of new real estate or industrial developments can be met promptly when it is forthcoming.

This combination of high fixed costs and excess capacity puts a public utility firm with a given plant in a "decreasing unit cost" position. Inasmuch as its capacity is not being fully utilized, and a large portion of its costs are not directly related to the quantity of its output, the average cost of producing an additional unit of service is less than the average per unit cost of its present output. This makes it possible and profitable for the firm to engage in discriminatory pricing practices in order to get new business, and if two competing public utility firms find themselves in this situation, there is a potential for a price war.[3]

Again, it must be pointed out that the capital needs of public utility companies are not unique. Large capital requirements, high fixed costs, and excess capacity are found in many types of businesses.

After considering the economic characteristics of public utility firms one is forced to conclude that all these characteristics are found in many other industries and that economic differences within the public utility field itself are at least as great as any differences that may exist between that field and other fields. How then are we to define or describe the public utility industry in economic terms? The answer is that we cannot! If no readily acceptable economic criteria exist for distinguishing a public utility from other types of businesses, then we must leave the economic area and look elsewhere for a definition.

LEGAL CHARACTERISTICS OF PUBLIC UTILITIES

Businesses traditionally classified as public utilities, even though they may be privately owned, have two major legal obligations not usually asked of other types of private businesses. First, they must serve all buyers within their market area without undue discrimination up to the limits of their capacity, and they may even be required to increase their capacity if demand for their product expands. Second, public utilities must sell their services at "reasonable" rates or prices; in application, reasonable prices are prices that will give the utility firm no more than "reasonable" earnings under prudent management.[4] In order to ensure that privately owned utility companies meet these two legal obligations, we have established a very thorough system of regulation of such companies by public officials.

The public utility concept, or the concept of "businesses affected with a public interest" and thus peculiarly subject to public regulation, has a long history in legal theory and practice. Privately owned "public corporations," with special obligations, were established in ancient Rome for the conduct of certain types of quasi-public enterprises, such as water supply, garbage disposal, and fire fighting services. In medieval Europe quality and prices of many commodities and services were strictly regulated by guilds of tradesmen and by the moral pressure of the Catholic Church's concept of the "just price." Close public regulation of many types of economic activity was continued under the doctrine of Mercantilism, which developed along with our modern nation-states. English common law, upon which a substantial portion of our modern American legal framework is based, has many decisions affirming the right of public authorities to regulate so-called common callings (i.e., occupations and businesses peculiarly "affected with a public interest"), such as blacksmiths, innkeepers, transportation, bakeries, and millers.[5]

Various legal theories have been advanced to justify the concept of certain businesses being especially "affected with a public interest." Among the more prominent of such theories is the "holding-out theory," which states that a person offering his services (holding himself out) to the general public thereby incurs an obligation to provide adequate services at a reasonable price. The "government function theory" justifies public utility regulation on the grounds that utilities actually supply services which otherwise would have to be supplied by the state, and thus, as agents of the state, they are liable to regulation in the public interest.[6] The "constructive grant theory" holds that those who engage in certain types of essential businesses thereby grant the general public an interest in the conduct of the operations of such businesses.[7] The "implied contract theory" maintains that the grant of special privileges to a company (such as an exclusive franchise, the right to occupy or use public properties like city streets or power dam sites, or the right of eminent domain[8]) obligates the business to submit to public regulation.[9] The "police power theory" upholds the right of any sovereign state to take whatever steps it feels necessary in order to protect and provide for the health and general welfare of its citizens.[10] All of these and other legal theories have been expressed and used at various times, although none by itself is, perhaps, entirely defensible. The police power theory seems most acceptable and most popular at the present time.

Throughout our history as a nation, and before, public regulation of business has been part of the American scene. Colonial lawmakers adopted English legal traditions, which later were transferred into our statutory laws. Public regulation of utility businesses, however, received a mighty push forward with the Grange movement.

THE GRANGER DEFINITION

The Grange ("Patrons of Husbandry") was a farmers' organization established in 1867. Although originally nonpolitical and designed to improve the economic lot of farmers by encouraging cooperative practices and sound farming methods, the Grange became politically powerful in several midwestern states during the early 1870's. Not only was this a period of general agricultural depression, but midwestern farmers were particularly provoked by discriminatory practices and alleged abuses perpetrated against farmers by railroads and "eastern financiers." At its height in 1875, the Grange movement had almost 22,000 local organizations with more than a half million members, heavily concentrated in Illinois, Iowa, Minnesota, Wisconsin, Kansas, Nebraska, and Missouri.

After they had achieved legislative control in several states, it is not surprising that the Grangers took steps to curb the abuses that they resented. The result was a series of so-called Granger laws, mainly establishing drastic (for the times) policies of state regulation of transportation and related activities. The regulated firms, naturally, protested the new laws, and several Granger cases reached the United States Supreme Court. For purposes of understanding the development of the public utility concept, the most important of these cases was *Munn v. Illinois*, 94 U.S. 113 (1877).

In 1871 the Illinois legislature passed a law declaring that grain elevators are public utilities and subject to price regulation by the state. Munn and Scott owned an elevator but failed to take out a license or post bond as required by law, and they charged rates higher than were legally permitted. They were found guilty and fined by the lower court, and they appealed to the United States Supreme Court. Munn and Scott maintained that they were engaged in a private business, that it had not been customary to regulate such businesses in the past, and that regulation forcing them to lower their rates was depriving them of their private property and thus was contrary to the United States Constitution. The historic decision of the Supreme Court, upholding the lower court, is here reproduced in part, along with portions of a strong dissenting opinion.

OPINION BY CHIEF JUSTICE WAITE: . . . When the people of the United Colonies separated from Great Britain, they changed the form, but not the substance, of their government. They retained for the purposes of government all the powers of the British Parliament, and through their state Constitutions or other forms of social compact, undertook to give practical effect to such as they deemed necessary for the common good and the security of life and property. All the powers which they retained they committed to their respective states, unless in express terms or by implication reserved to themselves. . . .

When one becomes a member of society, he necessarily parts with some rights or privileges which, as an individual not affected by his relations to others, he might retain. . . . This does not confer power upon the whole people to control rights which are purely and exclusively private . . . but it does authorize the establishment of laws requiring each citizen to so conduct himself, and so use his own property as not unnecessarily to injure another. This is the very essence of government. . . . Under these powers the government regulates the conduct of its citizens one towards another, and the manner in which each shall use his own property, when such regulation becomes necessary for the public good. In their exercise it has been customary in England from time immemorial, and in this country from its first colonization, to regulate ferries, common carriers, hackmen, bakers, millers, wharfingers, innkeepers, etc., and in so doing to fix a maximum of charge to be made for services rendered, accommodation furnished, and articles sold. To this day statutes are to be found in many of the states upon some or all of these subjects. . . .

From this it is apparent that, down to the time of the adoption of the 14th Amendment, it was not supposed that statutes regulating the use, or even the price of the use, of private property necessarily deprived an owner of his property without due process of law. Under some circumstances they may, but not under all. . . .

This brings us to inquire as to the principles upon which this power of regulation rests, in order that we may determine what is within and what without its operative effect. Looking, then, to the common law, from whence came the right which the Constitution protects, we find that when private property is "affected with a public interest, it ceases to be *juris privati* only". . . . Property does become clothed with a public interest when used in a manner to make it of public consequence, and affect the community at large. When, therefore, one devotes his property to a use in which the public has an interest, he, in effect, grants to the public an interest in that use, and must submit to be controlled by the public for the common good, to the extent of the interest he has created. He may withdraw his grant by discontinuing the use; but, so long as he maintains the use, he must submit to the control.

But we need not go further. Enough has already been said to show that, when private property is devoted to a public use, it is subject to public regulation. . . .

. . . Although in 1874 there were in Chicago fourteen warehouses adapted to this particular business, and owned by about thirty persons, nine business firms controlled them, and . . . the prices charged and received for storage were such "as have been from year to year agreed upon and established by the different elevators or warehouses in the city of Chicago, and which rates have been annually published in one or more newspapers printed in said city, in the month of January in each year, as the established rates for the year then next ensuing such publication." Thus it is apparent that all the elevating facilities through which these vast productions "of seven or eight great states of the West" must pass on the way "to four or five of the states on the seashore" may be a "virtual" monopoly.

Under such circumstances it is difficult to see why, if the common carrier, or the miller, or the ferryman, or the innkeeper, or the wharfinger, or the baker, or the cartman, or the hackney-coachman, pursues a public employment and exercises "a sort of public office," these plaintiffs in error do not. They stand, to use again the language of their counsel, in the very "gateway of commerce," and take toll from all who pass. Their business most certainly "tends to a common charge, and is become a thing of public interest and use." Every bushel of grain for its passage "pays a toll, which is a common charge," . . . if any business can be clothed "with a public interest, and cease to be *juris privati* only," this has been . . . it is by the facts.

. . . During the twenty years in which this peculiar business has been assuming its present "immense proportion," something had occurred which led the whole body of the people to suppose that remedies such as are usually employed to prevent abuses by virtual monopolies might not be inappropriate here. For our purposes we must assume that, if a state of facts could exist that would justify such legislation, it actually did exist when the statute now under consideration was passed. For us the question is one of power, not of expediency. If no state of circumstances could exist to justify such a statute, then we may declare this one void, because in excess of the legislative power of the state. But if it could, we must presume it did. Of the propriety of legislative interference within the scope of legislative power, the legislature is the exclusive judge.

Neither is it a matter of any moment that no precedent can be found for a statute precisely like this. It is conceded that the business is one of recent origin, that its growth has been rapid, and that it is already of great importance. And it must also be conceded that it is a business in which the whole public has a direct and positive interest. It presents, therefore, a case for the application of a long-known and well-established principle in social science, and this statute simply extends the law so as to meet this new development of commercial progress. There is no attempt to compel these owners to grant the public an interest in their property, but to declare their obligations, if they use it in this particular manner.

It matters not in this case that these plaintiffs in error had built their warehouses and established their business before the regulations complained of were adopted. What they did was, from the beginning, subject to the power of the body politic to require them to conform to such regulations as might be established by the proper authorities for the common good. They entered upon their business and provided themselves with the means to carry it on subject to this condition. If they did not wish to submit themselves to such interference, they should not have clothed the public with an interest in their concerns. . . .

. . . In countries where the common law prevails, it has been customary from time immemorial for the legislature to declare what shall be a reasonable compensation . . . or, perhaps more properly speaking, to fix a maximum beyond which any charge made would be unreasonable. . . .

. . . Mere common-law regulation of trade or business may be changed by statute. A person has no property, no vested interest, in any rule of the common law. That is only one of the forms of municipal law, and is no more sacred than any other. Rights of property which have been created by the common law cannot be taken away without due process; but the law itself, as a rule of conduct, may be changed at the will, or even at the whim, of the legislature, unless prevented by constitutional limitations. . . . To limit the rate of charge for services rendered in a public employment, or for the use of property in which the public has an interest, is only changing a regulation which existed before. It establishes no new principle in the law, but only gives a new effect to an old one.

We know that this is a power which may be abused; but that is no argument against its existence. For protection against abuses by legislatures the people must resort to the polls, not to the courts.

DISSENTING OPINION BY JUSTICE FIELD: . . . It would seem from its opinion that the court holds that property loses something of its private character when employed in such a way as to be generally useful. The doctrine declared is that property "becomes clothed with a public interest when used in a manner to make it of public consequence, and affect the community at large"; and from such clothing the right of the legislature is deduced to control the use of the property, and to determine the compensation which the owner may receive from it. . . . It is clear that the court intended to declare that, whenever one devotes his property to a business which is useful to the public—"affects the community at large"—the legislature can regulate the compensation which the owner may receive for its use, and for his own services in connection with it. . . .

If this be sound law . . . all property and all business in the State are held at the mercy of a majority of its legislature. . . . The public is interested in the manufacture of cotton, woolen, and silken fabrics, in the construction of machinery, in the printing and publication of books and periodicals, and in the making of utensils of every variety, useful and ornamental; indeed there is hardly an enterprise or business engaging the attention and labor of any considerable portion of the community, in which the public has not an interest. . . .

. . . The legislation in question is nothing less than a bold assertion of absolute power by the State to control at its discretion the property and business of the citizen, and fix the compensation he shall receive. . . . The decision of the court in this case gives unrestrained license to legislative will.

The importance of the Granger laws and the Granger cases is that they decisively affirmed the right of public regulation and established legal and administrative models and precedents which formed the basis for a continually expanding regulation of private businesses "affected with a public interest."

POST-GRANGER DEFINITIONS

Regulation of transportation companies and the traditional public utilities continued to grow more or less steadily after the 1870's, and the public utility concept was somewhat enlarged. In 1894 a North Dakota law regulating a large number of small and scattered grain elevators was upheld, even though no element of monopoly and no close connection with transportation (as had been found in previous cases) was alleged; instead, the nature of the business itself was held to be the determining factor in deciding whether or not regulation was applicable.[11] A Kansas law regulating the rates and other practices of fire insurance companies was upheld in 1914.[12] In 1921 a rent control act applicable in the District of Columbia was held to be constitutional.[13] Oklahoma cotton gins were held to come within the public utility concept in 1929.[14]

Following the *Munn v. Illinois* decision, however, for more than a half century the courts frequently were somewhat loath to extend the public utility concept to cover new types of business operations. For example, meat packing was held not to come within the public utility concept in a 1923 Kansas case.[15] A New York theater ticket brokerage business was held not subject to price regulation in 1927, although a substantial amount of monopoly of tickets for the best seats seemed to be involved.[16] In 1928, in a New Jersey case, employment agencies were declared not to be sufficiently affected with a public interest as to require regulation.[17] A Tennessee statute regulating the price of gasoline was held invalid in 1929.[18] In 1932 the manufacturing of ice was held not sufficiently affected with a public interest to permit the state of Oklahoma to regulate entry into this field.[19]

The severe economic depression of the early 1930's exerted a tremendous influence on the pattern of public regulation of private businesses. Not only was the concept of businesses "affected with a public interest" enlarged almost without limit but the goals of regulation were changed and enlarged. The case of *Nebbia v. New York,* 291 U.S. 502 (1934), virtually broke all bars limiting the public utility concept and regulatory objectives.

The New York legislature, to aid dairy farmers and presumably to assure an adequate supply of wholesome milk, in 1933 passed a law regulating the price of milk. The retail price of milk under this law was fixed at nine cents per quart. Nebbia, who owned a grocery store, maintained that he was being deprived of his property rights and denied equal rights under the law, but was convicted in the lower courts for selling two quarts of milk and a five-cent loaf of bread for eighteen cents. Upon appeal, the United States Supreme Court upheld Nebbia's conviction and the constitutionality of the New York statute. In its decision the court relied heavily upon the theory of the police power of the state. Key portions of the decision, as well as of Justice McReynold's strongly worded dissent, follow.

> OPINION BY JUSTICE ROBERTS: . . . Under our form of government the use of property and the making of contracts are normally matters of private and not of public concern. The general rule is that both shall be free of governmental interference. But neither property rights nor contract rights are absolute; for government cannot exist if the citizen may at will use his property to the detriment of his fellows, or exercise his freedom of contract to work them harm. Equally fundamental with the private right is that of the public to regulate it in the common interest. . . .
>
> . . . This court from the early days affirmed that the power to promote the general welfare is inherent in the government. . . . These correlative rights, that of the citizen to exercise exclusive dominion over property and freely to con-

tract about his affairs, and that of the state to regulate the use of property and the conduct of business, are always in collision. No exercise of the private right can be imagined which will not in some respect, however slight, affect the public; no exercise of the legislative prerogative to regulate the conduct of the citizen which will not to some extent abridge his liberty or affect his property. But subject only to constitutional restraint the private right must yield to the public need.

The Fifth Amendment, in the field of federal activity, and the Fourteenth, as respects state action, do not prohibit government regulation for the public welfare. They merely condition the exertion of the admitted power, by securing that the end shall be accomplished by methods consistent with due process. And the guaranty of due process, as has often been held, demands only that the law shall not be unreasonable, arbitrary, or capricious, and that the means selected shall have a real and substantial relation to the object sought to be attained. . . .

But we are told that because the law essays to control prices it denies due process. . . . The argument runs that the public control of rates or prices is *per se* unreasonable and unconstitutional, save as applied to businesses affected with a public interest; that a business so affected is one in which property is devoted to an enterprise of a sort which the public itself might appropriately undertake, or one whose owner relies on a public grant or franchise for the right to conduct the business, or in which he is bound to serve all who apply; in short, such as is commonly called a public utility; or a business in its nature a monopoly. The milk industry, it is said, possesses none of these characteristics. . . .

We may as well say at once that the dairy industry is not, in the accepted sense of the phrase, a public utility. . . . But if, as must be conceded, the industry is subject to regulation in the public interest, what constitutional principle bars the state from correcting existing maladjustments by legislation touching prices? We think there is no such principle. . . .

It is clear that there is no closed class or category of businesses affected with a public interest. . . . The phrase "affected with a public interest" can, in the nature of things, mean no more than that an industry, for adequate reason, is subject to control for the public good. . . . There can be no doubt that upon proper occasion and by appropriate measures the state may regulate a business in any of its aspects, including the prices to be charged for the products or commodities it sells.

So far as the requirement of due process is concerned, and in the absence of other constitutional restriction, a state is free to adopt whatever economic policy may reasonably be deemed to promote public welfare, and to enforce that policy by legislation adapted to its purpose. The courts are without authority either to declare such policy, or, when it is declared by the legislative arm, to override it. If the laws passed are seen to have a reasonable relation to a proper legislative purpose, and are neither arbitrary or discriminatory it does not lie with the courts to determine that the rule is unwise. With the wisdom of the policy adopted, with the adequacy or practicability of the law enacted to forward it, the courts are both incompetent and unauthorized to deal. . . . The legislature is primarily the judge of the necessity of such an enactment. . . .

The Constitution does not secure to any one liberty to conduct his business

> in such fashion as to inflict injury upon the public at large, or upon any substantial group of the people. Price control, like any other form of regulation, is unconstitutional only if arbitrary, discriminatory, or demonstrably irrelevant to the policy the legislature is free to adopt. . . .
>
> DISSENTING OPINION BY JUSTICE MCREYNOLDS: . . . This is not regulation, but management, control, dictation—it amounts to the deprivation of the fundamental right which one has to conduct his own affairs honestly and along customary lines. . . . This is but to declare that rights guaranteed by the Constitution exist only so long as supposed public interest does not require their extinction. To adopt such a view, of course, would put an end to liberty under the Constitution. . . .
>
> . . . Here, we find direct interference with guaranteed rights defended upon the ground that the purpose was to promote the public welfare by increasing milk prices at the farm. . . .
>
> Not only does the statute interfere arbitrarily with the rights of the little grocer to conduct his business according to standards long accepted—complete destruction may follow; but it takes away the liberty of twelve million consumers to buy a necessity of life in an open market. It imposes direct and arbitrary burdens upon those already seriously impoverished with the alleged immediate design of affording special benefits to others. To him with less than nine cents it says—you cannot procure a quart of milk from the grocer although he is anxious to accept what you can pay and the demands of your household are urgent! A superabundance; but no child can purchase from a willing storekeeper below the figure appointed by three men at headquarters! And this is true although the storekeeper himself may have bought from a willing producer at half that rate and must sell quickly or lose his stock through deterioration. . . .
>
> . . . The legislature cannot lawfully destroy guaranteed rights of one man with the prime purpose of enriching another, even if for the moment, this may seem advantageous to the public. And the adoption of any "concept of jurisprudence" which permits facile disregard of the Constitution as long interpreted and respected will inevitably lead to its destruction. Then, all rights will be subject to the caprice of the hour; government by stable laws will pass. . . .

The precedent established by *Nebbia v. New York* is extremely important for two reasons. First, it affirms the right of a state to declare any type of business sufficiently affected with a public interest to be brought under public regulation. Second, it upholds the right of regulation designed to protect producers as well as consumers. Early legal controls were primarily concerned with protecting consumers in situations where a monopoly of an essential service or product resulted in undue exploitation or abuse of the general public. Today, regulation is equally concerned—or more concerned, it sometimes appears—with protecting the profits or vested interests of established concerns. This new objective is justified by the idea that protection of profits leads to stability in an industry and thus assures consumers of adequate quantity and quality or the maintenance of adequate service. Apparently, as long as the *Nebbia v. New York* decision is followed, the courts will take a hands-off policy in regard to such legislation as long as it is not "unreasonable, arbitrary, or capricious."

SUMMARY

We have seen that there are no valid universal criteria by which we can define a public utility in economic terms. Legally speaking, the situation is almost as vague. The courts have been somewhat erratic and inconsistent in applying the concept of "businesses affected with a public interest," and they now seem to have abandoned this function to legislative bodies. For practical purposes, then, it would not be far wrong to assume that a public utility is any business which an appropriate legislative body declares to be a public utility! Nevertheless, we commonly think of public utility operations as being confined to certain privately owned or publicly owned organizations in the areas of communications, energy, transportation, and water supply, and sometimes sewage and garbage disposal.

The discussion in this chapter of economic and legal public utility definitions, together with an understanding of the role of utilities in our economy, as developed in Chapter 1, prepares the way for Part II, where a detailed examination of the regulation of privately owned utilities will be undertaken.

NOTES

1. Intercity and long-distance transportation of all types traditionally has been classified as a public utility service also, but since transportation is usually considered a separate specialized field, it is treated only incidentally in this text.
2. We describe roughly here a situation which economists refer to as "price inelasticity." The same comments might be made in reference to "income inelasticity"; that is, small changes in family incomes typically do not significantly affect the quantities of public utility services consumed. Over a long period of time, of course, changes in prices or incomes do affect consumption.
3. So-called destructive price wars and cut-throat competition in the public utility field generally have been frowned upon by regulatory authorities, on the assumption that such competition may ultimately result in a deterioration of consumer services. It is likely, however, that the evil effects of price wars, and even the likelihood of their occurrence, have been overemphasized. After all, businessmen usually are not fond of such wars, and if only two or three large companies are involved, it is logical to expect that they will come to terms before competing themselves out of business. Paradoxically, we often justify the regulation of public utilities because they are "monopolies," yet a large part of our regulatory effort is spent in preventing them from competing with each other! Pricing is discussed in detail in Chapter 14.
4. See Chapter 8 for some interpretations of reasonable earnings.
5. Common law is based on a body of precedents or judicial decisions handed down from generation to generation. Statutory law, on the other hand, is based upon specific codes of laws formally enacted by legislative bodies. Common law frequently, and somewhat misleadingly, is referred to as "unwritten law."

UNIVERSITY OF BRISTOL

6. For examples, see *Olcott v. The Supervisors,* 83 U.S. 678, 694–695 (1873); *Smyth v. Ames,* 169 U.S. 466, 544 (1898); *Southwestern Bell Telephone Co. v. Public Service Commission of Missouri,* 262 U.S. 276, 291 (1923).
7. See *Munn v. Illinois,* 94 U.S. 113 (1877), below.
8. Eminent domain is the right to acquire private property for public use through legal condemnation proceedings and the payment of a just compensation. The state often grants this right to privately owned public utilities.
9. For an expression of this theory in denying the right to regulate a particular business, see *Charles Wolff Packing Co. v. Court of Industrial Relations,* 262 U.S. 522 (1923).
10. This theory was strongly argued in the dissenting opinion of Justice Brandeis in *New State Ice Co. v. Liebmann,* 285 U.S. 262, 301–302 (1932), and was upheld in *Nebbia v. People of the State of New York,* 291 U.S. 502 (1934). Pertinent portions of the latter case are reproduced below.
11. *Brass v. State of North Dakota ex rel. Stoeser,* 153 U.S. 391 (1894).
12. *German Alliance Insurance Company v. Lewis,* 233 U.S. 389 (1914).
13. *Block v. Hirsh,* 256 U.S. 135 (1921).
14. *Frost v. Corporation Commission of the State of Oklahoma,* 278 U.S. 515 (1929).
15. *Charles Wolff Packing Co. v. Court of Industrial Relations,* 262 U.S. 522 (1923).
16. *Tyson and Brother v. Banton,* 273 U.S. 418 (1927).
17. *Ribnik v. McBride,* 277 U.S. 350 (1928).
18. *Williams v. Standard Oil Company,* 278 U.S. 235 (1929).
19. *New State Ice Co. v. Liebmann,* 285 U.S. 262 (1932).

ADDITIONAL READINGS

1. Barnes, Irston R., *The Economics of Public Utility Regulation* (New York: F. S. Crofts, 1942), ch. 1, "The Public Utility Concept," pp. 1–22.
2. Buck, Solon Justus, *The Granger Movement* (Cambridge, Mass.: Harvard University Press, 1913), chs. 4, 5, 6, "Granger Railway Legislation," pp. 123–237.
3. Clark, John M., *Social Control of Business* (New York: McGraw-Hill, 1939), ch. 3, "Business: Private Right or Public Interest?" pp. 32–50.
4. Garfield, Paul J., and Wallace F. Lovejoy, *Public Utility Economics* (Englewood Cliffs, N. J.: Prentice-Hall, 1964), ch. 1, "The Public Utility Concept," pp. 1–15; ch. 2, "Economic Characteristics of Public Utilities," pp. 15–27.
5. Glaeser, Martin G., *Public Utilities in American Capitalism* (New York: Macmillan, 1957), ch. 12, "Evolution of the Public Utility Concept," pp. 195–205.
6. Jones, Eliot, and Truman C. Bigham, *Principles of Public Utilities* (New York: Macmillan, 1937), ch. 2, "Characteristics of Public Utilities," pp. 62–101.
7. Phillips, Charles F., Jr., *The Economics of Regulation,* rev. ed. (Homewood, Ill.: Richard D. Irwin, 1969), ch. 2, "The Economic Concepts of Regulation," pp. 19–44; ch. 3, "The Legal Concept of Public Regulation," pp. 45–82.
8. Trachsel, Herman H., *Public Utility Regulation* (Chicago: Richard D. Irwin, 1947), part I, "Nature of a Public Utility," pp. 2–69.
9. Troxel, Emery, *Economics of Public Utilities* (New York: Rinehart, 1947), ch. 1, "The Legal Concept of a Public Utility," pp. 3–24; ch. 2, "Economic Characteristics of Public Utilities," pp. 25–48.

10. Wilson, G. Lloyd, James M. Herring, and Roland B. Eutsler, *Public Utility Industries* (New York: McGraw-Hill, 1936), ch. 1, "The Characteristics of Public Utilities," pp. 1–25.
11. Wilson, G. Lloyd, James M. Herring, and Roland B. Eutsler, *Public Utility Regulation* (New York: McGraw-Hill, 1938), ch. 1, "Regulation Before the Establishment of State Commissions," pp. 1–20.
12. *Encyclopaedia of the Social Sciences.* Articles on "Common Law" and "Public Utilities."
13. *Brass v. State of North Dakota ex rel. Stoeser,* 153 U.S. 391 (1894).
14. *German Alliance Insurance Co. v. Lewis,* 233 U.S. 389 (1914).
15. *New State Ice Co. v. Liebmann,* 285 U.S. 262 (1932).
16. *Charles Wolff Packing Co.v. Court of Industrial Relations,* 262 U.S. 522 (1923).

Part Two

The Regulation of Privately Owned Utilities

3

The Legal Basis for Regulation

Our system of government is based on a distribution of powers among state governments and the federal government. Public utilities are regulated at both of these government levels. To understand utility regulation, therefore, it is necessary to understand the specific powers and limitations of each regulatory level.

The individual states, as sovereign bodies, exercise all authority not assigned to the federal government by the United States Constitution or prohibited to the states (that is, retained by the people) by the various state constitutions. The federal government, on the other hand, has only the powers granted it by the states in the United States Constitution. The authority delegated the federal government by the states is permanent, however, and cannot be recalled without a constitutional amendment.

In effect, the United States Constitution is a document granting specific powers to a government, while the various state constitutions are documents which limit the powers of otherwise sovereign bodies. The relation between the federal government and state governments is expressed in Article X of the United States Constitution, which reads, "The powers not delegated to the United States by the Constitution, nor prohibited by it to the States, are reserved to the States respectively, or to the people."

THE CONSTITUTIONAL BASIS OF FEDERAL REGULATORY POWERS

The authority of the federal government to regulate public utility businesses, as well as other businesses, is based upon specific constitutional clauses. Historically, the most important of these clauses has been the "commerce clause,"[1] which gives to Congress the power "To regulate Commerce with foreign Nations, and among the several States, and with the Indian Tribes."

For public utility regulatory purposes, the commerce clause is probably still of the greatest importance, but during the past generation the "welfare clause"[2] has assumed increasing importance. This clause says, "The Congress shall have Power to lay and collect Taxes, Duties, Imposts and Excises, to pay the Debts and provide for the common Defence and general Welfare of the United States."

Additional specific regulatory authority of importance in the public utility field found in Article I, Section 8, of the Constitution includes the following powers:

> To borrow Money on the credit of the United States;
> To establish . . . uniform Laws on the subject of Bankruptcies throughout the United States;
> To . . . fix the Standard of Weights and Measures;
> To establish Post Offices and post Roads;
> To promote the Progress of Science and useful Arts, by securing for limited Times to Authors and Inventors the exclusive Right to their respective Writings and Discoveries.

Also, several clauses found in Article I give the federal government paramount control over navigation, including all navigable inland waters,[3] and Article II grants the President the ". . . Power, by and with the Advice and Consent of the Senate, to make Treaties. . . ."

The federal government, as any other government, has the right of eminent domain and the right to manage and control its own lands and properties in any manner that it sees fit. This latter right is of considerable importance, because of the extensive federal holdings of public lands and natural resources, and in the absence of any constitutional restrictions on the right of the federal government to acquire, own, and possess any type of property.

JUDICIAL INTERPRETATION

The enumerated powers of the federal government at first glance appear to be ridiculously few in view of the tremendous amount of federal regulatory authority now exercised. Actually, however, our Constitution has been kept a living and flexible document through custom, which makes gradual evolutionary changes, and through judicial interpretation, which tends, with some lag perhaps, to adapt the relatively short, written document to the needs of an ever-changing economy. There is a great deal of truth in the adage that United States Supreme Court decisions follow the election returns.

Article III, Section 1, of the Constitution states, "The judicial Power of the United States, shall be vested in one supreme Court, and in such inferior Courts as the Congress may from time to time ordain and establish." Nowhere in the Constitution is any authority given to the Supreme Court to rule on the constitutionality of laws passed by Congress. This practice, though, has become a traditional and generally unquestioned prerogative of the Court under our unusual governmental system of checks and balances, and it has provided a method by which our Constitution can be made relevant to changing conditions without the need for formal amendment.

In early England the courts were the ultimate source of appeal; they could invalidate legislative acts contrary to England's "unwritten" constitution. Following the Revolution of 1688, the British Parliament became supreme, but the concept of legislative supremacy never pervaded American jurisprudence. From our beginning as a nation judges have insisted on their right of judicial review of legislative actions. A New Jersey court declared a law of its state legislature unconstitutional in 1780, and a Rhode Island court took similar action in 1786 (note that this was prior to the adoption of the Constitution). It was under the great John Marshall, however, whose strong personality dominated the United States Supreme Court during its formative period (Marshall was Chief Justice from 1801 until 1835), that the Court gained its position as final arbitrator in the American governmental structure.

It was in the case of *Marbury v. Madison,* 1 Cranch 137 (1803), that the basis for judicial review was firmly established. Marbury had been appointed a Justice of the Peace for the District of Columbia, but for political reasons his commission of office had not been delivered. Under a law of 1789, Marbury brought suit to compel Secretary of State Madison to deliver his commission, although the Constitution did not explicitly authorize such suits to be brought to the Supreme Court. The key issue involved was whether the 1789 statute or the Constitution was to be dominant. Portions of the opinion upholding the Constitution over the statute follow.

> OPINION BY CHIEF JUSTICE MARSHALL: . . . All those who have framed written constitutions contemplate them as forming the fundamental and paramount law of the nation, and, consequently, the theory of every such government must be, that an act of the legislature, repugnant to the constitution, is void. . . .
>
> It is emphatically the province and duty of the judicial department to say what the law is. . . . If two laws conflict with each other, the courts must decide on the operation of each.
>
> So if a law be in opposition to the Constitution; if both the law and the Constitution apply to a particular case, so that the court must either decide that case conformably to the law, disregarding the Constitution, or conformably to the Constitution, disregarding the law, the court must determine which of these conflicting rules governs the case. This is the very essence of judicial duty.
>
> If, then . . . the Constitution is superior to any ordinary act of the legislature, the Constitution, and not such ordinary act, must govern the case to which they both apply. . . .
>
> . . . The particular phraseology of the Constitution of the United States confirms and strengthens the principle, supposed to be essential to all written constitutions, that a law repugnant to the Constitution is void; and that courts, as well as other departments, are bound by that instrument. . . .

Following decisions have so firmly entrenched the precedent of *Marbury v. Madison* in our legal traditions that today no one seriously opposes the right of judicial review, even though such a right, in its practical effect, gives the United States Supreme Court the power to create new law. The lengths to which we are sometimes willing to go to retain this tradition are seen in the famous attempt of President Franklin D. Roosevelt to "pack" the Supreme Court with Justices favorable to his social concepts during the 1930's, and the devious legal maneuvering of several Southern states to avoid educational desegregation during the 1950's and 1960's.

IMPLIED POWERS

The so-called "elastic clause" of the United States Constitution,[4] which has been interpreted very broadly both by Congress and the courts, has served as an extremely important instrument for expanding the authority of the federal government within the framework of the Constitution. This clause creates the "implied powers" of the federal government by giving Congress the power "To make all Laws which shall be necessary and proper for carrying into Execution the foregoing Powers, and all other Powers vested by this Constitution in the Government of the United States, or in any Department or Officer thereof."

The leading decision on the elastic clause was given in the case of *McCulloch v. Maryland,* 4 Wheaton 316 (1819). The State of Maryland brought suit to collect state taxes on bank notes issued by the National Bank, chartered by the United States Government. The constitutional issue involved was whether or not the federal government had the authority to charter a bank. The Supreme Court upheld the implied powers of the federal government under the elastic clause, which was interpreted as being an additional power of government. Pertinent portions of the decision follow.

> OPINION BY CHIEF JUSTICE MARSHALL: . . . This government of the Union . . . is acknowledged by all to be one of enumerated powers. . . .
>
> Among the enumerated powers, we do not find that of establishing a bank or creating a corporation. But there is no phrase in the instrument which, like the articles of confederation, excludes incidental or implied powers; and which requires that everything granted shall be expressly and minutely described. . . . A constitution . . . requires, that only its great outlines should be marked, its important objects designated, and the minor ingredients which compose those objects be deduced from the nature of the objects themselves. . . .
>
> . . . A government, intrusted with such ample powers, on the due execution of which the happiness and prosperity of the nation so vitally depends, must also be intrusted with ample means for their execution. The power being given, it is the interest of the nation to facilitate its execution. It can never be their interest, and cannot be presumed to have been their intention, to clog and embarrass its execution by withholding the most appropriate means. . . .
>
> The government which has a right to do an act, and has imposed on it the duty of performing that act, must, according to the dictates of reason, be allowed to select the means; and those who contend that it may not select any appropriate means, that one particular mode of effecting the object is excepted, take upon themselves the burden of establishing that exception.
>
> . . . To have prescribed the means by which government should, in all future time, execute its powers, would have been to change, entirely, the character of the instrument, and give it the properties of a legal code. It would have been an unwise attempt to provide, by immutable rules, for exigencies which, if foreseen at all, must have been seen dimly, and which can be best provided for as they occur. . . . Sound construction of the Constitution must allow to the national legislature that discretion, with respect to the means by which the powers it confers are to be carried into execution, which will enable that body to perform the high duties assigned to it, in the manner most beneficial to the people. Let the end be legitimate, let it be within the scope of the Constitution, and all means which are appropriate, which are plainly adapted to that end, which are not prohibited, but consist with the letter and spirit of the Constitution, are constitutional.

Since the decision of *McCulloch v. Maryland,* there has been no real question regarding the implied powers of the federal government as such. Those legal problems which have arisen under the elastic clause have dealt instead with defining just how much elasticity is available to the government. The tendency has been, in general, towards more and more elasticity.

RESTRICTIONS ON FEDERAL REGULATORY POWERS

THE RESERVATION OF POWERS TO THE STATE OR PEOPLE

Since the United States Constitution is a permissive document only, one of the principal restrictions on federal powers is that powers other than those enumerated or implied in the Constitution are reserved to the sovereign states or to the people, as expressed in Article X. In many respects this is, or could be, a serious limitation. The courts have ruled, though, that Article X does not conflict with, or limit, federal powers under the elastic clause,[5] and since this clause has been interpreted broadly, it has tended to some extent to nullify the effect of the reserved powers of the states.

DUE PROCESS AND EQUAL RIGHTS: FEDERAL

The concept of due process of law, or following the spirit and procedures of the laws of the land, has been a vital part of Anglo-American jurisprudence at least since the granting of the Magna Carta (A.D. 1215). The "due process clause" of the United States Constitution (a part of the celebrated Fifth Amendment) states that no person shall ". . . be deprived of life, liberty, or property, without due process of law; nor shall private property be taken for public use, without just compensation."

Although the wording is clear, the concept of what constitutes due process is both debatable and flexible. In application, we have the traditional version of procedural due process, which deals with such outward manifestations of justice as the right of an accused to face and cross-examine his accusers and to have a public trial before a jury. Substantive due process, on the other hand, deals with less tangible aspects, such as whether a law itself is reasonable and fair, and is much more vague. Laws have been held in conflict with substantive due process because they allegedly violated the "spirit of free enterprise."[6]

The due process clause, in both interpretations, has been a strong source of refuge for businesses attempting to escape regulation. In recent years, however, substantive due process has not provided the haven of earlier days. Much of the social legislation of the 1930's and later years would without doubt have foundered on the rock of due process during earlier decades. This does not necessarily mean that the courts have entirely abandoned substantive due process, but rather that the courts either have been less willing to impose their own economic and social ideas in their decisions, or that the ideas of the personnel of the courts have been more in harmony with the ideas of the legislators. Well-written laws and efficiently operated administrative agencies seldom make the mistake of violating procedural due process.

Potentially, the "equal rights clause" of the Constitution, Article IV, Section 2, is a restriction on federal regulatory powers. This clause states, "The Citizens of each State shall be entitled to all Privileges and Immunities of Citizens in the several States." In practice, however, there has been little violation of the concept of equal rights under the law by the federal government.[7]

STATE REGULATORY AUTHORITY AND RESTRICTIONS

As stated above, under our system of government the individual states are sovereign political bodies. As such, they have police power, the right of eminent domain, the right of taxation, and control over their own lands, properties, and natural resources. This means that states are limited mainly by their own constitutions and by the powers which they have conferred upon the federal government in the United States Constitution. As state constitutions differ widely in detail, the following discussion will be limited to the restrictions placed upon states by the United States Constitution.

Within its range of jurisdiction, the United States Constitution, as stated in Article VI, ". . . and the Laws of the United States which shall be made in Pursuance thereof; and all Treaties made, or which shall be made, under the Authority of the United States, shall be the Supreme Law of the Land; and the Judges in every State shall be bound thereby, any Thing in the Constitution or Laws of any State to the contrary notwithstanding."

DUE PROCESS AND EQUAL RIGHTS: STATE

Article XIV, Section 1, of the United States Constitution places upon the states an "equal rights" or "equal protection" restriction, similar to that placed upon the federal government by Article IV, Section 2, as well as a "due process" restriction similar to that placed on the federal government by the Fifth Amendment. Section 1 states, in part, "No State shall make or enforce any law which shall abridge the privileges or immunities of citizens of the United States; nor shall any State deprive any person of life, liberty, or property, without due process of law; nor deny to any person within its jurisdiction the equal protection of the laws."

The due process clause of the Fourteenth Amendment provides an interesting example of the flexibility of the United States Constitution. This amendment was added after the Civil War for the protection of the rights of recently freed Negroes of the Southern states. Smart attorneys, however, soon turned it into a bulwark for the protection of corporations against regulatory governmental encroachment. Long before the Fourteenth Amendment was passed, it had been established that a corporation is a legal "person," with many of the legal rights and privileges of a natural person.[8] As such, a corporation may no more be deprived of its rights of due process than may an individual. Actually, at least until quite recently, corporations have received much more protection under the Fourteenth Amendment than have the Negroes for whom it was designed. It has only been since the 1930's that due process has ceased to be an effective shield against exercise of the police power of the state.

The equal protection and equal rights clauses have been, and are, of considerable importance in preventing discrimination, particularly against out-of-state businesses. This has been especially true in taxation cases, in which outside businesses have alleged that they have been discriminated against. The equal rights clause does not require that a person residing in one state and doing business in another be entitled to the same privileges in his business state as in his home state, however. A common example is found in the gasoline tax, which varies widely among states. A person traveling in a state other than his home state must pay the gasoline tax required in the state where he is traveling, but he cannot be forced to pay more than residents of the latter state.

Neither does the equal rights concept mean that all persons or groups must be treated in exactly the same manner. Classifications of individuals into groups based upon occupational or other factors may not be discriminatory, providing such classifications are not unreasonable, arbitrary, or capricious. The United States Supreme Court has held, "The equal protection of the laws does not mean that all occupations that are called by the same name must be treated in the same way."[9] And again, "A law which affects the activities of some groups differently from the way in which it affects the activities of other groups is not necessarily banned by the Fourteenth Amendment."[10] Inhabitants or businesses of an outside state, though, cannot be discriminated against unduly merely on the basis of nonresidency. The Court has ruled that ". . . one of the privileges which the clause guarantees to citizens of State A is that of doing business in State B on terms of substantial equality with the citizens of that state."[11] Note that the key word in this interpretation is "substantial," which is not the same as "identical."

In practice, the courts have been fairly liberal in allowing legislative bodies to operate flexibly within the concept of substantial equality. For example, a Texas law exempting farmers from state antitrust laws has been held valid,[12] as has a New York law imposing a tax on public utility businesses which was not levied on other businesses,[13] an Indiana tax on chain stores based on the number of stores in the chain,[14] and the federal Social Security law which exempted certain categories of employers and employees while taxing others.[15] On the other hand, a New York law giving income tax exemptions to residents which were denied to nonresidents has been held invalid,[16] as has a Kentucky gross sales tax in which the burden of taxation increased progressively with the amount of sales.[17]

It should be pointed out that the concepts of equal rights and equal protection do not take precedence over the police power of a sovereign state, and with the growing popularity of the police power concept there has been a consequent weakening of Article IV, Section 2, and Article XIV, Section 1, as well as of Article V, of the United States Constitution.

FULL FAITH AND CREDIT

Article IV, Section 1, of the Constitution requires, "Full Faith and Credit shall be given in each State to the public Acts, Records, and Judicial Proceedings of every other State." This requirement, obligating the several states to respect the laws and judgments of all its neighbors, is a necessity for our system of government. Although restrictive in effect, in practice it does not today create many difficulties except in the field of "quickie" divorces.

SANCTITY OF CONTRACTS

The "sanctity of contract clause" of the United States Constitution, Article I, Section 10, states, "No State shall . . . pass any . . . Law impairing the Obligations of Contracts. . . ." It is interesting to note that no similar restriction is placed upon the federal government, but court interpretation generally has made the clause equally applicable to federal and state statutes.

The leading case upholding the sanctity of contracts is *Sturges v. Crowninshield,*[18] in which a New York law relieving bankrupt debtors of obligations incurred before the law was enacted was held invalid. Chief Justice Marshall, in his decision, said, "A contract is an agreement in which a party undertakes to do, or not to do, a particular thing. The law binds him to perform his undertaking, and this is, of course, the obligation of his contract," and ". . . contracts should be inviolable. The Constitution therefore declares that no state shall pass 'any law impairing the obligation of contracts. . . .'"

Contracts are binding upon states, as well as upon individuals.[19] Contract rights are not absolute, however. To be binding, of course, a contract must be made for a legal purpose and must meet all the legal tests of validity. Also, states in granting contracts, such as charters and franchises, can reserve the power to alter them later. In addition, the sovereign police power and the equally sovereign right of eminent domain take precedence over contract rights, and even the state itself cannot contract away these powers. The tax power, while an attribute of sovereignty, is not as strong as the police power and the right of eminent domain, and may be contracted away by the state.

Although it has long been understood that contract rights must give way to the police power in case of urgency, the economic depression of the early 1930's provided a clear-cut example of the supremacy of the police power. The State of Minnesota passed a law prohibiting the foreclosure of mortgages for a certain time. Although this did not discharge the debt nor relieve the debtor of any of his ultimate obligations, it did destroy the contractual right of the creditor to foreclose promptly for nonpayment. In upholding the Minnesota statute, the Court stated,

> . . . It does not follow that conditions may not arise in which a temporary restraint of enforcement may be consistent with the spirit and purpose of the constitutional provision and thus be found to be within the range of the reserved power of the State to protect the vital interests of the community. It cannot be maintained that the constitutional provision should be so construed as to prevent limited and temporary interpositions with respect to the enforcement of contracts if made necessary by a great public calamity such as fire, flood, or earthquake. . . . If state power exists to give temporary relief from the enforce-

> ment of contracts in the presence of disasters due to physical causes . . . that power cannot be said to be non-existent when the urgent public need demanding such relief is produced by other and economic causes. . . .[20]

As mentioned before, although there is no specific constitutional sanctity of contract requirement for the federal government, courts generally have read such a requirement into the Constitution. In the early 1930's, however, after the United States went off the gold standard, a suit was brought by a holder of a corporation bond calling for payment in gold. The bondholder alleged that his contractual rights were impaired because it was no longer legal for him to be paid in gold. The Court upheld the federal statute, however, on the grounds that no contract could be allowed to hamper Congress in the exercise of its constitutional authority (in this instance, the authority to control monetary standards).[21]

Article I, Section 10, of the United States Constitution further restricts the powers of states by prohibiting any "ex post facto Law," forbidding states from entering into "any Treaty, Alliance, or Confederation," and requiring the consent of Congress before any state can "enter into any Agreement or Compact with another State, or with a foreign Power."

LOCAL POWERS

The authority of local government bodies and subdivisions, such as counties, municipalities, school and public utility districts, and similar political units, is derived directly from the state. Generally, the state constitution or statute creating such a subdivision specifies its powers and jurisdiction, and like the federal government, the local government is limited to its expressly granted or implied powers. Implied local government powers, however, are generally not as broadly interpreted as implied federal powers. Since a considerable amount of public utility regulation in some states occurs at the local level in many fields, details of the acts creating such local political units and defining their powers are of particular importance to utility firms. Such details vary widely, of course, not only among states but within any individual state.

SUMMARY

Individual states are sovereign political bodies within our federal system, with both federal and local powers being derived from the states. The federal Constitution, like the local government charter, is permissive in nature, while state constitutions are limiting documents. For a federal action to be valid, it must come within the powers granted the federal government under the United States Constitution, while a state act is presumed to be within state powers if it has not been expressly prohibited by the state constitution or surrendered to the federal government. Because of the irrevocable grant of powers under the United States Constitution, however, and the judicial interpretation and expansion of that document, the federal government has considerable regulatory power over numerous aspects of our economy and paramount powers in many other areas.

Public utilities are regulated either by federal or state (including local) government, and often by both. In many instances, regulatory powers are divided clearly between these different government levels. In many other instances, however, as will be shown in Chapter 4, regulatory authority overlaps or is not clear-cut, leading to conflicts between federal and state juristictions. Public utilities are often caught in the middle of these conflicts.

NOTES

1. Found in Article I, Section 8, U.S. Constitution.
2. Found in Article I, Section 8, U.S. Constitution.
3. Some very small streams, with little or no history of navigation, have been held to be navigable waters.
4. The last clause of Article I, Section 8.
5. For an example, see *Case v. Bowles,* 327 U.S. 92 (1946).
6. For examples, see *Allgeyer v. Louisiana,* 165 U.S. 578 (1897); *Lochner v. New York,* 198 U.S. 45 (1905); *Adkins v. Children's Hospital,* 261 U.S. 525 (1923).
7. Most cases hinging on equal rights or equal protection have been based on actions of individual states and have been decided in whole or in part under the Fourteenth Amendment, discussed later.
8. The classic definition of a corporation, given by Chief Justice John Marshall and memorized by succeeding generations of college students, begins "A corporation is an artificial being, invisible, intangible, and existing only in contemplation of law." *Dartmouth College v. Woodward,* 4 Wheaton 518 (1819).
9. *Dominion Hotel, Inc. v. Arizona,* 249 U.S. 265 (1919).
10. *Kotch v. Board of River Port Pilot Commissioners,* 330 U.S. 552 (1947).
11. *Toomer v. Witsell,* 334 U.S. 385 (1948).
12. *Tigner v. Texas,* 310 U.S. 141 (1940).
13. *New York Rapid Transit Corp. v. New York,* 303 U.S. 573 (1938).
14. *State Board of Tax Commissioners of Indiana v. Jackson,* 283 U.S. 527 (1937).
15. *Stewart Machine Co. v. Davis,* 301 U.S. 548 (1937).
16. *Travis v. Yale and Towne Manufacturing Co.,* 252 U.S. 60 (1920).
17. *Stewart Dry Goods Co. v. Lewis,* 294 U.S. 550 (1935).
18. Found in 4 Wheaton 122 (1819).
19. For examples, see *Fletcher v. Peck,* 6 Cranch 87 (1810), and *Dartmouth College v. Woodward,* 4 Wheaton 518 (1819).
20. *Home Building and Loan Association v. Blaisdell,* 290 U.S. 398 (1934).
21. *Norman v. B. & O. R.,* 294 U.S. 240 (1935).

ADDITIONAL READINGS

1. Anderson, Ronald A., *Government Regulation of Business,* 3d ed. (Cincinnati: South-Western Publishing Co., 1966), ch. 1, "The Division of Power," pp. 1–16; ch. 2, "The Courts as Guardian of the Constitution," pp. 17–23.

2. Anshen, Melvin, and Francis D. Wormuth, *Private Enterprise and Public Policy* (New York: Macmillan, 1954), ch. 2, "Constitutional Principles," pp. 30–58.
3. Carr, Robert K., *The Supreme Court and Judicial Review.* American Government in Action Series (New York: Farrar and Rinehart, 1942), ch. 3, "The Genesis of Judicial Supremacy: The Federal and State Conventions," pp. 37–56.
4. Cook, Franklin H., *Principles of Business and the Federal Law* (New York: Macmillan, 1951), ch. 1, "Distribution of Government Powers," pp. 3–23.
5. Corwin, Edward S., *John Marshall and the Constitution.* The Chronicles of America Series, XVI (New Haven: Yale University Press, 1921), ch. 1, "The Establishment of the National Judiciary," pp. 1–24; ch. 5, "The Tenets of Nationalism," pp. 121–146.
6. Glaeser, Martin G., *Public Utilities in American Capitalism* (New York: Macmillan, 1957), ch. 13, "The Constitutional Basis of Public Utility Regulation," pp. 206–219.
7. Hall, Ford P., *Government and Business,* 3d ed. (New York: McGraw-Hill, 1949), ch. 2, "Constitutional Limitations Upon the Control of Business," pp. 18–28.
8. Jackson, Robert H., *The Supreme Court in the American System of Government* (Cambridge, Mass.: Harvard University Press, 1955), ch. 2, "The Supreme Court as a Law Court," pp. 28–52.
9. Pegrum, Dudley F., *Transportation: Economics and Public Policy,* rev. ed. (Homewood, Ill.: Richard D. Irwin, 1968), ch. 2, "The Agencies of Regulation," pp. 255–286.
10. Rohlfing, Charles C., Edward W. Carter, Bradford W. West, and John G. Hervey, *Business and Government,* 6th ed. (Brooklyn: Foundation Press, 1953), ch. 1, "The Constitution and Business," pp. 1–37.
11. Wilcox, Clair, *Public Policies Towards Business,* 4th ed. (Homewood, Ill.: Richard D. Irwin, 1971), ch. 2, "Methods and Limits of Control," pp. 17–45.

4

Conflicts Between Federal and State Regulatory Powers

Although the federal government, under the Constitution, has been given the power to regulate interstate commerce, with intrastate regulation presumably left to the several sovereign states, there remains a considerable area of conflict between federal and state regulatory powers. Before regulation can be applied, a number of knotty questions must be answered: What is "commerce"? What is meant by "interstate" and "intrastate"? What regulatory authority, if any, do states have over interstate commerce? What power, if any, does the federal government have over intrastate commerce? What about those borderline cases, in which intrastate and interstate commerce are so mixed that one cannot be regulated effectively without regulation of the other? These questions, and similar ones, must be answered by the courts. Thus, to find the answers one must look at leading court decisions dealing with these problems.

REGULATION OF INTERSTATE COMMERCE

Among the first questions that had to be answered in applying the commerce clause of the United States Constitution was, What is meant by "commerce among the several states"? This is what Congress has the power to regulate. Chief Justice Marshall, in a famous 1824 decision, defined both "commerce" and "among the several states."

Robert Fulton and Robert R. Livingston had been given the exclusive right by the state of New York to operate steamboats on the waters of that state. This right had been assigned to Ogden. Two steamboats, however, were operated by Gibbons between New Jersey and New York, partly in New York State waters. Ogden obtained an injunction against Gibbons, which was upheld by the New York courts. The case was brought to the United States Supreme Court upon appeal, and it turned in part upon whether or not the operation of steamboats is commerce, and whether or not operations affecting only two states is "among the several states." Obviously, his attorneys felt, if Gibbons was engaged in interstate commerce, this business could not be regulated by the state of New York. Pertinent parts of the decision in *Gibbons v. Ogden,* 22 U.S. 1 (1824), upholding Gibbons, follow.

OPINION BY CHIEF JUSTICE MARSHALL: . . . The subject to be regulated is commerce; and . . . commerce, undoubtedly, is traffic, but it is something more: it is intercourse. It describes the commercial intercourse between nations, and parts of nations, in all its branches, and is regulated by prescribing rules for carrying on that intercourse. . . .

To what commerce does this power extend? The Constitution informs us, to commerce "with foreign nations, and among the several States, and with the Indian tribes."

The word "among" means intermingled with. A thing which is among others, is intermingled with them. . . .

Comprehensive as the word "among" is, it may very properly be restricted to that commerce which concerns more states than one. . . . The completely internal commerce of a State, then, may be considered as reserved for the state itself.

. . . Commerce among the States must, of necessity, be commerce with the States. . . . The power of Congress, then, whatever it may be, must be exercised within the territorial jurisdiction of the several States. . . .

. . . What is this power?

It is the power to regulate; that is, to prescribe the rule by which commerce is to be governed. This power, like all others vested in Congress, is complete in itself, may be exercised to its utmost extent, and acknowledges no limitations, other than are prescribed in the Constitution. These are expressed in plain terms. . . . The power over commerce with foreign nations, and among the several states, is vested in Congress as absolutely as it would be in a single government. . . . The wisdom and the discretion of Congress, their identity with the people, and the influence which their constituents possess at elections, are . . . the sole restraints on which they have relied, to secure them from its abuse. They are the restraints on which the people must often rely solely, in all representative governments.

. . . When a State proceeds to regulate commerce with foreign nations, or among the several States, it is exercising the very power that is granted to Congress, and is doing the very thing which Congress is authorized to do. . . .

. . . The sole question is, can a State regulate commerce with foreign nations and among the States, while Congress is regulating it?

In our complex system . . . contests respecting power must arise. . . . This, however, does not prove that the one is exercising, or has a right to exercise, the powers of the other.

. . . Congress may control the State laws, so far as it may be necessary to control them, for the regulation of commerce.

The *Gibbons v. Ogden* decision provided a foundation upon which the following interpretations have been based. The concept of what constitutes interstate commerce generally has expanded constantly to include new industries and new situations. For example, a later Chief Justice, in speaking of congressional regulatory powers under the United States Constitution in a telegraph case, said, "The powers thus granted are not confined to the instrumentalities . . . known or in use when the Constitution was adopted, but they keep pace with the progress of the country. . . ."[1]

Similarly, articles of commerce originating in one state and going nonstop through another state and back to the first state, or through offshore waters or a foreign

UNIVERSITY
OF BRISTOL
LIBRARY
W.M.L.

country and back to the originating state, are in interstate commerce. Even goods transported across state lines without any intent of sale come under the interstate commerce clause—the act of crossing state boundaries alone is determining.[2]

Although Chief Justice Marshall may have said more in the *Gibbons v. Ogden* case than was absolutely necessary in deciding the points at issue, he did not have the final word on the matter of federal versus state regulation of commerce. This case marked a beginning rather than an ending.

THE "INDIVISIBLE THEORY" VERSUS THE "SEPARATION THEORY"

Marshall's argument, by implication at least, held that the power to regulate interstate commerce is indivisible, and since that power is given to Congress by the Constitution, the federal government necessarily has the sole right to engage in such regulation and states have no rights (subject to the qualifications of the police and tax powers of states, of course, both of which may be applied to interstate commerce, but not primarily for regulatory purposes). This argument sometimes has been called the "indivisible theory of regulation."

In opposition to the indivisible theory, a "separation theory of regulation" has been developed. This holds that two types of regulatory problems may exist in interstate commerce: *general* problems, which are best handled in a uniform way and thus are subject only to federal regulation, and *local* problems, which, because of their diversity, are best handled at the state level and thus may be regulated by states if Congress has not taken regulatory action already. The separation theory is the most popular today.

The leading separation theory case was decided in 1851. Pennsylvania enacted a law requiring ships sailing from Philadelphia to utilize the services of an approved pilot in leaving port, or as an alternative, to pay an amount equivalent to one half the pilotage fee into a fund to be used for the "relief of Distressed and Decayed pilots, their widows and children." Cooley, under federal license, operated ships between Philadelphia and New York, and he refused either to use local pilots or to pay the alternative pilotage fee. Cooley maintained that his own pilots were capable, and citing the *Gibbons v. Ogden* precedent, he said that he was engaged in interstate commerce and thereby subject only to congressional regulation. After losing in the lower courts, Cooley appealed to the United States Supreme Court. Portions of the decision in *Cooley v. The Board of Wardens of the Port of Philadelphia*, 53 U.S. 298 (1851), unfavorable to Cooley, are given here.

> OPINION BY JUSTICE CURTIS: . . . If the Constitution excluded the States from making any law regulating commerce, certainly Congress cannot regrant, or in any manner reconvey to the States that power. . . . On the other hand, if it were admitted that the existence of this power in Congress, like the power of taxation, is compatible with the existence of a similar power in the States, then it would be in conformity with the contemporary exposition of the Constitution . . . that it is not the mere existence of such a power, but its exercise by Congress, which may be incompatible with the exercise of the same power by the States,

and that the States may legislate in the absence of Congressional regulation. . . .

. . . When it is said that the nature of the power requires that it should be exercised exclusively by Congress, it must be intended to refer to the subjects of that power, and to say they are of such a nature as to require exclusive regulation by Congress. Now the power to regulate commerce, embraces a vast field, containing not only many, but exceedingly various subjects, quite unlike in their nature; some imperatively demanding a single uniform rule, operating equally on the commerce of the United States in every port; and some, like the subject now in question, as imperatively demanding that diversity, which alone can meet the local necessities of navigation.

Either absolutely to affirm, or deny that the nature of this power requires exclusive legislation by Congress, is to lose sight of the nature of the subjects of this power, and to assert concerning all of them, what is really applicable but to a part. Whatever subjects of this power are in their nature national, or admit only of one uniform system, or plan of regulation, may justly be said to be of such a nature as to require exclusive regulation by Congress. . . . The nature of this subject is such, that until Congress should find it necessary to exert its power, it should be left to the legislation of the States. . . . It is local and not national. . . .

A more concrete exposition of the separation theory was given in 1880, in *County of Mobile v. Kimball,* 102 U.S. 691. The County of Mobile, Alabama, refused payment for harbor construction work performed by a contractor. One of the defenses for nonpayment was that the contract was invalid from the beginning because such improvements were in an area subject to the commercial regulation of Congress. The Supreme Court, however, held that this was a local matter. Parts of the Court's decision follow.

OPINION BY JUSTICE FIELD: . . . The subjects, indeed, upon which Congress can act under this power are of infinite variety. . . . Some of them are national in their character, and admit and require uniformity of regulation, affecting alike all the States; others are local, or are mere aids to commerce, and can only be properly regulated by provisions adapted to their special circumstances and localities.

. . . Where from the nature of the subject or the sphere of its operation the case is local and limited, special regulations adapted to the immediate locality could only have been contemplated. State action upon such subjects can constitute no interference with the commercial power of Congress, for when that acts the State authority is superseded. Inaction of Congress upon these subjects of a local nature or operation, unlike its inaction upon matters affecting all the States and requiring uniformity of regulation, is not to be taken as a declaration that nothing shall be done with respect to them, but is rather to be deemed a declaration that for the time being, and until it sees fit to act, they may be regulated by State authority.

The legal principle is well established, then, that states as a rule can deal with local problems of interstate commerce if Congress has taken no regulatory action on such problems. Conflicts continue to arise regarding matters of *fact* (that is, what is a local and what is a general problem), but the matter of *law* appears to be fairly clear.

STATE CONTROL OF GENERAL PROBLEMS

Now, what about general problems in interstate commerce? Can states also regulate such problems in the absence of congressional regulation? The *Gibbons v. Ogden* case, of course, did not recognize a distinction between local and general problems, but it held that all interstate commerce was subject exclusively to Congressional control. The implication of the *Cooley v. Board of Wardens* case, although it did not deal specifically with this point, also appears to be that states cannot regulate general problems, that is, that by not acting, Congress actually has taken a form of action and has expressed its desire that no regulation be exercised.

Decisions given in the Granger cases (see Chapter 2) assumed that states *can* regulate general aspects of interstate commerce if Congress has not undertaken such regulation. Apparently, the reasoning behind these decisions was that there are things which "should" be regulated and that it is better to have state regulation than no regulation at all. After ten years of individual state regulation of interstate railroads, however, it became clear that such local regulation was leading to chaos in the transportation field. Consequently, in the *Wabash* case, dealing with an Illinois law prohibiting railroads from charging more for shorter than for longer hauls of similar commodities over the same route, much of the Granger legislation was reversed by the Supreme Court's declaration that

> . . . if each one of the states through whose territories these goods are transported can fix its own rules for prices, for modes of transit, for times and modes of delivery, and all the other incidents of transportation to which the word "regulation" can be applied, it is readily seen that the embarrassments upon interstate transportation, as an element of interstate commerce, might be too oppressive to be submitted to.[3]

With effective state regulation of railroads abolished, Congress could no longer ignore the transportation problem. One result of the prohibition of state regulation of general aspects of interstate commerce, then, was the passage, in 1887, of "An Act to Regulate Commerce" (Part I of today's Interstate Commerce Act), which put the federal government into the regulatory field on a large scale for the first time. Although the original Interstate Commerce Act applied only to interstate railroads (since extended to other forms of domestic interstate transportation, except air, which is regulated under separate, similar legislation), it has provided a model for succeeding federal and state regulation in many fields, including the public utilities field, just as earlier Granger legislation to a considerable extent had formed a pattern for the Interstate Commerce Act itself. Also, many of the legal and administrative principles applicable to present-day public utilities, and other regulated businesses, have grown out of federal experience with the Interstate Commerce Act.

The *Wabash* case established the principle that states cannot regulate general aspects of interstate commerce even if Congress has taken no regulatory action. There are certain exceptions or near-exceptions to this principle, however. It has been pointed out that states may exercise their sovereign police powers even though interstate commerce may be involved. Similarly, states may tax interstate commerce, although not in a discriminatory or burdensome manner (for example, a traveler may be required to pay a higher gasoline tax in a neighboring state than in his home state, but he cannot be required to pay a higher tax than that paid by citizens of the neighboring state). Although these two exceptions are, in effect, regulation of interstate commerce, they are permissible on the grounds that regulation is not the primary intent.

In addition, states traditionally have exercised a fairly broad and strict control over natural resources within their boundaries. For example, in preserving wildlife, states have been permitted to charge higher license fees to out-of-state hunters and fishermen than to their own residents. Oil and natural gas production quotas have been established by state regulatory authorities in the name of conservation (critics sometimes allege that such quotas are more for the conservation of high prices than for the conservation of resources), and at least one state (Oregon) requires a person to obtain a permit for cutting Christmas trees off his own land for sale in interstate commerce. In water resource matters, however, states have been less successful in retaining control, as will be seen in the section of this chapter that deals with navigable waters and federal lands. Arizona, despite twice calling out its National Guard to "protect its water from Californians," was unable to prevent construction of Parker Dam, a diversion facility below Hoover (Boulder) Dam.

Finally, Congress may specifically permit the individual states to regulate or control general matters of interstate commerce which would otherwise be subject only to federal control. Such permission is granted only by duly enacted statutes. Notable examples are found in state regulation of transportation and trade of intoxicating liquors, of interstate insurance companies, and of tidelands (submerged lands below the low-tide mark).

In review, then, primary authority over the general aspects of interstate commerce rests with the federal government, but states may regulate local problems involving interstate commerce and may even regulate some general aspects of such commerce under specified conditions.

REGULATION OF INTRASTATE COMMERCE

According to the United States Constitution states have the sole regulatory authority over matters of intrastate commerce. This general rule is qualified by many exceptions, however.

Early experience in the transportation field indicated that the federal government must be allowed to regulate intrastate commerce when such regulation is necessary for adequate regulation of interstate traffic (safety appliances on railroad cars used interchangeably in intrastate and interstate transportation, for example). Also, where intrastate and interstate traffic are so mixed that they cannot be separated, the federal government may regulate both. An example of this is found in the "rules-of-the-road" for airplane flight, which apply both to long-distance and local flights. In addition, if intrastate traffic is dangerous to interstate commerce, as poorly packed dynamite shipments or diseased livestock or vegetables might be, for example, the federal government may exercise regulatory authority.

THE SHREVEPORT DOCTRINE

The federal government may regulate intrastate commerce under certain other conditions. The famous Shreveport Doctrine, upheld by the United States Supreme Court in 1914, permits federal regulation of intrastate commerce in instances where a burden would be placed on interstate commerce by the absence of such intrastate regulation. The original Shreveport case was brought on by railroad rates which were substantially higher from Shreveport (in western Louisiana) to points in eastern Texas than the rates from Houston and Dallas to the same points. Shreveport distributors protested that their Houston and Dallas competitors had an unfair advantage. The Interstate Commerce Commission, on the basis of an investigation which found the rates from Shreveport reasonable, ordered the rates from Houston and Dallas raised on the grounds that they were discriminatory and burdensome on interstate commerce. The Texas Railroad Commission, however, maintained that this traffic was entirely within Texas and refused to permit the railroads to raise their rates. This deadlock between the federal and the Texas regulatory commissions was broken by the decision in *Houston, East and West Texas Railway Co. v. United States,* 234 U.S. 342 (1914), quoted in part here.

> OPINION BY JUSTICE HUGHES: . . . Whenever the interstate and intra-state transactions of carriers are so related that the government of the one involves the control of the other, it is Congress, and not the State, that is entitled to prescribe the final and dominant rule, for otherwise Congress would be denied the exercise of its Constitutional authority and the State, and not the Nation, would be supreme in the national field. . . .
>
> . . . Congress in the exercise of its paramount power may prevent the common instrumentalities of interstate and intra-state commercial intercourse from being used in their intra-state operations to the injury of interstate commerce. . . .
>
> . . . Congress is entitled to maintain its own standard as to these rates and to forbid any discriminatory action by interstate carriers which will obstruct the freedom of movement of interstate traffic over their lines in accordance with the terms it establishes. . . .
>
> . . . When . . . unjust discrimination against interstate trade arises from the relation of intra-state to interstate rates. . . . Such a matter is one with which Congress alone is competent to deal. . . .

Further concrete enunciation of the Shreveport Doctrine was given in a later case, in which the Interstate Commerce Commission required a railroad rate increase on both interstate and intrastate shipments of building materials that placed some Louisiana communities at a competitive disadvantage with Texas communities. In upholding the commission's order, the Supreme Court said,

> Congress . . . has empowered the Interstate Commerce Commission . . . to require the carriers to make and apply on intra-state transportation such reasonable charges as will produce its fair share of the amounts needed to pay operating expenses, provide an adequate railway system and yield a reasonable rate of return on the value of the property used in the transportation service.[4]

It appears from this decision that an intrastate rate which is insufficient to cover actual direct operating expenses plus something additional for the maintenance of required facilities (that is, some contribution to overhead or fixed expenses) may be considered burdensome on interstate commerce if both intrastate and interstate business is being conducted by a transportation or public utility firm. The concept of undue burden on interstate commerce was applied to the abandonment of intrastate railroad services in the Transportation Act of 1958; that is, if permission to abandon had been denied by a state commission, the Interstate Commerce Commission, under certain circumstances, could override the state's veto.

The Shreveport Doctrine, however, does not give blanket authority to the federal government to remove all inequalities between intrastate and interstate commerce. Instead, only "undue or unreasonable advantages, preferences, or prejudices" or "unjustly discriminatory" inequalities may be removed by federal action. This has been pointed out in a still later case dealing with the Shreveport Doctrine, in which the Interstate Commerce Commission ordered North Carolina intrastate railroad passenger fares to be increased to the same level as interstate passenger fares. In reversing the commission's order on the grounds that no finding of unreasonable or unjust discrimination had been made, the Court stated,

> Intra-state transportation is primarily the concern of the state. . . . The finding that interstate passengers paid higher fares than intra-state passengers for the same facilities is an inadequate support for nullifying state rates. . . . The power of the Commission to require states to raise their intra-state rates depends upon whether intra-state traffic is contributing its fair share of the earnings required. . . . The Commission must make findings on that issue. . . . Without such findings supported by evidence, the Commission was not authorized to find that the intra-state rates discriminated against interstate commerce.[5]

It seems clear, then, that although the federal government may regulate intrastate commerce to remove burdens from interstate commerce, the mere existence of inequality does not necessarily constitute a burden.

THE *DARBY* CASE

One of the broadest expressions of congressional regulatory power over both intrastate and interstate commerce came in a decision under the Fair Labor Standards Act of 1938. Darby, a Georgia lumber manufacturer, refused to abide by the wages and hours provisions of this federal law, alleging that manufacturing is not commerce (as had previously been held by the United States Supreme Court). The Court, however, while continuing to agree that manufacturing is not commerce, ruled against Darby on the grounds that manufactured goods may enter interstate channels and thus affect interstate commerce, and that consequently they may be regulated by the federal government. Key portions of the decision of *United States v. Darby,* 312 U.S. 100 (1941) follow.

> OPINION BY JUSTICE STONE: . . . While manufacture is not of itself interstate commerce, the shipment of manufactured goods interstate is such commerce and the prohibition of such shipment by Congress is indubitably a regulation of the commerce.
>
> The motive and purpose of a regulation of interstate commerce are matters for the legislative judgment upon the exercise of which the Constitution places no restriction and over which the courts are given no control. . . . Whatever their motive and purpose, regulations of commerce which do not infringe some Constitutional prohibition are within the plenary power conferred on Congress by the Commerce Clause. . . .
>
> . . . The power of Congress over interstate commerce is not confined to the regulation of commerce among the states. It extends to those activities intrastate which so affect interstate commerce or the exercise of the power of Congress over it as to make regulation of them appropriate means to the attainment of a legitimate end, the exercise of the granted power of Congress to regulate interstate commerce.
>
> Congress . . . may choose the means reasonably adopted to the attainment of the permitted end, even though they involve control of intra-state activities.

The *Darby* case seems to imply that the United States Supreme Court will take a hands-off attitude on whatever Congress chooses to do in the interstate commerce field, and that the same attitude applies to the intrastate field if it can be shown that intrastate commerce may affect interstate activities in any way. There is no implication here, of course, that specific constitutional restrictions (such as due process, for example) are being abandoned, but Congress apparently is given a relatively free hand in regulating for any reason and in any way that it sees fit so long as it does not conflict with such constitutional limitations.

NAVIGABLE WATERS AND FEDERAL LANDS

As mentioned earlier in this chapter, states have not been able to exercise as much control over their waters as over other forms of natural resources. The federal government's paramount rights over navigable streams have been upheld over both private and state claimants. This became especially important with the development of hydroelectric power generation. In an early case involving a private power company's right to construct a dam in a stream at a point where the private firm owned the banks of the stream on either side, the United States Supreme Court said, "That the running water in a great navigable stream is capable of private ownership is inconceivable," and further, "The use of the fall of such a stream for the production of power may be a reasonable use. . . . But every . . . structure in the water of a navigable river is subordinate to the right of navigation . . . and must be removed if Congress in the assertion of its power over navigation shall determine that their continuance is detrimental to the public interest. . . ."[6]

It is not enough to admit that Congress has final authority over navigable waters. As in the case of interstate commerce, it is necessary that we have a workable definition of what is meant by "navigable waters." Such a definition, with elaboration upon congressional powers, was given in *United States v. Appalachian Electric Power Co.*, 311 U.S. 377 (1940), a case dealing with the scope of the Federal Power Commission in the licensing of a dam. The pertinent portions of this decision follow.

> OPINION BY JUSTICE REED: . . . A waterway, otherwise suitable for navigation, is not barred from that classification merely because artificial aids must make the highway suitable for use before commercial navigation may be undertaken. . . . Nor is it necessary that the improvements should be actually completed or even authorized. . . .
>
> Nor is it necessary for navigability that the use should be continuous. . . . Even absence of use over long periods of years . . . does not affect the navigability of rivers in the Constitutional sense. It is well recognized too that the navigability may be of a substantial part only of the waterway in question. . . .
>
> . . . Nor is lack of commercial traffic a bar to a conclusion of navigability where personal or private use by boats demonstrates the availability of the stream for the simpler types of commercial navigation.
>
> . . . The respondent cannot, by seeking to use a navigable waterway for power generation alone, avoid the authority of the Government over the stream. The authority is as broad as the needs of commerce. . . . Navigable waters are subject to national planning and control in the broad regulation of commerce. . . . The plenary power of Congress over navigable waters would empower it to deny the privilege of constructing an obstruction in those waters. It may likewise grant the privilege on terms. . . .
>
> . . . There is no private property in the flow of the stream.

According to the definition given in the *Appalachian Electric* case, federal control includes some very small streams!

Federal and state laws conflicted in an Iowa case in which an organization was denied a license for a dam by the Federal Power Commission because of the organization's failure to comply with an Iowa licensing law. The United States Supreme Court, in holding that such a state requirement could nullify a federal law, stated, "To require the petitioner to secure the actual grant to it of a state permit . . . as a condition precedent to securing a federal license for the same project under the Federal Power Act would vest in . . . Iowa a veto power over the federal project." And further, "Where the Federal Government supersedes the state government there is no suggestion that the two agencies both shall have final authority. . . . A dual final authority . . . would be unworkable."[7] If state and federal water laws conflict on navigable streams, the former must yield.

In the *First Iowa* case, the Federal Power Commission agreed with the state until ordered to do otherwise by the Supreme Court. In the Oregon Fish Commission case,[8] however, a state commission and a federal commission were in direct conflict. The Oregon Fish Commission, under state law, denied permission for a private power company to build a dam on a non-navigable Oregon stream, alleging that the private firm's proposed facilities for protecting migratory salmon were inadequate. The Federal Power Commission authorized construction of the dam. The United States Supreme Court upheld the federal commission on the grounds that, among other things, the proposed dam was to be built on a federal reservation (that is, in a location where the federal government owned the land on either side of the stream).[9]

In a strongly worded dissent in the Oregon Fish Commission case, Justice Douglas maintained that ". . . the United States cannot give what it does not have" and further pointed out that ". . . it has been the long-term policy of Congress to separate western land from water rights" and that ". . . in the West, the United States owns a vast amount of land. . . . If by mere Executive action the federal lands may be reserved and all water rights appurtenant to them returned to the United States, vast dislocations in the economics of the Western States may follow."

The words of Justice Douglas are filled with significance, particularly for the West. More than 21 per cent of the entire land area of the United States is owned by the federal government, and another 3 per cent (mainly Indian reservations) is held in trust by it.[10] In four western states (Nevada, Utah, Idaho, and Oregon), excluding Indian reservations, the federal government owns more than one half of the total land area. If agencies of the federal government are to claim, and be sustained in, an absolute control over all waters in their reservations, despite state laws, it is very likely that "vast dislocations" may occur in the economics of western as well as other states.

CONTINUITY OF MOVEMENT

"Continuity of movement" involves movement from a point in one state to a point in another state, and thence to a second point in the latter state (or alternatively, from a point in one state to a second point in the same state, and thence to another state). For regulatory purposes the question arises as to where (if at all) interstate movement stops and intrastate movement begins (or vice versa). The answer to that question determines the respective regulatory jurisdictions of the state (or states) concerned and the federal government. The decision regarding whether or not a portion of such a movement is intrastate will depend on whether or not the movement "came to rest" at any point. "Coming to rest" is not necessarily a physical condition. It may be held that commodities legally have come to rest even though physical movement has never stopped. On the other hand, even though physical movement may have ceased entirely at some point, a movement may be held to be interstate commerce from beginning to end.

The leading utilities case concerning continuity of movement arose in connection with the movement of natural gas from Oklahoma to Kansas. A gas company piped its gas from interstate pipelines into the mains of local distributors, who sold the gas on a commission basis. The Kansas Public Utility Commission disallowed in part a requested rate increase, and the interstate gas company brought suit on the grounds that Kansas was interfering with interstate commerce. The gas company maintained that orders were placed for gas before movements started, that movement began in one state and never stopped until it ended at the consumer's burner in another state, and that the local distributors never actually owned the gas but only acted as commissioned representatives of the interstate firm. The United States Supreme Court, however, although agreeing that the original portion of the movement was interstate, held that for legal purposes the interstate movement ended (that is, the gas "came to rest") when it entered the distributor's mains (even though actual physical movement continued) and that the movement thereafter became intrastate and subject to state regulation. In the words of the Court, "Interstate commerce is a practical conception and what falls within it must be determined upon consideration of established facts and known commercial methods. . . . Interstate movement ended when the gas passed into local mains. . . ."[11]

In a later gas case the Court held that gas originating in West Virginia and moving into Pennsylvania, with custody changing at the state boundary, is interstate commerce, but that gas originating in Pennsylvania and mixed with West Virginia gas in known proportions for sale in Pennsylvania is intrastate commerce.[12] Also, a company producing and buying gas in Louisiana and selling it in the same state to three interstate pipeline companies, who in turn sold the gas in other states, was held to be subject to federal regulation.[13]

In the electric utilities field the Supreme Court has held that transmission of electric current from one state to another, with title and custody passing at the state line, is interstate commerce and not subject to regulation by either state,[14] and in a still later decision based upon this precedent, the Court has declared, "We see no distinction between a sale at or before reaching the state line."[15]

SUMMARY

Although the United States Constitution places the regulation of interstate commerce in congressional hands, and leaves the intrastate commerce to the states, there are many areas of conflict between state and federal authority. Intrastate and interstate affairs cannot be separated clearly under all circumstances. In practice, states regulate some aspects of interstate commerce and the federal government regulates some aspects of intrastate commerce. The United States Supreme Court, as the ultimate referee of constitutional relations between the states and the federal government, has established a substantial body of legal principles concerning such relations.

Although new situations continually arise, and precedents are sometimes reversed, most cases of conflict today turn upon questions of fact rather than upon points of law. In conclusion, two generalizations seem appropriate. First, even though the states are sovereign in our system of government, there is much more federal control of intrastate commerce than state control of interstate commerce. Second, because of the increasing complexity of our economic life, the overall long-term trend appears to be in the direction of more rather than less federal control, regardless of which political party is in office.

NOTES

1. Chief Justice Waite in *Pensacola Telegraph Co. v. Western Union Telegraph Co.,* 96 U.S. 1 (1877). Also see *Telegraph Company v. Texas,* 105 U.S. 460 (1881), which says, "A telegraph company occupies the same relation to commerce as a carrier of messages that a railroad company does as a carrier of goods. Both companies are instruments of commerce, and their business is commerce itself. . . ."
2. See *Hanley v. Kansas City Southern Railway Co.,* 187 U.S. 617 (1903); *United States v. Delaware, L. & W. R. Co.,* 152 Fed. 269 (1907); and *United States v. Simpson,* 252 U.S. 465 (1920).
3. *Wabash, St. Louis and Pacific Railway Co. v. Illinois,* 118 U.S. 557 (1886). Actually, in an earlier case, *Pensacola Telegraph Co. v. Western Union Telegraph Co.,* cited in note 1, the state of Florida had been prohibited from interfering with interstate commerce in the telegraphic field.
4. *Louisiana Public Service Commission et al. v. Texas and New Orleans Railroad Co. et al.,* 284 U.S. 125 (1931).
5. *North Carolina et al. v. United States et al.,* 325 U.S. 507 (1945).
6. *United States v. Chandler-Dunbar Water Power Co.,* 229 U.S. 53 (1913).
7. *First Iowa Hydro-Electric Cooperative v. Federal Power Commission,* 328 U.S. 152 (1946). In a somewhat similar 1972 decision, the Court prohibited the State of Minnesota from requiring more safety standards for a nuclear generating plant than the standards set by the U.S. Atomic Energy Commission.
8. *Federal Power Commission v. The State of Oregon,* 349 U.S. 435 (1954).
9. Article IV, Section 3, of the United States Constitution states, "The Congress shall have power to dispose of and make all needful Rules and Regulations respecting the Territory or other Property belonging to the United States. . . ."
10. Statistics in this paragraph are from General Services Administration, *Inventory Report on Federal Real Property,* prepared for the Senate Committee on Appropriations (Senate Document No. 100, 84th Congress, 2d Session).
11. *Public Utilities Commission For the State of Kansas et al. v. Landon, Receiver of the Kansas Natural Gas Company et al.,* 249 U.S. 236 (1919).
12. *Peoples Natural Gas Company v. Public Service Commission of Pennsylvania et al.,* 270 U.S. 550 (1926).
13. *Interstate Natural Gas Company, Inc. v. Federal Power Commission et al.,* 331 U.S. 682 (1947). A somewhat similar set of facts was involved in *Phillips Petroleum Co. v. Wisconsin et al.,* 347 U.S. 672 (1954), one of the most controversial utility decisions of its time. This case, however, was decided upon a determination of congressional intent rather than upon continuity of movement.
14. *Public Utilities Commission of Rhode Island et al. v. Attleboro Steam and Electric Company,* 273 U.S. 83 (1927).
15. *Jersey Central Power and Light Co. v. Federal Power Commission,* 319 U.S. 61 (1943).

ADDITIONAL READINGS

1. Anderson, Ronald A., *Government Regulation of Business,* 3d ed. (Cincinnati: South-Western Publishing Co., 1966), ch. 19, "The Commerce Power and the States," pp. 272–304.
2. Barnes, Irston R., *The Economics of Public Utility Regulation* (New York: F. S. Crofts, 1942), ch. 5, "State and Federal Responsibilities in Regulations: Jurisdictional Conflicts Between Federal and State Authority," pp. 156–167.
3. Cook, Franklin H., *Principles of Business and the Federal Law* (New York: Macmillan, 1951), ch. 11, "The States and Commerce," pp. 220–246.
4. Jones, Eliot, and Truman C. Bigham, *Principles of Public Utilities* (New York: Macmillan, 1937), ch. 13, "Local Versus State Regulation: State Versus Federal Regulation," pp. 619–669.
5. Sampson, Roy J., "Federal-State Conflicts and Utility Regulation," *Public Utilities Fortnightly,* vol. 68, no. 10 (November 9, 1961), pp. 729–740.
6. *Federal Power Commission v. The State of Oregon,* 349 U.S. 435 (1954).
7. *First Iowa Hydro-Electric Cooperative v. Federal Power Commission,* 328 U.S. 152 (1946).
8. *Jersey Central Power and Light Co. v. Federal Power Commission,* 319 U.S. 61 (1943).
9. *Louisiana Public Service Commission et al. v. Texas and New Orleans Railroad Co. et al.,* 284 U.S. 125 (1931).
10. *North Carolina et al. v. United States et al.,* 325 U.S. 507 (1945).
11. *Pensacola Telegraph Co. v. Western Union Telegraph Co.,* 96 U.S. 1 (1877).
12. *Peoples Natural Gas Company v. Public Service Commission of Pennsylvania et al.,* 270 U.S. 550 (1926).
13. *Public Utilities Commission for the State of Kansas et al. v. Landon, Receiver of the Kansas Natural Gas Company et al.,* 249 U.S. 236 (1919).
14. *Public Utilities Commission of Rhode Island et al. v. Attleboro Steam and Electric Company,* 273 U.S. 83 (1927).
15. *Telegraph Company v. Texas,* 105 U.S. 460 (1881).
16. *United States v. Chandler-Dunbar Water Power Co.,* 229 U.S. 53 (1913).
17. *Wabash, St. Louis and Pacific Railway Co. v. Illinois,* 118 U.S. 557 (1886).

5

Regulatory Methods and Principles

As indicated in Chapter 1, the special obligations imposed on public utility businesses and legal regulation of their economic activities have a long history. Many devices, affecting many aspects of utility operations, have been and are used for regulation.

At one extreme, free competition, that is, the complete absence of government constraints, might be considered a sort of regulatory device, since generally accepted economic theory holds that completely free competition, under "perfect" circumstances, leads to the "best" allocation of resources, the lowest prices, and the highest quality of service.[1] Perfect competitive conditions are seldom found in any type of economic endeavor, however, and particularly not in the public utilities area.

It is generally thought (based upon logic and history) that unrestricted competition between utility firms leads to expensive duplication of facilities, rate wars, financial instability, and poor service, or alternatively, to an eventual overt or covert conspiracy to divide or monopolize the market. Also, unregulated utilities, like other businesses, have been known to engage in stock watering, stock market manipulations, securities frauds, and other activities harmful to the consuming and investing public. Consequently, little reliance is placed upon free competition as a regulator of public utilities in our society.

At the opposite extreme, public ownership has been widely used as a regulatory device. This device is discussed at some length in Part Four.

Between the two extremes of free competition and public ownership are the methods of judicial, legislative, franchise, and commission regulation as well as some minor and indirect forms of control. All of these methods have been used, and still are used to some extent, although regulation by commission is now dominant.

JUDICIAL REGULATION

Under the common law, as pointed out in Chapter 1, public utilities and other businesses "affected with the public interest" are required to provide adequate and nondiscriminatory services at reasonable rates. Within this regulatory framework, even in the absence of legislation, an aggrieved customer or one denied service would have the right to start a court action against an offending utility. Until well into the nineteenth century this was the customary method, and usually the only available method, by which a consumer could obtain his legal rights from a recalcitrant utility.

Judicial regulation, however, is an inadequate and inefficient method of consumer protection. This became particularly apparent with the development of large transportation, communications, and energy firms beginning in the early part of the last century. Court actions are slow and costly. Judges are often not well informed on utility matters, and despite the oft-mentioned flexibility of the common law, they tend to render legalistic decisions or to stick closely to narrow precedents rather than to give decisions based upon contemporary economic situations. Also, common law procedures are designed to correct past wrongs rather than to control future conduct. Because of these weaknesses, judicial regulation in the form discussed here is not very important today. This does not mean, though, that the courts do not play an important role as reviewers of present-day regulatory laws and procedures.

DIRECT LEGISLATIVE REGULATION

Attempts to exercise direct legislative regulation over public utility (and other) businesses became widespread during the nineteenth century, although this device has an ancient origin.[2] These nineteenth-century efforts were mostly attempts to cope with the inadequacies of judicial regulation in an environment of new technologies, growing businesses, and corporate enterprise.

Basically, direct legislative regulation takes three forms: special charters of incorporation, general incorporation laws, and specific "thou shalt and thou shalt not" statutes. All may have some advantages over judicial regulation, but they also have significant weaknesses.

A special charter of incorporation granted to a particular firm by a legislative body can certainly specify the firm's duties and rights in considerable detail. Most early corporations in England and the United States were specially and individually chartered.[3] It may be difficult to amend such a corporate charter promptly if economic conditions change, however. And most legislators are not sufficiently aware of the technicalities of a particular type of business to prepare or evaluate a specific charter of incorporation. Many special charters were obtained through political influence or outright graft or bribery. Finally, in a rapidly expanding business environment, it became difficult or impossible for any legislative body to consider the formation of corporations individually.

General incorporation laws, that is, legislative statutes providing terms and conditions under which corporate charters could be obtained through state administrative channels, were enacted by all states during the first half of the nineteenth century. By that time, the corporation movement had grown so large that it was impossible for legislatures to handle each request for incorporation on an individual basis. General incorporation laws, though, must be designed to apply to all forms of business and to provide for a wide variety of contingencies over a long period of time. This means that they must be so broad and general that they can accomplish little effective regulation of a specific form of business in a specific locality and with peculiar operating conditions.

Consequently, many states attempted to regulate public utility businesses by special statutes specifying in some detail what must and must not be done. These statutes, in reality, were little more than an application of common law regulatory principles. As there was no continuous observation of operations when the legislature was not in session, and enforcement was dependent upon the courts, this method differed from judicial regulation mainly by making it somewhat easier for a customer to prove unreasonableness under some conditions. For example, if a rate or charge was higher than permitted by statute, a customer could eventually expect to win his suit. As might be supposed, though, few utilities openly violated the letter of the law. So far as the spirit of the law was concerned, however, violations were difficult to prove or correct.

In addition to most of the disadvantages of judicial regulation, special regulatory statutes had most of the disadvantages of special charters of incorporation. Even honest and intelligent legislators with the best of intentions could not be expected to enact a detailed regulatory law covering a wide variety of local conditions and adaptable to a rapidly changing technological, economic, and operating environment.

REGULATION BY FRANCHISE

Franchises, usually issued by local or state governments, became a popular regulatory device beginning in the 1830's. They have remained important at the local level. In most states local franchises are required by most types of public utility businesses, even though they have state incorporation and operating rights.

A franchise is a contract between a private business and a government body, and it normally cannot be broken by either party.[4] Provisions for amendments may be included in a franchise as a part of the contract, of course, but even so, franchises are relatively inflexible.

A franchise usually specifies what benefits a business is to receive from the issuing body. This may include such things as the right to use city streets for mains, tracks, or poles and lines. Provisions for protecting the public in matters of safety, service, and rates are included. Finally, the contract may provide a method or amount of payment by the business to the issuing government. Franchises often, but not always, grant an exclusive or monopoly right to provide specified services in a given area. Because of its grant of rights a franchise is considered a valuable property and sometimes may be transferred to another firm. The usual modern practice, however, is to state in the contract that it cannot be transferred to another firm without prior approval of the granting body.

Franchises may be classified as perpetual, short-term, long-term, and indeterminate. If no mention is made of expiration dates, courts have usually held that franchises are perpetual. In most cases, perpetual grants have been unintentional, and they are no longer common. Because of inevitable economic changes, the inflexibility of perpetual franchises is usually undesirable, from the viewpoints both of the issuing body (the public) and of the firm.

A long-term franchise typically runs from twenty-five to fifty years. Such contracts permit management to make and carry out long-range plans for orderly expansion and improvement of facilities with reasonable expectations of realizing profits on investments during the contract life. On the other hand, management, at least during the early life of a long-term franchise, may feel so secure that it becomes indifferent to public needs and complaints.

Short-term franchises, usually running for ten years or less and providing the firm an option for negotiating a renewal if services have been satisfactory, provide considerable incentive for management to remain responsive to public needs and attitudes. On the other hand, if management has doubts regarding the possibility of renewing a franchise, long-range planning and investment may be discouraged.

The indeterminate franchise, or terminable franchise or permit as it is sometimes called, is the newest development in the franchise field. Because it combines most of the advantages of the long-term and the short-term franchises without having their disadvantages, it is becoming increasingly popular.

This type of franchise has no termination date if the service remains satisfactory. There may be some dispute, of course, as to what constitutes satisfactory service, and a well-drawn contract will include some criteria for evaluation of service. If it is determined by whatever criteria are applicable that satisfactory service is not being rendered, the local granting body has the right to terminate the franchise by buying the utility's properties at a fair value. This requires some procedure for determining fair value within the terms of the contract, of course.

The indeterminate franchise thus provides a maximum of protection for both the consuming public and the utility firm. Management, if it wishes the business to continue, has an incentive to be responsive to public demands. In addition, there is no reason for management to be reluctant to undertake long-range planning and investment projects, since any properties acquired in such programs will be purchased by the granting body at a fair price if the franchise is terminated. Also, the political problems involved in the periodic renewal of fixed-term franchises are avoided.

Although local franchises are required in all except a few states, the details of their use vary widely. Indeterminate franchises, for example, may be issued in about one third of the states and exclusive rights to operate may be given in about one half. Some states permit either indeterminate or fixed-term and either exclusive or nonexclusive franchises, while others are less flexible. To answer any specific franchise problem, careful study of the applicable state and local laws may be necessary.[5]

COMMISSION REGULATION

Use of the "independent" regulatory commission, at both state and federal levels, is the latest public utility regulatory device. The Interstate Commerce Commission, the Civil Aeronautics Board, and the Federal Maritime Commission, all regulating transportation industries; the Federal Power Commission (energy industries); and the Federal Communications Commission (communications industries) are the best known of the national (interstate) commissions. Each state has a similar commission or commissions with various names (like Public Utilities Commission, Public Service Commission, Railroad Commission, etc.) regulating intrastate utility activities.[6] Local governments sometimes use a similar regulatory technique, but usually local powers are somewhat limited.

Regulatory commissions are created by legislative statutes (by Congress or state legislatures). Legislation outlines the broad policies to be followed, while the commissions are authorized to carry out these policies on a day-to-day basis. These commissions are said to be independent because they are created by, and primarily responsible to, the legislative rather than the executive branch of government.[7]

Courts have consistently held that the establishment of regulatory commissions to operate within a broad policy framework defined by statute is not an unconstitutional delegation of legislative powers. In practice, though, regulatory commissions do exercise a combination of legislative, executive, and judicial powers, and within the limits set by legislatures and courts, they have developed a considerable body of administrative law and procedures to the point where they may almost be considered a fourth branch of government, operating alongside the legislative, executive, and judicial branches.

Regulatory commissions are relatively small in size. At the federal level they usually vary from five to eleven members. State commissions vary from one to seven members, with more than three fourths of the states having a three-man commission. Every commission, of course, has a permanent staff, mostly composed of civil service employees. Depending upon the location of the commission and its duties and applicable laws, the permanent staff may vary from a few dozen up to several hundred people—federal commissions, of course, usually have a considerably larger number of permanent employees than their state counterparts.

Federal commissioners are appointed by the President, subject to Senate confirmation. The picture is more mixed among the states, however. In about one third of the states, commissioners are elected by the people, in another third they are appointed by the governor; and in the remainder they are appointed by the governor subject to legislative ratification. A few states still use other methods of choosing their commissioners.

State commissioners hold their offices for periods ranging from four to ten years, with six years the tenure in the majority of states. Laws regarding removal of commissioners prior to the expiration of their terms vary, but generally this is a difficult and little-used procedure. State salaries typically fall within the $15,000 to $19,000 per year bracket, although some states pay their commissioners less than $10,000 and others more than $20,000 per year. It is often said that salary levels, especially at the state level, are inadequate to obtain and retain top-level commissioners.

Usually there are no specific technical qualifications for commissioners, either at the state or federal levels. Permanent commission staffs are designed to maintain technical and other expert competence. Supposedly the commissioners themselves are competent administrators who are willing to act without political bias or favoritism, but this is, of course, not always true.

It may be unreasonable to expect that persons receiving high office through political processes, whether directly elected by the people or appointed by elected politicians, will completely forget politics immediately after assuming office. In fact, if "politics" is interpreted in the broad sense of carrying out the will of the public, it might be considered desirable that commissioners not be fully isolated from politics as long as their decisions are not blatantly partisan or arbitrary in nature.[8] In any case, many commissioners do have an active political background, and legal training is quite common among them.

Regulatory commissions reach their major decisions on the basis of evidence brought out by proceedings as specified in their governing statutes. Depending upon the circumstances, these proceedings may range from full-dress highly formal hearings, involving hundreds of witnesses and thousands of pages of testimony and exhibits (all subject to cross-examination or rebuttal by adversaries), down to very informal evidence collection and routine approval or disapproval of proposed actions by commission staff members. Further discussion of these procedures follows.

COMMISSION DEVELOPMENT

Commission history in the United States is often divided into three eras. From their beginnings during the 1830's until around 1870, they were mainly advisory in nature. That is, their principal or only function was to investigate conditions and report to, or advise, legislative bodies. Legislative action might or might not be taken upon commission recommendations.

The rise of the Grange movement led to strong state commissions. Most of these were concerned with railroad regulation during an entire generation; thus the period from around 1870 to the first decade of the twentieth century is often referred to as the era of the railroad commission. It was during this era that the federal government first entered the regulatory field in a substantial way, with the Interstate Commerce Commission. This agency, established in 1887, originally regulated only interstate railroads, but other forms of domestic transportation, except air, have since been brought into its domain.

The period from the first decade of this century to the present can be called the era of the public utility commission. Shortly after the turn of the century states began to reorganize their existing railroad commissions or to create new commissions to bring public utilities under state regulation. A little later, the federal government began establishing the forerunners of its own present regulatory commissions for the communications and energy utilities.

Although state regulation of public utilities evolved directly out of experiences with transportation, today public utility regulation is much more important than transportation regulation at the state level. So much of transportation regulation now falls under federal jurisdiction that most states have relatively little left to regulate in this field. This superseding of state by federal regulation has not gone as far in the traditional public utilities areas as it has in transportation, in part, perhaps, because public utility businesses can be more effectively regulated at the state and local level, without unduly hampering interstate commerce, than can transportation.

THE ADVANTAGES OF COMMISSION REGULATION

Compared to the earlier forms of regulation already discussed, commission regulation has several clear advantages, both for the public and for the utility firms themselves. It provides continuous regulation, under relatively well-known rules of the game, by full-time commissioners. The tenure of office is usually of sufficient length to allow commissioners to become experts in their fields of concern if they wish to do so. In fact, commissioners and commission personnel have been known to move from government service into high positions in the industries which they have been regulating.

As mentioned before, commissions are staffed with a permanent force of full-time, nonpolitical personnel, who usually enjoy civil service status. Although these personnel have no authority to make major decisions, they do develop a great amount of expertise in technological, legal, and other matters involving the work of their commissions. Their staff work provides continuity as well as essential assistance, and it may be extremely useful in educating new commissioners and in preventing them from making hasty or rash decisions.

Flexibility is one of the great advantages of commission regulation. Operating under broad general statutes, commissions have considerable latitude in exercising judgment and adapting regulation to particular situations. In other words, decisions are not as restricted as they might have been under direct legislative or judicial regulation. This is particularly important in an era of rapid technological, economic, and social change such as we have seen for several generations.

It might be argued that too much flexibility has disadvantages, that it tends to promote rule by men rather than rule by law. If this is a disadvantage, however, it is minimized by the opportunities given those harmed by commission decisions or actions to appeal to the courts for redress.

RELATIONS BETWEEN REGULATORY COMMISSIONS AND THE COURTS

Under our theory of government the legislative function is to make laws, the executive function is to administer or carry out these laws, and the courts' function is to determine and protect private rights which may be adversely affected by legislative or executive actions. In this context the regulatory commission's role is primarily executive,[9] although, as suggested before, in effect legislative and judicial elements are included in commission regulatory activities.

Commission decisions and actions, as well as the federal or state statutes under which actions are taken, may be overruled by the courts under some circumstances. An appropriate court of jurisdiction may hold that a statute itself is unconstitutional.[10] Even if a statute is constitutional, it may be held that a commission has exceeded its jurisdiction; that is, that it has exercised authority beyond that given by the controlling statute or statutes. Finally, commission actions may be overruled if the court finds that the commission has acted without due process of law.[11]

Among the most common grounds for reversal under due process today is a finding by the court that the commission has acted upon insufficient evidence or contrary to evidence. Naturally, commissions usually go to great lengths in building a record of evidence in their procedures to avoid possible court reversals on these grounds. This adds to the length and cost of many hearings and often leads commission critics to allege that procedures are unnecessarily bogged down in minor details and technicalities. Few of the critics, however, would be willing to give up the protections of due process in exchange for more rapid decisions. This might indeed lead to rule by men rather than rule by law. Unfortunately, there are costs attached to most benefits, even the cherished benefits of our traditional legal rights.

Appeals from rulings of federal regulatory commissions go to federal courts and eventually may reach the United States Supreme Court.[12] Review of state regulatory decisions varies depending upon the various state laws. In many instances, the original reviewing court is the state's Supreme Court or its highest trial court, but other courts may be specifically designated to perform this function. Courts do not automatically review statutes or commission actions, of course. It is a principle, under the so-called doctrine of primary jurisdiction, that commissions must act and that someone must appeal an action on the grounds that they are injured by it before an action or a statute will be reviewed.

Another principle, sometimes called the doctrine of administrative finality, limits court review to points of law only. That is, courts recognize the role of commissions as experts and normally accept their findings of fact (if commission facts are based upon substantial evidence) even though the facts as seen by those complaining of commission action may be quite different.[13]

As an illustration of the difference between fact and law, a commission might find that a given schedule of prices is likely to yield an annual return of 7 per cent on investment to a utility and that this rate of return is reasonable. The utility firm, on the other hand, might maintain that it is entitled to a price increase because the prices in question are likely to yield only 6 per cent and that anything less than 8 per cent is unreasonably low.

Under such circumstances, it is quite likely that the courts would uphold the commission's finding of fact that the prices will yield 7 per cent. The commission might be overruled on its contention that 7 per cent is a reasonable return, however. Reasonableness is a matter of interpretation or a point of law to be decided by the courts rather than being a fact subject to administrative finality. This does not imply, of course, that reversals of commission decisions on grounds of unreasonableness are widespread. Usually, based upon experience in similar cases, commissions have a fair idea of what courts will accept as reasonable, and they attempt to make their decisions accordingly.

Following chapters will contain a number of specific illustrations of commission and court interrelations.

INDIRECT METHODS OF REGULATION

From time to time other less direct methods are or have been used to influence the activities of public utilities. It might be argued that these methods are not regulation in the sense of our previous discussion of that term. But because they try to influence activity patterns along lines thought desirable by the public, it may be legitimate to consider these devices as indirect forms of regulation.

The use of publicity, perhaps through an investigation and public report by a fact-finding board or by a legislative committee or other governmental body is one such device. Even though such investigators may not have any actual power to compel firms or industries to follow their recommendations, they may have considerable indirect influence.

Businesses already subject to heavy government regulation or even direct government competition may fear that disregarding recommendations of "impartial" and respected investigators may ultimately lead to even more government regulation or ownership. In addition, it is reasonable to assume that the managers of public utility businesses, like other business managers and people in general, prefer to do right because it is right and prefer social approval over disapproval—at least if it does not cost too much.

Occasionally, businesses, including public utility businesses, have attempted voluntary self-regulation of prices, output, market divisions, and various other operating practices. Unless this has government blessing (as in the case of the N.R.A. codes of the 1930's, which eventually were declared unconstitutional), it is likely to lead to charges of conspiracy to monopolize and to result in prosecution under the antitrust laws. Further, unless there is a strong community of interest and tradition of cooperation among the firms involved, voluntary self-regulation without legal enforcement is likely to be ineffective. This device has worked reasonably well in the field of transportation but less successfully in most other major industries.

Government may also indirectly influence business practices through various kinds of promotional activities and subsidies, including laws designed to encourage consumer-owned cooperatives or even direct government ownership of facilities competing with privately owned businesses. Public ownership, which will be further discussed in Part Four, serves as a rough yardstick against which private performance may be measured, and it may provide competition and pose a threat to private utilities, which makes them much more sensitive to customer desires.

THE PRINCIPAL UTILITY ACTIVITIES SUBJECT TO REGULATION

Various kinds of activities of all types of businesses are subject to government regulation to some extent. These regulated activities include monopoly or restraint of trade, unfair competition, security issues, employer-employee relations, nondiscriminatory employment policies, social security, public health and safety (including water or air pollution), and zoning restrictions. Also, businesses are often required to keep certain kinds of records in specified form and to file regular or occasional reports or furnish certain types of information on demand. Sometimes, in some kinds of businesses, production quotas may be established by regulation.

Public utility businesses, like others, must comply with all these forms of regulation. In addition, though, some aspects of utility businesses are regulated which are not normally regulated in other industries, or utilities are more closely regulated in some of those activities in which regulation is common to all types of businesses. The most important of these special forms of utility regulation are mentioned in the following paragraphs.

Most of these special regulations are applicable to most utilities at the federal level if interstate commerce is involved or at the state level in most states for intrastate activities. It should be borne in mind, however, that federal regulation varies, depending upon the type of utility concerned, and that state regulation is far from uniform. The following discussion, therefore, treats general principles only. To answer a specific regulatory question concerning a particular type of utility in a given locality, thorough familiarity with the pertinent statutes and with court interpretations of these statutes is essential.

One of the most common regulations of utilities is the requirement that a firm secure a "certificate of convenience and necessity" or similar operating rights permission before beginning operations. This requirement, first established late in the nineteenth century, is in addition to the requirements of a corporate charter and franchises. The certificate may be granted by a federal or state regulatory agency, depending upon whether the proposed operation is interstate or intrastate. It is not considered a property or a contract (as is a franchise), and it cannot be transferred to another without permission of the granting agency. Like a franchise, it may be either for a fixed or indeterminate term, and either exclusive or nonexclusive, depending upon the pertinent statutes. The certificate is normally required for a large-scale extension of service as well as for original entry.

In order to obtain a certificate an applicant must show that there is a demand for the proposed service and that he has the necessary resources and qualifications to render adequate service at reasonable rates. Usually, an application will be denied if another firm operating in the area is giving, or can expand its operations to give, adequate service. Also, states often require that local authorities give their prior consent on matters affecting municipalities or local areas.

A certificate is clearly of considerable benefit to a firm, particularly if it grants exclusive operating rights in a given geographic area. Its primary purpose is protection of the public rather than conferring benefits on a firm, however. It is intended to prevent the economic waste of duplicate facilities, rate wars, and other forms of instability which might lead to financial hardship for a firm with consequent inadequate service or pressures for unreasonably high rates.

Among other things, too, certification allows a regulatory agency to review an applicant's financial resources, qualifications, and general business reputation and character with a view toward determining his fitness for giving good and reasonably priced services. If more than one application is being considered, the award will supposedly go to the most fit. If applicants are equally suited to give the demanded service, of course, the regulatory decision may be a tough one. It is reasonable to expect that political influence may sometimes be brought into such cases. The relative immunity of most commissions from direct political pressure, however, plus the ever-present possibility that a decision may be challenged in the courts by a rejected applicant, hopefully makes for a minimum of political decision-making by regulatory bodies in awarding operating rights.

Corresponding to the restriction on entry into the public utility business is the prohibition against abandoning service without permission. Besides complete withdrawal from all business, abandonment may include withdrawal from a portion (as a geographic area) of operations or the substitution of one kind of service for another (as electricity for gas, or buses for streetcars).

Certainly a firm cannot be forced to remain in business indefinitely if it is unprofitable and there are no prospects for earning profit. This would be considered a form of taking property without due process of law and would lead to inadequate service and ultimate bankruptcy. Usually, however, regulation can force a firm to continue operating an unprofitable portion of its business as long as its overall operations are profitable (this is not always done, of course, even if such regulatory authority exists). Even when overall operations are unprofitable, a firm may be forced to continue operations for a time or to change its operating procedures in order to see if its financial situation will not improve. The idea behind this regulation is that the service obligations of a public utility firm require it to take the poor as well as the good business, the milk with the cream.

One of the basic responsibilities of a public utility is to provide service that is adequate in quantity and quality as well as safe and continuous. It is often difficult to measure adequacy by objective standards, of course, but where inadequacy can be proved to the satisfaction of the regulators (and ultimately the courts, perhaps) a firm may be forced to make whatever procedural changes or additional investments in facilities that seem necessary to provide adequate service. This includes things like extending service into newly developing geographic areas, such as subdivisions, although a utility cannot be forced to expand its service into areas which it has never contemplated serving (its certificate of convenience and necessity or its corporate charter might be used as evidence of intent).[14] Similarly, a firm cannot be forced to provide a new and completely different service from that originally contemplated.

Another general regulatory restriction on public utilities is the prohibition of discrimination against any part of the public. Again, difficult questions may arise as to what constitutes the public and discrimination. As a generalization, discrimination might be defined as treating similar customers significantly differently, or as treating significantly differing customers similarly.

Actually, no two customers are identical, so some discrimination is inherent in doing business. Laws against discrimination, therefore, are interpreted according to some rule of reasonableness which places emphasis on undue discrimination rather than on all discrimination. It may even be difficult to define "undue," however. As a practical matter, customers may be grouped into different classes, like residential or industrial, and charged different rates without necessarily violating the prohibition against discrimination. Also, it is commonly accepted that charges may be made on a sliding scale according to quantities of services purchased, in effect quantity discounts, at least within some limits, without violation of the discrimination concept.

Price or rate regulation is perhaps the most discussed topic and generates the most controversy in the public utilities field. Rates must be reasonable, whatever that may mean. By implication, every rate charged every customer should meet this criterion, but as a practical matter utility rate regulation (except in transportation) generally involves regulation of the rate of return obtainable from some schedule of prices. Rate regulation will be examined in considerable detail in following chapters. It should be borne in mind, though, that regulation of service and discrimination cannot be divorced from rate regulation. It is impossible to regulate any one of these adequately without regulating the others.

Similarly, regulation of accounting practices is necessary for effective rate regulation. Accounts must be kept uniformly over time and among the various firms if competition is involved, in order to supply regulators with the information required to evaluate the financial condition of firms and make decisions on rate levels. In particular, asset and expense accounts must be treated uniformly. This means that the accounting systems of most utility businesses are, to a considerable extent, prescribed by regulatory necessity.

Finally, financial practices and procedures of most utility firms are closely regulated, again requiring considerable accounting uniformity. As indicated above, security issues of businesses in general are subject to some regulation, but financial regulation for public utility businesses is far more encompassing than for other types of enterprises. This, too, will be further discussed in a following chapter.

REGULATORY AGENCY PROCEDURES

The Federal Power Commission (F.P.C.) and the Federal Communications Commission (F.C.C.) are the principal federal agencies involved in utility regulation. In addition, each of the states has at least one regulatory commission, and in some states some kinds of utilities are regulated by local government bodies. Obviously, then, there is no one procedure which can be described as *the* regulatory procedure. Instead, there are numerous specific procedures. But most of these several regulatory agencies do have many similar procedural features.

All regulatory agencies, federal, state, or local, are charged with protecting the public interest. They are concerned with reasonable and nondiscriminatory rates, and they operate subject to the constraints of due process and statutory laws. Utility regulatory statutes in many instances do not differ greatly from one jurisdiction to another, and precedents decided in courts have brought considerable procedural uniformity. Further, the Federal Administrative Procedure Act of 1946 and similar acts by various states have contributed to similarity of regulatory procedures.

It is not quite true that one who is thoroughly familiar with the procedures of any one federal or state regulatory agency would be completely at home with the procedures of another, but neither would he be a complete stranger in any jurisdiction. A person who is well-acquainted with the general principles of regulatory laws and with the procedures followed by one agency can, with a little study of the appropriate statutes and published rules of procedure (if any) of another agency, perform effectively before or within this other agency.

For our present purposes, therefore, it is preferable to speak of regulatory procedures in general rather than to concentrate on the specific procedures of any one agency. Our discussion can be subdivided into the general topics of kinds of proceedings, formal hearings, and admissible evidence.[15]

KINDS OF PROCEEDINGS

The three principal kinds of proceedings before regulatory agencies are (1) applications or petitions, (2) complaints, and (3) investigations. A regulated utility, for example, may make application or petition to increase its rates. Those opposing such an application are protestants. Or some person, group, or organization may make a complaint that rates are unreasonably high or discriminatory or that service quality is poor. Then the utility becomes a respondent before the regulatory agency. Or finally, the regulatory body may, on its own initiative or under pressure from others, institute an investigation into rates, services, or other matters.

Generally, those advocating a change in the existing situation bear the burden of proof. That is, they must present convincing evidence to support their position. Opponents, of course, attempt to demolish this evidence or to present contrary evidence. This is particularly true in the case of applications or complaints. The location of the burden of proof is less clear in investigations initiated by the regulatory agencies themselves, but in most cases, if an agency decides a change is necessary, it places the burden of proof on the utility by ordering it to show cause why the change should not be made.

Although a regulatory proceeding is often called an adversary proceeding, it is not the exact equivalent of a trial in a court of law. In a criminal trial, for example, an accused is presumed innocent until proven guilty beyond the shadow of a doubt by an adversary process. A jury interprets the facts introduced into the trial, and a judge rules on points of law. In a regulatory proceeding, on the other hand, the regulatory agency acts as both judge and jury.

In addition, since its primary concern is with the overall public interest, a regulatory body attempts to make sure that both "adversary" parties introduce sufficient evidence to provide grounds for an appropriate decision; it may even have its own staff experts introduce evidence. Regulatory decisions made on insufficient evidence may be overturned if challenged by appeals in courts of law; obviously, no agency wants to leave itself vulnerable to such challenges.

Regulatory proceedings may be very informal or highly formal procedures. Often prehearing conferences are held at which representatives of all the contending parties meet with regulatory authorities. These preliminary conferences sometimes satisfactorily settle the issues involved and sometimes expedite future necessary proceedings by reducing the number of points under dispute. Most regulatory matters do not go into full-scale formal public hearings, but such hearings are the most publicly visible form of proceedings.

FORMAL PUBLIC HEARINGS

Formal public regulatory hearings are nearest in their procedures to the trappings of a court adversary trial. These hearings usually, but not always, are presided over by a hearing examiner (a high-level regulatory agency civil service employee who specializes in conducting hearings and preparing reports and recommendations based on the evidence presented). Sometimes a member or members of the regulatory agency, or the entire agency (that is, the commissioners themselves), will conduct a hearing.

Advance announcements are made as to the time, place, and scope of a public hearing. At the hearing's beginning, all parties who have indicated an intent to participate are identified—this includes representatives of applicants and protestants or complainants and respondents as well as intervenors who may favor one or the other side or who may intervene "as their interests appear" without specifically choosing sides.

Normally, witnesses for the side having the burden of proof appear first, followed by those opposed and other witnesses. Testimony and exhibits supporting their side's position are introduced by witnesses during direct examination by the person or persons (usually attorneys) conducting their side's case. Witnesses then are subject to cross-examination by those conducting the opposition case. Then rebuttal witnesses may be called. Finally, the case is summed up in oral arguments by representatives of each side.

Hearings vary considerably in length and strictness of procedures followed. Typically, they last only a few hours or a few days, but in some cases they have lasted for weeks or months and produced as many as 20,000 pages of transcribed testimony. Examiners differ considerably in what they will allow to be submitted as evidence. Some do not deviate very far from the rules of evidence followed in courts of law, while others are very permissive (see the following discussion of admissible evidence).

After the public portion of the hearing has ended, representatives of each party submit written legal briefs. These briefs state the party's case, present an abstract of its evidence, sum up the argument for its position, and request the findings desired from the regulatory agency. Then in due course—that is, after considering the evidence and briefs—the examiner prepares a report and recommendation on the matters involved.

This report goes to the regulatory body (commissioners), and exceptions to it may be filed by any of the concerned parties. Sometimes, also, short oral arguments may be made before the regulatory body itself. Finally, based upon the examiner's report and exceptions to it and oral arguments, if any, plus whatever portions of the evidence it wishes to consider, the regulatory agency issues its decision and an appropriate order.

But the process may not stop here. Any party not satisfied with the order may petition the regulatory agency for reconsideration, reargument, or even a rehearing on the grounds that (1) the decision is in error, (2) new evidence which could not have been brought out before has been found, or (3) conditions have changed substantially while the matter has been pending. If such appeals still do not produce satisfactory results, a party having substantial interest in the matter may then appeal to the courts for review. This may involve months or years of litigation.

ADMISSIBLE EVIDENCE

As already stated, regulatory proceedings are not conducted as strictly as court proceedings. This is particularly so insofar as admissible evidence is concerned. Hearings examiners have considerable discretion as to what kinds of evidence they allow to be introduced by testimony or exhibits of witnesses. Some are strict and some are lenient. It is safe to say that anything which can be introduced into a court under the accepted legal rules of evidence can be used in a regulatory proceeding. But not everything allowable in a regulatory proceeding may be used in a courtroom.

To be admissible in a regulatory proceeding, as in a court, evidence must be from a competent source and must be relevant to the case under consideration. But competency and relevance, in part at least, are matters of human judgment.

The competence of a witness may be shown by direct examination, especially in establishing his qualifications to testify, or its lack may be revealed by cross-examination. The introduction of irrelevant information, even though it may be factually correct, is frowned upon, because at best it is time-consuming and costly and at worst it may interject confusion into the real issues involved. Material which at first glance may appear irrelevant, though, may be shown to be pertinent by skillful direct examination or testimony prior to its presentation—or its relevance may be argued before the examiner if an opponent objects to its use on the grounds of irrelevance.

Hearsay evidence—"what someone else said"—is always excluded in courts and is usually excluded in regulatory proceedings. The "hearsay exclusion" is derived from the right of cross-examination. A person not present cannot be cross-examined; thus his testimony, even if submitted as a sworn affidavit, is normally not allowed. This does not mean, though, that routine business entries (such as accounting records, receipts, and the like), public documents, and certified statements may not be submitted as evidence in regulatory proceedings, although they are subject to challenge and rebuttal, of course.

Regulatory procedures, like court procedures, distinguish sharply between opinion testimony given by laymen (nonexperts) and that given by experts. A layman's statement must be as basic and simple as possible so that the hearing examiner can form his own opinion. Expert witnesses, however, are widely used in regulatory proceedings, even though much of what they say is clearly opinion and may even verge on hearsay insofar as expertise is based on education obtained from past exposure to books, university lectures, and the like.

Expertise is obtained and demonstrated in various ways, and one posing as an expert must be qualified to testify by some kind of acceptable build-up of the formal knowledge in his field and his own place in that field. An expert in one field of knowledge (like economics, finance, accounting) is not competent to testify as an expert in another field. Outside his own specialty, an expert is only another layman.

Hearings examiners, like judges, often consent to take official notice of events having some bearing on the case at hand, although not directly a part of the evidence. This may consist of such things as decisions rendered in similar cases in other jurisdictions, the basic intent of regulatory statutes as revealed by legislative hearings, or matters of "common knowledge," such as the fact that the Mississippi River flows generally north to south between St. Louis and New Orleans. Such notices are not legally binding but are given such consideration and weight as the examiner thinks appropriate.

It has been said that the rules of evidence have been devised more to exclude than to admit evidence. To a certain extent this is true. But the real purpose of these rules is to prevent the record of a proceeding from becoming cluttered with incompetent, irrelevant, and generally worthless information. It is not often that useful evidence is kept out of a regulatory proceeding simply because of procedural rules.

SUMMARY

More aspects of public utility businesses are regulated in more stringent ways than is true for businesses in general. This regulation may be federal, state, or local, or a combination of these. Many regulatory methods have been and are being used, but the franchise method at the local level and the commission method at the state and federal levels are most widespread today.

Under the commission method broad general rules are made by legislators, applied in detail in concrete cases by commissions, and may be reviewed for legality by the judiciary. This system results from a long period of trial-and-error evolution and, despite its acknowledged limitations, appears to be the best available regulatory method for our economy at the present time.

The social aim of public utility regulation is to ensure that the consuming public receives adequate service at reasonable rates and without discrimination (however these terms may be defined). In furtherance of this aim, many aspects of utility operations are closely controlled by representatives of the general public. Different jurisdictions, however, utilize a wide variety of regulations and regulatory methods. Thus, although one can discuss general methods and principles, it is necessary to consult the appropriate legislation, regulatory policies, and court interpretations to find a specific answer to a given problem in a given geographic area, and new problems, requiring new legislation, policies, and interpretations, are constantly arising.

One might legitimately criticize specific aspects of utility regulation or even debate whether or not such regulation in general is necessary or desirable. Although changes in details may be expected in the future as in the past, there are no indications of any lessening of regulation or of major changes in regulatory concepts and practices within the foreseeable future.

Although it is certainly worthwhile to consider "what ought to be," it is equally worthwhile for all those concerned with utilities—investors, managers, employees, suppliers, regulators, and customers—to be informed as to "what is." One cannot obtain one's rights or meet one's responsibilities unless one is aware of the nature of these rights and responsibilities.

Regulatory agency procedures are drawn from long-established legal principles designed for court trials based on the adversary process as used for the protection of individual rights. But these principles are somewhat relaxed in regulatory proceedings. The purpose of a trial is to discover guilt or innocence, while the purpose of a regulatory proceeding is to discover what is in the public interest. Well-known rules of the game, tempered with discretion, are valuable aids in accomplishing this. Such a compromise combines the rule of law with the judgment of informed men, which is a distinguishing characteristic of commission regulation. It is not perfect, but few things are. At least it works fairly well.

NOTES

1. For a brief discussion of perfect competition, see Lorie Tarshis, *Modern Economics* (Boston: Houghton Mifflin, 1967), pp. 132–141, or any number of similar textbooks on introductory economics.
2. The Code of Hammurabi, dating back almost 4,000 years, contains many specific regulations applicable to carriers and other public businesses. See C. H. W. Johns, *The Oldest Code of Laws in the World* (Edinburgh: T. & T. Clark, 1903), pp. 1–59. Similar legislative (or monarchial or church) regulations can be traced through succeeding Mediterranean and Western European societies to contemporary times. See Lester S. Levy and Roy J. Sampson, *American Economic Development* (Boston: Allyn and Bacon, 1962), chs. 18, 21, and 22.
3. Our modern corporation evolved directly from the English joint-stock companies of the seventeenth and eighteenth centuries, although its origins can be traced to earlier Italian city-state silent partnerships and perhaps to Ancient Roman and Greek business organizations for semipublic undertakings. See Armond B. DuBois, *The English Business Company After the Bubble Act 1720–1800* (New York: Commonwealth Fund, 1938); Bishop Carlton Hunt, *The Development of the Business Corporation in England 1800–1867* (Cambridge, Mass.: Harvard University Press, 1936); and Lester S. Levy and Roy J. Sampson, *American Economic Development* (Boston: Allyn and Bacon, 1962), ch. 17.
4. See *Dartmouth College v. Woodward,* 17 U.S. 518 (1819).
5. The "blue pages" of *Moody's Public Utility Manual* (New York: Moody's Investor's Service, annual) contain brief summaries of some pertinent points of the individual state franchise laws.
6. At present, almost three fourths of the pertinent state commissions are titled either Public Service Commission or Public Utility (or Utilities) Commission. The remainder operate under a variety of titles.

7. Although in many instances commissioners are appointed by the executive (President or Governor), they are usually subject to legislative confirmation.
8. Such decisions would probably be overturned by the courts upon appeal by aggrieved parties. See later, discussion of the relations between commissions and courts.
9. Note that there is a distinction between the executive function, as used here, and the office of the Chief Executive (President or Governor). As explained earlier, independent regulatory agencies are usually responsible to the legislative rather than to the executive branch of government.
10. See *Marbury v. Madison,* 1 Cranch 135 (1803), discussed in Chapter 3, as a leading case concerning the review of federal statutes for constitutionality.
11. See the discussion of due process as a restriction on federal and state authorities in Chapter 3.
12. The channels of appeal are to a United States District Court, thence to a Court of Appeals, thence to the United States Supreme Court. For details, see any one of several standard law texts, as Bernard F. Cataldo, and others, *Introduction to Law and the Legal Process* (New York: Wiley, 1965), ch. 5.
13. In the Oregon Fish Commission case, *Federal Power Commission v. The State of Oregon,* 349 U.S. 435 (1954), cited in Chapter 4, where the "facts" of a state commission conflicted with the "facts" of a federal commission, the United States Supreme Court appeared to show a preference for the federal "facts." The case was not decided entirely on these grounds, however.
14. See *Interstate Commerce Commission v. Oregon-Washington Railroad and Navigation Company,* 288 U.S. 14 (1933), for a leading case holding that a transportation company is not obliged to enter new territory. For a required extension of service within a firm's territory, however, see *Woodhaven Gas Light Co. v. Public Service Commission,* 269 U.S. 244 (1925).
15. The discussion of regulatory procedures in this text necessarily is brief as well as general. Anyone planning to participate in any way in a regulatory proceeding should, as a minimum general background, consult references like the two books by Francis X. Welch, *Preparing for the Utility Rate Case* (Washington, D.C.: Public Utility Reports, 1954) and *Conduct of the Utility Rate Case* (Washington, D.C.: Public Utility Reports, 1955).

ADDITIONAL READINGS

1. Barnes, Irston R., *The Economics of Public Utility Regulation* (New York: F. S. Crofts, 1942), ch. 6, "The Instruments of Regulation," pp. 168–217; ch. 7, "Franchises," pp. 218–241.
2. Cataldo, Bernard F., C. W. Gillam, F. G. Kempin, Jr., J. M. Stockton, and C. M. Weber, *Introduction to Law and the Legal Process* (New York: Wiley, 1965), ch. 5, "Federalism and the Legal System," pp. 163–192; ch. 7, "Judicial Procedure," pp. 209–249.
3. Clemens, Eli Winston, *Economics and Public Utilities* (New York: Appleton-Century-Crofts, 1950), ch. 3, "The Nature of Commission Regulation," pp. 38–71.
4. Garfield, Paul J., and Wallace F. Lovejoy, *Public Utility Economics* (Englewood Cliffs, N.J.: Prentice-Hall, 1964), ch. 3, "The Development and Scope of Utility Regulation," pp. 27–35; ch. 4, "Administrative Procedure and Review," pp. 36–43.
5. Glaeser, Martin G., *Public Utilities in American Capitalism* (New York: Macmillan, 1957), ch. 15, "The Administrative Commission," pp. 237–253.
6. Jones, Eliot, and Truman C. Bigham, *Principles of Public Utilities* (New York: Macmillan, 1931), ch. 3, "Regulation by Franchises," pp. 102–156; ch. 4, "Regulation by Commissions," pp. 157–190; ch. 9, "Regulation of Service," pp. 387–442.
7. Phillips, Charles F., Jr., *The Economics of Regulation,* rev. ed. (Homewood, Ill.:

Richard D. Irwin, 1969), ch. 4, "The Independent Regulatory Commissions," pp. 83–119.

8. Thompson, C. Woody, and Wendell R. Smith, *Public Utility Economics* (New York: McGraw-Hill, 1941), ch. 12, "Techniques of Regulation," pp. 236–254.
9. Trachsel, Herman H., *Public Utility Regulation* (Chicago: Richard D. Irwin, 1947), part II, "Agencies of Regulation," pp. 73–231.
10. Troxel, Emery, *Economics of Public Utilities* (New York: Rinehart, 1947), ch. 3, "Local Regulation and Franchises," pp. 49–66; ch. 4, "State Commissions," pp. 67–88.
11. Welch, Francis X., *Cases and Text on Public Utility Regulation* (Washington, D.C.: Public Utilities Reports, 1961), ch. 3, "The Utility's Duty to Serve," pp. 137–192; ch. 12, "Jurisdiction, Powers and Duties of the Commissions," pp. 543–577.
12. Welch, Francis X., *Conduct of the Utility Rate Case* (Washington, D.C.: Public Utility Reports, 1955), pp. xvi, 383.
13. Welch, Francis X., *Preparing for the Utility Rate Case* (Washington, D.C.: Public Utility Reports, 1954), pp. xi, 323.
14. Wilcox, Clair, *Public Policies Toward Business,* 4th ed. (Homewood, Ill.: Richard D. Irwin, 1971).
15. Wilcox, Delos F., *Municipal Franchises* (New York: McGraw-Hill, 1911).
16. Wilson, G. Lloyd, James M. Herring, and Roland B. Eutsler, *Public Utility Regulation* (New York: McGraw-Hill, 1938), ch. 9, "Regulation of Service," pp. 204–227.

6

Rate Regulation: Valuation

One of the principal obligations of a public utility or other business significantly affected with the public interest has traditionally been to charge only reasonable prices or rates. Many more economic and legal problems, and much more controversy and litigation, arise from regulation designed to enforce this obligation than from regulation of any other of the customary public utility duties. These problems stem from a constant tug-of-war between consumers and producers. Consumers want good service, but at low rates. Producers (utility firms or their investors) want profits and protection of their capital. Thus, what appears reasonable to one group may appear to be unreasonably high or unreasonably low to the other.

From the long-run point of view, of course, rates that are excessively above the value of the service to consumers will lead to decreases in consumption and perhaps to the development of substitute services. Similarly, rates below the cost of providing service will ultimately lead to a firm's bankruptcy. But no customer, utility investor or manager, or regulator desires either of these extreme results. Thus, the regulatory objective is to assure rates which are reasonable to all concerned at the present time. Consumers must not be overcharged, but regulation must not be so stringent that it in itself prevents a utility from earning a fair return.

In actual utility regulatory practice the terms "reasonable rate" and "fair return" have become virtually synonymous. An unfairly high return, by definition, means that rates are unreasonably high and should be lowered, while an unreasonably low rate, by the same definition, cannot yield a fair return.

This does not mean, of course, that regulation guarantees, or even attempts to guarantee, that every utility will earn a profit under all circumstances. Instead, it means, on the one hand, that regulation is expected to prevent excessive profits attributable to unreasonably high prices, and on the other hand, that regulation cannot keep prices below the level necessary for an otherwise viable firm to continue in business. There may be demand or operational conditions under which a firm cannot maintain itself at any price level. If so, regulation cannot solve the firm's problems. This situation has become notably widespread in street transportation.

Unlike intercity transportation, where intermodal and intramodal competition usually exists and rates are usually uniform for a particular mode in a sizable geographic area, rates for the communications and energy utilities are usually established at the individual firm level. Further, instead of being carefully scrutinized on a service by service or price by price basis, except in street transportation utility rates are normally examined primarily for their overall effect on the utility's rate of return.

In determining a fair or reasonable rate of return, three major questions must be answered. First, What is it that the rate is a return on; that is, what is the value of the utility's property, or its "rate base"? Second, What portion of the utility's gross revenues or income is to be considered its return? Or, stated another way, What deductions from gross revenues, in the form of operating expenses, depreciation, and taxes, must be made to arrive at the net revenue figure? Finally, After appropriate deductions from gross revenues are made, what percentage relation between the remaining net revenues and the rate base is fair? That is, What per cent should the firm be allowed to earn on its property investment?

The following two chapters consider the problems of determining net returns and percentage rates of return. The remainder of this chapter deals with various methods of determining the rate base or evaluating the firm's properties. This discussion does not involve the complex technical questions of property appraisal as such but confines itself to the equally complex economic and legal methods of valuation. The philosophy of the evaluators is of much greater practical effect and causes much greater controversy than the specific technical engineering and accounting techniques of appraisal.

ORIGIN AND EVOLUTION OF THE FAIR VALUE CONCEPT

The case of *Munn v Illinois* (see Chapter 2), which reaffirmed the right of public regulation of businesses peculiarly affected with the public interest, implied that the right to regulate also included the right to fix specific prices or rates of return. With the proliferation of regulation and regulated businesses, however, it soon became clear that there is a great difference between the right to regulate and the right to fix rates which cannot be appealed.

If rates are kept too low, a firm cannot continue to render adequate service or may even be forced completely out of business. Further, if regulation forces rates below some minimum level, the property of investors is being taken from them without due process of law, which is prohibited by the United States Constitution. Eventually, then, it was recognized that the regulators themselves (the commissions) must be subject to the higher regulation of the courts.

The United States Supreme Court held in 1890 that the reasonableness of a rate is a matter of law and thus subject to judicial review,[1] and in 1894 commission-established rates were actually overruled by the Court on the grounds that they were too low.[2] Neither of these cases, however, provided guidelines for the commissions' first step in establishing reasonable rates.

In 1898, though, in the celebrated and often quoted case of *Smyth v. Ames,*[3] the Court held that reasonable rates must be based upon "the fair value of the property being used." Further, the decision spelled out the factors to be considered in determining the fair value, as follows:

> . . . the original cost of construction, the amount expended in permanent improvements, the amount and market value of its bonds and stock, the present as compared with the original cost of construction, the probable earning capacity of the property under particular rates prescribed by statute, and the sum required to meet operating expenses. . . .

Apparently to make sure that nothing would be omitted, the opinion added, "We do not say that there may not be other matters to be considered. . . ."

A substantial portion of the *Smyth v. Ames* valuation rule very soon came under attack from many quarters, on the grounds that it was composed of verbose economic and legal nonsense.

It was rightly pointed out that the "probable earning capacity" cannot sensibly be used to establish a rate base, since the earning capacity itself is based upon the rate; in effect, the Court said that "the rate must be based upon the property value, which must be based upon the rate." This is so clearly "circular reasoning" that it is unworthy of all the learned discussion that has since been given it.

The "market value of its bonds and stock" is no more a satisfactory component of a rate base than is "probable earning capacity," since market value is normally closely related to earnings, which depend upon rates. In specifying "market value" rather than "book value" or "capitalization," the Court unfortunately ensured that this standard would not be seriously considered.

It is and was equally apparent that "the sum required to meet operating expenses" is not a part of the rate base but is, as it says, the operating expenses, which must be deducted from gross revenues to obtain the net return. Apparently, the Court's accounting background was somewhat weak.

Despite its much criticized clauses, however, the *Smyth v. Ames* rule contained enough substance to continue to dominate regulatory thinking and practice. Aside from the above-mentioned worthless verbiage, it spelled out two still important valuation methods. One, "original cost of construction" plus "the amount expended in permanent improvements," is the basis of the well-known original cost or actual cost method of valuation. The other, "the present as compared with the original cost of construction," supports the reproduction cost method. Variations of these two methods of valuation have prevailed since the turn of the century.

The fair value concept, vague though it is, was widely adopted and is still used in some form by almost one third of the states. Its application, of course, is extremely flexible and varies so much from state to state that generalization is almost impossible. Some fair value states give most weight to original cost, while others are more favorable to reproduction cost. Presumably all consider "other matters" (whatever these may be) and include a large element of judgment and compromise.

The fair value method can hardly be described as a specific method of valuation. Instead, it is a composite of methods, a pinch of this and a dash of that, which hopefully minimizes dissatisfactions of customers and utility firms or, if dissatisfactions become too acute, meets the reasonableness criteria of the appropriate reviewing courts.

THE ORIGINAL COST METHOD

The original cost method of valuation is now used by the Federal Power Commission and the Federal Communications Commission as well as by more than one half of the states. No doubt, a part of its popularity is based upon its relative straightforwardness. In comparison with the fair value approach it is easy to understand, explain, and administer, and unlike the reproduction cost method its seemingly inherent justice appeals to consumers—especially during periods of rising prices, when it is likely to result in lower rates than are obtainable under the reproduction cost method.

Even the original cost method of establishing a rate base is not simple, however. Original cost may be determined in various ways, with differing results. A firm's book cost as shown by its accounts, representing either the amount of money put into the company by investors or the actual historical cost of the facilities purchased (the two may be quite different), could be used. Often, though, existing records are inadequate, especially for properties acquired many years ago when regulation was lax or nonexistent. Also, for various reasons, properties may have been acquired at excessive prices. These devices have been used in valuation but have not proved satisfactory.

Today, the generally accepted definition of original cost is the "useful and used" version. That is, only those properties actually useful in and used in rendering utility services are included, and these at the price actually paid at the time they were first devoted to utility service, less accrued depreciation.

This version excludes properties which may be acquired by a firm for nonutility purposes or which may have been retired from service even though still having some value. Also, if one utility acquires properties from another at a higher price than that paid by the first utility owner, only the first cost may be included. Not many people would question the deduction for accrued depreciation on such properties, as depreciation is a cost of doing business, although the depreciation method used and the appropriate amount to be deducted may be debatable.

Several states further refine the original cost method by a "prudent investment" standard. That is, those expenditures or portions of expenditures for properties which the regulators find to be "imprudent" cannot be included in the rate base. Imprudent expenditures are apparently unwise, excessive, or even fraudulent payments for assets. In the absence of outright fraud, however, imprudence may be difficult to establish. A transaction which appeared prudent at the time it was made may later prove to have been unwise. Regulatory authorities, however, cannot use hindsight to penalize utilities for honest managerial mistakes, nor can regulators substitute their own judgments for the judgments of corporate managers.[4]

Although the courts have upheld the prudent investment standard, and no one could object to its intent if the original cost method of valuation is being employed, its usefulness is at best limited. Other existing laws apply to fraudulent misuse of corporate funds, and in the absence of fraud the prudent investment standard should not make any significant difference in an original cost valuation. This is particularly true now that the accounting, financial, and operational practices of most utilities in most jurisdictions have been closely regulated and scrutinized for many years.

As indicated, the original cost valuation method has the advantage of administrative practicality and popular understanding. It has other advantages, and some disadvantages as well. Since it provides a relatively fixed rate base, not influenced by price changes except as additional investments are made or assets replaced, it tends to result in relatively stable or only gradually changing rates. Stable rates have some inherent appeal, but they may be advantageous or not, depending upon one's circumstances and point of view.

During a long period of rising prices a relatively fixed rate base, resting on assets acquired at lower than current prices, produces lower rates than would an evaluation based on more recent price levels. Obviously, then, during inflationary periods informed consumers would prefer the original cost rate base method. At the same time, investors could rightly complain that their "sound" dollar investments are yielding returns in "depreciated" dollars of lower purchasing power. The reverse situation would be true during a long period of declining prices. It is not surprising, therefore, that the positions of utility firms and consumers with respect to the appropriateness of the original cost rate base have been known to shift with fluctuations in price levels.

During the past generation, of course, price trends have been upward; thus the major complaints against original cost valuation have come from utility investors (or their spokesmen, utility managers). It could be argued with some logic that inflation and corresponding decreases in real income are legitimate business risks to be considered and borne by utility investors. On the other hand, it could be argued with equal logic that consumers have no legal or just entitlement to the windfall benefits of unreasonably low rates enjoyed at the expense of investors in regulated businesses which cannot adjust their prices to account for price fluctuations with the same freedom as nonregulated firms.

Aside from the personal welfare of consuming and investing groups, however, original cost valuation poses some serious economic problems of resource allocation and use. If general price levels increase more rapidly than utility rate levels, it may be expected (assuming some relative price elasticity of demand) that consumption of utility services will increase more rapidly than consumption of other goods and services. But if investor returns and real incomes lag, new investment in utility facilities may be discouraged, and utility firms may even find it difficult to replace presently existing low-cost assets as they wear out or become obsolete.

In other words, inflexible rates and consequent fixed dollar returns to utility stockholders, during periods of increasing prices, are likely to encourage a greater consumption of utility services while at the same time discouraging the development or even the maintenance of the facilities necessary to provide these services. A similar line of reasoning, of course, leads to the conclusion that stable rates and increasing investor real income during periods of declining prices results in lowered consumption of utility services and increased investments in facilities.

The economic effects of stable rates are not confined to the utility industry itself.

In an environment of limited resources and incomes greater consumption of one type of product or greater investment in one type of industry necessarily means less consumption or investment in other products and industries, and vice versa. Thus, regulatory decisions concerning telephone rates may have repercussions on investments in supersonic aircraft or the consumption of hula hoops. The world of economics is one in which the parts are interlocking and interdependent.

The original cost method of utility property valuation, then, despite its merits and its widespread use, clearly does not provide ideal allocation and use of resources during periods of changing price levels. Since an ideal pattern of consumption and resource flow is based upon quick price adjustments in a competitive environment, we cannot expect similar results from a regulatory system designed in considerable part to promote stability rather than change. But at least we can recognize the price we pay for stability, its contrasting demerits and merits, in evaluating it. Intelligent choices between one alternative and another can only be made by comparing the benefits and disadvantages of the alternatives.

THE REPRODUCTION COST METHOD

A few states rely upon the reproduction cost method of valuation, while many of the states using the fair value concept make considerable use of reproduction cost in arriving at their versions of fair value. This method certainly is as fair (whatever that may mean) in establishing property values as is any other current or past regulatory device. In addition, it results in closer conformity to the ideal market-determined allocation of resources than does the rival original cost method.

Basically, the most generally accepted version of reproduction cost is the cost that would be required to reproduce the existing utility facilities, in substantially their present form, at current price levels. This sum may be calculated in various ways, including appraisals, estimates of the cost of equivalent new facilities less the appropriate deductions for depreciation necessary to account for the fact that existing facilities are not new, or by the original costs of existing facilities adjusted upward or downward by price indices reflecting price changes since the acquisition of particular assets.[5]

Insofar as reproduction costs are calculated accurately (and there is no reason why they cannot be as accurate as costs obtained by any other method) rates and returns based upon this method will fluctuate more with price level changes than under the original cost method. If rates (and returns) increase in exact proportion to overall price increases, investors could not legitimately complain of decreased real returns, nor could consumers complain of increased real rates. By the same token, if prices decrease, consumers faced with decreasing incomes will obtain decreased rates, and the decreased dollar returns of investors will be offset by the increased purchasing power of the dollar.

It is extremely unlikely that a reproduction cost rate base will exactly and continuously reflect changes in the general price level. (The general price level itself is only a rough approximation and changes continually.) But at least, despite the necessary lags in utility pricing and regulatory actions, reproduction cost valuation is normally more closely related to the current economic scene than is original cost valuation. This means that utility revenues during periods of increasing prices should be more adequate for maintaining and replacing facilities as well as for attracting new investment capital. Further, during periods of falling prices and decreased revenues investors are less likely to be scared away, and worn out facilities can be replaced at lower prices.

It would be hard to argue that the reproduction cost method does not provide for better resource allocation and use (in an economist's sense) and for more fairness to both consumers and investors during eras of fluctuating prices than does the original cost rate base. It is not at all strange, however, that consumers seem to prefer the original cost method during price upswings and reproduction cost during down-swings, while utilities prefer original cost when price levels are low and reproduction cost when prices are high.

Although the reproduction cost method appears to meet the tests of equity and economic allocation somewhat better than does the original cost method, it is subject to at least one major conceptual criticism: Its emphasis upon reproducing facilities in substantially their present form is highly unrealistic. The physical plant of most utilities is composed of a mixture of new, semiobsolete, and almost obsolete equipment, with varying degrees of efficiency, acquired and added to the existing plant piecemeal over a long period of time. Very few existing utility plants, if rebuilt from scratch, would be rebuilt with facilities in substantially their present form. Instead, they would be rebuilt completely with more modern and more efficient equipment, and the various pieces would be better integrated into a whole. This certainly would in most cases result in a different rate base (and different operating costs), although its effect on rate levels might vary depending upon the firm's particular circumstances.

Therefore, although the reproduction cost method as used at present is more relevant in economic and equity terms than the original cost method, a replacement cost variation would be even more relevant. Replacement cost in this sense would be the current cost of replacing the utility plant with another plant that would provide substantially similar services but that would not necessarily be made up of substantially similar facilities.

Since a major aim of a public utility business, like any other business, is to perpetuate its existence by supplying what its consumers want, and since this is consistent with a major aim of regulation, a good argument can be made for a still different version of replacement cost. This would be the costs (estimated, of course, like all other reproduction costs) of future replacement of existing facilities as they wear out or become economically obsolete.

If current and future revenues plus past internal savings do not provide sufficient funds for future replacements of facilities (and this is very possible during a long period of rising prices), a firm's services to its customers necessarily must deteriorate and eventually cease, or the firm must enter the capital market when replacement of presently used facilities becomes necessary. One might argue in opposition, of course, that the rates charged present consumers should not be used to help pay for facilities to be used by future consumers or even that the capital market should be utilized for facility replacement as well as for the acquisition of additional facilities.

The arguments and counterarguments must all be based largely upon subjective value judgments, as is any position concerning methods of establishing a rate base. But at least the alternatives should be understood, compared, and considered. As noted, reproduction cost as used at present and in the past is generally based upon the estimated cost of reproducing substantially similar facilities. Replacement cost, as defined here, has been discussed little and used less. This lack of consideration appears to have been based more upon regulatory expediency than upon deliberate judgment. (The same statement might be made about almost all regulatory devices.)

THE END RESULT CONCEPT

Following the *Smyth v. Ames* case regulatory commissions became particularly sensitive to Supreme Court preferences in establishing valuations and valuation methods. Since commission actions were subject to judicial review, commissions were forced to use methods acceptable to the courts and were in effect court-dominated in this phase of regulation.

For more than a generation the United States Supreme Court and lower courts, which necessarily followed its lead, tended to favor the reproduction cost method.[6] The *McCardle* case, in 1926, has been referred to as the high point of the Court's emphasis on this method.[7] In that decision, the court stated:

> . . . Consideration must be given to prices and wages prevailing at the time. . . .There must be an honest and intelligent forecast as to probable price and wage levels during a reasonable period in the immediate future. . . . It must be determined whether the rates . . . are yielding and will yield . . . a reasonable rate of return on the value of the property at the time of the investigation and for a reasonable time in the future.

The pendulum had begun to swing away from reproduction cost by 1933, however. In that year, the California Railroad Commission was upheld in its use of an original cost valuation based upon historical costs.[8] Although the Court did note that the method used did not appear to undervalue the firm's plant, since much of the plant had been built during a period when prices were higher than in 1933, it did give a hint of things to come by saying:

> We do not sit as a board of revision. . . . The legislative discretion . . . necessarily extends to the entire legislative process, embracing the method used in reaching the legislative determination, as well as that determination itself. . . . The judicial function does not go beyond the decision of the constitutional question. That question is whether the rates as fixed are confiscatory.

From this position it was not a long step to the final abandonment of judicial control over specific valuation methods. In the 1942 *Natural Gas Pipeline* decision[9] it became apparent that regulatory commissions, operating within the framework of their ruling legislation, were to be given a relatively free hand in rate base determination insofar as the United States Supreme Court was concerned. In expressing its changed viewpoint, the Court stated:

> The Constitution does not bind rate-making bodies to the service of any single formula or combination of formulas. Agencies to whom this legislative power has been delegated are free, within the ambit of their statutory authority, to make the pragmatic adjustments which may be called for by particular circumstances. Once a fair hearing has been given, proper findings made, and other statutory requirements satisfied, the courts cannot intervene in the absence of a clear showing that the limits of due process have been overstepped. If the commission's order, as applied to the facts before it and viewed in its entirety, produces no arbitrary result, our inquiry is at an end.

Although the *Natural Gas Pipeline* decision freed regulatory commissions from court-imposed valuation formulas (at least by the United States Supreme Court), it did not provide any complete explanation of what kind of "pragmatic adjustments" could be made or what the Court might consider an "arbitrary result." Two years later, however, the *Hope Natural Gas* case did provide such workable guidelines.[10] In that decision, to date the ruling expression of the United States Supreme Court on valuation methods and rates of return, the Court stated:

> . . . It is the result reached, not the method employed, which is controlling. . . . It is not theory but the impact of the rate order which counts. If the total effect of the rate order cannot be said to be unjust and unreasonable, judicial inquiry . . . is at an end. . . . Rates which enable the company to operate successfully, to maintain its financial integrity, to attract capital, and to compensate its investors for the risks assumed certainly cannot be condemned as invalid, even though they might produce only a meager return on the so-called "fair value" rate base.

The outcome of the end result concept as stated in the *Hope* case is that regulatory commissions are no longer bound by any rigid valuation formula or by any rigid percentage rate of return criteria (see Chapter 8) insofar as the federal courts are concerned. A return, however arrived at, unless procedural or substantive due process violations can be demonstrated, will not be overruled as long as it enables a firm to maintain its financial integrity—that is, if it enables the firm to maintain and attract the capital necessary to provide the services demanded of it by the public. In other words, regulatory actions can now be based more upon economic than upon legal standards.

This does not mean, of course, that all problems of valuation and rate-making have been solved, even from the legal viewpoint. No judgments of the future are infallible. A return which one person judges will maintain financial integrity may be judged by another as leading to financial ruin. Further, in order to make any intelligent judgments as to what return will maintain a firm's financial integrity, some method or methods of valuation must be used. Actually, most regulatory commissions are still bound by specific statutes, court interpretations, or long-established practices to some particular method of valuation.

As indicated, more than half the state commissions as well as the Federal Power Commission and the Federal Communications Commission now use the original cost method (including the prudent investment and other variations). Fair value is a poor second, and reproduction cost an even poorer third. Several states are not tied to any particular method. It must be remembered, however, that many of those states not bound to any method as well as many of the so-called fair value states may and do use original cost or reproduction cost in some variation or combination to establish valuations.[11]

VALUATION OF INTANGIBLE ASSETS

In addition to its physical properties a utility firm, like other firms, usually possesses a number of nonphysical or intangible assets. Since these have value, utilities often wish to have them included in their rate bases.

Franchises are a commonly owned utility property, definitely valuable, and often taxed. Franchise taxes, however, are deductible from gross revenues as operating expenses in arriving at net returns. Further, it is clear that a franchise has no earning capacity apart from the firm's physical plant. To allow a franchise value based upon earning capacity, therefore, would be circular reasoning of the celebrated *Smyth v. Ames* type.

Some confusion was created by the 1909 *Willcox* case,[12] wherein a franchise value was allowed. This was for a particular circumstance, however, and was not intended to, and did not, establish a precedent. The United States Supreme Court definitely ruled against franchise values in a rate base in a leading 1923 case.[13] Commissions and courts now generally allow franchise values in a rate base only at the actual cost of acquisition, including, of course, reasonable attorneys' fees and similar expenditures if these are not otherwise classified as operating expenses.

Considerable variation is found in the treatment of water rights as a component of the rate base. There are many alternative uses of water, which is increasingly being considered a scarce and valuable resource, and its value does not always depend upon its use by a utility. There is no question about the valuable nature of water rights and the fact that they may be included in the rate base.[14] The valuation may vary with circumstances, however.

The ownership of water rights may take at least three different forms. A firm may have complete ownership of its water, including the source of supply; it may have riparian rights to a flow which cannot be diminished; or it may have only public permission to make use of publicly owned waters. In the last situation federal regulations and most state regulations permit water rights to be valued only at cost of acquisition. If the utility has complete ownership or even riparian rights, however, it may be entitled to more, depending upon the state of jurisdiction. Sometimes water rights are included as a part of the land valuation, while sometimes a separate and additional valuation is made. The state trends seem to be favoring a cost of acquisition value only, but state water laws differ greatly and change slowly.

Patents may also be costly but often may have a commercial value much greater than their cost of acquisition or development. On the other hand, the use of a new patent may force a substantial amount of currently used equipment into obsolescence, or large sums may be spent on developing or attempting to develop patents which prove to be worthless. The proper treatment of patents in the rate base is therefore debatable. Should the cost of equipment made obsolete by a patent be considered? Or should the cost of developing unused patents or research costs which do not lead to patents be included?

No doubt, the most convenient method of handling patent costs is to treat research expenditures and equipment obsolescence simply as operating expenses and to include purchased patents at acquisition cost or to write them off over a period of time as operating expenses. Although the courts agree that patent costs, in some form, may be a legitimate part of the rate base, there is little commission uniformity and no really definitive Supreme Court decision on this matter. [15]

Contracts and leaseholds, for various reasons, often become much more valuable than their acquisition cost with the passage of time. For example, oil or natural gas may be discovered on land, or a new subdivision may be developed. Although, again, regulatory treatment has not been uniform, most commissions have held that it is a utility's duty to enter into the most favorable possible contracts and that consumers should not be penalized by higher rates resulting from a rate base expanded by a favorable contract or an unearned increment. The courts generally have accepted the inclusion of contracts and leaseholds at acquisition cost only or even sanctioned their exclusion from the rate base.[16]

The "going value" of a utility, despite or because of its nebulous nature, has given rise to many valuation problems and much discussion. Presumably, going value is the difference between the value of a firm already in operation and one with similar facilities which is not in operation. Or it might be defined as the value of a firm's organization and experience. Utility firms often have taken the position that a sum for going value should be included in the rate base and have put forth various methods, none very satisfactory, for measuring this alleged value.

Early developmental costs, including but not always limited to such items as incorporation fees and charges and construction interest and other expenses incurred before the firm could actually start selling its services, are often suggested as legitimate for inclusion within the rate base as a part of going value. Insofar as such costs are not reflected in the value of the firm's properties, and if they are not treated simply as operating expenses or amortized over the first few years of operation (as is customary with most nonregulated businesses), this version of going value is perhaps the most acceptable one.

Operating losses, if any, during the first few years of a firm's existence sometimes have been offered for inclusion in going value. It can be argued, though, that the risk of loss is included in the price paid by a firm for its capital and that a reflection of early losses in the rate base would be double counting.

Some regulatory commissions have never accepted the going concern concept, but many have given it some consideration, and some still do. As a generalization, the courts will usually allow going value as a part of the rate base if a regulatory commission finds it appropriate but will not require its inclusion.[17]

From the economic viewpoint it can be argued that going value ultimately depends upon a firm's earnings and that if it is capitalized and included in the rate base, this resembles the *Smyth v. Ames* circular reasoning regarding earning capacity as a part of the rate base upon which earnings are to be based. The regulatory trend is to disallow going value as a part of a firm's value for rate-making purposes, while the Supreme Court viewpoint appears to be that this is a matter of public policy rather than a legal question.

Good will is often considered a valuable asset of a nonregulated company and may be included as an important part of selling price. It has been defined as growing out of "the fixed and favorable consideration of customers" toward "an established and well-known and well-conducted business."[18] In other words, this concept is based generally upon the superior earning capacity of a firm resulting from its voluntary patronage in a competitive arena. Since good will is based upon earning capacity, however, and since public utility services often are exclusive within a given market, regulatory commissions and courts have consistently denied this item as an appropriate part of the rate base.[19]

In conclusion, intangible assets certainly may be valuable to a company, regulated as well as nonregulated. Regulation designed to produce reasonable rates of return, however, will usually not allow these intangibles to be capitalized on the basis of their alleged earning capacity for rate-making purposes. Instead, if they are considered at all, they are generally valued only at acquisition costs. Complete regulatory uniformity does not exist, and the courts have allowed some flexibility. The overall pattern, however, is fairly clear and consistent.

SUMMARY

Determination of reasonable rates, or fair rates of return, is the most difficult and controversial aspect of public utility regulation. The first step in this determination is the establishment of a property value, or rate base, against which net returns can be measured.

Physical properties may be valued either on an original cost or a reproduction cost basis, with several variations possible for each of these methods. Normally, original cost considers useful and used properties at their acquisition cost at the time they were devoted to utility service, while reproduction cost attempts to establish a present value for these same properties. Depreciation is deducted in both methods, and sometimes acquisitions deemed imprudent by regulators will not be allowed. The so-called fair value concept may make use of some type of original or reproduction cost method, or both, and may include various other factors in its valuation.

Original cost methods tend to provide more rate stability as well as lower rates during periods of rising prices. Reproduction cost, on the other hand, tends to reflect current economic conditions more accurately and to approximate more closely resource use and allocation criteria as commonly accepted among economists. Neither of these methods is entirely satisfactory from all viewpoints, but either is workable and generally acceptable.

Between the 1898 *Smyth v. Ames* decision and the late 1920's or early 1930's, because of court-imposed constraints, reproduction cost dominated. Then original cost became more popular, and finally, in 1942 and 1944, in the *Natural Gas Pipeline* and *Hope* cases, the end result doctrine was established. Under this currently prevailing concept regulators are not closely bound (except by their applicable specific statutes, customary practices, and state court interpretations) to any particular method of valuation as long as the net effect does not violate procedural or substantive due process. At present, among those regulatory bodies identifiable as favoring a particular method or concept, the most popular are original cost, fair value, and reproduction cost, in that order.

Intangible or nonphysical properties, insofar as they are valued at all for rate base purposes, are generally considered at acquisition cost only. That is, this category of assets is valued more nearly on an original cost than upon a reproduction cost or present value basis.

Finally, it must be emphasized that regulatory practices vary considerably, even among those jurisdictions where methods and practices nominally are the same, and that regulation even in a given jurisdiction is continually evolving. Generalizations like those contained in this chapter (and elsewhere in this and other texts) are possible and useful, but specific answers must be sought in the particular statutes, practices, and decisions applicable in a given jurisdiction. Even then, tomorrow's answer may be somewhat different in detail from yesterday's. The past does not foretell the future, any more than a general highway map shows all the obstacles on a particular road. But a knowledge of the past, like the possession of a map, may aid one in following the generally correct course.

NOTES

1. *Chicago, Milwaukee and St. Paul Railway v. Minnesota,* 134 U.S. 418 (1890).
2. *Reagan v. Farmers' Loan and Trust Company,* 154 U.S. 362 (1894).
3. Found in 169 U.S. 466 (1898).
4. See *Southwestern Bell Telephone Co. v. Missouri Public Service Commission,* 262 U.S. 276 (1923).
5. One theoretically and practically troublesome issue, regardless of the method of calculation, is the evaluation of land. If it is assumed that the present utility has not previously existed, the calculated value of its land might be considerably lower. That is, if land is valued at its actual present market price, this value necessarily includes the effects of the existence of the present utility, and thus the utility is entitled to a higher rate simply because of its previous existence—if utility services had never before been available to the community, land values, the rate base, and rates, would be lower! No generally satisfactory solution to this problem has been found. Usually, land is valued in such circumstances by a process of comparison and compromise.

6. For leading examples see: *San Diego Land and Town Co. v. National City,* 174 U.S. 739 (1899); *Willcox v. Consolidated Gas Co.,* 212 U.S. 19 (1909); Minnesota Rate cases, 230 U.S. 352 (1913); *Bluefield Water Works v. West Virginia Public Service Commission,* 262 U.S. 679 (1923); *Southwestern Bell Telephone Co. v. Missouri Public Service Commission,* 262 U.S. 276 (1923).
7. *McCardle v. Indianapolis Water Co.,* 272 U.S. 400 (1926).
8. *Los Angeles Gas and Electric Corporation v. Railroad Commission of California,* 289 U.S. 287 (1933).
9. *Federal Power Commission v. Natural Gas Pipeline Co. of America,* 315 U.S. 575 (1942).
10. *Federal Power Commission v. Hope Natural Gas Co.,* 320 U.S. 591 (1944).
11. The "blue pages" of *Moody's Public Utility Manual* (New York: Moody's Investor's Service, annual) provide an up-to-date summary of the principal valuation methods used in each state. This classification is very general, however. The specific state statutes, commission decisions, and court interpretations must be reviewed for a relatively complete understanding of the applicable rules in any particular state.
12. See note 6.
13. *Georgia Railway and Power Co. v. Railroad Commission of Georgia,* 262 U.S. 625 (1923).
14. See the *McCardle* case, note 7.
15. For example, in *Pacific Gas and Electric Co. v. San Francisco,* 265 U.S. 403 (1924), the United States Supreme Court ruled that the utility's specific patent in question should be valued at more than its development cost but did not define a method of valuation.
16. See *Colorado-Interstate Gas Co. v. Federal Power Commission,* 324 U.S. 581, and *Panhandle Eastern Pipe Line Co. v. Federal Power Commission,* 324 U.S. 635, both 1945. Also, *Interstate Commerce Commission v. New York, New Haven, and Hartford Railroad Co.,* 287 U.S. 178 (1932).
17. As illustrative prominent examples, the United States Supreme Court upheld the inclusion of going value in *Knoxville v. Knoxville Water Co.,* 212 U.S. 1 (1909), *Des Moines Gas Co. v. Des Moines,* 238 U.S. 153 (1915), and the *McCardle* case, note 7, but did not require its inclusion in the *Los Angeles Gas and Electric* case, note 8, *Dayton Power and Light Co. v. Public Utilities Commission of Ohio,* 292 U.S. 290 (1934), or the *Natural Gas Pipeline* case, note 9.
18. *Des Moines Gas* case, note 17.
19. For examples, see the *Willcox, Des Moines Gas,* and *Los Angeles Gas and Electric* cases, cited in notes 6 and 17.

ADDITIONAL READINGS

1. Barnes, Irston R., *The Economics of Public Utility Regulation* (New York: F. S. Crofts, 1942), ch. 11, "The Present-Fair-Value Concept of the Courts," pp. 370–403; ch. 12, "Original Cost," pp. 404–415; ch. 13, "Reproduction Cost," pp. 416–499.
2. Bonbright, James C., *Principles of Public Utility Rates* (New York: Columbia University Press, 1961), ch. 14, "The Rate Base: Replacement Cost as an Alternative Standard," pp. 224–237.
3. Clemens, Eli Winston, *Economics and Public Utilities* (New York: Appleton-Century-Crofts, 1950), ch. 7, "The Valuation Problem," pp. 140–161.
4. Garfield, Paul J., and Wallace F. Lovejoy, *Public Utility Economics* (Englewood Cliffs, N.J.: Prentice-Hall, 1964), ch. 6, "The Rate Base," pp. 56–83; ch. 7, "Valuation Procedures," pp. 83–94.
5. Glaeser, Martin G., *Public Utilities in American Capitalism* (New York: Macmillan, 1957), ch. 17, "The Problem of the Rate Base," pp. 270–286.

6. Phillips, Charles F., Jr., *The Economics of Regulation*, rev. ed. (Homewood, Ill.: Richard D. Irwin, 1969), ch. 8, "The Rate Base," pp. 216–259.
7. Trachsel, Herman H., *Public Utility Regulation* (Chicago: Richard D. Irwin, 1947), ch. 12, "The Valuation of Public Utilities," pp. 235–260.
8. Welch, Francis X., *Cases and Text on Public Utility Regulation* (Washington, D.C.: Public Utilities Reports, 1961), ch. 6, "The Basis of a Reasonable Rate," pp. 272–322.
9. *Federal Power Commission v. Hope Natural Gas Co.*, 320 U.S. 591 (1944).
10. *Federal Power Commission v. Natural Gas Pipeline Co. of America*, 315 U.S. 575 (1942).
11. *Los Angeles Gas and Electric Corporation v. Railroad Commission of California*, 289 U.S. 287 (1933).
12. *McCardle v. Indianapolis Water Co.*, 272 U.S. 400 (1926).
13. *Smyth v. Ames*, 169 U.S. 466 (1898).

7

Rate Regulation: Deductions From Operating Revenue

Consideration of utility operating expenses, depreciation charges, and tax payments is a second and vital part of rate regulation. These three costs combined, although they may vary considerably depending upon the kind of utility service furnished and the particular operating conditions, typically absorb 75 to 90 per cent of a utility firm's operating revenues. The percentage rate of return or fair return on the rate base (however that base may be established), that is, the amount allocated to interest payments, dividends, and surplus, must therefore come from the remaining 10 to 25 per cent of operating revenues.

No one disputes the need for deducting operating costs from operating revenues in determining a fair rate of return. But the amount and method of deduction may be very controversial. Clearly, even a relatively small change in cost categories that absorb as much as 90 per cent of a firm's revenues may have a palpable impact on consumer prices or stockholder dividends. Actually, regulation of what may be deducted is as important, or often far more important, in determining reasonable rates and fair returns as regulation of the rate base or of the percentage rate of return. In this chapter, then, we consider some of the major problems and techniques involved in regulatory disposition of operating expenses, taxes, and depreciation.

OPERATING EXPENSE DEDUCTIONS

It must be understood that the managers of a utility firm are primarily accountable to the firm's stockholders for their actions, unless the firm's ability to supply adequate services at reasonable rates is threatened. This means that a regulatory body cannot normally prohibit expenditures. Rather, with a few statutory exceptions for special cases, the regulatory role is to disallow improper expenditures for rate-making or fair return purposes. If improper expenditures are made and disallowed, they are borne by investors in the form of lower profits; management is answerable only to stockholders.

The legal right of regulatory authorities to scrutinize and disallow improper expenditures, even though not specifically mentioned in regulatory statutes, was recognized by the United States Supreme Court early in the history of commission regulation. In an 1892 decision the Court stated that regulatory authorities ". . . should be fully advised as to what is done with the receipts and earnings of the company," and that the regulatory power is not ". . . subservient to the discretion of any railroad corporation which may, by exorbitant and unreasonable salaries, or in some other improper way, transfer its earnings into what it is pleased to call 'operating expenses.'"[1]

Despite their legal right to do so, however, regulators made little effective use of operating expense controls before the 1930's. Perhaps there was some feeling during a less sophisticated era that the interests of management coincided with the interests of investors and consumers in keeping costs as low as possible.

Further, although the fact of regulation itself may be considered an invasion of "management prerogatives," there was some reluctance on the part of commissions to invade the managerial field of cost control. This reluctance was no doubt reinforced by a 1923 Supreme Court decision holding that a commission should not ". . . substitute its judgment for that of the directors of the corporation," and that it could not ". . . ignore items charged by the utility as operating expenses unless there is an abuse of discretion in that regard by the corporate officers."[2] Given the choice between accepting expenditures as made and proving "an abuse of discretion," most commissions followed the path of least resistance.

Subsequent investigation of utility holding company proliferation and manipulation during the 1920's, however, plus consumer demands for lower rates during the depressed 1930's, brought strong pressures for more effective regulation of utility expenditures. This process was facilitated by uniform systems of accounting and auditing, established originally for valuation purposes, and perhaps was indirectly aided by income tax requirements. Commission action in disallowing improper operating expenses was generally upheld by the courts on the grounds that consumers should not be "made to compensate extravagant or unnecessary costs. . . ."[3]

REGULATION TECHNIQUES

Commissions cannot arbitrarily disallow expenditures, of course. The assumption is that management acts honestly and in good faith, and its actions cannot be judged by hindsight. When an expenditure is challenged as improper, the firm must be given an opportunity to rebut the challenge. If the expense can be shown to be actual, necessary, and reasonable, it must be allowed. In this context, "actual" may be either a past expenditure or an unavoidable future expenditure, while "reasonable" is determined by the prevailing circumstances and alternatives as seen by a "prudent" manager. "Necessary" is subject to varying and often conflicting interpretations, as will be seen in the following section.

Operating expenses may be disallowed either after or before they are made, depending upon the statutes and regulatory practices under which the various agencies operate. In most jurisdictions disallowance occurs after the fact; thus the consumer is protected at the expense of the investor. Aside from the relative equities involved, this raises the question of adequacy of service. If investors do not get adequate returns, the firm may be unable to retain and attract the necessary capital for maintaining its financial integrity, and ultimately service may suffer. On the other hand, astute managers are normally well informed on the allowable and disallowable policies of particular commissions and can act accordingly. It is likely that the possibility or probability of disallowance, and consequent adverse effects on profits and on creditor or stockholder reaction, tends to curb improper expenditures considerably.

Disapproval of nonallowable expenditures in advance would seem to be more satisfactory from the firm's viewpoint. This can be accomplished in two ways. Certain types of described expenditures can be prohibited by statute or administrative ruling, or commissions can scrutinize utility budgets in advance, indicating what they consider to be unjustified or excessive proposed expenses. Outright prohibition has not been widely used, although the legal authority for it seems clearly established. Advance budgetary control is used, either formally or informally, by more than one third of the state commissions, and it is increasing in popularity. Since most utility firms budget well into the future, this method places no particular administrative burden upon either the firm or the commission.

A common method for checking whether expenditures are excessive either before or after they are made, is to compare them with some previously prepared set of standard costs or ratios. These standards may be based upon industry averages in a given area or upon a particular firm's past performance. This is useful primarily for screening, of course. There are many reasons why a particular expense of a given firm may deviate considerably from its past or industry averages. But wide deviations without obvious cause may alert both regulators and managers to the need for closer scrutiny.

One troublesome problem in examining expenditures is that of segregating legitimate operating expenses from legitimate capital expenses or expenses for other nonoperating purposes. For example, a capital facility may be replaced by another designed to do the same job, but the replacement may be more valuable or capital-intensive than the older facility. Thus, some portion of the expenditure could be considered as a routine operating expense, but some portion would be a net addition to previous capital and would be appropriately included in the rate base. Or noncapital expenditure, such as propaganda against public ownership or in support of rate increases, may be of definite value to investors but not necessary for providing required services. These and similar problems of expense segregation, despite uniform and consistent accounting systems and more or less known rules of the game, often generate controversy.

PROBLEMS WITH PARTICULAR EXPENDITURES

Most operating expenses incurred or proposed are proper and allowable, of course. Some particular kinds of expenditures, however, are often questioned. Although the carefulness of examination and regulatory practice itself vary considerably from jurisdiction to jurisdiction, it is possible to identify some widespread controversial areas and to make some general statements concerning them.

Payments to employees and management in the form of wages, salaries, expense accounts, bonuses, pensions, and other so-called fringe benefits conceivably can be used to conceal unusually high profits.[4] Generally, employee wages, pensions, and fringe benefits are accepted without question, as they are normally set by collective bargaining. Sometimes employee bonuses are questioned as a form of profit-sharing, however.

Management payments are more often challenged, especially if they are large in proportion to total revenues and if the receiving official is connected with a holding company or affiliated corporation or if he is an important stockholder (particularly in a small firm). A majority of the commissions, though, seldom if ever question executive compensation. Apparently, the belief prevails that except in peculiar circumstances interindustry competition for good managers requires competitive compensation and that most managers are worth what they are paid. This belief is reinforced by the fact that managerial compensation generally is not higher, nor does it represent a larger proportion of total revenues, in the regulated industries than in nonregulated businesses.

The existence of regulation creates additional operating expenses for a utility. Normal or routine costs arising from the fact of regulation, including the costs of preparing and presenting evidence supporting proposed rate increases, are usually accepted as proper. Sometimes, though, large expenditures in rate cases are amortized over a period of several years instead of being charged completely to the year in which they occurred.[5] Penalties or fines imposed for violations or noncompliance with statutes or commission orders are usually disallowed.

Several states under various circumstances have disallowed costs involved in protracted and expensive court appeals of commission rate orders, especially if these appeals have not been successful. Clearly, utility firms have the legal right to appeal commission orders and even the implied duty to their stockholders to do so if these orders appear unjustified. Appeal litigations costs, then, are obviously regulatory costs.

On the other hand, one might question the justice of requiring consumers to finance, in effect, through higher allowable operating costs and ultimately higher rates, court appeals designed to bring about rate increases. Also, there is a strong presumption that if appeal litigation financed indirectly by consumers rather than directly by investors is allowed, such appeals might become much more numerous, lengthy, and expensive than necessary. The United States Supreme Court has not ruled directly on disallowance of appeal litigation costs, but several state courts have upheld the practice under certain circumstances. State procedures and court rulings vary so widely, however, that any particular question in this area can be answered, if at all, only by reviewing what has happened in the particular jurisdiciton concerned.

Advertising and promotional costs, including minor servicing and repair of consumers' utility appliances, are allowable expenditures if their legitimate object is sales increase. Expenditures for propaganda, such as attempts to influence public policy on utility ownership or similar legislative matters, generally are not allowable. It is often very difficult to draw the line between legitimate "soft-sell" or institutional advertising and political propaganda, however.

Charitable donations and contributions, including financial support to a variety of community service organizations, are allowed by many commissions if not obviously excessive. Reasonable expenses for worthy causes are often justified as requirements of good corporate citizenship or institutional advertising or good public relations.

Some have maintained, nonetheless, that such expenditures are borne by consumers (or by investors, if disallowed) and that consumers (or investors) should have the privilege of choosing their own charities or even of refusing to make charitable contributions. Also, some argue that well-publicized "worthy donations" may be an indirect method of influencing public opinion on political matters affecting utility interests. If contributions are allowed, commissions often reduce the amount given by the firm's resulting decrease in income tax liabilities. Courts generally are neutral on the matter of charitable contributions, accepting the discretionary authority of the appropriate commissions.[6] It should be noted that in response to this criticism utility management may often be more willing to lend executives to work on worthy community projects than to make cash contributions. In effect, the lending of personnel is a "contribution in kind" and serves the same objective of good corporate citizenship without appearing on the books of account as a controversial operating deduction.

Political contributions are prohibited by federal and most state laws and thus are generally both disallowable and illegal. Reasonable lobbying expenses, however, are normally acceptable on the grounds that legislators need the organized opinions of affected industries in enacting legislation. Lobbying activities, though, are closely regulated by the federal government and by many state governments. The lobbyists' profession—and it may be dignified by that name—has a somewhat tarnished popular image because of occasional abuses. An honest lobbyist, however, may be regarded as an indispensable resource person for legislators rather than as a dispenser of illegitimate largesse.

In times past, many utilities, especially electric and gas firms, have operated appliance businesses or services, sometimes attracting sales by underselling independent competitors. Sales of utility services associated with the appliances might thus be increased, and appliance sales losses could be charged as operating expenses of the parent utility company. This practice was objectionable to independent appliance dealers, who felt that it was an unfair trade practice. Also, many consumers objected to subsidizing appliance sales by higher rates. Commissions now rule, with only a few exceptions, that nonutility expenses and revenues must be carefully segregated and that nonutility operations of a utility firm must stand or fall on their own.

Intercompany payments, that is, payments made by utility operating companies to parent holding companies or to affiliated firms, were formerly extensively used to disguise profits. Following the utility holding company investigations and stringent laws of the 1930's, however, commissions began to scrutinize interfirm transactions very carefully. Generally, such intercompany payments are now allowable only on the basis of the actual costs (including reasonable profits) of the company to which payments are made. Or alternatively, a firm cannot pay more for the services received by it from an affiliated company than it would have to pay a nonaffiliated firm for an equivalent service. The whole matter of the regulation of intercorporate relations is discussed in more detail in Chapter 9.

Research and development costs in this era of nuclear power and communications satellites have attracted attention, even though these may not be major expenditures for any one firm. Where these expenditures have been questioned, they have generally been found desirable and allowable (see, however, the discussion of patents in Chapter 6).

Sometimes questions have been raised as to whether consumers in general should be required to bear the costs of service rendered to customers who do not pay their bills. Some commissions on some occasions have disallowed uncollectibles, but the general practice is to recognize that any large business will have some uncollectible accounts and that this is a normal cost of doing business. Frequently, though, commissions impose or suggest operating procedures by which uncollectibles can be minimized, or they establish percentage standards beyond which uncollectible amounts may be considered as stemming from the faults or inefficiencies of the firm.

Finally, it has been suggested that "operating inefficiencies" as such provide grounds for reducing portions of particular operating expenses. In principle this seems to be valid, but not many commissions are eager to undertake the burden of proof necessary to establish outright inefficiency. Actually, this is generally unnecessary, since commissions can apply the same kind of sanctions by finding that actual or proposed expenditures are unnecessary or unreasonably extravagant.

In brief review, this section has identified several questionable utility operating expenses and stated some of the problems connected with allowing or disallowing them. This discussion has by no means dealt with all questionable areas but has been confined to the principal items of controversy. Many of these and similar costs will be discussed further, from managerial and other viewpoints, in several following chapters. The management of the two other major deductions from operating revenue, taxes and depreciation, are discussed in the immediately following sections.

UTILITY TAXATION

There is a great deal of interest in utility taxation for several reasons. First, the privately owned or investor-owned utilities have emphasized their tax payments as a matter of public relations. This is particularly true for electric utilities, where the tax issue is important in the private- versus public-ownership argument. Second, since utilities generally control large amounts of fixed capital, their rates of taxation and tax effects on local tax districts are of importance. Many school districts wish for electric generating plants or natural gas pipelines in their jurisdictions. Those local districts containing utility property generally count themselves quite lucky—and, it might be added, occasionally take advantage of the circumstances. Finally, many scholars writing in the utility area, as well as utility management, are concerned with the growth of the tax burden over time on an industry supplying an essential public service. One presentation of this problem noted that taxes as a percentage of gross revenue had grown from 9 per cent in the 1920's to over 23 per cent in the 1960's.[7] This growth is clearly a function of increasing tax rates as well as of the various types of taxes which utilities must pay.

KINDS OF TAXES

Utilities are subject to six separate types of taxes. Some of these are special taxes, while some are the same as taxes assessed on other businesses.

Ad Valorem or Property Taxes

Traditionally, the most important tax laid on utilities is the ad valorem or property tax. Since a utility uses a very large amount of fixed capital, property taxes are typically quite heavy.

Historically, the property tax on local utilities evolved out of the taxation of railroads, a business which has many similar economic characteristics. Railroads were the first example of "big business" in the United States using a large mass of fixed capital. As such, they were important taxpayers, and the manner in which taxes were assessed was of great importance to the various tax districts. But problems arose because the taxable property was usually in several tax districts or even in several states. In addition, rolling stock over an entire railroad system was difficult to assess in one individual tax district. Finally, the whole of the business as a "going concern" was often more valuable than the sum of its parts or the sum of the values assessed by all the tax districts.

Out of this historical background, and in response to these problems of taxation, the "unit rule" emerged.[8] Basically, this means that the property as a whole, irrespective of state or local government lines, is assigned a value. This total value is then allocated or prorated among the various tax districts according to some unit measure such as mileage. A similar type of procedure is used for utilities.

Often assessment of the value of a utility for tax purposes is placed in the hands of a state tax commission or board. This may be because of lack of expertness on the part of local tax authorities or because of possible inequities which could arise if each tax body assessed the property in its particular district. Also, a state board can often assess the "going concern" value, whereas a local assessor, faced with but one specific unit of property, cannot. Where utilities cross state lines, as in the case of telephone, natural gas pipelines, and some electric companies, statewide assessment can be made in conference with other states having jurisdiction to establish a total assessed value.

We will not discuss in detail how assessed value is allocated among the states and among tax divisions in a state. Basically, some agreed-upon unit of measure, such as the mileage of telephone lines, pipelines, power lines, or the like, is used. Within a state the location of the physical property is given prime consideration, and some additional factor is usually added to this figure to reflect total business done or the particular tax district's share of the whole as well as its individual share of the property. The state or the local district then applies its particular tax rate to this assessed value in order to determine the amount of taxes due. Since the property tax is controlled by the assessed value of the capital involved, it is often called an ad valorem tax.

Gross Receipts Taxes

In some tax jurisdictions a special utility gross receipts tax is used in lieu of the property tax. This came about historically because of the difficulty of assessing a value by the unit rule or because of the ease of collecting such a tax. This tax applies only to the business done within a single state. In a few states it is used in addition to a property tax.

Where this tax is used, it is typically a small percentage of gross income or receipts of the utility. Sometimes this tax will be assessed against one kind of utility, such as water companies, and not against others. Again, this may be done for administrative convenience. Sometimes this will be the only state tax on a utility, or sometimes it is but one of a series of taxes.

The gross receipts tax has the advantage of ease of administration but is generally objected to on "ability to pay" grounds. All utilities are not equally efficient, nor do all utilities require equal investment to produce a dollar of revenue. The high capital-intensive utilities generally do not object to a gross receipts tax as a substitute for a property tax, but low capital-intensive utility companies do. From the tax authorities' viewpoint the yield of this tax is quite predictable, remaining relatively the same or steadily growing over time. However, from the utilities' viewpoint the tax overlooks changes in efficiency or in technology that might affect physical property, and it is generally viewed as an unfair tax. This is particularly true where no sales tax is levied on other businesses—the gross receipts tax resembles the sales tax in many ways.

Income Taxes

Utilities pay corporate net income taxes to the federal government, as do other businesses. In addition, some states also assess corporate net income taxes on all businesses. Typically, net income taxes are not special to the utilities and are considered one of the burdens business must bear in our complex economy.

It is generally conceded that the corporate net income tax is more equitable than the gross receipts tax. This is because it more nearly reflects one of the popular canons of taxation, that is, ability to pay. Basically, the tax is assessed against profits and reflects the efficiency level of the business. It is, unfortunately, difficult to administer this tax, because judgments must be made as to which expenses may be deducted for tax calculation purposes and which may not. These judgments, usually made by the United States Internal Revenue Service, may be different from similar judgments of state regulatory commissions made for purposes of rate regulation. Some expense deductions are allowable for tax purposes but are not allowable for purposes of calculating the rate of return.

Tax rates on federal corporate net income taxes have varied in recent times as Congress has used fiscal policy to control the economy. Typically, state corporate net income tax rates, where this tax is used, have been more steady. The yield to the federal government tends to vary as a function of rulings of the Internal Revenue Service, the rate of taxation applied, and the profits made by utilities. For states, the main variable is the profits made by utilities.

At one time, the corporate income tax was considered a substitute for ad valorem or property taxes. Although some states officially took this position, the proposition was objected to on the grounds that the ad valorem tax reflects the "benefit" theory of taxation while the corporate net income tax reflects the "ability to pay" theory. In other words, the two taxes were based on different concepts and could not be substitutes for each other. It is fairly common today for both property taxes and income taxes (both state and federal) to be assessed against utilities.

Excise Taxes and Emergency Taxes

Many utilities are subject to excise taxes similar to gross receipts taxes. Starting as a wartime measure to influence use of scarce resources during an emergency, federal excise taxes of a stated percentage of utility bills became an important revenue source in the post-World War II period. (Emergency taxes of a similar nature were also used during World War I.) While different rates were applied to different utility services (15 per cent on some telephone service, 25 per cent on toll service), this was but one of a series of wartime taxes placed on various goods and services. Luxury items were also heavily taxed, as were amusements, women's handbags, transportation freight bills, and a myriad of other items. Most of these wartime taxes were slowly removed after the emergency, but utility taxes have tended to hang on.

One reason why such taxes are retained even after the original justification for their existence has long passed is that they are relatively easy to administer and are steady revenue producers for the federal government. In effect, utilities collect taxes for the government, and if demand for the particular services being taxed is relatively inelastic, consumption is not adversely affected. These taxes are called "nuisance taxes," not only because of their original intent to restrict consumption of scarce resources during an emergency but also because they are clearly passed on to consumers and are a nuisance for utilities to collect.

A similar excise tax was imposed by the federal government during the depression of the 1930's. Here the purpose was solely to collect revenue, and given the slow change in demand patterns for essential utility services, these depression excise taxes did help raise emergency revenues for the public purse. In addition, an excess profit tax on all businesses was used late during the depression and again during World War II and the Korean War. The idea here was to remove wartime profits arising out of emergency conditions. Since the tax was very difficult to administer and was considered unfair by many, it was removed after the emergency had passed. This was not, of course, a special tax, since it applied to all businesses.

Franchise and Privilege Taxes

These types of taxes are used primarily by state and local governments. The franchise tax, typically used by local government, is based upon giving a utility the right to use a franchise or to use city streets and alleys. Sometimes such a tax is based upon a measure of use, such as mileage of track in a transit system, number of poles in a telephone or power distribution system, and the like, and sometimes it is a simple lump sum. When it is a single sum, the tax may be thought of as a license tax or as a payment for the privilege of doing business in a city. It should be added that some states have a privilege tax as well and may base this on gross receipts, shares of capital stock, or some similar basis.

The franchise tax historically was not only a source of income to the city but may have been devised as a way to force local monopolies to share a portion of their profits with the cities in which they operated. In earlier developmental stages of utilities cities sometimes granted franchises to the utility corporation agreeing to pay the highest tax or to provide the city with the most free services. Services are never really free, of course, and such provisions were actually taxes in the sense that any contribution to government is a tax. Finally, it should be noted that these taxes are special taxes, which typically apply only to utilities.

Nonfiscal Taxes

The final type of taxes paid by utilities are considered by some not to be taxes at all, even though they appear as such in utility reports. These are the nonfiscal or nonrevenue taxes laid upon all businesses to support that broad category of government expenditures sometimes called social insurance.

The federal government requires utilities to collect from its employees and to match with corporate funds contributions to the Old Age and Survivors Insurance program, known popularly as social security. Similarly, businesses are required to contribute to unemployment compensation funds and other plans known by similar names. These are usually paid to the federal government but administered by states to benefit certain groups of unemployed workers. These nonfiscal taxes are levied on all businesses.

INEQUITIES OF UTILITY TAXATION

Tax Inequities Between Utilities and Other Types of Businesses

From a survey of utility taxes it is apparent that nonfiscal, property, and corporate net income taxes are applied to all businesses; excise taxes are special utility taxes among a group of special business taxes; and gross receipts taxes and franchise or privilege taxes are special to utilities alone. Thus, an argument can be made that the tax system treats utilities inequitably by applying special taxes to them that are not applied to other businesses.

Tax Inequities Among Utilities

In addition to the alleged inequity of taxation of utilities as compared to other businesses, it can be argued that the burden of taxation is inequitable among the various utilities themselves. With such a wide variety of taxes, differences among tax jurisdictions, and different economic and operating characteristics, some utilities must devote more of their revenues to paying taxes than other utilities. This burden is often measured by noting all taxes as a percentage of operating revenues.

These differences among utilities are illustrated by noting that nationally the total tax bill takes 20 to 22 per cent of the operating revenues of electric utilities, but only about 13 per cent for natural gas distribution utilities, and about 7 per cent of natural gas transmission utilities' operating revenues. Similarly, telephone companies pay about 22 per cent of their operating revenues in taxes, but domestic telegraph companies pay only about 4 per cent and international telegraph companies about 10 per cent. Water utilities pay about 22 per cent of operating revenues in taxes, while the figure is only 6 per cent for urban transit companies.[9]

These percentages naturally reflect the degree of fixed capital in each utility category, tax jurisdiction differences, special taxes imposed on one utility but not on others, differences in assessments of values, and the like. The point is that competing types of utility services do not always pay the same level of taxes.

It should be noted also that different tax burdens apply to different firms within a single class of utilities. For example, some electric utilities will be taxed in one state at a much higher rate than other electric utilities operating in another state. (The percentages of operating revenue noted previously are national average percentages.) Clearly, some firms pay much smaller percentages of gross revenue to tax districts than do others.

Property Tax Inequities

Even though all businesses pay property or ad valorem taxes, alleged inequities may arise because of differing valuation procedures and tax rates.

Utilities are more susceptible to high tax valuation than many other businesses. Utility capital is typically fixed in one place, is readily measurable and assessable, and exists in tremendous quantities. Further, local utilities tend to operate in a monopolistic environment—at least they have exclusive service territories—and tax assessors often assume that high valuations cannot adversely affect demand. Finally, utilities are often considered to be "tax collectors," since the tax bill is usually passed on to consumers by law; thus local and state tax authorities feel less restraint about valuing property higher for utilities than for other businesses.

The same reasoning applies to tax rates. Some states have classified property taxes with different percentages of taxable value applied to various classes of property. Usually, utility property will be placed in one of the highest property classifications, along with railroads and perhaps a few other selected businesses. It is not unusual in such instances to find utility property taxed at 50 to 60 per cent of assessed value, while other business assets are taxed at 20 to 30 per cent, and homes and personal property at 15 to 20 per cent.

But even if the percentage of assessed value and the assessment procedure is the same for all businesses, the fact that utilities are one of the largest users of fixed capital means that the tax burden will be heavier per dollar of sales for utilities than for most other businesses.

Taxation of Competing Utility Firms

Taxation may affect competition in two ways. First, all tax-paying utilities which compete do not always pay the same rate of taxes. Second, some utilities may pay taxes while others do not, or some may make different types of contributions to government.

The matter of different rates between competing utilities, such as electric power companies and natural gas companies, or telephone and telegraph, has been noted. Similarly, differences between firms in a given type of utility, such as power companies operating in adjacent or different states or portions of a state, have been noted. Because of these differences, extreme caution must be exercised in comparing bills or rates charged by competing utilities or by utilities of the same class. While adjustments because of variations in taxation are possible, typically such adjustments are not made when comparisons are drawn.

The fact that some utilities make contributions to government in the form of taxes, while others make larger or smaller contributions, or sometimes no contributions, is part of the public- versus-private-ownership argument. Publicly owned utilities typically do not pay taxes, although some of them make payments in lieu of taxes. The federal government does not collect income taxes from its own enterprises, and one agency of government does not tax another agency. Hence, a state does not tax a federal project, nor does the federal government collect income taxes from a municipal utility.

The matter of government-owned utilities will be discussed further in Part Four. It is sufficient to note here that comparisons between privately owned, tax-paying utilities and government-owned, tax-exempted utilities are extremely hazardous. To some degree the two are not comparable, and policy decisions made solely on unadjusted data as to lower rates of the one relative to the other are to be avoided. This is especially true in the electric power and telephone areas, where taxes make up approximately 22 per cent of the bill, as already noted. Unfortunately, such comparisons are inevitable and are made regularly without proper adjustment to reflect different tax situations.

THE CASE FOR LOWER TAXATION

A case can be made for lower utility taxation in general. This case rests on three propositions: (1) Utilities provide essential services. (2) Utilities are decreasing-cost industries. (3) Services which compete should be treated alike.

Essential Service Argument

If the services of utilities are truly essential to economic growth and the American standard of living, such services should be priced as low as possible. Taxes raise the prices of utility services, and given any degree of price elasticity at all in the demand for utility services, high taxes result in less of the essential services being used.

Similarly, some groups may be deprived of a portion of these services because of the higher prices they must pay because of high taxes, and other groups may use less than they would if taxes were lower. Basically, this argument rests on the proposition that essential services should be as inexpensive as possible.

Decreasing Cost Argument

Utilities are generally considered decreasing cost industries. The more services sold, the lower per unit costs become. At least this appears to be true for most utilities. Taxes raise prices and hence affect demand. This decreased demand may force utilities to operate at higher per unit costs. Or to state it another way, a lower tax level may allow a utility to gain more economies of scale as it moves down its decreasing cost curve. This means that prices may be even lower than the decreased tax, or conversely, price increases because of taxes will actually be higher than the amount of the taxes. A tax on a decreasing cost industry results in a burden made up of the amount of the tax plus the lost economies of scale. Alfred Marshall noted this effect of taxation on decreasing cost industries as early as 1890.[10]

Equity in Competition Argument

Investor-owned utilities which compete with publicly owned utilities often make a case for lower taxes on the equity argument that the tax system should not be used as a competitive weapon but should rather be a neutral force in the natural struggle of the marketplace. Here the philosophy of equity is used with some force. The counter-argument is often made that there is rarely a direct competition between the two types of ownership and that the equity argument is based on an erroneous assumption of price competition. On the other hand, it must be noted that public policy decisions whether to go public or remain private do often turn on comparative rates. However, investor-owner utilities are as apt in publicizing how much tax they pay as the publicly owned utilities are at publicizing how their rates are lower. This argument applies principally to electric and telephone utilities when a struggle over ownership exists.

INCIDENCE OF TAXES

Many people are not impressed with the argument about how high utility taxes are, or that a case can be made (on various grounds) for lower utility taxes. They point out that utilities pass their taxes on to consumers.[11] In effect, such people are talking about the "incidence" of the tax burden.

The term "impact" is used to refer to the place where taxes are initially paid, and "incidence" refers to the place where the burden finally comes to rest. The difference between "impact" and "incidence," if any exists, comes from "shifting." In the case of utilities there are two approaches to this problem, legal incidence and actual incidence.

Legal Incidence

From the legal viewpoint there is little question that utility taxes are shifted and the incidence is with the consumer. All businesses try to shift taxes, but utilities, because they are regulated, have the legal right to so do. This unusual situation rests on a 1922 United States Supreme Court decision, in which Justice Brandeis said:

> In calculating . . . a proper return, it is necessary to deduct from gross revenue the expenses and charges; and all taxes which would be payable if a fair return were earned are appropriate deductions. There is no difference in this respect between state and federal taxes, or between income taxes and others.[12]

This has led one scholar to state, ". . . utility industries are tax collectors par excellence,"[13] and another to write that ". . . the utility company is made to serve, essentially, as a tax-collecting conduit between users of utility service and the government. . . . Higher taxes mean higher rates; lower taxes, lower rates."[14]

The matter of legal incidence is well settled in law–utility taxes are to be passed on to the customer.

Actual Incidence

In practice, the actual incidence may or may not be the same as the legal incidence. While utilities have the legal right to shift all types of taxes, they may not always do so for at least the three following reasons.

(1) *Management Prerogative:* Management may prefer to absorb a tax increase (literally shifting the amount of the tax to the stockholders) if some corporate disadvantage would arise by shifting to the consumer. Fair value determination of rate levels are not made each year. A utility might be earning its full allowable profit, or more important, management might feel that asking for an increase in rates to cover increased taxes might open up the whole question of the level of rates. If earnings are high, it might not be worth the risk and the better policy could be to "let sleeping dogs lie."

Similarly, small tax increases might be absorbed for a period of time simply because it is easier to pay the taxes than to go to the expense of making a case to a commission for a rate increase. This would be a short-term decision, of course, and given a series of small increases over time, management would undoubtedly come back to the clearly settled legal incidence.

(2) *Regulatory Lag:* Legal and actual incidence may be different because of regulatory lag. Rate cases take time. Preparation is necessary, hearings are involved, delays in decisions are common, and delays in implementing regulatory decisions are well known. All of these are involved in regulatory lag. Thus, a tax increase might not be immediately reflected in utility rates, not only because management elects to wait but because of this additional lag.

(3) *Adverse Effects:* Actual incidence may be different from legal incidence because of the adverse effects of a tax. In some instances, a price increase because of

shifting a tax may adversely affect demand for the service. Here it may be best for the utility to absorb or pass on to the stockholders any tax increase. This may be the case with parts of the urban transit system, where following the legal incidence would merely compound an already difficult problem.

Similarly, management may feel that substantial economies of scale would be lost if rates were increased to reflect a tax increase. Management or regulatory authorities may recognize the decreasing cost argument noted in the preceding section and feel that the loss in economies of scale is so great that everyone is better off if the tax is absorbed.

Incidence of a Tax Decrease

While it is true that taxes historically have tended to increase, the possibility of a tax decrease does present itself. This becomes more important as the federal government places more emphasis on fiscal policy as a tool of general economic control. The federal net corporate income tax, one of the major tax payments made by utilities (and other businesses), both decreased and increased during the 1960's. Further, national economic policy and the "new economics" give every indication that this tax rate will continue to vary over time. Hence, one can properly ask, What is the incidence of a tax decrease?

The legal incidence is undoubtedly the correct one for a tax decrease. All of the reasons why actual incidence would not be the same as legal incidence are canceled in the case of a decrease. As to management's fears of opening up the question of rate levels, passing on a decrease would tend to delay a question of rates being too high and thus would be in management's interest. While additional revenues from a tax decrease might be held by the corporation for a time, it eventually would have to justify this to regulatory commissions. Thus, a fair value and rate level determination would be hastened by not passing a tax decrease on to customers. For a tax increase, passing the tax on might hasten a hearing; for a tax decrease, not passing the decrease on would have the same effect.

The question of regulatory lag is of less importance for a tax decrease. Commissions rarely delay a decrease in prices. And adverse effects become just the opposite. A lowering of rates should stimulate demand and allow for economies of scale. Accordingly, this should be welcomed by responsible utility management.

Unfortunately, all utility managements do not recognize the advantages of passing on tax decreases and that it is in their interests in the long run to adopt the legal incidence. Regulatory authorities have sometimes had to act in order to make the self-interests of utilities clear to utility management.[15]

There is one problem with a tax decrease which may call for regulatory interference. The question of who gets the tax decrease may be of some importance. Management undoubtedly would prefer to give the lowered rates to customers with the most elastic demand curves—preferably industrial customers, who have access to alternative utility sources and for whom lower prices might stimulate demand. Regulatory authorities, existing in a political climate, might wish to see a tax decrease reflected in lower residential rates—where there are more customers. Both sides would have rational but conflicting views on the matter of where the benefits of a tax decrease should come to rest.

Compliance Costs

It should be recognized that for utilities to act as tax collectors, which in effect they do unless actual incidence varies greatly from legal incidence, is not without costs. Firms must make collections, handle funds, pay the taxes to various units of government, and keep track of the income due. Rarely is credit given to utilities for these free services. Instead, the costs of this compliance with tax laws are absorbed by the firms and passed on to consumers in the form of higher overhead costs or passed back to stockholders as lower earnings.

Equity would seem to demand that the governments involved reimburse utilities (and other businesses) for being tax collectors. However, this factor is rarely considered when new taxes are proposed. Compliance costs fall proportionately more heavily on utilities than on other businesses because of the special taxes on utilities and the large burden of ad valorem taxes on a capital-intensive industry.[16]

TAXATION AS A SUBSTITUTE FOR REGULATION

It has been argued that taxation can be a substitute (or at least a supplement) for regulation. The idea is that taxation will take away the excess profits of a local monopoly or will attend to those economic matters missed by regulation. To some degree, the early franchise tax was based on this argument.[17]

This argument is spurious. Taxation and regulation have entirely different goals. They are not similar or comparable. The tax system tends to be inflexible, while regulation can be flexible. Regulation can allow some incentives for efficiency and good management, while a straight utility tax to capture profits may decrease incentive and good management. As Professor Clemens stated years ago: "If excess profits are being made it would be better to lower rates to the direct benefit of the consumers than to drain off the revenues into the government coffers."[18]

DEPRECIATION EXPENSES

Without doubt, depreciation is the most complicated and controversial of the operating cost deductions. The methods used to calculate this item vary, as do the ways of accomplishing depreciation deductions. Practically everyone is interested in this item—consumers, utility management, regulatory officials, owners of utility stock, owners of utility bonds, creditors who lend utilities funds, the general public, and the tax collector.

The customer is interested in depreciation deductions because they are operating costs for which he must eventually pay. If they are too high, he pays too much. Since depreciation expenses affect a firm's ability to borrow, consumer service levels eventually may suffer if rates are too low. Utility management sees depreciation as having an effect on the cost of capital. Regulatory authorities view depreciation as a deduction before fair value is determined. Clearly, their work can be subverted if the amount deducted for depreciation is not proper. Since depreciation is a cost, it affects the levels of profits. Hence, owners of utility stocks want only proper depreciation deducted before profits are calculated. Bondholders and creditors look to depreciation to protect their funds and expect that the total amount deducted will replace the funds lent by them. Finally, income taxes are collected on the net income, after costs are deducted, so that tax authorities are concerned over proper depreciation, too. In recent times it has often been the tax collector's interest in proper depreciation that has caused much of the inquiry into depreciation accounting. Nevertheless, all parties are interested in having the proper deduction for depreciation made. The controversy comes, of course, over what is proper.

A DEFINITION OF DEPRECIATION

It follows that the definition of depreciation must be important. Regulatory authorities have tried to define depreciation for their work. The following definition seems readily acceptable to most groups:

> (1) Depreciation is the expiration or consumption, in whole or in part, of the service life, capacity, or utility of property resulting from the action of one or more of the forces operating to bring about retirement of such property from service.
>
> (2) The forces so operating include wear and tear, decay, action of the elements, inadequacy, obsolescence, and public requirements.
>
> (3) Depreciation results in a cost of service.[19]

This definition emphasizes several things. First, it notes the loss of service life of assets. Thus, depreciation is not solely a physical matter, as sometimes supposed, but rather an economic or pecuniary matter. As Professor Glaeser has said, "Depreciation is a device adopted for measuring the exhaustion or disintegration of physical capital in terms of monetary or pecuniary capital."[20]

Second, the definition emphasizes the causes of depreciation. Typically, these are grouped under the two broad headings of physical and functional.

Physical depreciation is basically of two types—depreciation due to use and depreciation due to time. Capital wears out as it is used; indeed some people stress the "capital consumption" idea in depreciation. But in addition to wear and tear, rust and rot, capital deteriorates simply with the passage of time. Idle and unused capital is depreciating even though it is maintained. As one authority puts it, "Most property, whether used or not, is on its way to the scrap heap and to the time when it will have no value."[21]

Functional depreciation is divided into the three subgroups of inadequacy, obsolescence, and public requirements or action of public authority. Property may be fit for service but be too small or inadequate for the service area. At times, demand grows faster than anticipated, and perfectly good capital must be replaced because of its inadequacy. This is sometimes called the "market factor" in depreciation. On the other hand, changes in technology may cause equipment which still has remaining service life to become obsolete. This is called the "progress factor" in depreciation, and since technological changes cannot be predicted, this is a most frustrating matter for utility management and regulators. Public requirements or government action sometimes cause depreciation of capital even though the property is still fit for use from a physical viewpoint. An example of this "social factor" in depreciation is the requirement that telephone and power lines be placed underground. The capital replaced has further physical life, but society has required that it be scrapped.

There is also a third cause of depreciation, which may be called "contingent casualties," such as unforeseen and uninsurable accidents and disasters which destroy capital. This is a relatively minor cause, however.

The importance of these various causes of depreciation is difficult to assess, yet past evidence suggests that functional depreciation is far more important than physical depreciation. One well-known utility engineer once suggested that the functional causes were as great as 80 per cent, while only 20 per cent of past replacement of capital had been required because of physical causes.[22]

Depreciation and maintenance are sometimes confused, since both are costs of operation. Maintenance is designed to keep equipment in good operating condition, while depreciation is designed to recover the capital used up in operation. The distinction was carefully drawn by Chief Justice Hughes in 1934 when he wrote:

> Broadly speaking, depreciation is the loss, not restored by current maintenance, which is due to all the factors causing the ultimate retirement of property. These factors embrace wear and tear, decay, inadequacy, and obsolescence. Annual depreciation is the loss which takes place in a year. In determining reasonable rates for supplying public service, it is proper to include in the operating expenses, that is, in the cost of producing the service, an allowance for consumption of capital in order to maintain the integrity of the investment in the service rendered.[23]

Certainly this emphasizes the idea that depreciation is a cost of service and is something beyond proper maintenance.

Finally, it should be apparent that depreciation is designed to recoup the capital invested and *not* to provide a fund for replacement of capital. Accountants note that depreciation is "cost recovery" and the United States Supreme Court has settled the issue.[24] As far as regulation is concerned, only the original cost of the capital may be recouped, regardless of changes in the value of the dollars expended as compared to the value of the dollars later allocated to depreciation. The discussion of the need for economic depreciation–whereby depreciation accounts reflect changes in the value of the dollar and provide, at the end of the useful life of an asset, a sum sufficient to replace the capital–remains, for public utilities at least, just a discussion.

THE IMPORTANCE OF DEPRECIATION

The interest of various groups in depreciation stems from the fact that it is an operating expense. As such, it affects the prices of services, the profits of corporations, and the taxes based on profits. Further, since the credits taken for depreciation affect the cost of capital, depreciation also affects investment.

From a statistical point of view depreciation can be quite important. Again, in dealing with a capital-intensive industry, depreciation becomes a substantial sum. In the electric power industry more than 11 per cent of operating revenues go to depreciation; in natural gas transmission, between 8 and 9 per cent; in water and telephone, more than 8 per cent; and in natural gas distribution, about 5 per cent.[25] When these percentages are related to the substantial revenues of these utilities, it can be seen that literally billions of dollars are involved in utility depreciation accounting. It should also be noted that these percentages of operating revenues taken by depreciation are substantially larger than for most nonutility industries, reflecting once more the capital-intensive nature of utilities.

PROCEDURES FOR DEDUCTING DEPRECIATION EXPENSES

There are several procedures for deducting depreciation expenses. Some are very complex and beyond the scope of this book. Since disagreement among honest men is possible, almost all of the methods are controversial. Disagreement more often than not revolves around either the tax ramifications of depreciation accounting or the regulatory effect of depreciation methods. Both the Internal Revenue Service and the state regulatory commissions in each jurisdiction will have something to say about the method used by a specific public utility corporation. On some occasions, the approved depreciation method for tax purposes may be different from the approved method for regulatory purposes.

The procedure for accounting for this important deduction from operating revenues involves three factors: the depreciation base, the estimated probable life of the asset, and the method of allocating the depreciation base over the probable life.

Basically, the depreciation base is the original cost of the asset minus an estimate of its scrap or reclaimable value. As noted, the question of using an original cost or another base was settled in the 1940's. In addition, if depreciation is properly understood as a device to *recover* capital and not to *supply* capital, only original cost may be used. Scrap or reclaimable value is deducted from the base, so that only the actual value of the capital committed is involved.

While probable life can only be an estimate, it is surprising how accurate such estimates can be. Because depreciation is a large dollar amount in the utilities and also because it has long been regulated, rather good historical records exist. From these records relatively good estimates of probable life can be drawn.

The establishment of a depreciation base and the estimate of probable life are relatively simple operations. Determination of the method to be used in allocating the depreciation base over the probable life is not so simple. Several alternatives exist, and there is controversy about which is proper because of public policy variations introduced in recent years.

The simplest method in use is the "straight line" method. This method distributes the depreciation base equally over the estimated life of the asset. Hence, the use of an asset with an original cost of $11,000, scrap value of $1,000, and probable life of ten years would result in a depreciation entry of $1,000 per year. This method is easy to understand and administer. It may not, however, be the most logical from an economic viewpoint.

A second method is the "sinking fund" method. The theory is that depreciation reserves are not kept as idle balances; thus it is assumed that the annual charges earn a rate of interest. Under the straight line method, no consideration is given to this earning power effect; in the sinking fund method this earning effect is considered. Basically, an amount is charged off yearly that equals annual depreciation less the interest earned on the previous balance. Thus, less is charged off for depreciation yearly, because it is assumed the funds earn income.

A third method is the "retirement reserve" procedure. The assumption here is that reinvestment occurs at a relatively stable rate and that it is unnecessary to maintain large depreciation balances. It should be noted that under the straight line method, if the estimates of probable life are correct, the depreciation account would average 50 per cent of the depreciation base over time. While the depreciation balance would be less under the sinking fund method, it would still be substantial. From the point of view of providing funds for replacement, it is doubtful that such substantial balances would ever be needed.

The retirement reserve method is analogous to reserves in banking. A small percentage of the asset value of the whole plant is set aside under the assumption that no more than this will be needed in one year for replacement. This type of depreciation accounting was once popular but is generally considered improper today. The reasons for its abandonment are as follows: (1) It subverts the idea of depreciation because it considers capital replacement rather than capital recovery. (2) Abuses were common in an earlier and less regulated period when ridiculously low balances were maintained on the books of account. (3) Once the tax factor became important, depreciation as a deduction before income tax liability was calculated had new meaning to the industry, the regulator, and the customer.

Public policy variations in recent years have tended to further complicate depreciation accounting and to add considerable controversy. Two public actions are of prime importance in this regard, the accelerated depreciation allowable since 1954 and the investment tax credit allowable since 1962.

Under the Revenue Act of 1954 an industry can elect to use accelerated depreciation for income tax purposes on assets acquired subsequent to 1954. In effect, this means that a firm may depreciate new property more rapidly than under the straight line method by applying either the "declining balance" method or the "sum of the digits" method. While the calculations vary somewhat, the effect of these methods of accelerated depreciation is to allow larger depreciation deductions early in the life of the asset and smaller deductions later in the asset's life. This affects the tax liability of a firm and is particularly important in the capital-intensive public utilities. Since depreciation is deducted prior to the calculation of tax liability, larger balances lead to a tax savings early in the probable life of the asset and smaller tax deductions later in the life of the asset.[26] This tax deferral is, in effect, an interest-free loan to the utility, since depreciation allowances are normally reinvested in the firm.

This tax effect has caused problems for regulatory authorities. They have a choice of "normalizing" the effect of accelerated depreciation or of using the "flow-through" method. In a normalized situation an adjustment is made for rate-making purposes to reflect the differences in tax liability coming from the accelerated depreciation method. That is, the commission allows a utility to calculate depreciation for tax purposes on the accelerated basis but calculates depreciation for rate-making purposes on a straight line basis. The difference between the two is credited to a special reserve account which should receive balances early in the life of an asset and pay out balances late in the life of the asset. In the flow-through method actual tax payments are used for rate-making purposes, thus giving customers the advantage of accelerated depreciation (lower rates) during the early years of the asset's life. In the later years of the asset's life taxes and rates rise.

There has been a great deal of controversy, including court cases, over which method should be used. Both federal and state commissions vary in their treatment of accelerated depreciation. A discussion of the various positions of commissions, courts, and the accounting profession is beyond the scope of this book. But this controversy illustrates the importance of depreciation in a capital-intensive industry like the public utilities.[27]

The other public policy variation tending to complicate depreciation is the Revenue Act of 1962, which provided a 3 per cent maximum deduction of the value of new investment from corporate income taxes. The intent was to stimulate investment. Nonregulated firms were granted up to 7 per cent, while regulated firms (with the exception of natural gas producers and pipelines) were allowed 3 per cent. Again, tax liability and rates are affected. The same issues as to normalization or flow-through are involved, and again treatment by commissions varies. While the intent of the tax variation is different with regard to accelerated depreciation and investment tax credit, the effects are the same, and the controversy over how to handle the item on the books of account is the same.

SUMMARY

This chapter has considered the important matter of deducting operating costs from operating revenues in order to determine a fair rate of return. These costs account for up to 90 per cent of operating revenues, and a small change in these deductions is often as important as a change in the rate of return insofar as rates are concerned.

These deductions fall into three main groups: operating expenses, taxes, and depreciation, each of which has engendered much disagreement.

Operating expenses are by far the largest deduction. While the right of regulatory commissions to scrutinize and disallow operating expenses has long been legally established, it is only since the 1930's that commissions have exercised this right. Even now, they sometimes fear to infringe on "management's prerogatives". Generally, the normal costs of doing business are allowable for purposes of operating expense deductions. Commissions may not prohibit a utility from spending its funds as it wishes, but they may disallow certain expenditures for rate-making purposes. In this fashion, commissions prevent a utility from charging these expenses to consumers and, in effect, require investors to stand these costs. Donations to charity, lobbying and propaganda activities, regulatory costs, appealing commission decisions, retail sales activities, and intercompany payments have often been challenged as allowable deductions.

The second largest deduction is for taxes. Since utilities are capital-intensive industries, they are particularly susceptible to taxation. Utilities pay special taxes as well as general taxes, and all do not pay equally. Further, since utilities are allowed by law to pass taxes on to their customers, tax authorities do not hesitate to levy special taxes on utilities. It should be noted that there is a difference between the legal incidence and the actual incidence of utility taxes and that a strong case can be made for lower taxes on essential utility services.

Depreciation expense deductions are the smallest of the operating revenue deductions but the ones around which the most controversy has arisen. Everyone is interested in proper depreciation, but not everyone can agree on what is proper. Almost every commission has had to make difficult judgments as to proper depreciation procedures. Misunderstanding sometimes arises because depreciation is not properly understood as capital recovery and the causes of depreciation are not always properly identified. In recent times, changes in public policy have led to disagreement over the handling of accelerated depreciation and investment tax credit, with a resulting difficulty in deciding whether to normalize or flow-through. Practice varies on these matters, and expert opinion differs. At least the frequency of disagreement illustrates the importance of depreciation deductions in capital-intensive utilities.

NOTES

1. *Chicago and Grand Trunk Railway v. Wellman,* 143 U.S. 339 (1892).
2. *Southwestern Bell Telephone Co. v. Missouri Public Service Commission,* 252 U.S. 276 (1923).
3. *Acker v. United States,* 298 U.S. 425 (1936).
4. See *Chicago and Grand Trunk Railway v. Wellman,* cited in note 1.
5. See *Driscoll v. Edison Light and Power Co.,* 307 U.S. 104 (1939).
6. See *West Ohio Gas Co. v. Public Utilities Commission of Ohio,* 294 U.S. 63 (1935).
7. *Moody's Public Utility Manual, 1967,* pp. 9–24. Readers may wish to check *Moody's* for current ratios of taxes to operating revenues.
8. See *Adams Express Co. v. Ohio,* 165 U.S. 194 (1896).
9. Estimated by the authors using *Moody's.*
10. Alfred Marshall, *Principles of Economics,* 8th ed. (London: Macmillan, 1930), p. 469.

11. For an interesting discussion of this problem, see Lee Metcalf and Vic Reinemer, *Overcharge* (New York: David McKay Co., 1967), ch. 5.
12. *Galveston Electric Company v. Galveston,* 258 U.S. 388, 399–400 (1922). See also *Georgia Railway and Power Co. v. Railroad Commission of Georgia,* 262 U.S. 625 (1923).
13. Eli Winston Clemens, *Economics and Public Utilities* (New York: Appleton-Century-Crofts, 1950), p. 526.
14. Ben W. Lewis, "The Duty of a Public Utility to Reduce Its Income Tax Liability by Using Accelerated Depreciation," *Land Economics,* vol. 35, no. 2 (May 1959), p. 110.
15. For a discussion of the problems of a tax decrease, see Martin T. Farris, "Tax Reductions and Utility Rates," *Public Utilities Fortnightly,* vol. 74, no. 5 (August 27, 1964), pp. 30–38.
16. These costs are not small. The *Wall Street Journal* has noted that the costs to utilities of collecting a 4 per cent Los Angeles tax on utility bills would be over $1 million for the first year and $500,000 annually in subsequent years. The city council imposing this tax voted against reimbursing the utilities for these costs. See "Los Angeles Tax on Utility Bills Stirs Controversy," *Wall Street Journal,* October 4, 1967.
17. See C. Lowell Harriss, "Taxation of Public Utilities: Considerations for the Long Run," *Proceedings of the Fourth Annual Iowa State Conference on Public Utility Valuation and Rate Making Process,* May 1965.
18. Clemens, p. 546.
19. National Association of Railroad and Utility Commissioners, *Report of the Committee on Depreciation, 1943* (Washington, D.C.: 1943), p. 14.
20. Martin G. Glaeser, *Public Utilities in American Capitalism* (New York: Macmillan, 1957), p. 345.
21. Clemens, p. 189.
22. L. R. Nash, "A New Depreciation Fallacy," *Public Utilities Fortnightly,* vol. 30, no. 12 (December 3, 1942), p. 761.
23. *Lindheimer v. Illinois Bell Telephone Co.,* 292 U.S. 151 (1934).
24. See *Federal Power Commission v. Hope Natural Gas Co.,* 320 U.S. 591 (1944).
25. Estimated by the authors, using *Moody's.*
26. It has been pointed out that as long as a utility continues to grow and add depreciable capital assets, its tax payments will continue to be deferred. See Eugene F. Brigham and James L. Pappas, *Liberalized Depreciation and the Cost of Capital,* M.S.U. Public Utilities Studies (East Lansing, Mich.: Institute of Public Utilities, Michigan State University, 1970), p. 2.
27. Readers may wish to consider the review of this matter appearing in Charles F. Phillips, Jr., *The Economics of Regulation,* rev. ed. (Homewood, Ill.: Richard D. Irwin, 1969), pp. 201–206, or Paul J. Garfield and Wallace F. Lovejoy, *Public Utility Economics* (Englewood Cliffs, N.J.: Prentice-Hall, 1964), pp. 109–114.

ADDITIONAL READINGS

1. Barnes, Irston R., *The Economics of Public Utility Regulation* (New York: F. S. Crofts, 1942), ch. 18, "Regulation of Utility Expenses," pp. 600–627.
2. Brigham, Eugene F., and James L. Pappas, *Liberalized Depreciation and the Cost of Capital,* M.S.U. Public Utilities Studies (East Lansing, Mich.: Institute of Public Utilities, Michigan State University, 1970).
3. Clemens, Eli Winston, *Economics and Public Utilities* (New York: Appleton-Century-Crofts, 1950), ch. 6, "Operating Expenses and Their Regulation," pp. 127–139; ch. 9, "Depreciation," pp. 189–216; ch. 20, "The Taxation of Public Utilities," pp. 522–547.

4. Garfield, Paul J., and Wallace F. Lovejoy, *Public Utility Economics* (Englewood Cliffs, N.J.: Prentice-Hall, 1964), ch. 5, "The Regulation of Operating Expenses," pp. 44–56; ch. 8, "Depreciation," pp. 94–113; ch. 17, "The Economics of Taxation," pp. 385–395.
5. Glaeser, Martin G., *Public Utilities in American Capitalism* (New York: Macmillan, 1957), ch. 21, "Depreciation Policies," pp. 345–366; ch. 33, "The Problem of Taxation," pp. 574–586.
6. Phillips, Charles F., Jr., *The Economics of Regulation,* rev. ed. (Homewood, Ill.: Richard D. Irwin, 1969), ch. 7, "Operating Expenses, Depreciation, and Taxes," pp. 178–215.
7. Troxel, Emery, *Economics of Public Utilities* (New York: Rinehart, 1947), ch. 11, "Control of Expenditures," pp. 236–257; ch. 15, "Depreciation," pp. 328–351; ch. 16, "The Special Problem of Obsolescence," pp. 352–371.

8

Rate Regulation: Percentage Returns

Determination of a fair percentage rate of return is a third vital element of utility rate regulation. This percentage rate is calculated by dividing the amount of total operating revenues remaining after deductions from operating revenue by the amount of the firm's rate base. The actual net dollar revenue remaining after deductions is, of course, the ultimate consideration of the utility and its regulators, but for convenience, comparison, and control, this amount is customarily expressed in percentage terms. In practice, the allowable percentage rate of return is established, and then price levels are adjusted in an attempt to obtain a yield at least approximating this allowed rate.[1]

A firm's rate base, deductions from operating revenue, and percentage rate of return are necessarily interdependent. For example, imagine a firm with a rate base of $100 million, with annual total operating revenues of $30 million and allowable operating revenue deductions of $24 million. The firm's net return would be $6 million, or 6 per cent. But if the same firm's rate base should be valued at $120 million, with the same operating revenues and deductions, its same $6 million net return would be only 5 per cent. Similarly, with the same $100 million rate base and $30 million total revenues, but with $26 million rather than $24 million allowable operating revenue deductions, the yield would be only 4 per cent.

It is clear, then, that none of the three major factors in determining a fair rate of return can be considered in isolation from the others. Further, a specific percentage rate of return in one jurisdiction with a particular method or philosophy of valuation and particular rules concerning allowable deductions may mean something quite different from the same percentage return in another jurisdiction with different methods and rules. Or, as valuation methods and deductible rules change with the passage of time in a given jurisdiction, the reasonableness of a specific percentage rate of return may be affected.

When a rate base and rules for operating revenue deductions have been established, however, it is the percentage rate of return which determines the amount of net revenues a firm is entitled to earn (if it can) and which consequently establishes the level of consumer prices. In this chapter, therefore, in discussing the importance of the percentage rate, the evolution of concepts regarding it, and some of the problems and effects of its administration, it is assumed that the rate base and operating revenue deductions, however they may have been determined, are not being questioned.

THE IMPORTANCE OF THE RATE OF RETURN

There are no purely economic grounds, and at best only weak and ill-defined legal or moral grounds, upon which it can be argued that any firm or industry is entitled to any particular level of return, or any return at all, as a matter of abstract right.[2] Rather, any valid argument for a particular level of return must be based upon need.

In evaluating needs the interests of three groups must be considered: investors (that is, the utility itself), consumers of the utility's product, and the general public (including, but not limited to, the utility's customers). Certainly the interests of these three groups are intertwined, and in a perfectly competitive world might be identical. But in the real world intergroup conflicts arise. Various interests must be weighed, traded off against each other, and settled by compromise, and this is the essential task of commission regulation and judicial review. It follows, then, at least within some range of judgment, that the philosophies of regulators and reviewing courts may be of much more importance in determining what level of earnings a utility firm is entitled to strive for than any abstract theory, legal doctrine, or regulatory method.

The firm's basic net revenue need is for income sufficient to cover the capital costs necessary to provide the services required and expected of it.[3] Owners of capital must be paid for making it available to the firm, for supervising its organization and use in conjunction with other capital and human resources, and for the risks which they assume.[4] These payments take the form of interest, which may include discounts or other marketing costs involved in security sales and profits which go into dividends or corporate surpluses.[5]

Investors are not expected to be any more altruistic than other people. Without reasonable expectations for the preservation of their capital and payment for its use, they will not supply capital to an enterprise. Further, if anticipated risks and other investment circumstances are approximately the same, investment will flow into those enterprises where anticipated yields are highest. Although self-evident, these statements highlight a very real problem faced by businesses whose earnings may be limited by regulation.

In a private enterprise economy, or in a private and public enterprise economy such as that which characterizes the utilities segment of our economic system, an individual firm must compete for the always limited amount of available capital resources. Every firm must compete with every other firm, not only in its own field but in every other field of endeavor. Potential investment capital is extremely mobile and very sensitive to very minor differentials in the prices paid for its alternative uses. Only the most uninformed person could assume that potential investors in utility firms do not consider, among other factors which may affect the safety and yield of their capital, the regulatory environment in the jurisdiction in which a firm operates. In evaluating or comparing regulatory environments attention must clearly be given to past regulatory practices as well as to current laws and philosophies.

In summary, in order to begin a utility business or to continue it investors must be convinced that their capital will earn at least as much in a utility firm as it would earn in another firm with similar risks and surrounding conditions. This is not to say that all utility firms, even in the same utility industry or geographic area, need the same percentage rate of return nor that the percentage rate needs of a particular firm do not change with the passage of time and changing economic conditions. Every firm during every time period has individual needs. It is the determination of these specific needs that create most of the problems and controversies of rate regulation.

Consumers of utility services have no more abstract right to any level of prices than utility firms have to any level of earnings. Legally, however, consumers are in a somewhat stronger position than those who supply their services. As emphasized in preceding chapters, a long line of judicial decisions and statutory laws have confirmed consumers' legal right to reasonable prices for utility services. In contrast, utility firms only have a legal right to attempt to make profits at these reasonable prices. Strictly speaking, that is, no more than reasonable prices may be charged regardless of a firm's adverse profits condition. But since earnings cannot be unreasonably high, continued extremely favorable earnings must lead to pressure for price reductions.

This "heads I lose, tails I don't win" aspect of regulation sometimes galls utility investors and managers. It should not. Regardless of its moral or philosophical implications or economic effects, it is a fact of economic life that rate regulation has a built-in consumer bias. It was and is designed to favor consumers and, like other rules of the game established by society, must be adapted to as long as it remains a rule. The utility firm's role, like the consumer's role, is to make the most of the opportunities provided within these legal constraints. As indicated, regulatory rules are not completely inflexible, and commission regulation, despite its legal bias, is concerned in considerable part with judgment reconciliation of conflicting interests or claims of legal rights. Actually, as noted in Chapter 6, except for unusual circumstances, the expressions "reasonable prices" and "reasonable earnings" have become almost interchangeable in regulatory practice.

The third interest group, the general public apart from the specific consumers of a utility's services, is not directly represented as an interest claimant in rate regulatory proceedings. Consequently, it is generally ignored though never unaffected.

The general public certainly has a vital economic interest, if no legally definable rights, in how the economy's capital and human resources are allocated. Since economic resources are limited, more resources devoted to one purpose means that less are available for other uses. Further, the prevailing combination or mixture of all resources among various possible alternative uses affects the overall efficiency, productivity, property values, and consumer satisfactions of the economy.

As a simplified example, the expansion of an automobile plant in Michigan may mean that funds will not be available for expanding electric services in New Jersey or for building a plywood mill in Oregon, even though the electric services would have provided more consumer satisfaction in New Jersey and the unbuilt plywood mill would have created more employment in Oregon than is obtained from the additional automobile output. One cannot say, given the facts as stated, that the results of this particular allocation are desirable or undesirable in an overall sense, but one can say that the results are quite different from those that would have been obtained from an alternative allocation.

In the fictional perfectly competitive world of economic theory resource allocation is adjusted toward optimal results by the profit mechanism and consumer sovereignty.[6] Even in the less perfect real world profits must be considered as the major allocator within the unregulated sector of the economy. But in the regulated world of public utilities, profits themselves, and thus interindustry and intraindustry allocations, are influenced in undetermined directions by the regulatory process. Every rate decision by every commission is likely to affect persons other than those investing in, or consuming the services of, the utility firm directly involved. The cumulative effects of all decisions by all commissions could be quite significant.

We do not argue that the allocative results of rate regulation are either good or bad from the viewpoint of the general public. Aside from the difficulties of defining "good" or "bad" and identifying the "general public," the fact is that we simply do not know the effects of regulation. We can say, however, that a sizable group other than those people directly concerned are affected and that this group has no direct representation and receives no direct consideration.

Nor is this an indictment of regulators or of the other two interest groups. Instead, it is a reflection of an omission from the rate regulatory process as it is now constituted. Legally, regulators are only primary adjudicators between adversaries, with no responsibilities or powers for protecting the interests of the entire public. Perhaps this is as much as can be expected of public officials within a private ownership framework.

LEGAL VIEWS OF THE PERCENTAGE RATE OF RETURN

Many court appeals have been made, and are still being made, on the grounds that commissions have set rates of return at unduly low levels. The courts consistently have taken the position that there is a minimum level below which commissions cannot force rates without violation of due process. But although the courts must rule upon whether a particular rate is reasonable at a given time and under existing circumstances, they have never said specifically where the minimum level is located. At best, court-established guidelines are somewhat vague—perhaps as vague as the expressed judgment processes used by most commissions in determining (or disguising how they have determined) reasonable rates. Perhaps the greatest area of agreement is that reasonableness varies with economic conditions, geographic areas, and a variety of individual operating circumstances and environments as well as with individual regulators, judges, and changing viewpoints.

All is not chaos, however. An evolutionary line of legal thought on reasonable rates of return and how they may be determined can be traced at least from the 1898 *Smyth v. Ames* case[7] to the present. In that case the court said:

> If the company is deprived of the power of charging reasonable rates for the

> use of its property . . . while other persons are permitted to receive reasonable profits upon their invested capital, the company is deprived of the equal protection of the laws.

Even before this, the United States Supreme Court had affirmed that commission-established rates are subject to judicial review and had actually overruled commission rates in the *Milwaukee* and *Reagan* cases.[8] Neither of these earlier cases established useful rate of return guidelines, however. Crude guidelines appeared in the 1909 *Willcox* case,[9] though, with the following statement:

> There is no particular rate of compensation which must in all cases and in all parts of the country be regarded as sufficient for capital invested in business enterprises. Such compensation must depend greatly upon circumstances and locality . . . the amount of risk . . . and the rate expected and usually realized there upon investments of a somewhat similar nature. . . .

COMPARATIVE EARNINGS STANDARD

The *Willcox* decision gave the first hint of what may be called the comparative earnings standard. This standard was fully developed in 1923, in the *Bluefield* case,[10] when the Court said:

> A public utility is entitled to such rates as will permit it to earn a return . . . equal to that generally being made at the same time and in the same general part of the country on investments in other business undertakings which are attended by corresponding risks and uncertainties; but it has no constitutional right to profits such as are realized in highly profitable enterprises or speculative ventures.

The comparable earnings standard is a useful legal device, particularly since it approximates the decision process used by potential investors in deciding where to invest their funds. It has unavoidable conceptual and administrative weaknesses, however, both for regulators and investors.

It is at least questionable whether a valid comparison can be made between regulated and nonregulated businesses for rate determination purposes. Presumably the regulated businesses are different from the nonregulated in some way or they would never have been regulated. Even if this presumption is not correct, the mere fact of regulation itself creates differences which may make comparisons invalid.

Further, regulated utilities in one jurisdiction cannot be compared with regulated utilities elsewhere, because this would be circular reasoning. Fair returns for regulated utilities in general cannot be deduced from the returns of utilities in general. In addition, as already noted, regulatory methods of handling valuation and operating revenue deductions vary so widely from jurisdiction to jurisdiction that nominal returns must be viewed with considerable skepticism.

Finally, how does one compare or rank the relative risks of one company, regulated or not, with those of another? Many risks, involving varying degrees of probabilities, are a part of any business. Public utility businesses as a group are generally thought to be less risky than wildcat oil-drilling firms. But the decline of the street transportation industry, and of many individual firms in other utility fields, cannot be forgotten, any more than can the great successes of many wildcat drillers. What kind of trade-off is necessary between the small likelihood of great success and the great likelihood of modest stability?

Despite its weaknesses, which have been discussed at length in many scholarly volumes, the comparable earnings standard is a useful tool. It has not been replaced but has rather been incorporated into the currently prevailing financial integrity standard.

FINANCIAL INTEGRITY STANDARD

The financial integrity criterion was presented in the same *Bluefield* case which developed the comparable earnings standard. Continuing its opinion, the Court stated:

> The return should be reasonably sufficient to assure confidence in the financial soundness of the utility and should be adequate, under efficient and economical management, to maintain and support its credit and enable it to raise the money necessary for the proper discharge of its public duties.

The landmark *Hope* case,[11] in 1944, gave the fullest expression to date of the financial integrity standard. Here the court held that in addition to requiring revenues sufficient to cover operating expenses, a utility firm is entitled to returns sufficient for its capital costs. These capital costs were said to include

> . . . service on the debt and dividends on the stock. . . . By that standard the return to the equity owner should be commensurate with risks on investments in other enterprises having corresponding risks. That return, moreover, should be sufficient to assure confidence in the financial integrity of the enterprise, so as to maintain its credit and to attract capital.

It is clear that the financial integrity standard is a logical and necessary outgrowth of the comparable earnings standard and that, as stated, the comparable earnings criterion is an essential part of financial integrity. Basically, the two approaches have the same philosophy and differ only in administration. The comparable earnings standard emphasizes a mechanical comparison, while the financial integrity standard emphasizes the determination of capital costs. If correctly performed, either method should give the same ultimate result as the other. But capital cost determination, while difficult, imprecise, and controversial, is in most cases probably less so than comparing the earnings of "similar" investments.

ADMINISTRATION OF THE FINANCIAL INTEGRITY STANDARD

The differing points of view of regulators and the regulated, or of consumers and producers, give rise to many complex problems in rate of return regulation. For simplicity, we group the most important or controversial of these problems under four general headings. These include the differences between confiscatory and reasonable returns, capital cost determination, fluctuating earnings, and incentive earnings.

Other categorizations could be made, of course, and there may be problems which do not fit neatly into this classification. But at least this is a convenient grouping for general discussion purposes, and one which includes most of the important problems. The order in which these groups are named is not intended to suggest any relative ranking of the importance of the problems themselves. Also, it is not suggested that all of these problems are unique to the administration of the financial integrity standard. Rather, most of them would exist under any method of earnings regulation, and certainly they are interrelated with each other.

REASONABLE RETURNS

Most of the percentage rates of return which commissions and courts have held to be not unreasonably low have been bunched between 6 and 8 per cent, although there are exceptions both upward and downward. During the present generation, until recently, the concentration has been more in the direction of 6 per cent than 8 per cent. Historically, there have been gradual trends upward and downward, again with many exceptions. During the prosperous 1920's returns were allowed to move up, but they declined during the less prosperous 1930's. There is some evidence, although mixed, that percentage rates started moving up again as far back as the mid-1950's.

This recent upward movement may reflect more liberal commission attitudes towards utilities or the acceptance of some degree of continuing inflation as a permanent rather than a temporary phenomenon. The new generation of regulators can have only slight personal memories of the depression psychology of the 1930's and the accompanying investigations of utility holding company practices during the 1920's.

Some of the recent increases in permitted percentage rate of return levels, though, may be attributable to the swing toward the original cost rate base following the *Hope* decision. Insofar as an original cost rate base produces a lower valuation than the reproduction cost, fair value, or some other method, a correspondingly higher percentage rate of return is required to yield the same net return on the same property. Thus, some increases may be more apparent than real. It is as hazardous to generalize about real rate of return movements over the years as it is to compare contemporary real rates of return in jurisdictions with differing rate base and operating revenue deduction methods.

Much of the controversy about reasonable versus confiscatory rates grows out of the fact that reasonableness covers a range of rate levels. That is, any rate between the low level which would constitute confiscation under the due process clause and the high level which would constitute undue profits may be considered reasonable.

This range could vary as much as several percentage points. Thus, since the courts only rule on whether or not a commission ruling will lead to confiscatory (or unduly high) returns, there is a so-called zone of reasonableness between unduly low and unduly high within which commissions have discretionary powers to fix rates of return at any level.[12]

For example, under a given set of circumstances, a reviewing court might hold that a return of less than 6 per cent is confiscatory or that a return of more than 8 per cent is unduly high. This would mean that a commission could establish rates expected to yield 6 per cent, 8 per cent, or anything between without being overruled by the court. (Court rulings cannot be predicted with certainty, of course, but established precedents may provide useful guidelines.)

The difference between a 6 per cent and an 8 per cent rate of return for a firm with a rate base of $100 million, a medium-sized utility firm, would represent annual profits of $2 million, or $100,000 for each 0.1 per cent. The importance of even small changes in percentage rates of return can be appreciated by realizing that the fifty largest utility corporations in the United States possess net assets of around $132 billion.[13] It is not surprising that rate cases are usually carefully presented and considered and often bitterly contested.

Some commissions have acquired the reputation of tending to favor a "bare bones" or minimum nonconfiscatory approach toward earnings regulation, while others are reported to be somewhat more liberal toward higher earnings. Utility companies complain that the "bare bones" approach hampers the accumulation of retained earnings and makes it more difficult and costly to attract necessary new capital for improving or expanding services. There is some validity to this complaint, but the record of recent years does not indicate that utility services in general have been inadequate because of lack of financing.

It probably is true that a substantial cushion of retained earnings or surpluses, by reducing risks from the viewpoint of potential new investors, makes it easier and less expensive to acquire the new capital upon which many utilities rely heavily for expansion. This has been recognized by the courts.[14] On the other hand, consumers may legitimately argue that retained earnings actually represent increases in stockholders' equities and thus, if stockholders are receiving adequate dividends, represent excessive earnings. Further, it can be argued that insofar as surpluses reduce the cost of future financing and presumably lead to future lower rates, they represent a subsidy by present and past consumers to future consumers. Also, there are strong arguments against using retained earnings to increase a utility's rate base. In effect, this makes consumers involuntary investors in the firm without entitling them to receive dividends or other prerogatives of voluntary investors.

Few would dispute the desirability of some cushion of retained earnings for a firm which must seek funds in the capital market from time to time. The size of the cushion may be debated, however. For example, how large a safety cushion is necessary to reduce financing costs by a specific amount? There is no certain answer for all circumstances. Even in a particular circumstance an answer at best must be only an informed opinion, and even based on the same information opinions may vary widely.

The need for retained earnings or surpluses is much less obvious in static or declining industries or firms. In such situations the problem is not one of attracting new capital but rather one of retaining, or perhaps gradually phasing out, existing capital. No safety reserves for new investors are necessary under these conditions. There can be no serious objection if management or stockholders choose not to distribute all current earnings in current dividends, but higher rates simply to provide higher retained earnings cannot be justified either on economic or legal grounds. Such situations, of course, are rare.

CAPITAL COSTS

A fairly accurate determination of a utility's capital costs is essential if the firm's financial integrity is to be maintained and rates are not to be unduly high. This is not easy, even for past periods. It is particularly difficult in rate cases, in which future costs must be considered.

In addition to its common stocks a typical utility may have outstanding several classes of preferred stocks and a variety of long-term and intermediate-term bonds and short-term debt obligations, incurred at different times and with different maturity dates, involving different degrees of risk to investors, and requiring the payment of different dividend or interest returns. The firm's debts must be refinanced on a more or less continuous basis as old obligations mature, and improvement or expansion of services may require new equity or debt capital.

The cost of new capital or of capital for refinancing will clearly depend, among other factors, on the degree of risk as seen by investors. The risk aspect, in turn, will be influenced both by anticipated future earnings and by the relative ranking within the firm's capital structure—that is, whether a senior or junior obligation in claims against earnings or assets—of the financial instrument issued by the corporation for this financing.

One might suppose that among the numerous possibilities for financing there is some ideal combination of a capital structure which would give, for a particular firm in a particular situation, the lowest possible capital costs. The dead hand of past financing, however, strongly influences future financing. Any future obligation must be fitted into the already existing financial framework. Further, even if the ideal structure, with lowest costs, should be attained, the erratic nature of the future money market probably would make it impossible to maintain. It should be clear, then, that practical regulation cannot be based upon some ideal capital cost concept. Instead, it must be based upon a realistic evaluation of what already exists, modified, of course, by the best available insights into future conditions.

There is considerable debate concerning how much attention should be devoted to the relative proportions of equity and debt capital in a utility firm's financial structure in rate of return determination. As an illustrative example, imagine a firm with a rate base of $100 million and with a financial structure made up of $60 million in 5 per cent bonds and $40 million in common stock. If the firm is allowed 8 per cent earnings on its rate base, equity earnings will be $5 million, or at a rate of 12.5 per cent. On the other hand, if the firm's financial structure contains $40 million in 5 per cent bonds and $60 million in common stock, equity earnings will be $6 million, but at a 10 per cent rate of return.

Because the type of assets held by most utilities is particularly well suited for debt financing, there are strong inducements for holders of common stock to favor heavy debt financing and consequent higher percentage yields on equities. During a recent year, for example, the ratio of the aggregate net assets to the aggregate equity was approximately 2.5 to 1 for the nation's fifteen largest electric and electric-gas utilities. In contrast, the asset to equity ratio was approximately 1.6 to 1 for the nation's fifteen largest manufacturing firms.[15]

It is often argued that the pertinent capital costs of a utility for rate determination purposes are composed only of its actual interest charges and its preferred stock dividend rates (if any), plus earnings on common stock comparable to those of similar industries or degrees of risk. This method, which is designed to limit increased common stock earnings by "playing on the equity," has been used and upheld. At first glance it seems entirely appropriate and desirable from the consumers' viewpoint and fair to investors.

There are counterarguments to this plan, however. If equity earnings are limited drastically, a firm may not be able to build up a reserve safety cushion of retained earnings or surpluses. This means increased risks for all classes of investors and is thus likely to lead to increased costs for both debt and equity capital in future financing. Also, from a logical standpoint, to say nothing of the implications for optimal allocation of real capital resources, it is difficult to reconcile earnings of 8 per cent from a particular asset if it is financed by equity funds and of only 5 per cent if it is debt-financed.

Most, if not all, regulatory commissions do take a firm's capital structure into account, in one way or another, in attempting to determine a reasonable rate of return. It is apparent, though, that some commissions, those following the "bare bones" approach, pay more attention to this factor than do others. As an illustration, the country's fifteen largest electric and electric-gas firms had average net earnings of approximately 4.3 per cent on aggregate net assets, and average net earnings on aggregate equity of about 10.7 per cent during a recent year. The range of net earnings on equity among these firms, however, was from a little more than 7 per cent to almost 15 per cent, with a median earning of more than 11 per cent.[16]

Regulatory folklore, expressed in many court and commission decisions and widely accepted, holds that utility businesses are more stable and less risky than businesses in general and that utility investors should therefore be satisfied with lower rates of return than is necessary in most other types of undertakings.[17] This belief has some basis in fact, but it must be accepted with considerable caution. It is only necessary to look back at the failures of individual utility firms—or even of entire utility-type industries, like stagecoaching, steamboating, street transport, or intercity railroad passenger service—to see that utility businesses and industries are far from risk-free.

It appears that relative inelasticity of demand tends to result in fewer adverse effects on utility revenues than on the revenues of some other types of businesses when prices increase or incomes fall. There are other types of enterprise equally favored by inelastic consumer demand schedules, however. Further, inelasticity usually works both upward and downward; thus utilities may not benefit from windfall increases in business if their prices are decreased or consumer incomes increased—and if volume increases do occur, earnings regulation is likely to limit profit increases.

It is often held that regulation protects utility firms from competition. This applies, however, only to competition from similar utility firms and not to other types of enterprises which may furnish competing services. Regulation did not protect the railroad passenger business from airplanes and automobiles, nor does it protect electric and gas utilities from the competition of oil and coal.

Utility enterprises have never been any more immune to the risks of technological change or consumer preference shifts than other businesses, and the rapid technological advances of the present era have multiplied these risks. Even now, for all we know, designs may be well along for a new and simple fuel cell, solar battery, or the like, which will revolutionize the technologies of energy production and distribution overnight and make obsolete many billions of dollars worth of plant and equipment in the "low-risk" electric and gas utilities. The nature and timing of revolutionary new technologies cannot be predicted, but one *can* safely predict that such advances will occur.

To some extent, it may be argued that close regulatory scrutiny of utility expenditures protects investors (as well as consumers) from improper management actions and that legal permission to increase prices when necessary makes such increases more palatable to consumers. Offsetting these possible advantages, however, are the limitations and inflexibility imposed on managers, which hamper them in making rapid, beneficial expenditures or price adjustments. This inflexibility may be particularly harmful during a period of rapidly rising costs. Further, a significant part of a utility's human resources must at all times be employed in grappling with regulatory problems.

Regulation is also accompanied by the ever-present possibility that important franchises may not be renewed, or renewed only under unfavorable conditions, or even that some or all of a firm's operations may be acquired by a public agency. Or the strictness of regulation may be increased, or competition from publicly owned utilities may be instituted. All in all, the special interest taken by government at all levels in those businesses considered to be "peculiarly affected with the public interest" seems more likely to increase than to decrease risks from the investors' point of view. To the extent that utilities are low-risk ventures, if they are, this may be despite, rather than because of, government intervention.

Finally, evaluation of the risk of losses without corresponding evaluation of the possibility for gains is a sterile exercise. All investors expect to face some risks and to receive some gains. The probabilities of gain and loss, insofar as information and intellect permits, are weighed against each other by the investor in deciding where and at what minimum price he will make his capital available. It seems logical to think, therefore, that with an equivalent degree of risk, capital will be supplied more cheaply in a venture where the possibilities of speculative gains (in addition to more normal returns) are greater than where such possibilities are smaller. Thus, insofar as regulatory and other factors limit the likelihood of speculative gains in the assumed low-risk regulated industries, the costs of equity capital may be increased.

In this brief discussion of the nature of some of the economic risks of utility businesses, we are not maintaining that utilities are more or less subject to risk than are businesses in general. We cannot prove generalizations in this area any better than anyone else can. The variables are too numerous and too little known. Most economic risks are much less subject to quantification than are most physical risks. This is an area ruled by judgment or opinion, and the opinions of regulators and regulated, or even of neutral observers, often differ substantially.

In summary, one can only say with reasonable confidence that all businesses, regulated and nonregulated, are subject to risks, that the nature and total impact of these risks vary considerably between industries and between individual firms within a particular industry, and that risks in an industry or a firm vary with the passage of time and changing conditions. Or, as a generalization, one might say that some kinds of risks are greater and some lower in regulated public utility firms as a group than in other businesses. But this cannot answer the question (despite the "answers" given by court and regulatory dicta) of whether or not total risks are greater or smaller in the utility businesses. We can only say, "It depends."

FLUCTUATING EARNINGS

The risks involved in fluctuating earnings, or rather the certainty that such fluctuations will occur, influence willingness to invest and cost of capital in the utility industries. Typically, a nonregulated firm has much more flexibility in adjusting prices to meet changing costs than does a regulated utility. Also, nonregulated firms are free to accumulate reserves from the higher earnings of fat years to stabilize dividends and other payouts during periods of low earnings. Effective earnings regulation of utilities, however, is designed to prevent unusually high earnings at any time; thus a utility's reserve cushion for lean years may be small or nonexistent.

Regulatory delays in allowing upward price adjustments when costs are rising rapidly can create a profits squeeze. Even when price adjustments are obtained, however, they cannot be calculated to offset past low earnings. Although utility investors are legally entitled to the right to attempt to earn a fair return, it is a well-established legal principle, based on many decisions, that rates cannot be averaged over time, either upwards or downwards. In the words of the United States Supreme Court, "Profits of the past cannot be used to sustain confiscatory rates for the future" and "Past losses cannot be used to . . . support a claim that rates for the future are confiscatory."[18]

The prohibition of averaging of rates does prevent forced subsidization of consumers of one time period by consumers of another time period. It also means, however, that if utility firms are to protect their investors against the adverse dividend effects of low earning years they must either be lucky enough or astute enough to enjoy unusually high earnings for a time before their prices are forced downward by regulation or they must provide a protective cushion out of ordinary reasonable earnings. One or both of these devices may be feasible under tolerant regulation but difficult under a "bare bones" approach.

Some regulatory attention and experimentation has been devoted to so-called equalization reserve plans, in which all or a portion of earnings above a certain level are set aside to be withdrawn during periods of lower earnings, thus stabilizing consumer prices and investor returns. These plans, though, generally have not satisfied regulators, investors, or consumers and have never been of practical importance.[19] The problem remains and must be met by management operating within the existing regulatory framework.

Fortunately from the utility's viewpoint, many commissions do recognize the importance of providing earnings sufficient to build up at least modest protective reserves, believing that such reserves tend to reduce risks and financing costs and that contributions to them can thus be legitimately included in reasonable earnings. This has been accepted by the courts.[20] But differences of opinion concerning the appropriate size of such reserves and what they may be used for are likely to persist.

INCENTIVE EARNINGS

The question of incentive rate of return plans, close to the hearts of many utility executives, is deceiving at first glance. Under such plans it is contemplated that unusually efficient firms will be rewarded by being allowed to earn something more than they would otherwise be entitled to expect. Presumably, inefficient firms would be penalized by lower earnings, while those not particularly efficient or inefficient would be allowed some in-between level of earnings.

It is argued that such a method of reward and punishment through profit levels is comparable to the workings of competition in the nonregulated sectors of the economy, and since most persons believe this leads to desirable economic results it should be applied in the regulated sectors as well. Greater rewards stimulate greater efforts, and it is only fair, the argument goes, that greater efforts should bring greater rewards. Investors, consumers, and the entire economy benefit from more efficient use of capital and human resources; thus inefficiency should be discouraged and efficiency encouraged by the regulatory process.

Various specific incentive plans have been proposed. For example, standards for ordinary performance and returns may be established and performance deviations rewarded (or punished) according to some determined scale. Or firms may be allowed higher earnings if they can increase their revenues while at the same time lowering consumer prices. These and similar devices have been adopted on a limited and experimental basis in some jurisdictions, but in general they have not worked very well and have not been widely accepted.

Serious operational and conceptual difficulties beset incentive earning plans. Measurements of efficiency are not notably precise, and deviations from performance and earnings standards cannot always be charged to managerial efficiency or inefficiency. The existence of reasonable earnings under effective regulation implies, unless there is strong evidence to the contrary, that a firm is efficient and thus needs no additional incentive stimulation. Further, if an "inefficient" firm's earnings and services already are inadequate, it is hard to explain how the penalty of even lower earnings could enable it to improve its services and maintain its financial integrity.

Managers of public utility firms are both morally and legally obligated, and expected, to operate these firms as efficiently as possible in any case. In return, these firms are protected against regulation which would deny them the right to earn reasonable returns. If regulation actually does restrict this right, the courts are available for appeal. On the other hand, if poor earnings are attributable to poor management rather than to regulation, this is a matter to be settled between stockholders and management.

It is contrary to the entire spirit and purpose of regulation to allow consumers to be charged higher prices as an incentive for managerial efficiency, as some plans have proposed. Such schemes are not comparable with the profits rewards of efficiency in nonregulated industries. An unusually efficient nonregulated firm usually attains superior earnings by providing its customers with a better product or service at the same price as its competitors, or by an equivalent product or service at a lower cost. Tying incentives to higher consumer prices involves a very peculiar definition of "incentive."

In short, commissions which refuse to accept schemes of regulatory reward and punishment and stick to the concept of "reasonable returns, under honest, efficient, and economical management," apparently stand on solid conceptual and practical grounds. Such a stand, of course, does not necessarily constitute a "bare bones" regulatory approach and does not imply that reasonable rates of return cannot include both adequate dividends and some contributions to surplus safety reserves under normal conditions. Nor does it mean that regulators should be unduly strict in quickly stripping away all additional earnings arising from efficiency improvements. As already indicated reasonableness is not a point on a scale but a zone within which discretion can be exercised. The proper concern of regulators is the administration of returns within this zone and not the administration of discipline to management. Managerial discipline is a stockholders' function.

Ultimately, the capital marketplace is the final and only vindicator of regulatory judgment concerning what rate or level of earnings is sufficient to maintain financial integrity. If judgment errs upward, excessive earnings may result, calling for downward readjustments. If the error is downward, decreased earnings, higher capital costs, service deterioration, and eventual bankruptcy could follow.

The experience of most utilities in attracting or maintaining the capital necessary to meet the growing service demands of a growing population during recent years suggests that if regulatory judgment has erred, it has erred, purposely or not, mainly in the upward direction. This does not seem undesirable, if errors are to be made (and they cannot be completely eliminated, of course). Higher than necessary earnings at least provide capital which can be used for service improvements if the firm wishes to do this. Also, once an error in judgment becomes apparent, it is probably easier to correct an upward than a downward error, with fewer adverse effects on both consumers and investors.

THE IMPACT OF EARNINGS REGULATION

Earnings regulation, like other regulation, is often criticized by those whose personal philosophies make them opposed to any economic regulation. This is a legitimate form of criticism, of course, as long as it does not lead the critic to ignore or distort pertinent evidence. Some critics, however, who agree with the principle of regulation point out many evils in its practice. It may be, too, that some allow their personal philosophies to color their observations. In any case, three major types of shortcomings in present practices are alleged by various critics.

One group alleges that regulators are too harsh with utility companies. That is, that in their zeal to keep consumer prices low, commissions unduly restrict earnings, with immediate adverse effects on investors and long-term adverse effects on consumer services. Needless to say, most of these complaints are not from consumers.

The record indicates that utility firms in general, except those adversely affected by drastically changed technologies or similar factors not attributable to regulation, have been able to maintain their financial integrity and to expand and improve their services. Specific instances of service deterioration and even of company failure can be cited, and similar failures will no doubt occur in the future, but it would be difficult to establish that regulation has played a major role in causing such failures.

At the opposite extreme are those who allege that regulators unduly favor the regulated firms at the expense of consumers. This alleged favoritism takes the form of protection against competition, thus allowing lax or inefficient management, and eventually requiring higher consumer prices to maintain a desirable rate of return. Or lax regulation may even allow returns to be unreasonably high.[21]

As pointed out in the preceding section, regulatory protection against competition is highly overrated. Further, comparison of price and earnings trends in the utilities industries with trends in other major industries do not substantiate the claim that regulation has been unusually lax or overly prejudiced in favor of regulated firms. Some lax management exists in every industry, but regulation seems more likely to discourage than to encourage this. As for the level of permitted rates, one person's "too high" may be another's "too low."

Finally, there is a group which, although not claiming conscious regulatory bias in any direction, maintains that earnings regulation has had no significant effect whatsoever on prices. This argument cannot be refuted by empirical data any more than it can be proved. Its empirical proof or refutation would involve comparing evidence of what actually has been against hypothetical evidence of what might have been under very different historical circumstances. Actual data may be available, but "might have been" data are entirely subjective.

Our opinion, based upon our observations and studies and reflecting our own biases if you will, is that rate of return regulation generally has been effective in keeping prices and earnings lower than they otherwise would have been, while at the same time allowing the regulated utilities to maintain sufficient financial integrity to support significant improvements in the quantity and quality of services rendered.

This is not to say that existing forms of regulation, or any regulation, is either good or bad, or that some different form of regulation would not be better, or that utility prices in general are too high or too low. These in considerable part are subjective evaluations, determined by one's individual philosophy and viewpoint. The overriding objective fact is that society in its collective judgment has instituted particular kinds of rules and charged certain agencies and individuals with their administration. We can only live with these rules, adapt to them as necessary, evaluate and criticize them if we wish, and work towards their elimination or modification if we do not like their results or intents.

It cannot be denied that regulatory mistakes, both in law and judgment, have been made, if we define "mistake" as a result different from or opposite to that intended. Nor can it be denied that some individual regulators have been incompetent, dishonest, or both. We can expect the same in the future. All human beings and human institutions are fallible. We believe, however—again, an opinion, based upon our study of the evidence—that most regulators are and have been as competent and honest as any other group of public servants and have conscientiously attempted to meet their responsibilities within the legal and economic framework in which they operate.

SUMMARY

It should be clear from the discussion in this chapter and preceding chapters that the regulation of public utility earnings is more of an art than a science, more a matter of judgment hopefully directed toward attaining approximate goals than a set of infallible rules leading to determinate results. Honest men, even if not particularly affected by outcomes, can reach quite different judgments from the same set of facts. It is not surprising, then, that public utility regulation, where many of those directly involved are directly affected by outcomes, gives rise to numerous controversies.

It is the primary duty of management to protect the interests of the firm and the investors. This does not mean that consumer interests can be ignored, since the firm depends upon its customers and exists to serve them, but a firm cannot be primarily a welfare agency in a profit-seeking economy. The primary duty of regulators, on the other hand, is to guard the interests of consumers. Similarly, this involves giving some attention, but not primary attention, to the welfare of the firm. To some extent, then, the responsibilities of managers and regulators overlap, but to some extent they deviate. It is the deviations, or supposed deviations, that create regulatory problems.

Present regulatory practices are the result of a long process of evolution in legal and economic thought and of trial and error. Several established and well-known statutes and precedents provide useful guidelines, but iron-clad rules are few. There is no reason to believe that the evolutionary process has stopped or that it will do so in the foreseeable future. Every answer seems to raise new questions and every solution to create new problems. This is an inherent part of a dynamic economic process. We can only hope that, whatever tomorrow's regulatory questions and problems, they will continue to be tackled by the good judgment of honest men, fairly representing consumer, investor, and hopefully even general public interests.

NOTES

1. Conceptually this is so. Actually, some commissions appear first to determine actual net revenue dollar needs, which are then translated into percentages.
2. The United States Supreme Court has stated that due process "... does not assure to public utilities the right under all circumstances to have a return upon the value of the property ..." and that due process "... cannot be applied to insure values or to restore values that have been lost by the operation of economic forces." See *Public Service Commission of Montana v. Great Northern Utilities Co.*, 289 U.S. 130 (1935) and *Market Street Railway Co. v. Railroad Commission of California*, 324 U.S. 548 (1945).
3. Since the quantity of services which the public is willing to consume is a function of the prices charged, some circularity of reasoning is involved in relating income needs to service expectations. As a practical administrative matter, however, service requirements and the facilities necessary to meet them, at least at some minimum level of adequacy, can be considered as fixed for any given short-run time period.
4. Strictly speaking, "risk" can be measured in probability terms and thus is "insurable," while "uncertainty" by definition is not measurable. As used here, however, as in most similar discussions, "risk" refers to both measurable and nonmeasurable possibilities of loss; that is, risk includes uncertainties. For a classic discussion of this fine point, see Frank H. Knight, *Risk, Uncertainty and Profit* (Boston: Houghton Mifflin, 1921).
5. "Profits," as used here, refers to the common or accounting concept of that term, rather than to the economic concept. For the distinction, see Knight, cited in note 4.
6. Elaboration of the meaning of "optimal" is outside the scope of this discussion. A good elementary treatment of the workings of perfect competition can be found in Lorie Tarshis, *Modern Economics: An Introduction* (Boston: Houghton Mifflin, 1967), ch. 4 and 5, or in similar sections of several other introductory economics textbooks.
7. 169 U.S. 466 (1898). Previously cited in Chapter 6.
8. 134 U.S. 418 (1890) and 154 U.S. 362 (1894), respectively, both previously cited in Chapter 6.
9. 212 U.S. 19 (1909). Previously cited in Chapter 6.
10. 262 U.S. 679 (1923). Previously cited in Chapter 6.
11. 320 U.S. 591 (1944). Previously cited in Chapter 6.
12. In *Banton v. Belt Line Railway Corp.*, 268 U.S. 413 (1925), the Court held that a commission "... in its discretion, may determine to be reasonable and just a rate that is substantially higher than one merely sufficient to justify a judicial finding in a confiscation case. ..."
13. Owners' equity, defined as the total of capital stock, surpluses and retained earnings, in these fifty largest firms is around $54 billion.
14. For example, see *United Railways and Electric Company of Baltimore v. West*, 280 U.S. 234 (1930).
15. Calculated by the authors from the latest available published statements at the time of writing.
16. See note 15. During the same year the fifteen largest manufacturing firms had average earnings of about 10.4 per cent on assets and 16.7 per cent on equity, with an equity earnings range from almost 8 per cent to almost 26 per cent, and an equity median of approximately 14.7 per cent.
17. For an example, see the *Bluefield* case, cited previously.
18. *Public Utility Commissioners of New Jersey vs. New York Telephone Co.*, 271 U.S. 23 (1926). This principle has been upheld in both earlier and later decisions.
19. Perhaps the most ambitious scheme of this type, and the most celebrated failure, was the so-called "recapture clause" of the Transportation Act of 1920, applicable to railroads under the regulatory administration of the Interstate Commerce Commission. After innumerable difficulties and complaints this plan was abandoned in 1933.
20. For one example, see the *United Railways* case, cited in note 14.
21. For a recent strong expression of this viewpoint and considerable other criticism of electric utility returns and activities, see Lee Metcalf and Vic Reinemer, *Overcharge* (New York: David McKay Co., 1967). This book, by a United States Senator and his executive secretary, was

advertised by the subtitle "How Electric Utilities Exploit and Mislead the Public, and What You Can Do About It." For a criticism of the research methodology upon which these authors base their "overcharge" claim, see Robert S. Stich, "Limitations to the Comparative Rate Approach," *Public Utilities Fortnightly,* vol. 80, no. 2 (July 20, 1967), pp. 21–27. The so-called A-J-W effect, a theoretical argument concerned as much with the philosophy of regulation as with specific rates of return, contends that resource allocation is distorted when regulated rates of return exceed actual marketplace capital costs. This is discussed in Chapter 10.

ADDITIONAL READINGS

1. Barnes, Irston R., *The Economics of Public Utility Regulation* (New York: F. S. Crofts, 1942), ch. 15, "The Rate of Return," pp. 516–544.
2. Blatz, Richard B., "Efficiency Incentives for Telephone Companies," *Public Utilities Fortnightly,* vol. 72, no. 6 (September 12, 1963), pp. 19–27.
3. Bonbright, James C., *Principles of Public Utility Rates* (New York: Columbia University Press, 1961).
4. Clemens, Eli Winston, *Economics and Public Utilities* (New York: Appleton-Century-Crofts, 1950).
5. Cootner, Paul H., and Daniel M. Holland, "Rate of Return and Business Risk," *The Bell Journal of Economics and Management Science,* vol. 1, no. 2 (Autumn 1970); pp. 211–226.
6. D'Ambrosio, Charles A., "Some Risk Concepts in Utility Rate Making," *Public Utilities Fortnightly,* vol. 87, no. 4 (February 18, 1971), pp. 28–35.
7. Davis, Blaine R., "Investment and Rate of Return for the Regulated Firm," *The Bell Journal of Economics and Management Science,* vol. 1, no. 2 (Autumn 1970); pp. 245–270.
8. Garfield, Paul J., and Wallace F. Lovejoy, *Public Utility Economics* (Englewood Cliffs, N.J.: Prentice-Hall, 1964), ch. 9, "Rate of Return," pp. 114–134.
9. Glaeser, Martin G., *Public Utilities in American Capitalism* (New York: Macmillan, 1957), ch. 23, "Fixing the Fair Return," pp. 384–402.
10. Gutmann, Peter M., "The Fair Rate of Return: A New Approach," *Public Utilities Fortnightly,* vol. 87, no. 5 (March 4, 1971), pp. 41–44.
11. Jones, Eliot, and Truman C. Bigham, *Principles of Public Utilities* (New York: Macmillan, 1931), ch. 6, "Rate of Return," pp. 252–287.
12. Klevorick, Alvin K., "The 'Optimal' Fair Rate of Return," *The Bell Journal of Economics and Management Science,* vol. 2, no. 1 (Spring 1971), pp. 122–153.
13. Kolb, Burton A., "The Role of Risk in Public Utility Regulation—Technological Change and Risk," *The Economics of Regulation of Public Utilities.* Papers presented at a conference at Northwestern University, June 19–24, 1966 (Evanston, Ill.: Northwestern University, 1966), pp. 151–160.
14. Phillips, Charles F., Jr., *The Economics of Regulation,* rev. ed. (Homewood, Ill.: Richard D. Irwin, 1969), ch. 9, "The Rate of Return," pp. 260–302.
15. Rosenthal, Richard L., "Management and Regulatory Responsibility to Investors," *Public Utilities Fortnightly,* vol. 72, no. 4 (August 15, 1963), pp. 15–30.

16. Trachsel, Herman H., *Public Utility Regulation* (Chicago: Richard D. Irwin, 1947), ch. 16, "Rate of Return," pp. 322–340.

17. Trebing, Harry M., "Toward an Incentive System of Regulation," *Public Utilities Fortnightly*, vol. 72, no. 2 (July 18, 1963), pp. 23–37.

18. Trebing, Harry M., and R. Hayden Howard, eds., *Rate of Return Under Regulation: New Directions and Perspectives.* M.S.U. Public Utilities Studies (East Lansing, Mich.: Institute of Public Utilities, Michigan State University, 1969).

19. Troxel, Emery, *Economics of Public Utilities* (New York: Rinehart, 1947), ch. 17, "The Rate of Return," pp. 372–395; ch. 18, "Continuity of Earnings Regulation," pp. 396–418; ch. 19 "Cyclical Control of Earnings," pp. 419–440.

20. Welch, Francis X., *Cases and Text on Public Utility Regulations* (Washington, D.C.: Public Utilities Reports, 1961), ch. 10, "The Return Allowance," pp. 453–490.

9

Regulation of Intercorporate Relations

Practically all firms in the various utilities are organized as corporations. This form of business enterprise is necessary where large amounts of capital are used. As we have already seen, too, practically all utilities are regulated by public authorities. Only the publicly owned group, which will be discussed in Part Four, is an exception, and even within that group some selective regulation takes place. Since the 1930's the relations of one corporation with another have come under regulation. While the degree and type of regulation varies by utility and often by the public authority of jurisdiction, it is a fact of life for the modern public utility. Hence, our survey of the regulation of privately owned utilities would be incomplete without some consideration of this factor.

IMPORTANCE OF INTERCORPORATE RELATIONS

Society has long been interested in the relations existing between corporations, as evidenced by the antitrust laws of our nation starting in 1890 and continuing to the present. In the utilities field, however, one firm's relation with another is even more worthy of public interest than in most other businesses because of two reasons. First, as noted earlier, modern life in the West is so dependent on utility services that any corporate relations which adversely affect a utility's ability to serve is likely to affect a major segment of our society. Second, the fact that utility rates (prices) are regulated at least partly based on the operating expenses of the firm means that any factor affecting costs of the firm will be of public interest.

In addition, regulation of intercorporate relations has come about largely because of abuses and excesses connected with such relations in past decades. To understand why regulation is so important it is necessary to understand the problems which gave rise to it originally.

Finally, intercorporate relations have again assumed particular importance at the present time. It was suggested in Chapter 1 that at least the "Big Three" utilities—power, natural gas, and telephone—are currently in the cooperative stage of development, and this involves joint participation of two or more corporations in a single undertaking, such as an interconnected power or telephone system or joint ownership of natural resources. Activities of this nature have increased markedly in the past two decades, and consequently intercorporate relations have once again moved into the spotlight of public interest.

THE INTEGRATION MOVEMENT

Some writers approach the problem of intercorporate relations by tracing the development of the so-called "integration movement."[1] This approach allows one to appreciate how the problems involved developed over time and the manner in which they were partly solved.

Originally most utility firms were very small, served a small territory, and lacked capital and technical sophistication. Sometimes two or more firms served the same territory as various local governments attempted to protect their citizens during the "competitive era." However, this competition was often bought at a high price–high rates, poor service, inadequate plant. When it was recognized that economies of scale were possible with larger production units and larger service territories, formerly competitive firms often merged or consolidated. Sometimes one firm became bankrupt and sold out to the surviving competitor; sometimes the integration was a planned thing, with sound economies and engineering at its base. But whatever the route, most early utilities eventually found themselves part of a bigger unit, often of a city-wide system of power, gas, water, or telephone services.

The second phase of the integration movement came as the consolidated unit discovered that it needed modern equipment, capital, engineering and technical services, and modern management. Quite often these improvements were beyond the means available to even a consolidated company. Borrowing in complicated financial markets was not easy for these firms, and financial advisors were sometimes necessary. Engineering and management consultants also had to be hired. Finally, equipment had to be financed, because of the limited credit of the small and little-known utility firms.

This phase led to stock and bond ownership by various groups in many operating companies. A typical example was the experience of General Electric Company. In order to sell equipment to utilities General Electric began to accept stocks and bonds as part payment for heavy electrical equipment. A general lack of confidence in the soundness of the utilities and a lack of capital made this manner of financing customers almost mandatory for electrical equipment suppliers. By 1905 General Electric decided to establish a separate company to hold the securities it had acquired in financing its customers.[2] This company was appropriately called Electric Bond and Share and was subsequently to become one of the largest of the public utility holding companies.[3]

Several other holding companies were formed by various management and engineering consulting firms.[4] Initially securities were accepted as part of the consulting fee. Later, these firms sought to control the operating utilities, and the management and engineering service contract became a lucrative source of income. Apparently some investment banking firms also accepted securities as a part of their fees in raising capital for operating utilities.[5] Most of the utilities remained small consolidated city-wide systems until after World War I, when the third and speculative phase of the integration movement began.

The decade of the 1920's was the era of the public utility holding company. Table 9-1 indicates the popularity of this device by noting new holding companies incorporated in the electric power industry over several decades.

With a "return to normalcy," an apparently high level of prosperity, and the recognition that utilities were a growth industry providing almost indispensable service, the integration movement began to be dominated by speculators and financial manipulators. Large profits could be made from the holding company device, and huge economic power came to those who knew how to organize systems of utilities into financial giants. Professor Clemens, among others, has eloquently described the speculations of these times.[6]

The final result was extreme concentration in the hands of a very few companies. Integration became a fact of utility life, particularly in the electric power industry. By 1929 a small group of sixteen holding companies generated over 80 per cent of all electric energy in the United States, with three systems accounting for over 45 per cent of the total (see Table 9-2). The integration movement had led to a social problem of concentration of economic power.

Table 9-1 New Holding Companies Incorporated in the Electric Power Industry

Prior to 1900	5 companies
1900–1909	11 companies
1910–1919	7 companies
1920–1929	46 companies
1930–1935	2 companies

Source: *Public Utility Holding Companies,* Hearings on HR 5423, House Committee on Interstate and Foreign Commerce, 74th Congress, 1st Session, part III (1935), p. 2191.

Table 9-2 Percentage of Electric Energy Generated by Holding Company Groups, 1929

United Corporation Group	20.8
Electric Bond and Share Co.	14.3
Insull Group	10.3
Thirteen Other Large Holding Companies	34.8
	80.2
Small Holding Companies	2.1
Large Local Companies	12.1
Small Local Companies	5.6
	100.0

Adapted from Federal Trade Commission, *Utility Corporations,* 70th Congress, 1st Session, Senate Document No. 92, part 72-A, p. 38.

THE HOLDING COMPANY DEVICE

The extreme concentration of utility firms had been accomplished by use of the holding company. In a broad sense, a holding company is any firm holding or owning securities in any other company or companies. Practically all large businesses would fall under this definition. However, as used here and in the usual sense, ownership, either majority or minority, must be coupled with control. Hence, the classic definition of a holding company is "any company, incorporated or unincorporated, which is in a position to control, or materially to influence, the management of one or more other companies by virtue, in part at least, of its ownership of securities in the other company or companies."[7]

Many scholars attribute the growth of the holding company to increasing competition between states to be "state of origin" for corporations and hence to collect incorporation fees. The State of New Jersey seems to have begun issuing liberal corporate charters after changing its laws on incorporation in 1889 to allow one corporation to hold stock in a limited way in another corporation. In 1896 New Jersey again amended its laws to allow any corporation incorporated in that state to hold securities and exercise all rights of ownership in any other corporation.[8] Although there were some earlier holding companies in the utilities,[9] it was not until New Jersey allowed the device that this form of integration became popular.

THE STRUCTURE OF THE HOLDING COMPANY

The key to concentrating economic power in the hands of a few and reaping large profits on the investment of a small sum lay primarily in being able to sell stocks and bonds to the public while holding control with a small ownership. It is well to remember that the decade of the 1920's was a period of speculation in securities as well as of broad acceptance of utilities as a growth industry. Financial speculators and manipulators were adept at taking advantage of these two facts.

It should be recognized that many utility companies were both operating companies with properties that served the public and holding companies which held control of other utilities. It was, however, in the "pure" holding company, without properties other than security holdings in other companies, that the device found its ultimate power. Figure 9-1 presents a hypothetical holding company structure with three layers or degrees of companies to illustrate the device.

Assume, for the sake of illustration, that each operating company shown in this figure has $1 million in assets, represented equally by voting common stocks and bonds, and that holding companies are entirely financed by equity capital. Further assume that control can be exercised by 51 per cent of common stock ownership. (These are extremely conservative assumptions. Equity was often much less than 50 per cent, control normally can be exercised with much less than 51 per cent of equity ownership, and holding companies themselves used substantial debt financing.) Now, a little arithmetic will demonstrate that only a small investment at the top of the holding company pyramid can control very large assets at the bottom of the pyramid.

Figure 9–1 Hypothetical Holding Company Pyramid

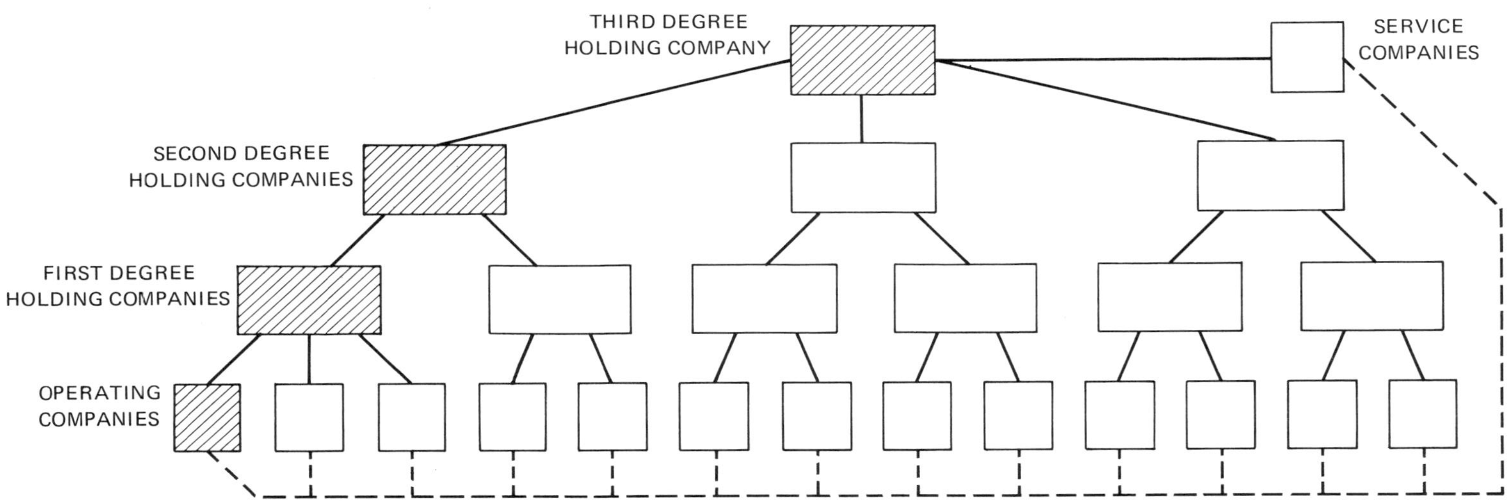

For example, under the above extremely conservative assumptions, the six first-degree holding companies could control $13 million in assets with investments of a little more than $3.3 million. The three second-degree companies could exercise control by investing less than $1.7 million. The top or third-degree holding company could control the operating companies, through its control of the lower holding companies, with an investment of about $862,000. The possibilities for controlling large quantities of assets with a very small investment at the top of the pyramid and for reaping enormous profits on this small investment are limited only by one's imagination. And some utility entrepreneurs of the 1920's were very imaginative!

THE ADVANTAGES OF THE HOLDING COMPANY

Because of the problems which arose from the holding company device, it is sometimes easy to overlook the fact that there were advantages from holding companies to operating utilities and investors. At least six probable advantages can be specified.

First, it is probable that better engineering and construction came from the holding companies. As noted, many early holding companies were formed by engineering consulting firms. Many smaller utilities could not have afforded the level of engineering and technical efficiency that arose from the service companies often attached to holding company pyramids.

Second, superior management may have come to operating utilities in the same manner. Many earlier holding companies were started by engineers and managers whose initial goal was not unusual profits or exploitation.

Third, some operating economies arose from bringing together units of the holding company where interconnection was possible. Larger units of production were sometimes possible through holding company arrangements. Both the utility and its customers benefited from this type of integration where it existed.

Fourth, undoubtedly the operating utilities obtained capital more easily and cheaply. Financial markets are complex, and holding company promoters knew how to raise capital and how to deal with financial institutions.

Fifth, there may well have been some real economies in purchasing and procurement because of integration. By ordering in large blocks several utilities in a holding company family could benefit from that association.

Finally, from the investors' viewpoint, there was a degree of safety in the diversification obtainable by owning holding company securities. The investor could literally own a small piece of many utilities scattered over a wide geographic area by investing in a holding company. For the investor, this was valuable.

It should be mentioned, however, that toward the end of the holding company period many of these advantages disappeared or were offset by disadvantages as the speculative fever increased and holding companies created more and more layers of intermediate holding companies or practiced some of the abuses of this device.

THE ABUSES OF THE HOLDING COMPANY

The abuses of the public utility holding company were many and have been minutely detailed time and time again. We will describe the investigations of this device by the federal government in a following section. Suffice it for now to say that the temptation to use the holding company device in an exploitive manner was apparently overwhelming.

Pyramiding

Pyramiding of control has already been mentioned. The amount of excessive profit increases markedly with each layer of intermediate holding companies. Our example shows only three layers, but federal investigation disclosed in one case six levels or layers of intermediate holding companies between the operating company and the holding company at the top of the pyramid. The profit potential was fantastic, as most of the operating company profits could be siphoned to the top through dividends and charges for "services."

It should be emphasized that many holding companies exercised control with minority ownership of common stock. Practically all of the major holding companies noted by name in Table 9-2 operated on a minority ownership basis. Control was possible with minority ownership because ownership of the majority of the common stock was widely dispersed and the use of the corporate proxy gave management control. Control with a small investment was furthered in some cases by having several classes of stock with variable voting power.[10] Voting trusts were established, and one holding company owned stock in an equal holding company in many instances.

Pyramiding led to separate salaries and offices for many people. Often the owners of the top holding company elected themselves as officers in all the underlying companies and drew salaries from each. Mr. H. D. Hopson testified that he was unable to recall the number of companies in which he served as an officer or the exact number of corporations involved in his Associated Gas and Electric Company pyramid. However, he stated there were "probably three hundred" separate corporations involved.[11]

Complex Financial Structure

The financial structure of the holding company pyramid was very complex. As noted, the whole scheme rested on selling bonds and stocks to the public. Bonds and debentures had a reputation of being less risky than common stock, as traditionally they are based on physical assets. Capitalizing on this reputation, manipulators of holding companies were able to concentrate control and earnings in their own hands by issuing large amounts of bonds and debentures and preferred stocks. In effect, "financial leverage" was carried to its extreme. Many different issues or classes of stocks and bonds were utilized.[12] Securities were issued for practically every purpose and on nearly every occasion, often with little regard for the value of the property or right acquired.[13] New issues of securities sold to the public seem to have been at least partly under the control of a small group of investment bankers, some of whom were also on the boards of directors of holding companies. The result was even further speculation and manipulation of security markets.[14]

Write-Up and Manipulation of Accounts

Property accounts apparently were written up and excessive stock issued upon acquisition of operating properties. Subsequent investigation showed that write-ups exceeded $1.4 billion.[15] Some of this occurred when the companies were organized,[16] some when properties were transferred from one corporation to another within the same holding company family,[17] some when affiliated firms were consolidated,[18] and some when they were reorganized.[19]

Write-ups also facilitated the paying of excessive dividends. In order for holding companies in the upper reaches of the pyramid to benefit most, dividends had to be paid by operating companies. Often dividends were paid and charged to capital surplus—an account which often was inflated by write-ups.[20] Excessive dividends prevented operating companies from maintaining adequate reserves; thus when earnings leveled off or dropped in the early 1930's, the whole house of cards tumbled.

Service Contracts and Exploitation of Operating Companies

Operating companies at the base of the pyramid were exploited in many ways, but one particular favorite of manipulators was the service contract. Based on the fact that operating companies often needed engineering, management, and financial services, practically all holding company families maintained a service company to provide this help. Of course, the service company was owned by the people in control of the pyramid, and much publicity was given to the fact that "superior" services could be attained by the use of this device.

Fees varied for these services, but a fixed percentage of income was popular. These fees were supposed to be negotiated between the parties by "arm's length bargaining." Since different corporations and names were involved, this appeared to be the case on the surface. Actually, with control vested in the same small group having control of the service company, little bargaining took place. While some services were performed on a sliding scale of variable fees, 2.5 to 5 per cent of income was a popular charge for management services, 3.75 to 9.75 per cent of cost for engineering services, and various per diem and out-of-pocket cost fees prevailed for other services. While the percentages seem small, the aggregate of these fees was considerable,[21] and service was given whether needed or not.

Operating companies were exploited in other ways as well. "Upstream loans" were used, whereby operating companies lent funds to their parent companies, which sometimes loaned the funds back to other operating companies in the family at excessive interest rates. Inadequate depreciation was recorded (in order to increase reported earnings and dividends), political contributions were made in the name of operating companies to gain influence on legislation, security prices were manipulated to build a base for the issuance of more securities, and so forth. The public knew very little of all this until afterwards. Corporate disclosure of information came in the 1930's (some suggest as a result of these excesses), and all of these transactions were among corporations with different names. It is also well to remember that these intercorporate relations usually affected the cost of the operating utility and hence were passed on in higher rates for power and gas.

THE FAILURE OF THE HOLDING COMPANY

With the change in economic conditions brought on by the 1930's depression, revenues for utilities leveled off or declined. This caused the overlying holding companies to face a financial crisis. From September 1929 to April 1936 a total of fifty-three holding companies with combined assets of almost $1.7 billion went into receivership or bankruptcy. In addition, twenty-three holding companies were forced to default on interest payments on bonds, and as of December 1938, $1.4 billion of the $2.4 billion in preferred stocks of holding companies were in arrears on dividends.[22] Many issues of stocks and bonds purchased by the public during the 1920's proved of little value and certainly did not provide the financial security that its owners had hoped. An extreme example of this problem was the $8.34 per $100 received by holders of debentures in the Insull system upon bankruptcy; other classes of security holders received nothing.[23] Many were disillusioned, and an extreme reaction set in.

REGULATION OF HOLDING COMPANIES

It is well to remember that the integration movement took place during the period of state regulation of utilities and prior to the advent of federal regulation. Indeed, it is often said that excesses of holding companies hastened or actually brought on federal controls over public utilities.

FAILURE OF STATE REGULATION

Generally, holding companies were beyond the control of the various state commissions. This was true for three reasons.

First, the immense size of the holding companies with their superior legal, engineering, and financial resources easily dominated understaffed state commissions. Most commissions accepted cost data given to them by utilities. Little effective accounting regulation existed. Also, little control was exercised over intercorporate relations.

Second, many state commissions lacked jurisdiction over the financial dealings of operating companies even if they had had the degree of expertise necessary to control holding company excesses. Clemens notes that up to 1931 only about half the state commissions had authority over mergers, consolidations, and the purchase and sale or exchange of securities or assets.[24] There was considerable question as to whether or not a state commission could control a holding company. Many holding companies did not serve the public but merely held assets. Holding companies rarely had authority to serve and rarely held a franchise or a certificate of public convenience and necessity.[25] In addition, there were legal questions of what constituted control–in 1930 the Supreme Court held that each corporation must be treated as a separate entity even though fully owned by a holding company.[26]

Finally, most holding companies were interstate in nature, whereas commissions could control only intrastate economic activities. When a state commission attempted to regulate the price paid for power purchased from a holding company affiliate in another state and transmitted across a state line, the Supreme Court held the action unconstitutional.[27]

This failure of state commissions to control holding companies caused two reactions. First, state commission jurisdiction was increased during the 1930's. Second, federal controls were instituted. There seems little doubt that the excesses of the holding companies during the 1920's brought about federal control over utilities during the 1930's.

FEDERAL INVESTIGATION

Holding company control and concentration in utilities was often investigated before the 1930's.[28] The relations of electrical equipment suppliers and utilities were the subject of two special reports.[29] However, it was the massive investigation by the Federal Trade Commission which finally uncovered most of the holding company abuses.

Beginning in 1928 the F. T. C. investigated holding companies for almost nine years. The final report was published in 1937.[30] More than eighty volumes of hearings and testimony are involved, constituting the most complete investigation of any industry ever attempted in the United States. Even before the investigation was complete, liberal writers had a field day and Congress was beginning to act to control holding companies.

FEDERAL REGULATION

Federal regulation of the utility industry is found in six separate acts,[31] but regulation of holding companies is involved directly in only three of these. These are the Securities Act of 1933, which created the Securities and Exchange Commission (S.E.C.) and gave it jurisdiction over all securities sold in interstate commerce, including those of public utilities; the Securities and Exchange Act of 1934, which enlarged the commission's powers; and the Public Utility Act of 1935, known as the Wheeler-Rayburn Act. This last statute has two parts. Part I is called the Public Utility Holding Company Act and is of major concern here.

Objective of the Holding Company Act

The object of Title I of the Public Utility Holding Company Act is to retain for the public the benefits of utility natural monopoly while providing protection against the public interest disadvantages of undue concentration of economic power.[32] This compromise of preserving what was in the public interest and prohibiting what was adverse to the consumer and the investor was not an easy task.

Definition of "Holding Company" and "Registration"

The first task was for Congress to declare gas and electric holding companies to be "affected with the national public interest" because of their sale of securities in interstate commerce and their use of the mails. This declaration required a definition of a holding company. A most stringent definition was used. A holding company was defined as (1) "any company which directly or indirectly owns, controls, or holds with power to vote, 10 per cent or more of the outstanding voting securities of a public utility company or of a company which is a holding company" and (2) "any person found by the Commission to exercise, directly or indirectly, a controlling influence over the management policies of any public utility or holding company."[33] All such persons or firms were required to register with the S. E. C., and it was declared unlawful for any unregistered firms to engage in any business in interstate commerce. Registration was to be accomplished by December 1, 1935, by filing a registration statement which contained a great deal of information about the operations of registering firms. Additional information could be required by the S. E. C. and usually was.

Firms could be declared exempt from the act on request to the S. E. C., and the statute provided guidelines for the exemptions.[34] Basically, any firm which was intrastate in character and under the jurisdiction of a state commission was exempted. The object of the act was to supplement state regulation, not replace it.

Specific Controls

A variety of specific controls, mostly dealing with the financial operations of the holding companies, was included in the statute. Accounts and reports were regulated, and a uniform system of accounts established. Intercompany loans were controlled, with the "upstream loan" prohibited and the "downstream loan" allowable only with S. E. C. supervision. Service, sales, and construction contracts had to be approved by the commission. Payment of dividends by registered holding companies or any subsidiary company needed commission approval; political activities, contributions and lobbying by registered holding companies were prohibited; security operations by officers and directors were controlled; the use of proxies was controlled; and competitive bidding on the issuance of securities was required. The commission was given extensive controls over the purchase and sale of assets by holding companies. This included not only the acquisition of the securities of other companies but also the acquisition of the holding companies' own securities and the purchase of physical assets.

The "Death Sentence Clauses"

The most devastating part of the act was contained in Section 11, the so-called "death sentence clauses." First, all holding companies were limited to two degrees or layers, and no holding company more than twice removed from the operating company was allowed to exist. Second, the holding companies were required to dispose of all their properties in such a way that only a single integrated system would remain. The statute provided in Section 11 (b) that "the Commission shall . . . limit the operations of the holding company system of which such company is a part to a single integrated public utility system, and to such other businesses as are reasonably incidental or economically necessary or appropriate to the operation of such integrated public utility system."[35] An "integrated public utility system" is defined as one whose assets "are physically interconnected or capable of interconnection and which under normal conditions may be economically operated as a single interconnected and coordinated system confined in its operations to a single area or region, in one or more states. . . ." Since holding companies typically held ownership and control in many scattered systems, this meant that they had to choose which one system they wished to retain and dispose of all other holdings.

Finally, the commission was instructed to require that each registered holding company and each subsidiary take steps to insure "that the corporate structure . . . of any company in the holding company system does not unduly or unnecessarily complicate the structure, or unfairly or inequitably distribute voting power. . . ."[36] The prohibition of holding companies more than twice removed is also contained in this "corporate simplification" section.

While most authors have labeled Section 11 the "death sentence clause," Professor Barnes has suggested that this requirement is far removed from a death sentence and has questioned whether or not a second-degree holding company can perform any necessary function which cannot be just as well performed by a first-degree company.[37]

THE EFFECTS OF THE HOLDING COMPANY ACT

There have been many effects of the Public Utility Holding Company Act. Some of these were relatively short-term in nature, while others have extended up to the present time.

SHORT-TERM EFFECTS

Naturally, the act was challenged in the courts; hence, a delay in registration and action took place until the constitutionality of the statute was upheld.[38] The S. E. C. moved cautiously and invited the companies involved to submit their own reorganization plans. Both of these factors meant that it was not until 1940 that proceedings before the commission began. During its first ten years of work 2,145 companies were subject to the act and 1,432 were eliminated by exemption, merger and consolidation, sale, dissolution or divestment.[39] Many companies were dissolved by distributing the assets (securities) to their owners. Others were merged to form new companies or were merged with companies in other holding company families. Many were sold to new stockholders. By whatever means, the first short-term effect was the virtual abolishment of the public utility holding company.

A second short-term effect was the reorganization of the companies and the utility systems. Some holding companies became investment companies, others reverted to service and consulting firms. Many simply disappeared. The operating companies were restructured slowly into new systems. The S. E. C. generally applied the act in such a way that the remaining systems were confined to a single state or to a single and adjacent state. Thus, a new pattern of utility firms emerged with integrated operations in a limited geographic region.

The third short-term effect of the act was to modify the capital structure of utilities. Write-ups were eliminated by replacing debt with stock. All new issues of securities had to be approved by the S. E. C., and the commission set as a criterion the lowering of the debt-equity ratio. Considerable influence over time was exerted on utility company capital structure, and a more realistic balance between long-term debt, preferred stock, and equity was sought.

The fourth short-term effect was to strengthen state commission control. As the federal investigation of holding companies pointed up the weaknesses of state commissions, many states gave greater authority to their commissions to deal with financial matters and intercorporate relations. While this effect was an indirect one, it is true that state control was strengthened by the holding company disclosures.

The final short-term effect of the act was also indirect. As a reaction to the disclosures of holding company excesses, the public ownership movement made great strides. More will be noted about this in Part Four, but it is more than mere coincidence that municipal, state, and federal ownership of the utilities progressed mightily during the 1930's. It was not hard to convince local voters to take over the distribution system of a local power company if it had been involved in the holding company fiasco. Similarly, Congress was easily convinced that one way to obtain a degree of control over the excesses of private enterprise was to construct competing, federally sponsored utility plants. The issue was a national one, and the matter of ownership of utilities became the subject of presidential addresses and party platforms. Without the disclosure of holding company excesses, it is doubtful that the matter of the ownership of utilities would have been so extensively debated; certainly the ownership of other types of businesses was not an issue of national concern.

LONG-TERM EFFECTS

At least three long-term effects of the Public Utility Holding Company Act can be enumerated. These can be called the structural effects, the operating effects, and the control effects.

The structure of the modern-day power and gas industry is a direct result of the holding company period. Modern power companies are organized on a one-area basis in a state or part of a state. Occasionally, a power or gas distribution company will serve in a portion of another state but rarely in more than part of an adjacent state. The systems are integrated and physically interconnected. While there may well be doubts that this type of structure is necessarily the most economical, nevertheless the single area confined generally to one state is the structure inherited from controls over the holding company.

From an operating point of view, utilities wisely chose to stress operating efficiency and public service. Utility finances have been ultraconservative since the 1930's. Memories are long, and many blamed much of the stock market crash on the utilities. The reputation of "wheeling and dealing" dies slowly. However, by stressing good service at a modest price and being good corporate citizens, utilities have by and large overcome the reputation of the 1930's. This was accomplished primarily by stressing engineering and efficiency; taking a most conservative financial stance on such things as dividends, stock issues, intercorporate dealings, and acquisitions; and by being constantly aware of the corporate public image. Much of the way utilities typically operate today is the direct result of trying to avoid excesses of the past.

Finally, the Holding Company Act was but one of the several federal statutes controlling utilities passed during the 1930's. The point is that the holding company left as one of its legacies a structure of federal control which had not existed prior to the 1930's.

CURRENT INTERCORPORATE RELATIONS

As suggested earlier, intercorporate relations may again be gaining importance. The utility of the 1970's finds itself involved with other corporations in a number of ways. Physical coordination and interconnection of power, gas, and telephone companies is quite common. This regional integration between firms, particularly in electric power, makes a great deal of economic sense and has been fostered by the action of federal authorities. Most of the power systems of the country are interconnected into one giant power pool or another. And as power or gas or messages go back and forth across interconnected systems, intercorporate dealings are once more a necessity.

Joint ownership of resources such as gas producing fields, gas pipelines, underground gas storage, coal fields, and so forth is common. Joint ownership of power plants is now common, even though it was a rare event a few years ago. Leasing facilities from other utilities or other corporations is not unknown. Arrangements with suppliers, which may or may not involve ownership, are also found in today's utilities. Joint planning and joint ventures in subsidiary companies is a well-established fact. All of these relations are based on a perplexing array of intercorporate relations, some of which are not completely controlled by state and federal authorities.

Indeed, it may well be that the controls and regulations set down by society in the 1930's to solve a particular problem are quite outdated in the changed environment of today's utilities. Perhaps an updating is needed. At least in some quarters it has been suggested that controls over utilities imposed during a past age are a limiting and undesirable factor in the technological progress of modern utilities.[40]

This is not to suggest that the abuses of the past have come to revisit us. However, it should be pointed out that growth and change in the utility industry during the last thirty to forty years has once more caused the regulation of intercorporate relations to become of some concern.

SUMMARY

A knowledge of intercorporate relations and their abuses and regulation is important to the understanding of utilities in five ways. First, abuses of holding companies provide the rationale for some of the continuing distrust of utilities. Memories are long and reputations pass away slowly. Second, the regulation of holding companies has a direct bearing on utility structures and operations. Third, regulation of holding companies is significant as the basis for some of the present utility controls, such as accounting controls, competitive bidding on securities, avoidance of political influence, and the like. Fourth, abuses of intercorporate relations contributed to the establishment of federal controls over utilities. Finally, intercorporate relations may once more be a significant factor in the control and regulation of utilities as the complexities of the latter third of the twentieth century call for more and more cooperation among utility firms in order to adequately serve the public.

NOTES

1. See Eli Winston Clemens, *Economics and Public Utilities* (New York: Appleton-Century-Crofts, 1950), pp. 486–491.
2. The Westinghouse Company, another large supplier of electrical equipment, also accepted securities as part payment for equipment. However, Westinghouse never formed a separate company to hold these securities.
3. The relations between the General Electric Company and the electric utilities were the subject of two special reports by the Federal Trade Commission. See *Electric Power Industry, Control of Power Companies,* 69th Congress, 2d Session, Document No. 213 (1927); and *Electric Power Industry, Supply of Electrical Equipment and Competitive Conditions,* 70th Congress, 1st Session, Document No. 46 (1929).
4. The Standard Gas and Electric System was built by H. M. Byllesby Company, a construction engineering firm. General Gas and Electric Company is identified with W. S. Barstow; Associated Gas and Electric Company with S. G. White Management Corporation; and Engineers Public Service Company with Stone and Webster, Inc., utility consultants (Clemens, p. 487).
5. The Central Public Service Corporation Systems seem to have been sponsored by A. E. Pierce and Company, investment bankers, while The United Corporation, the largest public utility holding company, was set up in 1929 by the three investment banking firms of J. P. Morgan and Company, Drexel and Company, and Bonbright and Company. See James C. Bonbright and Gardiner C. Means, *The Holding Company: Its Public Significance and Its Regulation* (New York: McGraw-Hill, 1932), pp. 124, 127.
6. Clemens, p. 490.
7. Bonbright and Means, p. 10.
8. Irston R. Barnes, *The Economics of Public Utility Regulation* (New York: Appleton-Century-Crofts, 1942), p. 65.
9. The first "pure" holding company in utilities was probably American Bell Telephone, created by a special act of Massachusetts in 1880 (Bonbright and Means, p. 63). The first holding company in the gas industry seems to have been The United Gas Improvement Company of Philadelphia, created in 1882 (Barnes, p. 66).
10. Many examples can be found in the literature on holding companies, but perhaps the most extreme was ownership control by H. M. Byllesby and Company of a particular issue of common stock which had unusual voting privileges in Standard Gas and Electric. In this case less than 0.3 per cent in an equity interest of $3 million controlled $1.2 billion of assets (Bonbright and Means, p. 116).

11. Clemens, p. 499.
12. One holding company had eighteen classes of bonds and ten classes of stocks, as well as stock purchase rights and "allotment certificates." Many of these were subject to callable or convertible provisions (Clemens, p. 499).
13. Professor Barnes has listed nine purposes for which holding company securities were issued, as follows: to affiliated interests for property or other securities; to nonaffiliated interests for property or other securities; for cash or book credit; for services; as dividends; as bonuses with other securities; in payment of contracts; for good will and other intangibles, such as going value, water rights, and franchises; to retire outstanding securities and refinance maturing obligations. Many of these purposes, of course, were quite proper, but there was a tendency to over-issue and to disregard actual values (Barnes, pp. 108–111).
14. Manipulation of utility stock prices by holding company insiders and investment bankers is detailed in Federal Trade Commission, *Utility Corporations,* 70th Congress, 1st Session, Senate Document No. 92, part 72–A, pp. 565–587.
15. *Ibid.,* p. 302. A write-up is an increase in the book value of an asset in excess of its actual cost.
16. Mohawk Hudson Power Company was made up of properties valued at $37.6 million, but it sold securities valued at $51.9 million, a $14.3 million write-up (*Ibid.,* pp. 226–229).
17. F.T.C. investigation showed that the Central and Southwest Utilities Company (controlled by Insull) had write-ups of $32 million, $23 million of which came from transferring properties among underlying holding companies. Cities Service Company had assets of $40 million; its parent Cities Service Power and Light issued $99 million in bonds, preferred and common stock to it for these properties and proceeded to record these same securities at $106 million, a 165 per cent write-up (*Ibid.,* pp. 239–241).
18. Minnesota Power and Light had write-ups of 126 per cent; Florida Power and Light, 103 per cent; Louisiana Power & Light, 109 per cent; and Mississippi Power & Light, 110 per cent, when they were each formed under subholding companies of Electric Bond and Share (*Ibid.,* pp. 259–260).
19. Omaha Electric Light and Power had assets of $3.7 million. It was reorganized into Nebraska Power Company as part of Electric Bond and Share's pyramid and issued securities with a face value of $11 million (*Ibid.,* p. 264).
20. Many examples were found during the F.T.C. investigation. Perhaps the most flagrant case was Insull Utility Investment, Inc., which paid $17.6 million in dividends between January 1929 and April 1932 on income actually received of $12.4 million while recording expenses of $14.4 million (*Ibid.,* p. 447).
21. Associated Gas and Electric had income of $6.5 million from service contracts with its affiliated companies from 1924 to 1929. This was 193 per cent of its costs. The service company of National Electric Power (Electric Management and Engineering Corporation) made a profit of $2.9 million, 171 per cent of its costs; while W. S. Barstow Management Association had an income of $4 million, or 321 per cent of its costs during the same period (*Ibid.,* pp. 662–663).
22. Clemens, p. 505.
23. Quoted in Charles F. Phillips, Jr., *The Economics of Regulation,* rev. ed. (Homewood, Ill.: Richard D. Irwin, 1969), p. 560.
24. Clemens, p. 504.
25. This line of reasoning is detailed in Barnes, p. 630.
26. *Smith v. Illinois Bell Telephone Co.,* 282 U.S. 133 (1930).
27. *Rhode Island Public Utilities Commission v. Attleboro Steam and Electric Co.,* 273 U.S. 83 (1927).
28. Barnes states (p. 83) that the first investigation of holding companies was in 1911.
29. See note 3.
30. Federal Trade Commission, *Utility Corporations,* 70th Congress, 1st Session, Senate Document No. 92.
31. The Federal Water Power Act, 1920; the Securities Act, 1933; the Securities and Exchange Act, 1934; the Federal Communications Act, 1934; the Public Utility Act, 1935 (two parts: Public Utility Holding Company Act and Federal Power Act); and the Natural Gas Act, 1938.

32. See Paul J. Garfield and Wallace F. Lovejoy, *Public Utility Economics* (Englewood Cliffs, N.J.: Prentice-Hall, 1964), pp. 440–441.
33. Found in 49 Stat 803 (1935), section 2.
34. One of the more detailed discussions of this area as well as of the entire act is found in Barnes, pp. 655–682.
35. Found in 49 Stat 803 (1935), section 11(b).
36. *Ibid.*
37. Barnes, p. 675.
38. The three pivotal cases upholding the Public Utility Holding Company Act were *Electric Bond and Share Co. v. Securities and Exchange Commission,* 303 U.S. 419 (1938); *North American Co. v. Securities and Exchange Commission,* 327 U.S. 686 (1946); and *American Power & Light Co. v. Securities and Exchange Commission,* 329 U.S. 90 (1946).
39. Clemens, p. 512.
40. A good summary of some of these ideas is found in Charles F. Phillips, Jr. "Growth, Technology and Competition in Regulation," *Public Utilities Fortnightly,* vol. 81, no. 9 (April 25, 1968), p. 34.

ADDITIONAL READINGS

1. Barnes, Irston R., *The Economics of Public Utility Regulation* (New York: F. S. Crofts, 1942), ch. 4, "The Corporate Structure of the Utilities: The Holding Company," pp. 61–148; ch. 19, "Regulation of Holding Companies and Intercorporate Relations" pp. 628–682.
2. Bonbright, James C., and Gardiner C. Means, *The Holding Company: Its Public Significance and Its Regulation* (New York: McGraw-Hill, 1932), ch. 1, "Significance of the Holding Company," pp. 1–20; ch. 2, "The Holding Company as an Alternative to Other Forms of Combination," pp. 21–54; ch. 3, "Early History of the Holding Company in America," pp. 55–64; ch. 5, "The Public Utility Company–Organization and the Major Systems," pp. 90–148; ch. 6, "The Public Utility Holding Company–Necessity of Regulation," pp. 149–199; ch. 7, "The Public Utility Company–Existing and Proposed Regulation," pp. 200–222.
3. Clemens, Eli Winston, *Economics and Public Utilities* (New York: Appleton-Century-Crofts, 1950), ch. 18, "Federal Regulation," pp. 422–450; ch. 19, "The Regulation of Accounting," pp. 451–463; ch. 20, "Regulation of Securities and Finance," pp. 464–485; ch. 21, "The Problem of the Holding Company," pp. 486–521.
4. Garfield, Paul J., and Wallace F. Lovejoy, *Public Utility Economics* (Englewood Cliffs, N. J.: Prentice-Hall, 1964), ch. 3, "The Development and Scope of Utility Regulation," pp. 29–35; ch. 20, "The Structure and Organization of Utility Industries," pp. 434–469.
5. Glaeser, Martin G., *Public Utilities in American Capitalism* (New York: Macmillan, 1957), ch. 9, "Regulation in the Twentieth Century," pp. 125–154; ch. 11, "The Structure of Public Utility Capitalism," pp. 178–194.
6. Phillips, Charles F., Jr., *The Economics of Regulation,* rev. ed. (Homewood, Ill.: Richard D. Irwin, 1969), ch. 15, "The Electric Power Industry," pp. 537–594.
7. Ripley, William Z., *Main Street and Wall Street* (Boston: Little, Brown, 1927), ch.

10, "More Light: And Power Too!" pp. 276–309; ch. 11, "Public Utilities: Still More About Them," pp. 310–353.

8. Ritchie, Robert F., *Integration of Public Utility Holding Companies*. Michigan Legal Studies (Ann Arbor, Mich.: University of Michigan Law School, 1954), p. 330.
9. Troxel, Emery, *Economics of Public Utilities* (New York: Rinehart, 1947), ch. 5, "Federal Regulation," pp. 89–114; ch. 8, "Corporate Integration," pp. 164–189.

10

Evaluation of the Regulatory Process

Evaluating regulation is an endless task but one which is being constantly undertaken. At any given time, considerable comment and writing on this subject is available. Our approach, therefore, is not to review all the literature evaluating regulation but rather to establish a framework within which current evaluation can be considered.

Basically, two approaches are possible: Evaluation of the idea of regulation itself and evaluation of the regulatory process. The latter is made up of consideration of regulatory agencies and their operations. In addition, some discussion of alternatives to regulation is necessary in order to place the evaluation process in perspective.

THE GOALS OF REGULATION

Why does society regulate the utilities to the degree that it does? Part of the answer has already been noted in the discussion in Part One. That is, utilities are a "halfway house" between society providing its own economic functions collectively through government ownership and allowing individual profit-seeking firms to perform these economic functions under a system of minimum social control. Further, there is a historical legal framework of regulation, developed over time, based on the assumption that the utility type of undertaking must be regulated in the public interest. One could argue that the historical reasons and the legal framework are no longer valid. However, a more fruitful approach is to consider the goals of regulation and evaluate the devices society has used to achieve these goals.

There are at least four goals of regulation: control of monopoly, protection of consumers, substitution for competition, and social allocation. This last goal, social allocation, seems to have two conflicting subgoals, namely, allocation for efficiency and allocation for ecological protection.

CONTROL OF MONOPOLY

Utilities traditionally have been organized in a monopoly form. While some authors say that this has come about because it is a "natural" form for utilities to assume, others say that historical practices like the granting of franchises and limiting entry have encouraged this form.[1]

The term "natural monopoly" suggests that most utility firms operate with a markedly decreasing cost function and have decreasing costs over a wide scale of operations. That is, in the first instance, per unit costs can be lowered considerably if a firm can operate near full capacity. Thus, either lower prices or higher profits can be derived from increases in production up to the limits of capacity. In the long run, economies of large scale seem available to most utilities. Hence, the larger the production unit, the lower the costs per unit of output and the lower the price or the higher the profit. Also, decreasing long-term costs for utilities result from technological progress over time. In all these instances most utilities are able to decrease costs per unit of production.[2]

It is felt that society will be better served by a monopolistic type of organization if such an organization does indeed take advantage of these economies. This principle has long been recognized and has led to social preference for one utility in a given service area. It is further widely believed that utilities move "naturally" toward a monopolistic type of structure if allowed to operate without social controls. This tendency has been recognized in the literature of economics for more than a century,[3] although some object to the use of the term "natural" to characterize this type of market structure.[4]

Controlled entry and operation only by permission of some agency of government are grounded in the concept that duplication of the large capital undertakings of utilities is socially wasteful and that competition among utility firms, which of necessity must use the public streets, is unduly disruptive. Under these circumstances it is logical to limit service to a single seller and thus avoid waste and disruption.[5] Thus, local monopoly has become the predominant form of market structure.

Traditionally, citizens of this country have had a strong preference for an economic system based on competition. While this philosophical preference may be more emotional than economically logical, it is nevertheless very real and exerts a social pressure to conform. Monopoly is considered undesirable as such, and many of our laws are designed to destroy monopoly or discourage monopolistic tendencies. But utilities present a paradox, for monopoly here seems to have desirable aspects in the form of lower costs, less social disruption, and better service; yet this violates our philosophical preference for competition. The answer, of course, has been to establish regulatory controls over monopoly, so as to receive the benefits of monopoly but avoid its disadvantages. In a very general way, this control of monopoly has been the goal of regulation from earliest times.[6]

PROTECTION OF CONSUMERS

Protecting consumers is a somewhat more sophisticated goal of regulation. It goes beyond monopoly control as a substitute for a philosophical preference for competition. Regulation here attempts to prevent specific monopolistic abuses, such as high prices, extraordinary profits, or undue discrimination and inequities among users. To be sure, this goal is also based upon the idea that utilities operate best as monopolies, but its emphasis lies on preventing more or less vaguely agreed-upon abuses which emanate from the monopoly form.

This goal is implicit in the whole idea of a "fair rate of return on a fair value." A utility should be prevented from taking advantage of its monopoly position to exploit consumers; it is within the public interest to limit earnings.[7] Not only will such a limitation prevent a utility from making excessive profits but it should also assure lower prices and less discrimination.

To be sure that this goal of consumer protection is attained, regulators are also charged with approving specific prices or rates. These are to be reasonable and by implication not too high nor discriminatory.[8] Anyone considering the goals or standards established in the legislation on regulation must be struck by the emphasis on protection of the consumer.[9]

The consumer protection goal also involves regulation of the quality of service. Entry control, earnings limitations, and prevention of discrimination historically proved to be incomplete devices for protecting consumers. Low earnings, low prices, and monopolistic market structures often led to poorer services. Thus, in order to fully protect consumers service levels had to be controlled. This control is one of the most difficult, though most essential, tasks of regulation.[10]

Monopoly control and consumer protection are interdependent goals. They overlap and blend into one another, and together they give rise to a third goal: regulation as a substitute for competition.

SUBSTITUTE FOR COMPETITION

Many think of regulation as being a substitute for competition. Starting from the ideal of the competitive marketplace within which firms operate with a limited amount of interference, economists try to set forth the results of such competition. These "competitive goals" are then used as goals of regulation. In a phrase, the aim is to "make the utilities act like competitive firms would act if competition were possible."[11]

Implied in this idea is the goal of controlling monopoly. If utility firms are to be made to act as competitive firms, no monopoly abuses will be allowed. Those espousing this goal do not favor actual competition. The theory recognizes the need for a monopoly type of market structure. It merely says that the goal of regulation is to approximate or simulate a "competitive result." Also implied in this idea is the goal of protection of consumers. Within broad limitations it is felt that competition is one of the best protective devices available to consumers and that among the results of a competitive environment will be good service and the prevention of excessive prices, unusually high earnings, and discriminatory rates. When the goal of regulation is substitution for competition, consumer protection follows naturally.

But the substitute for competition idea goes even further than the previous two goals which are embodied within it. The ideal of competition includes the concept that the economy as a whole possesses a mechanism which leads to some sort of efficient or ideal allocation of resources, both physical and monetary. Economists call this the "Pareto's optimum." By this they mean basically that only the proper amount of resources are used to produce the desired service and that society as a whole would be no better off if the resources committed to one use were shifted to an alternative use. The competitive ideal implies some sort of best resource allocation within the whole of society.[12]

While the ideal of substituting regulation for competition is easy to state, it is extremely difficult to practice. In order to have much effect on utilities regulatory authorities concerned with simulating competitive allocation of resources must have considerable control over investment policies of firms as well as over other inputs, such as labor and materials. Also, the process of choosing between alternative technologies must be very complete in order to truly simulate competition and effectively substitute for the natural marketplace. It is doubtful that regulatory jurisdiction extends this far or that regulatory decisions should replace managerial decisions.[13]

SOCIAL ALLOCATION

In recent times doubts have been expressed concerning the value of simulating competition for the purpose of allocating resources. It has been pointed out that allocation under a competitive market can sometimes be far from perfect. It is felt that competition can be too destructive at times.[14] Some say that the market mechanism must sometimes be supplanted as well as supplemented.[15] There is no general satisfaction with the performance of the unregulated sector of the economy, as our continuing struggle with antitrust problems discloses. Given the shortcomings of the competitive market as an ideal, it has been suggested that the goal of direct social allocation of resources and production be used in lieu of attempts to simulate what we think the competitive market might do.

Several questions arise concerning this. For instance, What methods and devices could be used to achieve direct social allocation? This raises many philosophical questions, which are difficult to answer, including the matter of ownership of utilities and to what particular objectives the proposed social allocation goal should be directed. In a very broad way, two somewhat conflicting objectives can be taken as the goal of social allocation: economic efficiency and ecology.

Economic Efficiency

The traditional goal of social allocation has been economic efficiency; it includes an evaluation of how well utilities have performed under regulatory restraints. While the standard of comparison is not always entirely clear, the implications of such an evaluation are: If utilities have not performed as well under regulatory restraint as they should have or could have, then the regulatory restraint needs to be reformed or changed.

Specific concern over the performance of the regulated sector of the economy is relatively new[16] and seems to be generated mostly by academic writers interested in welfare economics. By and large, these studies concern themselves with growth in productivity of the utility sector,[17] the use or abuse of scarce capital resources,[18] the specific level of prices or rates under control,[19] the regulatory process,[20] and the social costs involved.[21] In general, such studies hold that rates should be as low as possible, allocation of resources should be as close to a social optimum as possible,[22] regulation should be as effective as possible while causing a minimum of social dislocations—in a word, Pareto's optimum.

Ecology Goal

Somewhat opposing the economic efficiency goal is an even newer concern stemming from the so-called ecology movement. Since utilities are so universal in our society, and since they involve elaborate capital structures, they have considerable environmental or ecological effects. Given the projected future growth and development of utilities as a necessary part of future growth in the economy, the allocation of resources within and by utilities promises to have even greater future environmental effects. Those concerned with ecology have suggested that the regulatory process could have as a goal the minimization of adverse ecological effects of utilities.

The concern here is not with lower prices or more efficient resource allocation or even with the regulatory process. Instead, these goals are quite secondary to the goal of decreasing air, water, thermal, visual, and noise pollution. If a choice exists between pollution at a lower price and less pollution at a higher price, people concerned with ecology would, of course, argue for the latter. Economic efficiency would be seen as secondary to ecological considerations.

SUMMARY OF THE GOALS OF REGULATION

There may well be many other goals of regulation.[23] Some may stress one aspect of utilities and some another aspect. However, the four major goals seem to be the traditional one of control of monopoly, the more comprehensive one of protection of the consumer, the goal of regulation as a substitute for competition with its resultant concern with resource allocation, and the goal of direct social allocation itself. All of these goals blend into one another, and none seems to stand alone.

Finally, it may be questioned whether any of these goals can be completely achieved. The utility industry may be too complex and subject to too many forces within too many political jurisdictions to allow regulators complete success in achieving these goals. This does not preclude, however, the discussion of, and establishment of, goals towards which regulation can be aimed. The very fact that ideals are rarely attained is one of the reasons why they remain ideals.

COMMISSIONS AS REGULATORS

Once the goals of regulation are noted, the next logical question would be, Who exercises social regulation to achieve these goals? Viewed historically, the principal responsibility for regulation has devolved upon legislatures, then courts, and currently regulatory commissions. While all three have exercised social regulation more or less concurrently, each has been predominant in the regulatory process at different time periods.

Originally, courts attempted to regulate in the public interest by use of the common law, as noted earlier. However, this early device for regulation was quite ineffective. It will be recalled from the earlier discussion that the case-by-case method was used with the object of restoring the injured party or "making him whole" again. No social goal or concerted idea of regulation in the public interest existed. Individual private interest was paramount. Additional shortcomings of common law regulation have previously been noted.

LEGISLATIVE CONTROL

It was not until the era following the Civil War that conscious social goals for regulation emerged. These goals were principally embodied in the so-called Granger Acts of state legislatures during the late 1860's and early 1870's. Basically, it was the legislature itself which attempted to be the regulator, with prices and conditions of service directly established by state statute.

As noted before, this was the era of judicial noninterference. When the Supreme Court upheld these Granger laws as a proper exercise of the power of the state, it specifically avoided imposing its judgment on the legislature. In *Munn v. Illinois* (1877) the court explicitly stated, "We know that this is a power which may be abused; but that is no argument against its existence. For protection against abuses by the legislatures the people must resort to the polls, not the courts." [24]

Unquestionably, in this situation the legislature was the regulator and established the goals and procedures of regulation. By and large, the goal was the control of monopoly.

JUDICIAL SUPREMACY

From this concept of supremacy of the legislature, the judiciary slowly emerged as the regulator. In 1886 the Court began to have doubts about its position of noninterference when it stated, "This power to regulate is not a power to destroy, and limitation is not the equivalent of confiscation."[25] By 1890 the Court was adopting the idea that rates established by legislatures were subject to judicial review[26] and in 1894 it actually enjoined a state commission from setting rates too low.[27] However, it was not until its celebrated *Smyth v. Ames* decision (1898) that the Court finally stepped in as the regulator of utilities.[28]

The *Smyth v. Ames* decision has been discussed previously and need not be reviewed again. For our purposes here it is sufficient to note that this decision brought the full force of the judiciary into the determination and establishment of the goals of regulation. While state commissions were revived during the early 1900's,[29] their every action was subject to court review and interpretation.

Concurrent with judicial review of the fair value concept, the Court continued to pass upon which firms were "affected with the public interest." This matter also has been previously noted but is mentioned here again to reinforce the idea that the courts were the regulators between 1898 and 1944. This role of defining the scope of regulation as well as determining the results of regulation prompted the late Professor Commons to note that the Supreme Court "occupies the unique position of the first authoritative faculty of political economy in the world's history."[30]

COMMISSION REGULATION

The role of regulator has changed hands notably in recent times. While the courts continue to be final arbiters of what kinds of businesses can be regulated, it is state and federal commissions which are now charged with the actual regulation process. With the *Hope Natural Gas* decision (1944), already mentioned, the courts gave notice that they would limit their interest in utility pricing and performance to consideration of the end result of regulation, not the process itself. While this throws a considerable burden on commissions, it gives them great latitude. Since the *Hope* decision the role of regulator has been held by the various commissions.[31]

This is not to say that commissions can act without fear of review. The courts still stand ready to strike down commission actions under specific circumstances.[32] Similarly, legislatures are responsible generally for the establishment of commissions, their jurisdiction, and the enunciation of standards to be applied.[33]

It is within these broad judicial and legislative frameworks that various administrative commissions operate to put regulation into effect. Commissions determine fair value and find a fair rate of return, approve utility rate schedules with respect to permissible degrees of discrimination, allow operating expenses as part of the pricing process, specify depreciation schedules to be used, impose various service standards on the supplying utilities, pass upon the issuance of securities, issue certificates of public convenience and necessity, monitor utility intercorporate relations–in short, commissions are very active regulators, and they have often been called a fourth arm of government.

CRITICISMS OF COMMISSION REGULATION

Commissions as regulators have been subject to considerable criticism. Some of these criticisms have been briefly noted in previous chapters, but in order to give a more complete understanding of regulation many of these shortcomings should be discussed in more detail. (We do not pretend, however, to present a complete catalog of all the possible criticisms of regulation.)

Basically, criticism of regulation by commissions can be grouped into four categories: shortcomings of procedure, operational deficiencies, distrust of the political environment, and weaknesses of the concept of regulation. Each category possesses several subcategories.

Procedural Shortcomings

One group of criticisms turns on procedural matters. While specific complaints about procedures before a given commission are common, more important are the criticisms of commission procedures in general. These can be summarized as shortcomings due to adversary proceedings, imbalance of power, problems of impartiality, and regulatory lag.

Adversary Proceedings: A commission arrives at its judgments after adversary proceedings, as noted in Chapter 5. Representatives of a utility firm present a case for the desired commission action, and representatives of other groups protest or contend against the firm's position. Other parties may also join in support of the firm. Often the commission staff takes a position. Indeed, the commission itself can start the adversary proceedings on its own order or in the public interest. Regardless of how proceedings are initiated, though, there is almost always a pro and a con, a winner and a loser.

While this may be an effective way to bring out the various special interests of the parties involved, it can be questioned whether adversary proceedings always lead to the best decision. Some commissions have become highly formalized and the "rules of the game" of adversary proceedings may sometimes be used to exclude valid data. Matters may be left unconsidered or thrown out because of some quirk in procedures or because a petitioner has not filed his pleading correctly or within the deadline or in the prescribed form, and so on. The contest can become more a matter of observing the proper "rules of the game" than of making valid economic judgments.

Adversary proceedings tend to be lengthy and expensive. Expert witnesses are hired, substantial legal staffs are involved, sophisticated exhibits of economic data are prepared, detailed engineering studies are commissioned—the whole process is costly. This expense may exclude some parties from being heard. But of more importance, perhaps, is the fact that ultimately consumers pay, in their rates or taxes, for this complicated and highly institutionalized way of considering utility problems. Expenses of appearing before a commission are generally allowed as operating expenses; thus a utility recovers its cost of adversary proceedings whether it wins or loses its point of contention. Commissions are publicly supported; therefore the costs of commission proceedings ultimately appear as part of legislative appropriations.

In adversary proceedings there is always a winner and a loser, but the public always pays either in higher rates or in higher taxes. This is one of the few situations where the consumer does pay regardless of who wins or loses.[34]

Imbalance of Power: Adversary proceedings assume equality between adversaries—or at any rate, no marked inequality. In actual fact, the contending sides are rarely equal. Serious imbalances exist. Utility firms generally command more resources and experts than do protesting groups. In addition, the costs of proceedings can be recovered by utilities in consumers' bills. No such recovery device exists for users of utility services.

But commissions are charged with protecting the public interest. Here again, imbalance of power prevails. By and large, commissions do not have the resources, staffs, or expertise to present an effective battle to utility companies.[35] Although there may be exceptions, it is generally agreed that utility firms possess considerably greater power than either their opponents or commission staffs.[36]

Problems of Impartiality: Can a commission really be impartial? Basically, a commission has three more or less conflicting roles to play: prosecutor, judge, and jury. To some, a commission is administrator, judge, and legislator.[37] Regardless of the particular roles assumed, conflicts will always arise. One of the most frequent criticisms of commissions is their difficulty in remaining impartial while assuming conflicting roles. A commission is asked to do the job of judging a utility's performance while at the same time protecting the interests of the public and of the utility's owners and creditors, all the while maintaining a strictly neutral, unbiased, and fair attitude as a judge in a courtroom might do.[38] The task is probably impossible.

Regulatory Lag: Modern regulation is a time-consuming process. Adversary proceedings are usually drawn-out affairs. Even after all evidence is presented, a commission will often "take under advisement" the economic data and delay a decision for many weeks or even months. Also, a firm typically waits until it can amply demonstrate a poor financial condition before it comes to a commission for relief, and a commission rarely moves to limit the profits of a utility firm until it can show that excessive returns have been earned for several years. Higher than "fair rate of return" earnings for a year, or several years, rarely bring on immediate corrective action. These tendencies to wait until a clear-cut case for higher or lower rates is established, plus the considerable delay in decision-making, are known as regulatory lag.

Even though they themselves contribute greatly to regulatory lag, utility firms are very critical of commission regulation because of this lag. They point out that they are always behind comparable businesses in matters of cost, fair rates of return, and the like. Consumer interest groups are also critical of regulation because of lag. They point out that excessive earnings are not recaptured and that the "water over the dam" theory penalizes consumers.[39] It seems that everyone is unhappy abour regulatory lag, but little is done to correct it.

Regulatory lag can become extreme. In some historic electric power cases, and in a recent F. P. C. gas case, ten years elapsed before final decisions were reached. It should be noted that this is extreme and that many commissions are alert to this problem and attempt to expedite matters as much as possible.

The effects of regulatory lag are hard to analyze. At least one authority suggests that because of regulatory lag, utility firms can enjoy the financial benefits from new technology longer than if they were in a competitive market; hence they can be satisfied with a lower-than-ordinary rate of return for longer periods.[40] In effect, an incentive to be operationally efficient may be inadvertently built into the regulatory process by way of inefficiencies of regulation![41]

Perhaps such a paradox is possible. However, it is most difficult to measure the effect of regulatory lag or adversary proceedings or problems of impartiality or the imbalance of power. About all that can be said is that these procedural shortcomings do exist.

Operational Deficiencies

Another group of criticisms concerns the deficiencies in the operation of commissions. These concern problems of jurisdiction, qualifications of commissioners, inadequate budgets, problems of staff, and the alleged tendency for commissions to pass through predictable life cycles.

Jurisdiction: Commission jurisdiction is not the same in all states. With the exception of the "home rule states,"[42] most states ask their commissions to regulate electricity, gas, water, and telephones. [43] There are some variations among states in this group, but the major variations are in what powers are granted to commissions. Jurisdiction varies considerably. Some commissions have broad powers and discretion to be concerned with almost all utility operations, while others are extremely limited as to the matters that can be considered. Such diversity leads to uneven regulation.

Many states allow commissions to regulate transportation firms. In some instances, states have given jurisdiction to commissions to regulate many businesses other than the traditional local utilities and transportation companies.[44] Given the limited staffs and budgets of most commissions, this broad grant of jurisdiction may detract from the effectiveness of utility regulation just as much as the fact of having limited jurisdiction.

A favorite criticism of commissions is either that they lack proper jurisdiction or that their jurisdiction is so wide that their efforts are ineffective.

Qualifications of Commissioners: Generally few, if any, qualifications for commissioners are specified by law.[45] In thirty-eight states commissioners are appointed; in sixteen, elected by popular vote; and in two states elected by the legislature.[46] Qualifications of commissioners are generally left up to the person appointing them (usually the Governor) or the electorate to decide. This results in vastly different types and backgrounds of commissioners. It is alleged that since the pay of the commissioners is not exceptionally good, and no qualifications are generally established, the type of commissioner appointed or elected is not always the best. A frequent complaint is that commissioners simply do not understand what they are doing and are not qualified to pass judgments on utilities or to protect the public interest.

Budget: When it is considered that the typical consumer pays a considerable portion of his income for power, gas, telephone, water, and other services under commission regulation, adequate support for regulatory commissions should be readily forthcoming. Unfortunately, this is rarely the case. Most commissions operate under very limited budgets.

Actually, there are three ways in which a commission may be financed. The most common is an annual legislative appropriation. The second is charging fees or selling licenses or otherwise charging for specific regulations. The third is use of assessments. These assessments may be either general assessments, typically a small percentage of incomes of regulated firms, or special assessments levied to cover the costs of specific regulatory problems.

Assessments are often favored for four reasons. They remove commissions from complete reliance on general taxation and the whims of legislatures. There is justice in assessing the costs of regulation against the beneficiaries, be they utility stockholders or consumers. Commissions' budgets expand or contract as more or less regulation is undertaken. And finally, if the costs are assessed against a utility, the firm will have an incentive to avoid undue proceedings since it must stand the cost.[47]

To some degree these are valid reasons for favoring assessments. But it must be remembered that even though a firm initially pays the cost of regulation with special assessments, the cost ultimately will appear in the customers' bills. Further, general assessments are really nothing more than poorly disguised taxes.

Estimates of the amount expended on regulation vary, but it is considerable.[48] This has led some critics to question whether commission budgets are not too high, considering the results. This argument, of course, depends on the results of the regulation.

Staff: Good commission staffs are one factor that may offset lack of qualifications of commissioners. Well-trained and well-qualified staff personnel can do much to make regulation effective. It is sometimes said that it is most important to have "experts on tap, not on top." This stresses the need for good general judgment by commissioners and well-grounded expertise by staffs.

Unfortunately, there is evidence that most commission staffs are overworked, undertrained, and poorly paid. Restrictive budgets prevent the broad use of expert consultants. The result seems to be that too few people try to do too many jobs with too few resources.[49]

Commission Life Cycle: In addition to the operational deficiencies already mentioned, it has been observed that commissions tend to vary over time in their application and enthusiasm for the tasks of regulation. According to some critics, commissions progress through a four-period cycle of gestation, youth, maturity, and old age.[50] Gestation includes the events leading to the basic regulatory statute, often marked by scandal, deep public concern with a problem, and the creation of a regulatory body amid controversy over maintaining the *status quo* and agitation for reform. The statute typically is a compromise, and the first few years of the commission's life may be spent in clarifying and testing the basic foundations of regulation.

In the period of youth or growth, the commission is vigorous, although inexperienced. This leads to aggressive controls with a broad view of public responsibility. New issues are likely to be challenged, the commission staff is likely to be highly dedicated and ambitious, and public support is likely to be very high. Aside from limiting interpretations of courts, the commission is likely to achieve its greatest accomplishments during this phase.

Maturity slowly sets in as public support diminishes and political leadership turns to other problems. Controversy fades, commissions adjust to conflicts between parties, and procedures become more settled. A tendency to regulate by formula and routine becomes pronounced and institutionalized. There is a tendency for the commission to identify itself with the regulated industry as it settles down to the workaday tasks of regulation. Finally, old age comes as the commission assumes the role of protector of the industry it is charged with regulating. Attempts to maintain the *status quo* and failure to keep pace with changing economic conditions and technology are prevalent. The commission becomes sluggish and falls behind in its work, and its policies become obsolete.[51]

The Interstate Commerce Commission is usually singled out as an example of this life cycle idea. Perhaps in some instances the idea fits, but many questions have been raised about the theory. One can question that one phase absolutely and necessarily leads to another, or that association with and protection of the firms regulated comes only with maturity, and the like. Nevertheless, the life cycle idea does point to a shortcoming of commission regulation and may help explain other criticisms of the process.

Distrust of the Political Environment

A third set of criticisms revolve around the political processes within which regulation exists. These concern themselves with the politics involved in selecting commissioners, the solving of economic problems by political action, and the recent concept of "consumerism." In general, these criticisms evidence considerable distrust of the political environment of regulation.

Political Selection: As noted previously, commissioners are selected either by appointment or elections. The elective process involves the general electorate in all but two states, where the legislature elects commissioners. Where the appointive process is used, typically the Governor appoints, with confirmation by one of the houses of the legislature.

Considerable debate exists as to which process is superior. There is a tendency for appointed commissioners to be defeated candidates "rewarded" for their efforts by appointment to a commission. Yet this need not be the case, and appointment does allow governors wider choice of qualified persons who might not choose to stand for election. Since appointments must usually be confirmed by one house of the legislature, though, a politically acceptable commissioner is necessary. In the elective states real questions arise in situations where potential or incumbent commissioners campaign for public office on a platform of lower rates which they perhaps cannot deliver, a distressingly familiar tendency on the part of men wishing to be elected by popular vote.

Political Solutions to Economic Problems: One can always criticize regulation by noting its political origins. Regulatory statutes are usually born of political controversy. Commission decisions are often made with an eye to political consequences. Overzealous public support for control of utilities, or just the opposite, public apathy concerning the regulatory task, are both cited by critics of regulation.

While it is true that regulation exists in a political climate, we do live in a political world. As no better way to solve these problems has yet been suggested, the charge of "politics" apparently will be attached to commission regulation for some time.

Consumerism: Recently, considerable popular criticism of commissions has involved the idea that commissions tend to identify with the industry they are supposed to regulate and thereby neglect their task of protecting consumers. In a very general way, this movement has been connected with the name of Ralph Nader, although the same tendency has been pointed out for more than thirty years.[52] As suggested previously, this tendency may come from a confusion as to the goals of regulation as much as from overt political influence by regulated firms.

WEAKNESSES OF THE CONCEPT OF REGULATION

In addition to the shortcomings of commission procedures, operational deficiencies, and distrust of the political environment, critics have concerned themselves with weaknesses of the concept of regulation itself. Basically, they point to five weaknesses of the concept, noting that it is static, that it provides no incentives for efficiency, that it may lead to distortions, that it is based on a mistaken idea of monopoly, and that it is ineffective.

Static Nature of Regulation

It is often pointed out that the concept of regulation is oriented towards the past and does not take the future into account. That is, regulation sees events as they are at the present and gives little consideration to the consequences of its own actions or to events that might occur in the future.[53]

Using the case-by-case method of solving problems as they arise, and ignoring anything not brought to its attention, commission regulation is alleged to operate by formula relations isolated from the real world and with little concern for past experiences or future expectations.[54] In particular, critics allege that commissions ignore elasticity of demand. In changing rates, commissions by their own actions influence future consumption; yet traditionally rate decisions are undertaken with no consideration of demand elasticity. The data weighed are almost solely relevant to past economic relations, and commissions typically are concerned with reducing past wrongs.[55] While some commissions do attempt to practice continuous control of earnings or constant surveillance, these devices can be effective only if a sophisticated and expert staff assists enlightened commissioners operating without severe jurisdictional restrictions. Rarely are all these conditions present. Regulation tends to remain static and negative in its orientation.[56]

Lack of Incentives

A further criticism of regulation is that it does not provide any incentives for regulated firms to be efficient, innovative, dynamic, or technologically up-to-date.[57] If a utility firm should possess these characteristics and thereby increase its profits, the regulatory process takes away these gains. This assumes that regulation is effective and more or less continuous. Regulatory lag may allow a firm to enjoy the fruits of its efficiency for a short time, as noted, but eventually the rewards of efficiency will be taken away. Given this regulatory restriction of incentives, some feel that the utility managers adopt a "what's the use" attitude or fail to be as efficient as they could be.[58]

In spite of this tendency, it is felt by many that utilities are relatively efficient, have kept pace with technological growth, and have increased their productivity. Apparently some of this incentive to efficiency comes not only from regulatory lag but from managerial attitude and the built-in profit orientation of the American businessman. Such things are difficult to measure, so the utilities and the regulatory concepts remain under continuous criticism for this lack of incentive.

Distortions

Extending upon this criticism of lack of incentive, some authors have claimed that negative incentives actually exist and that, given the regulatory structure, an actual distortion in the allocation of resources by utilities exists or will exist. This is known as the Averch-Johnson-Wellisz (or A-J-W) effect.[59]

Briefly, this proposition holds that if the allowable rate of return is greater than the cost of capital but less than would be earned without regulation, a regulated firm will substitute capital for other production factors and operate at an output above minimum costs. Further, the firm will expand in its regulated markets and possibly drive out other, lower-cost competing firms—a clear case of economic misallocation of resources.[60]

This has been extended to include the somewhat older complaint of rate base padding[61] and various managerial preferences for expenses as well as voluntary restraints of profits.[62] Kahn lists eight possible reactions from the A-J-W effect.[63]

Other authors have pointed out the problems with this proposition. Most of these problems turn on the assumption of profit maximization and on the difficulties of finding overwhelming empirical evidence that the A-J-W effect has indeed operated.[64] Much analysis has gone into the possibilities of distortion under regulation. The record is still not clear at this point, but the tentative evaluation by Kahn that the effect has done "more good than harm"[65] seems realistic.

Monopoly Unrealistic

Another group of critics points to the fact that regulation is based on the assumption that utility firms are monopolists, when in fact considerable competition exists in the modern world. It is true that many regulatory concepts seem to assume a monopolistic firm. It is also true that there are all degrees and types of monopoly and competition. Probably neither of these extremes of market structure exists in a pure form.

Utilities compete in many ways. Some compete against one another in certain consumer uses, such as gas and electricity for cooking, water heating, and the like. Another type of competition is for the consumers' dollars, whereby utilities compete with all kinds of businesses. Also, large industrial firms can install their own power or communication systems, and the like; in effect, a regulated versus nonregulated type of competition. There may also be "fuel competition" between utilities and between industrial and regulated users. Other types of competition also exist.

However, the existence of these types and degrees of competition does not always mean that utilities are not monopolistic. Some utility markets are monopolistic, while some have various degrees of competition. But the exclusive service area concept remains, and one firm selling one product in one market is typically all that society allows. In this sense, at least, monopoly remains, and regulation based on this assumption is realistic.

Ineffectiveness of Regulation

Finally, other critics have attempted to measure the effectiveness of regulation. Some of these conclude that regulation has not made a great deal of difference in the past; therefore there is little reason to regulate in the future. Literally, these critics are saying, Why regulate at all, since it does not change anything?[66]

The problem with this approach is that it is extremely difficult to measure the effects of regulation, since it is so widespread in utilities that regulated versus nonregulated comparisons are questionable. The abandonment of regulation because of its alleged ineffectiveness requires more faith in the automatic operation of the market mechanism than many are willing to assume. These critics make a positive contribution, however, by calling attention to the necessity for constant reconsideration of the role of regulation and the alternatives to regulation.

Conclusions on Criticisms of Regulation

The process of regulation and the commissions that supervise it have many shortcomings and have drawn much criticism. This criticism concerns (1) procedural shortcomings, such as adversary proceedings, imbalance of power, problems of impartiality, and regulatory lag; (2) operational deficiencies, such as jurisdiction, qualifications of commissions, budget, staff, and commission life cycle problems; (3) distrust of the political environment, such as political selection of commissioners, political solutions to economic problems, and consumerism; and (4) weaknesses of the concept of regulation, such as its static nature, lack of incentives, possible distortions, unrealistic assumptions of monopoly, and questions of the effectiveness of regulation. All of these points call for an evaluation of the role of regulation and the alternatives to regulation.

ALTERNATIVES TO COMMISSION CONTROL

If all these criticisms have validity, and given the acceptance of the goals of regulation, we should look at alternative methods of achieving these goals. What are the available substitutes for the regulatory process?

Basically three alternatives present themselves. One is reliance on the free market, with an abandonment of regulation. Another is to change the ownership pattern and abandon the idea of allowing private firms to supply utility services. The third alternative is to reform present regulation and aim for more enlightened commission control.

While critics may question the effectiveness of regulation and point out its shortcomings, very few are willing to go all the way toward abandoning regulation. Similarly, the general public gives little evidence of being willing to turn monopoly loose without some restraining devices. The idea of some sort of social control over utilities is deeply ingrained, and the inadequacies of regulation will probably have to become considerably more extreme before much of a concerted movement develops for completely abandoning regulation and relying solely on natural market forces.

The alternative of government ownership is also fraught with problems. While there is considerable support for this alternative, and government ownership has progressed in certain of the utility fields, many philosophical and operational problems remain. Again, there is little evidence that the general public is ready to abandon the traditional role assigned to utilities as a "halfway house" between a relatively free market on the one hand and complete government ownership on the other. This is not to say that some compromise such as "institutional competition,"[67] with a great degree of public ownership in some types of utilities, is not possible. But for now, the built-in bias of the American public against government-supplied services is considerable, and we foresee no mass movement toward public ownership in response to dissatisfaction with regulation. The potential threat of public ownership, of course, may well be as effective as actual public ownership.

The only realistic alternative seems to be continued operation within the existing regulatory system, with efforts toward improving the performance of regulated firms and regulatory commissions.

It is clearly in the interest of all parties to make regulation work. For utility firms, the alternatives of unregulated competition or public ownership certainly are not desirable.[68] For regulatory commissions, greater efficiency, procedural reforms, and greater attention to public needs clearly are preferable. For consumers, more effective and enlightened commission control within the present system offers the greatest hope of protection when the results of the available alternatives are so unclear.

The choice is not easy, and the path to enlightened regulation is steep. However, given the alternatives, it is the only viable choice.[69]

NOTES

1. Both of these positions are reviewed in Alfred E. Kahn, *The Economics of Regulation: Principles and Institutions,* vol. 2, *Institutional Issues* (New York: Wiley, 1971), chs. 1, 4, and 5.
2. The telephone industry may be a possible exception. For a general review of factors of decreasing costs, see Kahn, ch. 5; William Iulo, *Electric Utilities: Cost and Performance* (Pullman, Wash.: Bureau of Economic and Business Research, Washington State University, 1961); William Iulo, "Problems in the Definition and Measurement of Superior Performance," in Harry M. Trebing, ed., *Performance Under Regulation* (East Lansing, Mich.: Institute of Public Utilities, Michigan State University, 1968), pp. 3–19; William H. Dodge, "Productivity

Measures and Performance Evaluation," in Trebing, pp. 20–32; and William R. Hughes, "Short-Run Efficiency and the Organization of the Electric Power Industry," *Quarterly Journal of Economics,* vol. 72, no. 4 (November 1962), pp. 592–612.

3. Paul J. Garfield and Wallace F. Lovejoy, *Public Utility Economics* (Englewood Cliffs, N. J.: Prentice-Hall, 1964), p. 15, observes that John Stuart Mill originally noted this tendency among utilities in 1848.
4. See Horace M. Gray, "The Passing of the Public Utility Concept," *Journal of Land and Public Utility Economics,* vol. 16, no. 1 (February 1940), pp. 8–20, or James R. Nelson, "The Role of Competition in the Regulated Industries," *The Anti-Trust Bulletin,* vol. 11, no. 1 (January 1966), pp. 1–36.
5. See James C. Bonbright, *Principles of Public Utility Rates* (New York: Columbia University Press, 1961), p. 11; Garfield and Lovejoy, p. 16; and Ben W. Lewis, "The Rationale of Regulation," in Harry J. Levin, ed., *Business Organization and Public Policy* (New York: Rinehart, 1958), p. 434.
6. This is verified by several early Supreme Court decisions, in which the existence of monopoly was one of the necessary prerequisites for a business to be "affected with the public interest." See *Munn v. Illinois,* 94 U.S. 113 (1877).
7. This concept is found in many court decisions and economic writings. One of the clearest statements can be found in Glaeser; he notes that the rate of return must be within a "zone of reasonableness," with such a zone being defined as falling between the upper "line of extortion" and the lower "line of confiscation." Martin G. Glaeser, *Public Utilities in American Capitalism* (New York: Macmillan, 1957), p. 284.
8. The standard of "just and reasonable" generally applies to control of the *level* of rates, while the standard of "nondiscrimination" and "not unduly preferential or prejudicial" applies to the *structure* of rates. But these phrases sometimes are interchanged or linked together in law and common usage.
9. Some authors give considerable emphasis to the consumer protection goal. See George J. Stigler, "The Theory of Economic Regulation," *The Bell Journal of Economics and Management Science,* vol. 2, no. 1 (Spring 1971), p. 3; Richard A. Posner, "Taxation By Regulation," *Ibid.,* p. 22; and Charles F. Phillips, Jr., *The Economics of Regulation,* rev. ed. (Homewood, Ill.: Richard D. Irwin, 1969), p. 124.
10. See Kahn, vol. 1, *Economic Principles,* pp. 21–25, and Phillips, pp. 400–438.
11. See Lewis, pp. 437–439, and Bonbright, pp. 48–62.
12. See Walter Adams and Joel R. Dirlam, "Market Structure, Regulation, and Dynamic Change," in Trebing, p. 134, for a quick summary of this allocation problem.
13. For an interesting discussion of the problem of where management can control and where commissions can control (plus a discussion of how much competition to allow between utilities), see James W. McKie, "Regulation and the Free Market: The Problem of Boundaries," *The Bell Journal of Economics and Management Science,* vol. 1, no. 1 (Spring 1970), pp. 6–26.
14. See Kahn, vol. 2, pp. 173–178.
15. See Ben W. Lewis, "Emphasis and Misemphasis in Regulatory Policy," in William G. Shepherd and Thomas G. Gies, eds., *Utility Regulation: New Directions in Theory and Policy* (New York: Random House, 1966), pp. 212–248.
16. See Trebing, p. vii; Shepherd and Gies; and Burton A. Kolb and Otis Lipstreu, eds., *New Concepts and Current Issues in Public Utility Regulation* (Denver: Peerless Publishing Co., 1963).
17. See William G. Shepherd, "Utility Growth and Profits Under Regulation," in Shepherd and Gies, pp. 3–57; William Iulo, "Problems in the Definition and Measurement of Superior Performance"; Dodge; and Max E. Fletcher, Charles Dibee, and Gilbert L. Gifford (three separate papers), "Functions of Profits in Public Service Industries," in Kolb and Lipstreu, pp. 154–170.
18. For examples, see James R. Nelson, "Pricing and Resource Allocation in the Public Utility Sector," in Shepherd and Gies, pp. 58–87, and Harold H. Wein, "Fair Rate of Return and Incentives–Some General Considerations," in Trebing, pp. 39–67.
19. See Alfred E. Kahn, "Inducement to Superior Performance: Price," in Trebing, pp. 88–102, and Kahn, *The Economics of Regulation,* vol. 1, chs. 3 and 4.
20. See Lewis, "Emphasis and Misemphasis in Regulatory Policy"; Roger C. Cramton, "The Effec-

tiveness of Economic Regulation–A Legal View," in Shepherd and Gies, pp. 249–263; Mark S. Massel, "The Regulatory Process and Public Utility Performance," in Trebing, pp. 113–127; Adams and Dirlam, pp. 131–144; and Martin T. Farris and Reuben A. Zubrow (two separate papers), "A Critical Appraisal of the Traditional Approach to Regulation of Public Service Industries," in Kolb and Lipstreu, pp. 191–218.

21. See Fred M. Westfield, "Methodology of Evaluating Regulation," *American Economic Review,* vol. LXI, no. 2 (May 1971), pp. 211–217; Boyd L. Nelson, "Costs and Benefits of Regulating Communications," *Ibid.,* pp. 218–225; and Ann F. Friedlaender, "The Social Costs of Regulating Railroads," *Ibid.,* pp. 226–234.
22. No more resources should be committed to utilities in a resource-scarce economy than are necessary to produce the desired level of service.
23. See Adams and Dirlam, pp. 131–144, for an alternative set of four "models of regulation," namely competition, static regulation, static regulation cum competition, and dynamic regulation.
24. See 94 U.S. 113, 134.
25. *Stone v. Farmers' Loan and Trust Company,* 116 U.S. 307, 331.
26. *Chicago, Milwaukee and St. Paul Railway v. Minnesota,* 134 U.S. 418, 456–457.
27. *Reagan v. Farmers' Loan and Trust Company,* 154 U.S. 362, 411.
28. See 169 U.S. 466.
29. The history of the establishment of state commissions is graphically illustrated by the statement that two thirds of the states had commissions by 1915 and three fourths by 1922. Concerning the date of establishment of commissions with jurisdiction over electric power, by decades, one article notes: Before 1910, six states; 1910–1920, twenty-nine states; 1920–1930, one state; 1930–1940, three states; 1940–1950, two states; 1950–1960, two states. See George J. Stigler and Claire Friedland, "What Can Regulators Regulate? The Case of Electricity," *The Journal of Law and Economics,* vol. 5, no. 1 (October 1962), pp. 1–16.
30. John R. Commons, *Legal Foundations of Capitalism* (New York: Macmillan, 1924), p. 7.
31. See Farris, p. 194.
32. For a concise discussion of the topic of judicial review, including the famous "Ben Avon Rule," see Garfield and Lovejoy, pp. 40–43.
33. See Eli Winston Clemens, *Economics and Public Utilities* (New York: Appleton-Century-Crofts, 1950), p. 56.
34. See Shepherd, "Utility Growth and Profits Under Regulation," p. 28.
35. For a popularized discussion of this point, see Lee Metcalf and Vic Reinemer, *Overcharge* (New York: David McKay Co., 1967), ch. 3. Also see Harry M. Trebing, "What's Wrong With Commission Regulation?" *Public Utilities Fortnightly,* vol. 65, no. 10 (May 12, 1960), pp. 660–670.
36. For many years the idea of a consumers' counsel has been discussed as an answer to this imbalance. Glaeser (p. 253) traces this movement to 1930. Also, note various issues of the *Congressional Record* since 1967 for efforts by Senator Metcalf to establish a consumers' counsel.
37. Newton W. Minow, former chairman of the Federal Power Commission, is quoted as saying: "I do not believe it is possible to be a good judge on Monday and Tuesday, a good legislator on Wednesday and Thursday, and a good administrator on Friday." See "Remarkable Remarks," *Public Utilities Fortnightly,* vol. 72, no. 12 (December 5, 1963), p. 11.
38. Phillips, pp. 113–114, has a good summary of this point.
39. Because of administrative difficulties in determining who should receive recaptured excessive earnings, commissions often consider past excessive earnings not subject to recapture. See Metcalf and Reinemer, pp. 36–41.
40. Bonbright, pp. 261–262.
41. See Wein, pp. 61–64.
42. Generally considered as Minnesota, Nebraska, South Dakota, and Texas.
43. Fifty states regulate telephone companies, forty-eight regulate gas utilities, forty-eight regulate water companies, and forty-seven regulate electric power utilities. See Federal Power Commission, *Federal and State Commission Jurisdiction and Regulation, Electric, Gas and Telephone Utilities, 1967* (Washington, D.C.: Government Printing Office, 1968).

44. The list of businesses regulated by commissions often includes express companies, warehouses, toll bridges, ferries, sleeping car companies, sewage systems, grain elevators, cotton gins, wharves, turnpikes, refuse collectors, port districts, coal slurry pipelines, CATV systems, and other undertakings.
45. Phillips, p. 96, states that only five states have specified educational or professional requirements for commissioners.
46. Several states have more than one commission which is concerned with utilities.
47. Clemens, p. 414.
48. Phillips, pp. 100 and 104, estimates that states spent $65 million during 1967 but notes that three fourths of that figure was spent by seventeen agencies, leaving an average of $403,000 annually for the remaining thirty-nine commissions. Federal commission budgets were $87 million during the same year.
49. Compare Phillips, p. 96.
50. For a detailed analysis of this point, see Marver H. Bernstein, *Regulating Business By Independent Commission* (Princeton, N.J.: Princeton University Press, 1955), ch. 3.
51. *Ibid.*, pp. 94–95.
52. See Gray. Bernstein also included this in his life cycle analysis during the 1950's. There are still other examples.
53. In their four models of regulation, Adams and Dirlam label "static regulation" as the "traditional regulatory model" and suggest that its operation is "boringly familiar."
54. See Massel.
55. See Emery Troxel, *Economics of Public Utilities* (New York: Rinehart, 1947), p. 231.
56. See Trebing, "What's Wrong With Commission Regulation?"
57. There has been wide concern with this point. For examples, see Wein; Iulo, "Problems in the Definition and Measurement of Superior Performance"; Dodge; Harry M. Trebing, "Toward an Incentive System of Regulation," *Public Utilities Fortnightly,* vol. 72, no. 2 (July 18, 1963), pp. 22, 23; and Shepherd, "Utility Growth and Profits Under Regulation," among many others.
58. See Trebing, "Toward an Incentive System of Regulation," p. 36, for a confirming quotation from a telephone company official.
59. The original work on this was published in Harvey Averch and L. L. Johnson, "Behavior of the Firm Under Regulatory Constraint," *American Economic Review,* vol. 52, no. 5 (December 1962), pp. 1052–1069, and S. H. Wellisz, "Regulation of Natural Gas Pipeline Companies: An Economic Analysis," *Journal of Political Economy,* vol. 71, no. 1 (February 1963), pp. 30–43. Kahn, *The Economics of Regulation,* vol. 2, pp. 49–59 and 106–107, carefully reviews this argument and its literature.
60. See Averch and Johnson, pp. 1052–1053.
61. See Gordon R. Corey, "The Averch and Johnson Proposition: A Critical Analysis," *The Bell Journal of Economics and Management Science,* vol. 2, no. 1 (Spring 1971), pp. 359–362, for a history of the idea of distortion of the rate base.
62. See Milton Z. Kafoglis, "Output of the Restrained Firm," *American Economic Review,* vol. 59, no. 4 (September 1969), pp. 583–589.
63. These are lack of consideration of peak load and marginal cost pricing; willingness to maintain excess standby capacity; resistance to regional planning and power pooling; resistance to introduction of capital-saving technology; reluctance to lease; excessively high standards of reliability; tendency to bargain less hard in purchasing; and tendency to reach out for additional business at a loss. See Kahn, *The Economics of Regulation,* vol. 2, pp. 53–54.
64. See Irwin M. Stelzer, "Rate Base Regulation and Some Alternatives," *Public Utilities Fortnightly,* vol. 84, no. 7 (September 25, 1969), pp. 17–25, for a good review. Kafoglis is particularly good on the assumptions of profit maximization. The assumptions of the A-J-W discussion are well reviewed in William J. Baumol and Alvin K. Klevorick, "Input Choices and Rate-of-Return Regulation: An Overview of the Discussion," *The Bell Journal of Economics and Management Science,* vol. 1, no. 2 (Autumn 1970), pp. 162–190, and in Alvin K. Klevorick, "The Optimal Fair Rate of Return," *Ibid.*, vol. 2, no. 1 (Spring 1971), pp. 122–153.
65. Kahn, *The Economics of Regulation,* vol. 2, pp. 50 and 107.

66. This group includes representatives of the "Chicago School" of economists, which places great reliance on the natural market mechanism to solve most problems. See Stigler and Friedland, and Harold Demetz, "Why Regulate Utilities?" *The Journal of Law and Economics,* vol. 11, no. 1 (April 1968), pp. 1, 3. For some contrary evidence, see Roy J. Sampson, "Comparative Performance of Electric Utilities Under State and Under Local Rate Regulation," *Land Economics,* vol. 34, no. 2 (May 1958), pp. 174–177.
67. See Walter Adams and Horace M. Gray, *Monopoly in America* (New York: Macmillan, 1955), ch. 3.
68. See Lewis, "Emphasis and Misemphasis in Regulatory Policy."
69. Phillips, pp. 720–736, discusses this as "A Continuing Challenge," while Kahn, *The Economics of Regulation,* vol. 2, characterizes it as "The Choice Among Imperfect Systems."

ADDITIONAL READINGS

1. Bernstein, Marver H., *Regulating Business by Independent Commission* (Princeton, N.J.: Princeton University Press, 1955).
2. Glaeser, Martin G., *Public Utilities in American Capitalism* (New York: Macmillan, 1957), ch. 34, "A Social Balance Sheet of Public Utility Economics," pp. 587–607.
3. Kahn, Alfred E., *The Economics of Regulation: Principles and Institutions,* vol. 2, *Institutional Issues* (New York: Wiley, 1971), ch. 1, "Monopoly and Protectionism," pp. 1–46; ch. 2, "Incentives and Distortions," pp. 47–94; ch. 3, "Positive Influences on Public Utility Performance," pp. 95–112; ch. 7, "The Institution of Regulated Monopoly: Reprise," pp. 324-329.
4. Krislov, Samuel, and Lloyd D. Musolf, *The Politics of Regulation: A Reader* (Boston: Houghton Mifflin, 1964).
5. MacAvoy, Paul W., "The Effectiveness of the Federal Power Commission," *The Bell Journal of Economics and Management Science,* vol. 1, no. 2 (Autumn 1970), pp. 271-303.
6. Phillips, Charles F., Jr., *The Economics of Regulation,* rev. ed. (Homewood, Ill.: Richard D. Irwin, 1969), ch. 4, "The Independent Regulatory Commission," pp. 83–119; ch. 5, "The Goals, Task, Phases and Procedure of Regulation," pp. 123–141; ch. 18, "An Appraisal of Regulation," pp. 691-726.
7. Shepherd, William G., and Thomas G. Gies, eds., *Utility Regulation: New Directions in Theory and Policy* (New York: Random House, 1966).
8. Stelzer, Irwin M., "Rate Base Regulation and Some Alternatives," *Public Utilities Fortnightly,* vol. 84, no. 7 (September 25, 1969), pp. 17–25.
9. Trebing, Harry, M., ed., *Performance Under Regulation* (East Lansing, Mich.: Institute of Public Utilities, Michigan State University, 1968).
10. Trebing, Harry M., "What's Wrong With Commission Regulation?" *Public Utilities Fortnightly,* vol. 65, no. 10 (May 12, 1960), pp. 660–670 (part I); vol. 65, no. 11 (May 26, 1960), pp. 738–750 (part II).
11. Williamson, Oliver E., "Administrative Controls and Regulatory Behavior," in Harry M. Trebing, ed., *Essays on Public Utility Pricing and Regulation.* M. S. U. Public Utilities Studies (East Lansing, Mich.: Institute of Public Utilities, Michigan State University, 1971), pp. 411–438, with "Comments" by Henry M. Boettinger, pp. 439–448, and Leland L. Johnson, pp. 449–454.

Part Three

The Management of Privately Owned Utilities

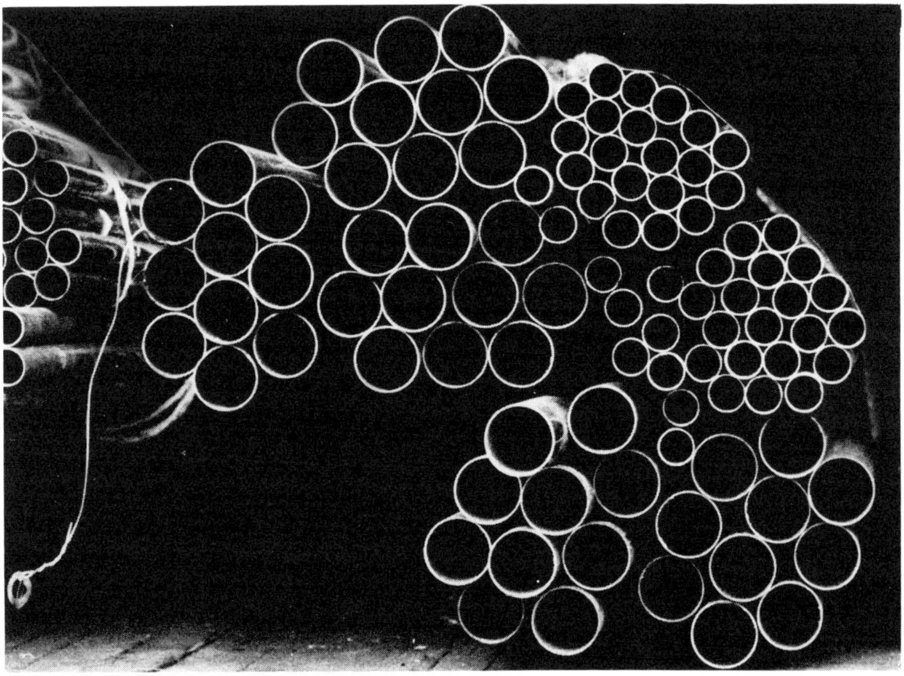

11

General Utility Management and Organization Principles

In Part Two of this book the regulation of privately owned utilities was discussed. Emphasis was upon what regulation currently exists and why and how it came about. Without a thorough grounding in these matters, the reader would be handicapped in understanding utility management, which must deal with regulatory constraints in making decisions. Fortunately, the general principles of existing regulation are reasonably straightforward and can be grasped without undue difficulty, although the details and boundaries of regulation may be less easily understood. Further, it can be assumed, based upon past experience, that these principles usually change in an evolutionary rather than a revolutionary pattern.

Any discussion of the process of management itself, though, must be mostly theoretical rather than descriptive, because universally accepted principles of management still are not firmly established. That is, in discussing management, it is necessary to place more emphasis upon "what ought to be" or "what could be" than upon "what is." Management must operate in an economic and social environment that increasingly imposes extralegal environmental constraints upon it. ("Environment," as discussed in this chapter, refers to institutional rather than to physical surroundings.) This is particularly true for public utility management.

This chapter deals with some of the general functions and problems of the management of privately owned utilities. The immediately following five chapters treat several important and highly specialized management functions in more detail.

We do not propose to engage in the fruitless debate as to whether management is an art or a science—perhaps it is a combination of both. Nor do we propose to discuss in detail the basic principles of organization and management in general. Those desiring more background in these matters will find an ample and growing literature readily available for reference.[1] For our present purposes a brief summary of the nature and functions of management, followed by consideration of management's institutional environment and its responsibilities and how these affect its processes, is sufficient.

THE NATURE AND FUNCTIONS OF MANAGEMENT

The primary social function of any business, whether nonregulated or regulated, is to provide something, goods or services, that the public desires at prices the public is able and willing to pay. All management efforts must be directed toward this aim.

Business is not primarily for the benefit of its owners, managers, employees, financiers, or suppliers. Certainly all these groups, and others, do have legitimate economic, legal, or moral interests in a business, but these interests are subservient to overall customer and social interests.

One of the major problems of management, then, is to operate the business in such a way that conflicts between these various interests are minimized. In other words, compromises must be made to protect the interests of all those concerned in any way with the organization insofar as possible without sacrificing the dominant social or customer interest. This is accomplished by adopting appropriate business strategy and tactics.

MANAGEMENT STRATEGY AND TACTICS

Management, whether of nonregulated or regulated businesses (or of public enterprises, for that matter), operates at two levels.[2] Strategy is established at the formulative level, while tactics, hopefully consistent with this strategy, are employed at the administrative level. Formulators in privately owned corporations are corporate boards of directors, directly responsible to stockholders, while administrators are corporate officials, professional managers, appointed by and directly responsible to their boards of directors (or, in the case of lower level administrators, appointed by and responsible to higher level administrators).

At the formulative level management's functions are (1) to establish overall goals or objectives of the organization, and (2) to establish general policies designed to meet these goals. The administrative or tactical function includes the four processes of (1) forecasting future needs of the organization, based on forecasted customer demands; (2) making plans to meet these needs; (3) acquiring and organizing the necessary resources (financial, human, and physical) to carry out these plans; and (4) the actual operation or supervision of these resources. This last administrative function, of course, includes constant checking to assure that the best possible use is being made of existing resources and investigating the possibilities of obtaining even better performance by varying the resource mix.

These two levels of management, formulative and administrative, call for quite different types of managerial knowledge, viewpoints, and skills. One is not necessarily of greater or lesser importance or higher or lower than the other. It takes both to do the job. Administration is professional management. Goal and policy formulation, on the other hand, is based primarily on a good perspective of the general social and economic environment and a feel for the pulse of the corporate stockholder. Administrators may have formulative abilities (in fact, most corporate formulators are current or former administrators), and formulators may have administrative abilities, but their functions are separate.

The formulation of good strategy requires good communication with tacticians. That is, the viewpoints of those who are going to be on the firing line, actually doing the job, must be sought and considered carefully. Similarly, tacticians must understand and conform to the prevailing strategy. This is why the top professional management of a firm usually sits on the corporate board of directors.

But the requirements of good communication and close cooperation between the formulative and administrative levels of management do not imply that the responsibilities of these two separate groups should be overlapped or intermingled. Formulators should formulate and administrators should administer. Those preparing business strategy cannot dictate tactics any more than those preparing global military strategy can control the details of military operations on a battlefield thousands of miles away. If tacticians do not perform properly, they should be replaced.

Similarly, the immediate battlefield viewpoint of the tactician, although it may be important, is not in itself sufficient for the formulation of strategy. This viewpoint is only one of many which must be weighed along with others. If the tactician cannot conform to the prevailing strategy, or is unwilling to do so, and if he cannot persuade the formulators to modify strategy, he should resign from his position.

WHAT MANAGERS MANAGE

Simply stated, in a broad sense, managers manage people. Or perhaps more accurately, managers provide the conditions and motivations under which people manage themselves in the process of manipulating financial and physical resources to achieve the goals of an organization. Financial and physical resources by themselves produce nothing. At the lower levels managers may be primarily technologists or specialists in some field, like engineering or accounting. As managers progress up the administrative ladder, however, specialization usually becomes less important in comparison to the generalized skills necessary for dealing with people and adapting to a broader and ever-changing environment. One might say that a top manager specializes in being a generalist.

In many respects, managerial skills, as opposed to technological or specialized skills, are readily transferable from one type of organization or industry to another. At least at the higher levels management is management, whether it is applied in a steel company, a regulated public utility, an educational institution, a government agency, or some other form of organization. There are differences in the details of management, however, because of the different institutional environments within which different organizations operate. An organization's environment imposes limitations or constraints upon what it can do. These constraints affect both the formulative and administrative levels of management; thus it is essential that managers at all levels understand their environmental limitations.

THE UTILITY MANAGER'S INSTITUTIONAL ENVIRONMENT

Our society, in order to facilitate the balancing of conflicting social and private interests, has provided for a variety of conditions under which economic activities can be undertaken. At one end of a range we have privately owned nonregulated businesses —that is, nonregulated in the economic sense, although all privately owned businesses are, of course, subject to various general laws. Proceeding along the range, we find other types of businesses, such as banks and insurance companies, that are subject to varying degrees of special economic regulation. The most complete form of economic regulation is that applied to privately owned public utilities.[3]

Law requires that the conduct of regulated businesses differ from that of the nonregulated in many respects, and public opinion expects different conduct in still other matters. These diverse external environmental constraints may or may not create more difficult managerial problems for public utility managers than for managers of nonregulated businesses, but at least they create some different types of problems. Also, the external environment creates some problems in utility internal environments.

THE EXTERNAL ENVIRONMENT

Perhaps the four most important external environmental constraints on public utility management are, in order of importance, profits, regulatory laws, general laws, and public opinion. The managements of nonregulated businesses, of course, are subject to all these constraints except regulatory laws, but some of them apply to a lesser degree for nonregulated than for regulated businesses. Also, since utilities have more constraints, and more rigid ones, than nonregulated firms, there is a greater likelihood that one constraint will conflict with another. The profits constraint, particularly, is likely to conflict with other regulatory limitations or with public opinion constraints in utility management.

Profits Constraint

Although profits cannot be called a social goal insofar as any particular business or industry is concerned, certainly profits are the predominant private goal and motive for a privately owned business, whether regulated or nonregulated. In a sense, too, profits can be called a major constraint because no privately owned business can indefinitely maintain or attract the capital resources necessary to continue its services or to expand or improve its services without profits.[4]

The economic environment, in other words, demands that a privately owned business be profitable if it is to survive, whereas the broader social environment may or may not demand that a particular firm or industry survive or expand. If society demands that a business be continued, obviously social goals and private profit goals are not in conflict.[5] If a business serves no useful social purpose, on the other hand, its private profit goals are clearly inconsistent with social goals. Such undesired businesses eventually expire, either because of outright prohibitory or restrictive laws or because of lack of profits.[6]

A nonregulated business, though, may build up reserves out of excess profits (that is, profits higher than necessary to maintain the business and satisfy dividend recipients) during good years sufficient to carry it through a series of several lean years or sufficient to expand its operations if this seems desirable. A regulated utility is usually not permitted to build a substantial reserve cushion; thus, either during periods of adversity or in case of contemplated expansion, its financial problems may differ from those of a nonregulated firm.

Legal Constraints

Profit-making, although necessary, is only one of several conditions essential for success in the modern business world. Every business, whether or not regulated as a public utility, must conform to various general laws enacted by society as a whole. These general laws, all of which limit managerial freedom in some way, typically impose equivalent kinds and degrees of constraints upon nonregulated and regulated businesses. In some instances, regulated businesses are actually exempt from certain kinds of general laws applicable to other businesses, but the managerial freedom gained by such exemptions is usually more than offset by specific regulatory laws which do not apply to businesses in general.

In short, with regard to legal constraints, utility businesses operate in a more restrictive environment than do most other businesses. In addition to the general laws to which all must conform, the nature of which is beyond the scope of this discussion, utilities must conform to many special regulatory limitations or requirements on such matters as profits, pricing, operating rights, service performance, financing, and the like. Many of these regulatory limitations were discussed in Part Two of this book.

As indicated, one type of regulatory constraint may even conflict with another. For example, utilities are required to provide their services at reasonable rates, but they also are required to provide adequate and continuous services. This can create problems in employer-employee relations. Obviously, a firm may not be able to furnish adequate and continuous services if its employees engage in a prolonged strike. But if wages and worker benefits must be increased substantially to avoid a strike and consequent service disruptions, the resulting decrease in profit prospects may call for higher rates, thus bringing objections from customers and resistance from regulatory commissions. Utility managers clearly have quite different problems in their employer-employee relations than do managers of nonregulated firms.

Although existing labor legislation is designed to minimize work stoppages in the utility industries, and regulatory processes supposedly provide for passing enough of necessary operating cost increases along to customers to prevent unreasonably low profits, this machinery does not always work perfectly. Fortunately, serious strikes in utility firms are rare, but they do occur. That more strikes do not occur is perhaps an indication that utility managers are adept in navigating courses between the constraints of profits or price regulations on the one side and service requirements on the other.

Public Opinion Constraint

Public opinion certainly has been considered seriously by most or all privately owned businesses during recent decades. This constraint, though, appears to be much more important for utility managers than for managers of most other types of businesses.

Managers of privately owned utilities are quite aware of the potential threats of public ownership, public competition, loss or cancellation of franchises, or the enactment of more stringent regulatory legislation (or perhaps more stringent enforcement of existing legislation). Also, the actions of utilities are often more immediately visible to the general public than are the actions of many other types of businesses. Thus, utility managers are by necessity very sensitive to public opinion.[7]

Yielding to the pressures of public opinion, however necessary or desirable this may be, is often costly and thus conflicts with the need to maintain adequate profits (or alternatively, for going through the regulatory process to obtain permission to establish higher rates). Even if public opinion is placated by conforming to various costly standards that society considers desirable, customers may be alienated if the utility is thereby forced to ask for higher rates in order to maintain adequate profits.

As the nation becomes more densely populated, more industrialized, more urbanized, and more affluent, the demand for utility services increases, but so do social desires for the beauties and amenities of "unspoiled" nature. Scenic areas must be preserved for present and future enjoyment. Telephone and electric firms are often pressured to place their wires and cables underground rather than overhead. Hydroelectric dams in some parts of the country must have fish ladders for migratory fish. The public may expect that lakes behind dams have boating, picnic, or other recreation facilities with suitable access roads. Smoke from coal-burning electric generating plants must be curtailed, and atomic generating plants must not discharge an excessive amount of water vapor into the air or too much hot water into streams. Decorative or concealing shubbery must be placed around certain kinds of plant facilities.

Utilities have long been looked upon as important financial contributors to various worthy causes, and their managers have been expected to play active roles in organizations concerned with community progress, charitable drives, and the like. More recently, emphasis on the private business training and employment of persons from the disadvantaged or hard-core poverty group, particularly racial minorities, has placed pressures on utilities as well as on other businesses. In a sense, social pressures now require that employee selection become more of a "screening in" than a "screening out" process insofar as minority groups are concerned.

All these and similar activities which society as a whole, probably including most utility managers, considers desirable, increase the operating costs of the firms involved. This, of course, decreases profits unless rates are increased correspondingly. This situation is not unique to utilities, of course, but because of the quasi-public nature and high public visibility of utilities, plus their peculiar susceptibility to the pressures of public opinion and their rate or profits regulation, the problem is somewhat different in degree from that faced by nonregulated businesses.

Clearly, the free-wheeling days of almost unlimited entrepreneurial or managerial freedom and flexibility are only a historical memory. In addition to outright legal restrictions on various kinds of activities, every business is expected to be a good citizen with a well-developed social conscience. But more legal restrictions are imposed on utilities, and more social consciousness is expected of them even in areas not actually covered by law, than is generally true for nonregulated businesses. This different external environment is necessarily reflected in the internal or intraorganizational environment and problems of a utility company.

THE INTERNAL ENVIRONMENT

One can easily see that a firm's external environment may have an important influence on its internal organizational structure, the kinds of people (in terms of backgrounds and interests) included among its personnel, and the kinds of activities in which its personnel engage. For example, a regulated utility might be expected to have some major division within its organization specializing in regulatory matters. This would require a staff of attorneys, cost analysts, and similar specialists. Similarly, public relations work might be expected to be relatively important among firms particularly sensitive to public opinion, and employee relations work, among firms who are expected to provide continuous and adequate services at publicly regulated reasonable rates. Conversely, it might be expected that nonregulated businesses, operating in less restrictive external environments, would have fewer needs for organizational and staffing patterns designed to deal with the particular kinds of constraints that weigh most heavily on utilities.

More managerial and other personnel resources of utilities must be devoted to problems arising out of legal constraints and public expectations than would be necessary if these constraints were less severe. This means either that less attention is given to other types of problems or that managerial and other personnel resources are greater than would otherwise be necessary. In either case, the costs of providing a given quantity and quality of utility services are higher than they would otherwise be. In other words, the social benefits resulting from the peculiar environmental constraints imposed on privately owned utilities, however worthwhile they may be, are achieved only by some loss of economic efficiency.

Although supporting evidence is scanty, it appears likely that external constraints, in addition to dictating a different type of personnel mix, typically lead to trade-offs in which more total resources are used and less attention given to other kinds of problems than would be true in a less restrictive environment. We are not suggesting that this is necessarily undesirable. Rather, we are simply emphasizing that social benefits cannot be obtained without cost and that a firm's internal organization cannot be considered completely apart from its surrounding conditions.

The external environment of regulated utilities has also given rise to an image which, although inaccurate, in our opinion, creates potentially serious internal problems for utilities. This is an image that we have often noted among those whom we have considered to be the best potential managerial material in our university classes—a conception of utilities as staid, conservative, highly regulated (frustratingly so), guaranteed-income, by-the-book organizations, providing little opportunity or reward for creative managerial talent and initiative.

Most able and dynamic individuals, interested in fully utilizing their abilities and in receiving recognition, promotion, and other rewards commensurate with their performances, are not attracted by such an image. Instead, those most interested in stability and job security with a reasonably adequate but never large income, those who are disinclined to rock the boat—that is, the picture (often wrong also) of the typical civil service employee—are most likely to gravitate toward public utilities.

As indicated, we feel that this image is incorrect and that utilities have as much need, room, and opportunity for aggressive and creative managers as do other types of business. Actually, utility environmental constraints would appear to offer even more challenges and opportunities for managerial ingenuity than are found in most other industries. A race over an obstacle course can be just as interesting, both to participants and viewers, as a race over an unobstructed track.

The histories of past and present successful utility managers demonstrate that opportunities and rewards exist in this field. (One wonders how these people found their way into utility management. Perhaps the image was not as fixed during earlier years, or perhaps alternative opportunities in other fields did not appear as abundant as they do today.) But unless the present stereotyped utility image is replaced by a more realistic and appealing one, it is quite likely that the quality of utility management will not be maintained and that in the future the utility industry will come to resemble the present image of it.

This threatened deterioration of the quality of the next generation of utility managers should be an important concern of present utility top management. The personnel officer recruiting on university campuses, often looking for specialists to fill particular vacancies, can select from among those who present themselves for employment interviews, but he cannot get the message across to the large number of potentially excellent managers who, through disinterest attributable to inadequate or incorrect information, fail to schedule interviews with him. Unfortunately, with a few notable exceptions, utility top managements have not particularly concerned themselves with the recruitment of able successors. Insofar as this is true, they have been neglecting one of their most important managerial responsibilities.

MANAGERIAL RESPONSIBILITIES AND PROBLEMS

Because of the difference in institutional environments, specific managerial responsibilities may be handled differently in utility than in nonutility businesses, but these differences are in degree or emphasis rather than in kind. Even within the utility industries, as in other kinds of industries, such differences in degree exist. But in general, managerial responsibilities in any privately owned business are the same.

Management's responsibilities are to its customers, to society in general, and to those directly or indirectly affiliated with the business. A useful economic function must be performed by providing goods or services at prices that customers are willing and able to pay. The business must be operated in conformity with existing laws and extralegal social values or constraints. Finally, the interests of those who depend on the business for incomes and employment must be served.

An overriding management responsibility, then, is to make every effort to see that the firm remains viable; that is, that it survives and that its customers and affiliates receive benefits from it at least commensurate with developments in technology, the "state of the art," and economic growth.

Management meets this primary responsibility in four general ways: (1) Conditions are established under which the ordinary operations of the firm are carried out efficiently. (Several of these operations are discussed specifically in Chapters 12 through 16.) (2) Management tries to secure its own succession. (3) Management attempts to protect the firm from the risks and hazards inherent in change and the passage of time. (4) Management seeks to provide for orderly economic growth in the context of ever-changing environmental conditions. The last three of these processes are worthy of additional comments at this point.

MANAGERIAL SUCCESSION

Good management is perhaps the most valuable asset and scarcest resource that any firm has. Not only must this resource be used wisely today, but if the firm is to remain viable, it must be replenished continually. Present management must provide the conditions under which future good management will be available when it is needed. This involves both the selection and the in-house development of future managers and is a proper concern of top management.

Future managers may be recruited from university campuses or hired away from other organizations. Management development may take any one or any combination of a variety of forms, including formal general or specific university programs on a full-time or part-time basis, company education courses, home study, and attendance at seminars and trade association meetings, as well as lateral or vertical moves within the organization.

There seems to be no one best method of recruiting and developing future managers. Various trade-offs between alternative methods may be made, depending upon the firm's needs and the amount of resources it has available for these purposes. Almost everyone who has been involved with this process, however, would agree that several basic principles must be followed to obtain the best results in management development programs.

Potential future managers should be allowed and encouraged to extend themselves as much as possible, even at the risk of making mistakes. Excellent performers should not be held back by organizational inertia or seniority rules. Achievement should be recognized when it occurs. When one goal is reached, the next should be clearly in sight. And finally, top management should take a personal interest in the systematic development of its successors. The survival and prosperity of the firm, insofar as it depends on a continuous stream of high-quality managers, is too important to be left entirely in the hands of training officers or the immediate supervisors of young employees.

PROTECTION AGAINST RISKS

Protection against physical risks, such as the loss of assets by fire, natural disasters, theft, and similar occurrences, is a technical matter, within the province of insurance specialists operating under general management guidelines. Time and change, however, inevitably bring more serious risks of a kind that cannot be covered by insurance. These uninsurable business risks, which may limit a firm's profitability or cause its failure, must be foreseen and offset insofar as possible by top management.

History does not support the common assumption that utilities are a low-risk form of economic activity. Nineteenth-century privately owned canals, steamboats, and toll roads are no more. Privately owned urban transit that still exists is barely surviving. Railroad securities are no longer considered blue-chip issues. In short, technological change can easily make obsolete billions of dollars of investment. The impact of an inexpensive and simple solar battery or some such "science fiction" device might, for example, be devastating to the present electric and gas utility industries. And those old enough to remember the Buck Rogers comic strips know that "science fiction" has a tendency to become scientific reality.

Utility investments are typically large. Utility assets have a long life with low capital turnover and usually are not readily adaptable to uses other than those for which they were designed. Actually, therefore, in the technological sense, and from a long-run point of view, it may be argued that utilities are a relatively high-risk industry.

The present era's emphasis on both basic and applied research has greatly accelerated the rate of technological change and increased the risks of technological obsolescence. Not only are more scientific breakthroughs occurring but the time gap between laboratory development and commercial application is narrowing rapidly. Utility management cannot prevent this and should not, of course, attempt to do so. But the adage "If you can't lick 'em, join 'em" is very applicable here. That is, in order to protect the firm and the industry management must stay ahead of current technology in its thinking and planning and introduce the new technologies itself (insofar as possible) rather than allow an entirely new and different competitive industry to develop.

The failure of railroad management to enter the trucking business on a large scale prior to the enactment of the Motor Carrier Act of 1935, which effectively limited railroad expansion in the trucking field, is a classic example of management's failure to think ahead and remain flexible. More recently, entry of established communications utility firms into the fields of data transmission and communications satellites provide examples of attempts to adapt to new technologies.

Obsolescence can occur in management and in organizations, of course, for other than technological reasons and may be just as devastating. The warning signals of managerial obsolescence are complacency, impatience with new ideas, especially if these originate from subordinates, and excessive reliance on policy manuals and organization charts. Any organization which believes that its current methods and procedures are the best within a given environment is asking for trouble. It will fail to attract the most creative potential managers or will lose them to more dynamic organizations. Successful management provides an atmosphere in which change is accepted as routine rather than resisted.

Inflation creates significant problems and risks for all types of businesses, but especially for utilities. Regulated rates of return on large long-lived fixed assets valued on an original cost basis may cause erosion of investors' real income and lead to difficulties in asset replacement. The management of an individual firm can do little to prevent inflation, and it often can do very little about the regulatory process, but it can take inflationary trends and prospects into account in planning for future growth or asset replacement.

The external environment within which utilities operate, by limiting both their earnings and their operational flexibility, hampers their ability to protect themselves against risks. The other side of the coin, of course, is that regulation does provide some protection against risk, particularly the risk of competition from similar utilities within a given geographic area. To the extent that this protection exists, though, it is short-term in nature. That is, it certainly does not protect against losses of markets to other types of substitute services which may be equally desirable from the consumers' viewpoint. Overall, it is debatable whether or not utilities in general are more or less risky than established major nonregulated industries, but it is at least correct to say that utilities are far from risk-free.

MANAGING FOR GROWTH

It is common knowledge that at any given time in any multifirm industry some firms are likely to be declining in relative importance, as measured by output, sales, profits, or other standards, in comparison with other firms in the industry or with the business community as a whole. Some firms remain relatively stable or grow at about the same pace as the industry or the national growth rate or that of the immediately surrounding economy. A few firms, however, surpass their own industry growth rate average or the national growth rate average.

Growth in itself may not be necessary for the continued survival of an established business. Those firms with records of greater than average growth, though, have advantages over less fortunate firms in attracting and retaining high-quality human resources and in acquiring capital resources for further expansion or the provision of better services. Winners tend to be more attractive than losers. Thus, in order to assure that a business will remain able to perform its social function—that is, to provide desired goods or services to its customers at reasonable prices and to protect the various interests of its employees, investors, and affiliated groups—responsible management must be concerned with growth.

Social environmental constraints, both legal and extralegal, certainly affect the amount, rate, and direction of growth. Since utilities are subjected to more of these constraints than businesses in general, utility management must choose its path carefully to avoid conflicts and to take as much advantage of environmental factors as possible.

For example, the construction of a nuclear electric generating plant in a particular community might be opposed strongly by local citizens on various grounds, such as safety or the thermal pollution of water. But if the utility's management can convince the community that the new plant will attract a cluster of power-using manufacturing industries, with consequent increased local employment, incomes, and business activity, the strong American community passion for economic growth may offset the opposition to the proposed development. (This passion has been weakened, but not wiped out, by the recent ecological or "no-growth" movements.)

Unfortunately, no one has produced any formula giving automatic assurance of growth. One can only say that in any given environment, growth is influenced by the qualities of management. It appears that many managers, perfectly capable of running a going concern successfully, do not have those intangible creative entrepreneurial qualities necessary to build or expand an organization. Growth-minded organizations must assure a succession of growth-minded leaders.[8]

In this age of glamorous growth industries based on recent scientific breakthroughs, the traditional utility industries are not normally considered as being among the growth industries. Because of their regulated earnings and other constraints, this picture is generally accurate insofar as speculative investment in utility common stocks is concerned. Utility stocks are more noted for stable dividends than for spectacular price increases on the stock market. But this picture certainly is inaccurate from the viewpoint of the potentials for output and market expansion. Increased population and affluence brings demands for more than proportionate increases in services. History and contemporary experience demonstrate that growth-minded utility managers, despite the constraints within which they operate, are able to satisfy their creative entrepreneurial instincts and provide more and better services for their customers and communities by taking advantage of growth opportunities.

SUMMARY

Management in a private enterprise economy has the same characteristics and the same general kinds of responsibilities and problems in all types of business. It provides the appropriate strategies and tactics, both motivating and facilitating, under which people in its organization provide goods and services to the public at a profit. If successful, this fills a public need and permits the firm to survive.

All industries and businesses, however, must operate within a complex of social constraints, legal and otherwise. These environmental constraints are more numerous and more rigid for utilities than for most other types of private economic activity.

This does not mean, though, that challenges and creative opportunities are fewer in the utilities industries than in other industries. It simply means that the challenges and opportunities are different because of a different institutional environment.

This chapter points out several basic differences between the utility social environment and the environment of businesses in general and relates this prevailing environment to several basic management responsibilities and problems. Following chapters in this part discuss in more detail a number of operational problems and techniques of privately owned utilities.

NOTES

1. Those interested in further reading on basic management concepts and practices are advised to consult sources such as Drucker, *Managing for Results;* Koontz and O'Donnell, *Principles of*

Management; and Sayles and Strauss, *Human Behavior in Organizations.* All these books are cited in "Additional Readings" at the end of this chapter.

2. The management of publicly owned utilities is discussed in Chapter 18.
3. See discussion of this range in Chapter 1. The publicly owned enterprise, discussed in Part Four, is at the opposite end of the range from the nonregulated privately owned business.
4. Readers may wish to refer back to the discussions of the rate of return in Chapter 8.
5. Social versus private goal conflicts still may arise, of course, concerning the amount of profits; that is, managers or owners may try to obtain profits higher than those necessary to assure continuance of the firm's desired services, or legitimate disputes about the level of necessary profits may arise. Such conflicts have been significant in bringing about earnings regulation for privately owned utilities.
6. But economic demand is only a part of broader social demand. The availability of some kinds or levels of services may be demanded by society even though a privately owned firm cannot make sufficient profits to survive by selling these services to the public. Such services are provided with the assistance of public subsidies or by public ownership.
7. Chapter 15 discusses public relations, which includes methods of informing and influencing public opinion. The present discussion is concerned with more general managerial problems relating to public opinion.
8. One well-known utility's approach to developing growth-minded managers is presented concisely in Frederick R. Kappel, *Vitality in a Business Enterprise* (New York: McGraw-Hill, 1960).

ADDITIONAL READINGS

1. Bailey, J. K., "Responsibility for Organizations as Followed by Leading U.S. Utilities," *Public Utilities Fortnightly,* vol. 73, no. 4 (February 13, 1964), pp. 15–31.
2. Dally, Kenneth L., "Developing Management for Today and Tomorrow," *Public Utilities Fortnightly,* vol. 71, no. 6 (March 14, 1963), pp. 35–40.
3. Davis, Keith, and Robert L. Blomstrom, *Business, Society, and Environment,* 2d ed. (New York: McGraw-Hill, 1971).
4. Drucker, Peter F., *Managing for Results* (New York: Harper and Row, 1964).
5. Garvin, Daniel F., "Impelling Signals of Tomorrow," *Public Utilities Fortnightly,* vol. 81, no. 2 (January 18, 1968), pp. 22–32.
6. Journey, Drexel D., "Beautification, Recreation, and the Utilities," *Public Utilities Fortnightly,* vol. 80, no. 5 (August 31, 1967), pp. 27–30.
7. Kappel, Frederick R., *Vitality in a Business Enterprise* (New York: McGraw-Hill, 1960).
8. Kolb, Burton A., "The Role of Risk in Public Utility Regulation—Technological Change and Risk," *The Economics of Regulation of Public Utilities.* Papers presented at a conference at Northwestern University, June 19–24, 1966 (Evanston, Ill.: Northwestern University, 1966), pp. 151–160.
9. Koontz, Harold, and Cyril O'Donnell, *Principles of Management,* 4th ed. (New York: McGraw-Hill, 1968).
10. Pinet, Frank S., "What Do Managers Manage?" *Public Utilities Fortnightly,* vol. 73, no. 2 (January 16, 1964), pp. 26–32.
11. Sayles, Leonard R., and George Strauss, *Human Behavior In Organizations* (Englewood Cliffs, N.J.: Prentice-Hall, 1966).
12. Stich, Robert S., "The Price of Efficiency," *Public Utilities Fortnightly,* vol. 81, no. 3 (February 1, 1968), pp. 19–23.

12

Marketing Utility Services

There are many definitions of marketing, but all authorities agree that certain basic principles, strategies, and tactics are applicable to the marketing of all types of goods and services. Since a large body of general marketing literature exists, we will not examine here the common elements and principles of marketing. Rather, we are concerned mainly with those aspects of marketing in which some degree of difference exists between marketing utility services and marketing tangible products. Those interested in basic marketing principles should consult other readily available sources.[1]

By any definition, marketing involves selling, but this is much more than merely satisfying existing consumer wants. Essentially, it involves making the consumer aware that the seller has something available which will bring the consumer more satisfaction for a given expenditure than can be obtained from any other product at the same price. The consumer may not know that the seller's product is available or even that he has a want to be satisfied unless he is informed by the seller.

Marketing also, in its broad sense, includes much more than selling. Utility marketing is closely connected with pricing, public and regulatory relations, forecasting and planning, and production and production costs. These interrelated aspects of marketing are discussed in following chapters (except production, which is an engineering matter largely beyond the scope of this book). This chapter, therefore, concentrates primarily on the selling aspect of marketing.

Since marketing does involve many functional areas, divisions, or departments of a firm, though, it is too important to leave entirely to the sales department or marketing experts. Proper coordination leading to the most effective use of a firm's resources and the greatest degree of profitability can come only through the leadership of a marketing-minded top management. Many managements in the past, and some today, have been more interested in engineering and financing problems than in marketing. There appears, however, to be a recent trend toward greater marketing emphasis on the part of top management. A firm lives, grows, and profits only through its sales, and sales of utility services do not keep pace with the rest of the economy without aggressive marketing.[2]

The first steps in marketing, or selling, are to obtain a thorough knowledge of the product and of its market. Only then can intelligent and effective consumer persuasion be undertaken. This chapter will discuss, in order, the general nature of utility products, the characteristics of its consumer markets, and finally the application of marketing techniques. Our discussion will necessarily be somewhat general and will emphasize features where utility marketing differs somewhat from other marketing.

THE NATURE OF UTILITY SERVICES

Utility services are intangible. The consumer cannot see, feel, or taste them, and he assumes that one unit of a given service is identical to every other unit. After the initial sales contact, sales and consumption generally occur on the consumer's premises, at his option, without further personal contact with the seller (except such services as street transit and sometimes telegraph and pay phones). Buyer-seller contact normally is only through the billing and payment process unless there is a breakdown in services, causing consumer complaints.

The utility customer expects immediate service at any time. Services generally cannot be stored nor their consumption deferred. If the service is not available for immediate consumption when demanded, the sale will probably be lost forever. If power failure causes lights to be off for an hour today, we will not usually keep our lights on an extra hour tomorrow.

From the seller's viewpoint, utility services are usually produced under short-term conditions of decreasing costs. Most utility services require large plant and equipment investments with consequent high fixed costs. The legal obligation to provide an adequate quantity of service at all times means that except during peak consumption periods, which may occur only a few days a year, or a few hours or minutes a day, the seller normally has considerable excess production capacity. Actually, most firms have some excess capacity even during peak periods, since capacity is usually installed in large blocks rather than in small increments. In addition, from the long-run point of view there may be substantial economies of large-scale production as a result of expansion in plant size.

This decreasing cost situation makes it profitable for sellers of utility services to increase their load factors through more complete utilization of facilities. At any time when capacities are significantly underutilized, increased sales may add very little to costs; thus revenues from these sales may go almost entirely to profits. Marketing efforts, or differential pricing, designed to increase sales during off-peak periods, when excess capacities exist, are therefore likely to be very profitable.

These consumption and production characteristics are not unique to the utility industries, of course, as pointed out in Chapter 2. But they are commonly found in these industries and are different from the characteristics of many other types of products. They significantly influence the type of market and the marketing techniques used in selling utility services.

THE CHARACTERISTICS OF THE MARKET FOR UTILITY SERVICES

As noted already, utility services cannot be considered necessary in a biological sense. Mankind could exist, and civilization could continue (even if on a different level), without any of the services provided by modern utilities. Individuals could obtain their own water, light, and fuel, carry their own messages, and provide their own transportation without relying upon any of our existing organizations for these services. Most people in most times and places have done this.

Self-supply, however, would be costly and inconvenient and would require drastic changes in our economy and our way of life. Having attained our present standards, most of us would be extremely reluctant to abandon them. In this sense, then, most utility services can be considered social necessities even if not biologically essential—perhaps of the same order as the "necessity" for clothing in a moderate climate. As with clothes, however, the socially necessary quantity and quality of utility services may vary greatly among individuals or groups. Utility marketing, then, like marketing of women's fashions, must be designed in part to arouse latent desires for more and different products.

VARIETIES OF COMPETITION

It has been emphasized that the provision of utility services, at least from a marketing viewpoint, cannot be considered a monopoly. Sometimes more than one seller of the same kind of service is located in one market area, and substitute services (in addition to self-supply) are almost always available. For example, heat may be obtained from electricity, natural or artificial gas, oil, coal, or wood; light from electricity, gas, oil, candles, batteries, or torches; messages can be sent by phone, telegraph, radio, letter, or even carrier pigeon; and so with other utility services. In addition, some sellers even compete with themselves by selling substitute products, such as gas and electricity.

In addition to competing with sellers of fairly close substitutes, every seller of utility services is competing with sellers of all kinds of nonutility products. Consumers have only a certain amount to spend. Money spent for nonutility items cannot be spent for utility services. If a family prefers movies to television, or a new automobile to an automatic dishwasher, or a summer vacation tour to an air conditioner, electricity sales will be reduced.

Finally, in some areas and for some types of services, ideological competition may exist. That is, consumers may have a choice between equivalent or substitute services supplied either by privately owned or publicly owned facilities and may have a definite preference for one or the other.

In summary, the often-heard statement that sellers of utility services have a monopoly of necessities is extremely misleading. No utility service can be considered a necessity except in the social sense for limited quantities, and every seller of utility services competes with all sellers of all goods and services and usually with sellers of equivalent services.

DERIVED DEMAND

Because of the nature of the utility product, the demand for utility services is a derived demand. That is, consumers do not want the service for itself but for what it can do to satisfy other wants. Consumers, for example, buy electricity for light, gas for heat, telephone services because they want to send messages, or street transit rides because they want to get from one place to another. These relations are quite obvious. Their effects upon the nature of the market and marketing techniques for utility services, however, which may not be so obvious, should be understood clearly.

Derived demand for utility services means that sales of these services are significantly influenced by consumer income levels and by family life styles and patterns as well as by the prices and financing terms of the instruments through which utility services are brought to the consumers. Suburban dwellers with large houses and lawns to mow and water, a host of appliances, widely scattered friends, and commuting jobs consume more utility services than apartment dwellers. Teenagers may influence a family toward an additional telephone, or large houses may be conducive to additional phone extensions. Small children make mothers wish for washing machines, just as large families stimulate dishwasher sales or the acquisition of more than one television set. Factors affecting incomes, living habits, and the availability and terms of housing and consumer credit, then, have a direct impact on the demand for all types of utility services. These factors are probably of much more importance than the prices charged by utilities.

ELASTICITY AND INELASTICITY

It is generally thought that the demand for utility services is relatively inelastic with respect to price changes; that is, that small price increases or decreases do not significantly change the quantities consumed. This is probably as true as most generalizations. Few people will consistently turn off their lights thirty minutes earlier each night merely because electricity rates are increased 10 per cent or burn them thirty minutes longer because of a decrease. For a particular residential consumer in a given short-term situation, demand can be considered relatively price inelastic within reasonable limits of price change.[3]

Like all generalizations, though, price inelasticity of utility services must be accepted with reservations. The exceptions are quite important in actual marketing practice. The nature of consumer demand will vary depending upon what use is being made of the utility service and what alternatives are available.

For example, if a residential consumer is already using an electric range, he may continue to use the same amount of electricity even if electricity rates are increased substantially. If he is building a new house, however, and has not yet incurred the expenses of wiring and purchasing a range, high electricity rates may cause him to decide in favor of gas or some other substitute. The same principle would apply for a commercial or industrial user. Once a sizable financial commitment has tied a consumer to a particular type of service, his demand may be relatively inelastic for a short-term period. If he is uncommitted, however, he may compare prices rather carefully. Further, in the long run, when his present facilities have to be replaced, he may switch to a substitute service.

On the whole, it is likely that the demands of commercial and industrial users are more elastic than those of residential users. Large consumers may have more knowledge of actual utility production costs and may be in a stronger position to bargain with alternative sources of supply. Or if prices become unduly high, they may have the capability of producing their own utility services. Few residential consumers have these alternatives.

The differing demand elasticities and other circumstances of various consumer groups must be taken into account in utility marketing and pricing policies. As an example, approximately 90 per cent of the nation's electricity customers are residential; they account for only 30 per cent of total consumption but for 40 per cent of the total electric utility revenues. Similarly, residential consumers are around 90 per cent of natural gas customers, accounting for about 25 per cent of total sales and 50 per cent of total revenues.[4] The higher residential rates indicated by these figures, of course, does not necessarily imply economic discrimination against residential users. There may be significant cost differences between supplying a large industrial purchaser and a small residential purchaser.

Electric pricing policies of publicly supplied power (discussed further in Part Four), beginning particularly during the 1930's, were based largely on the assumption of relative elasticity of demand. The result has been that per capita consumption of electric services in those areas where low-priced public power is available has exceeded consumption in higher-priced areas. This indicates that price elasticity for these services, at least on a long-run basis, may be of more importance than formerly supposed. It may be partly attributable, however, to more aggressive marketing, consumer organization, and publicity on the part of public power marketers in the areas concerned and to substantially increased relative income levels in some of these formerly chronically depressed areas. Even in a low-priced area, over a short time period, it is likely that other factors have more consumption impact than do small price changes.

It is generally assumed, too, that the demand for utility services is relatively inelastic with respect to income changes; in other words, that small changes in consumer incomes have little effect on the purchase of utility services. Again, as a generalization and over a short period of time this is probably correct. But like price elasticity, income elasticity cannot be assumed equal for all groups and for long periods of time.

Rising incomes allow individuals to purchase more appliances that require utility services (if they are acquainted with the availability and desirability of these appliances) and eventually may lead to new and larger houses, desires to emulate neighbors or higher income groups, and to quite different styles of family life—perhaps even to a greater number of children. Better and more favorable credit terms, a usual accompaniment of rising incomes, adds reinforcement. Similarly, a general increase in prosperity increases the consumption of industrial customers, who use utility services in producing many types of goods.

Generally, the market for utility services during the past generation has expanded tremendously. For example, since the mid-1930's electricity consumption has increased by 1,000 per cent; natural gas by 500 per cent; and the number of telephones in use and toll and long distance calls by 500 per cent. Water utility revenues have increased by 400 per cent and telegraph revenues by 300 per cent. The notable exception is street transit, with the number of rides down about 40 per cent since its World War II all-time peak.[5]

This expansion can be attributed partly to larger population, increased affluence, and the development of more devices which make use of utility services. More people are using more services than ever before. As incomes rise, a smaller percentage of total income goes for basic items like food, clothing, and shelter, leaving more for other purposes. In the electric utility field, for example, today's average residential customer uses seven times as much service as the average customer of a generation ago.

It would be a mistake, however, to assume that more people, higher incomes, and proliferating appliance technology by themselves have accounted fully for the great expansion in utility service consumption. Aggressive marketing by the sellers of utility services has also played an important role.

Despite the old saying, the world does not beat a path to the door of the man who invents a better mousetrap—not even that portion of the world plagued with mice and having the money to buy traps. Instead, the inventor must proclaim the merits of his innovation loudly and clearly from his housetop if he expects to avoid bankruptcy. Further, his proclaiming will be much more effective if it is aimed in the direction of those neighbors who have both mice and money.

Although the growth of utility service consumption during the past generation (except street transit) has been considerably more rapid than increases in population and Gross National Product, it has not been uniform among various groups of customers. In general, a more stable and consistent pattern has prevailed in residential markets. Industrial consumption tends to fluctuate more with changes in general economic conditions than does home consumption.

USE PATTERNS

The consumption of utility services, both residential and industrial, is characterized by wide periodic short-term fluctuations, daily, weekly, or seasonally. Street transit, for example, is used most heavily during the early morning and late afternoon, Monday through Friday. Electric lights, television sets, and ranges are used heavily during the evening. Gas and electric heating are used primarily in the winter. Business phones are little-used at night. Water is used for lawns during the summer. It is even claimed that sudden and temporary heavy use of water occurs during evening television commercials.

The patterns of peak and off-peak use can fortunately be predicted fairly accurately from past records. Thus, it is possible to adjust marketing and pricing policies to bring about a more equal distribution of use. It may be difficult, although not impossible, to reduce consumption significantly during peak periods, but it may be fairly easy to build up off-peak consumption.

All consumers like convenient service, and in an affluent society users are willing to pay more for extras, such as wide-area telephone dialing; numerous phone, electric, and gas connections; and the like. Also, among some groups, features of beauty (like colored telephones), unobtrusiveness (recessed connections), or novelty (musical doorbells or outdoor gas lights) are becoming increasingly popular. As the market for basic bread-and-butter services becomes more saturated, it is likely that marketing of these extra, aesthetic, or novel qualities will become relatively more important. This will require a detailed knowledge of the psychologies of different potential consuming groups.

Also in the area of consumer psychology, some individuals have strong prejudices against some kinds of utility service facilities. For example, many people greatly fear gas explosions, are afraid of electrocution or severe burning from electric blankets, maintain that electric heat is not as warming as other types of heat, or feel that air conditioning aggravates allergies or sinus problems.

A single seller of a particular utility service in a given geographic area is faced with a different problem in advertising and promoting his product than are most other sellers. If a territory is served by a dozen automobile dealers, for example, the cumulative effects of all their advertising aids in influencing customers in favor of new cars. The single utility seller, however, must undertake the entire burden of promoting his product himself. He may, of course, be aided considerably by appliance dealers, and he does get full benefit of whatever product acceptance he can create. It cannot be said as a generalization that the utility is either handicapped or benefited by such a situation. It can be said, however, that a unique situation exists and that therefore special tactics are appropriate.

SUMMARY OF MARKET CHARACTERISTICS

To recapitulate briefly, the demand for utility services is derived from the demand for other services; thus marketing must attempt to influence the consumer toward satisfying these other wants. Price and income inelasticity of demand probably is greater in the short run than over a longer time period. Even in the short run, however, elasticity varies among consumer groups and is lower for present than for potential customers and higher for nonresidential than for residential users.

Basically, the size of the market for utility services is determined by the size and income level of the population. Even though an affluent society spends relatively more on services than a poor society, however, full exploitation of market potential requires technological innovation and imaginative selling. Best cost and profit results are obtained by equalizing load factors through increased off-peak consumption.

A great expansion in the consumption of utility services has occurred in recent years. It appears that the existing market for basic uses is much nearer saturation than was true a generation ago. Barring technological breakthroughs which would change the nature of the utility product and its market significantly, selling efforts will probably be more and more directed toward satisfying the latent desires for convenience and luxury of an increasingly affluent society.

To be most effective, this future selling will require careful study and forecasting of trends in income levels, family life styles, and specific tastes and preferences of particular consuming groups. An efficient mousetrap will not be enough. It must be tailored for each using group according to that group's preferences for size, shape, design, and color, preferably self-baiting and disposing of its own catch, and advertised by an aromatic in-group cheese.

THE APPLICATION OF MARKETING TECHNIQUES

RESEARCHING THE MARKET

As has been continually emphasized, the first prerequisite for effective marketing of utility services (or any product) is a thorough understanding of the characteristics of the market and how the product can satisfy the existing or latent desires of customers. Only then can intelligent marketing approaches, fitting into the seller's overall goals, be designed.

Actually, there are several markets for each service sold by the typical utility organization. Determination of which among these holds out the greatest promise for profitable exploitation and of how this exploitation can best be accomplished is a task of marketing research. Detailed exploration of the procedures of marketing research is beyond the scope of this discussion, but a growing body of literature exists for those who may be particularly interested in pursuing it further.[6]

Very briefly, before undertaking a marketing research project it is desirable to decide what questions need answering, how much is available to spend in developing answers, and what sources and techniques are most likely to provide answers. Data sources may be primary or secondary, including government or trade publications, company or private files, or direct customer contacts. Techniques may include observation, surveys, or controlled experiments. Whatever the data or the techniques, it is necessary to develop standards for measuring or estimating the validity or reliability of the answers. As stated, this perhaps sounds simple and straightforward. In reality, however, marketing research is a complex specialty, containing many pitfalls for the unwary and untrained. Poorly conducted research often leads to worse decisions than those based on no research at all.

MARKETING METHODS

Marketing methods might be classified into the shotgun approach or the rifle approach. Shotgun marketing refers to the promotion of all possible service uses by all potential consumers without particular emphasis on any one feature or group. The rifle approach, on the other hand, aims at a specific service use by a specific group. Which of these approaches, or rather what combination of them, is most effective will vary, of course, with prevailing circumstances. Most sellers use both approaches, varying the emphasis of each one as results dictate.

Both advertising and personal selling are used in utility marketing. Personal selling is generally high-cost selling and thus is justified only where there are relatively good prospects of success or high payoffs in volume. Advertising, on the other hand, reaches a large number of potential customers at a lower per-customer cost but usually results in a lower percentage of sales among those exposed and a lower average volume of sales from those who do buy. An effective sales manager is constantly aware of the results and costs of these alternative selling methods and is prepared to make trade-offs between them as necessary to attain maximum benefits from his sales resource.[7]

An effective sales program, in addition to being based on the psychology, habits, and expressed and latent needs of potential purchasers, must be designed to communicate briefly, in a stimulating manner, and in terms of the consumers' interests. Its managers should have specific accomplishment goals for given expenditures as well as standards for evaluating performance both while the program is underway and at its conclusion. Also, they should know what kinds of media (newspapers, magazines, billboards, television, direct mailing, personal contact, etc.) or what combinations of media, do the best job, that is, where additional expenditures at any given time bring the most profitable sales.

Evaluation of sales programs should be continuous and as objective as possible. It is better to acknowledge mistakes and cut losses than to throw good money after bad. Evaluation, however, is not always easy. The total effects of a particular program may be both delayed and long continued. Also, it is probable that under most circumstances a continuing series of promotional or advertising expenditures has a cumulative effect; that is, greater results may be obtained from later than from earlier expenditures of the same magnitude.

A utility organization's own sales department, an independent advertising agency, or institutional advertising through trade associations may be used in sales programs. Many sellers use all of these. Also, a utility's own customers may be contacted directly and inexpensively by small pieces of advertising literature inserted with monthly bills.

The primary objective of utility sales efforts is, of course, to increase consumption of utility services. This objective usually must be attained in an indirect, or even an "indirect-indirect," manner, however. That is, potential consumers must first be persuaded to acquire, install, and use appliances operated by utility services or to increase the use of their present appliances. An example of the indirect approach might be to encourage sales of electric water heaters so that more electricity can be sold. An "indirect-indirect" example might be the promotion of automatic washing machine sales; this may require the installation of even larger water heaters and thus even larger electricity sales.

The great expansion in average residential electric power consumption during the past generation provides a clear example of the relation between appliances and consumption. During this time, for example, the annual sales of electric water heaters have increased 1,200 per cent, ranges 1,000 per cent, clocks and vacuum cleaners 500 per cent, washing machines 350 per cent, refrigerators and irons 250 per cent, and even radios 200 per cent.[8] Since World War II television sets have become almost universal home fixtures, and sales of air conditioners and dishwashers have grown from almost nothing to sizable numbers.

Some gas and electric utilities have engaged in direct appliance merchandising. Others have financed appliance purchases on favorable terms or have provided installation or repair services at low prices. Some have done all of these. For many reasons, including objections from independent appliance dealers and regulatory authorities, direct appliance merchandising by utilities is declining. Other methods of cooperation with manufacturers and dealers, including financing, servicing, and joint advertising and promotion, are widely used. Similarly, architects, home building contractors, and building code officials, who often influence or determine what kinds of fixtures and utility services go into new homes, are carefully cultivated.

In addition, many kinds of "free" consulting services are available to potential customers. These include home service representatives; culinary experts; illumination, heating, air conditioning, and communications engineers; and irrigation specialists, to name only a few. These services, besides being very useful to customers or potential customers, also aid in selling particular kinds of utility services.

Ideally, at least if a utility's peak load is near its full capacity, sales efforts should be designed to increase off-peak use. As examples, summer air conditioners can offset winter heaters, electric blankets can offset turned-down heaters, evening phone calls to Aunt Minnie can offset daytime business calls, or midday shopping housewives can offset early morning and late afternoon street transit riders. Many possibilities of these kinds exist for smoothing daily, weekly, or seasonal fluctuations in utilization, either through promotional activities or pricing differentials.

Selective load building, although it has obvious profit opportunities, must be carefully approached, however. If it is too successful, it may transform an off-peak period into a period with greater capacity demands than the peak period it is designed to offset. Or it may overlap other uses, so that it adds to the demands of the peak period. (As an illustration, television sets and lights are usually on at the same time, and electric ranges may be used during a considerable portion of this time.)

In order to avoid these dangers the utility's management must have accurate information and maintain constant checks on the load factor and have reliable forecasts, well into the future, of technological and consuming patterns which may affect load trends. Marketing programs which appear quite desirable under present conditions often are invitations for future trouble.

SUMMARY

Contrary to the opinions of many consumers, and even of some past and perhaps some present utility managers, marketing is a vital element in utility success as well as a method of reducing costs and providing lower consumer prices. Because of the environment in which utilities operate, though, marketing of their services appears to be more closely tied to several other managerial functions than is true of many other types of industries. This requires particularly close interfunctional coordination.

Characteristics of the utility product require a roundabout method of marketing, quite different in some respects from the sale of tangible goods. Also, there are several markets, each requiring thorough understanding and somewhat different techniques. Increasing population and affluence have made it relatively easy to market utility services in recent years, even though considerable marketing efforts have always been necessary. Future marketing is likely to be more difficult and to require different tactics, but its opportunities and rewards should be equal to those of the past. An increasingly affluent society will consume growing quantities of services if technology makes them available and if they are attractively presented by good marketers.

NOTES

1. Part I of J. B. Matthews, Jr., R. D. Buzzell, Theodore Leavitt, and R. E. Frank, *Marketing: An Introductory Analysis* (New York: McGraw-Hill, 1964) contains an interesting and well-written brief introduction to marketing and the modern concept of the marketing system. This was not written specifically for utility services marketing, but many of the principles discussed are generally applicable.
2. Even though earnings are regulated, it is not often that regulatory commissions on their own initiative force already established rates downward because of increased profits. Utility firms may be able to keep additional profits resulting from more efficient resource use for a considerable period of time, particularly if they do not have to apply for rate increases (see Chapter 8 for the earnings range of large utilities during a recent year). Also, firms often have earnings lower than allowed by applicable regulatory orders. Thus, more effective marketing may be motivated by definite profit incentives as well as by desires for expansion in firm sizes and services.
3. Various more or less controlled experiments have indicated that increases in street transit fares and pay phone charges have resulted in temporary patronage decreases (just as happened when the traditional five-cent cup of coffee passed from the scene). These declines soon disappear, however, and consumption patterns resume their previous trend.
4. These figures are rounded approximations, intended only to show general relations.
5. These figures, calculated by the authors from various published sources, do not purport to be exact. Rather, they are rounded approximations intended to indicate the general magnitudes and trends of changes. Note that the figures cited refer to consumption changes rather than revenue changes, except as indicated. Operating revenues have increased more rapidly than consumption in the natural gas and telephone industries but less rapidly for privately owned electric utilities.
6. Good brief introductions to marketing research, not designed particularly for the utility industries but nonetheless useful, can be found in Chapters 4 and 8 of E. J. McCarthy, *Basic Marketing: A Managerial Approach,* 4th ed. (Homewood, Ill.: Richard D. Irwin, 1971) and in Part I of F. T. Schreier, *Modern Marketing Research: A Behavioral Science Approach* (Belmont, Calif.: Wadsworth Publishing Co., 1963).
7. A good short introduction to advertising and personal selling is given in T. N. Beckman and W. R. Davidson, *Marketing,* 8th ed. (New York: Ronald Press, 1967), ch. 21 and 22. The literature on both these topics is voluminous.
8. Rounded approximations as calculated by the authors from various published sources. These figures are not intended to be precise but rather to indicate magnitudes of changes.

ADDITIONAL READINGS

1. Anshen, Melvin, "Introducing the Marketing Concept Through Management Development," in Lynn H. Stockman, ed., *Advancing Marketing Efficiency.* Proceedings of the 41st National Conference of the American Marketing Association (Chicago: American Marketing Association, 1959), pp. 250–257.
2. Beckman, Theodore N., and William R. Davidson, *Marketing,* 8th ed. (New York: Ronald Press, 1967), ch. 21, "The Selling Function: Advertising," pp. 566–589; ch. 22, "The Selling Function: Personal Selling and Sales Promotion," pp. 590–620.
3. Farmer, Richard N., "Marketing the Transit System," *Journal of Marketing,* vol. 28, no. 1 (January 1964), pp. 54–57.
4. Matthews, John B., Jr., Robert D. Buzzell, Theodore Leavitt, and Ronald E. Frank, *Marketing: An Introductory Analysis* (New York: McGraw-Hill, 1964), part I, "Marketing Today," pp. 3–32.

5. McCarthy, E. Jerome, *Basic Marketing: A Managerial Approach,* 4th ed. (Homewood, Ill.: Richard D. Irwin, 1971), ch. 4, "Gathering Market Information," pp. 89–114; ch. 8, "Consumers: A Behavioral Science View," pp. 188–221.
6. Schreier, Fred T., *Modern Marketing Research: A Behavioral Science Approach* (Belmont, Calif.: Wadsworth Publishing Co., 1963), part I, "Fundamentals of Marketing Research," pp. 3–55.
7. Thompson, C. Woody, and Wendell R. Smith, *Public Utility Economics* (New York: McGraw-Hill, 1941), ch. 24, "The Marketing of Utility Service," pp. 503–523.
8. Tuthill, O. W., "Modern Marketing Challenges Utility Management," in Lynn H. Stockman, ed., *Advancing Marketing Efficiency.* Proceedings of the 41st National Conference of the American Marketing Association (Chicago: American Marketing Association, 1959), pp. 267–274.
9. Wotruba, Thomas R., "Marketing Functions and Utilities' Sales Goals," *Public Utilities Fortnightly,* vol. 77, no. 6 (March 17, 1966), pp. 22–30.
10. Wotruba, Thomas R., "The Sales Promotion Function in a Public Utility," *Public Utilities Fortnightly,* vol. 72, no. 9 (October 24, 1963), pp. 42–46.

13

Utility Finance and Accounting

Utility finance and accounting are complex matters that are of primary importance to the operation of utilities. The object of this chapter is not to present a definitive analysis of finance and accounting problems. Such a task is better reserved for more specialized treatments. However, some preliminary understanding of these two areas is necessary in order to comprehend the tasks of utility management. Hence, the goal of this chapter is to give some appreciation of the problems involved, and an elementary understanding of each of these areas.

UTILITY FINANCE AND FINANCIAL PROBLEMS

Some understanding of utility financial management can be gained by considering the problem of capital acquisition, the financial environment within which utility firms operate, and managerial alternatives or choices in finance.

THE PROBLEM OF CAPITAL ACQUISITION

A public utility has a constant and recurring need for new capital. There are three reasons for this: the capital-intensive nature of the industry, the steady growth of demand for services over time, and the long history of the industry, which has made it necessary to refund past capital obligations.

Utilities are among the most capital-intensive firms in the American economy. While the use of people is important and resource inputs are necessary, services are primarily based on capital. A glance at the operations of an electric power company, a natural gas company, or a telephone or water company quickly reveals this. The capital utilized is in the form of generators, pipes, control panels, switchboards, reservoirs, meters, wires, control towers, and the like. A utility's capital is immense and is committed for long periods of time in specialized and physical things.

The demand for most utility services has shown a steady and remarkable growth over a long period of time. Use of many of these services has regularly doubled each ten years or less for many years. This steady growth in demand means a constant problem of obtaining capital for most utility firms. Just keeping up with the public demand for services means raising considerable amounts of new capital annually, to say nothing of the constant refunding need.

Some idea of the size of the capital problem for utilities is given by Table 13-1. In 1969 some $26.7 billion in new corporate securities were sold in the United States. When Communication ($2.2 billion) is added to the Electric, Gas, and Water group ($6.7 billion), one out of every three dollars in new corporate securities sold came from the utility industry ($8.9 billion of the $26.7 billion total).

Utilities raise capital by using every type of security. Indeed, needs are so great that all money markets must be tapped, along with considerable retained capital or plowed-back earnings. However, because of the long-term nature of the capital, the steady growth factor, and the financial reputation for stability, corporate bonds are a prime source of new capital. Table 13-2 illustrates this fact. Out of the $18.3 billion in new bonds issued in 1969, utilities sold $7.3 billion, or more than 40 per cent. Most (78 per cent) of the preferred stock issued came from utilities, although the total

Table 13-1 New Corporate Securities Offered in the United States in 1969, by Industry (Millions of Dollars)

Industry Group	Dollar Amounts	Per Cent
Electric, Gas, and Water	$ 6,736	25
Communication	2,187	8
Manufacturing	6,355	24
Extractive (Mines)	1,721	6
Rail	294	1
Other Transportation	1,851	7
Financial and Real Estate	4,409	16
Commercial and Other	3,188	12
Total	$26,744	100

Source: *Statistical Bulletin,* Securities and Exchange Commission (March 1970), p. 16.

Table 13-2 New Corporate Securities Offered in the United States in 1969, by Type (Millions of Dollars)

Type	Total	Utilities	Per Cent of Total Offered by Utilities
Bonds	$18,347	$7,372	40
Preferred	681	529	78
Common	7,714	1,020	13
Total	$26,743	$8,921	33

Source: *Statistical Bulletin,* Securities and Exchange Commission (March 1970), p. 16.

amount of capital raised was small. More than $1 billion was raised through common stock, which amounted to more than 13 per cent of all equity stock issues that year. However, bonds clearly dominate as the method of raising new capital for utilities.

With this huge need for new capital on a recurring basis, a clearly defined financial environment exists. The manager of this specialized and extremely important area must operate under definite constraints and within a set of historical conditions that affect his actions.

THE UTILITY FINANCIAL ENVIRONMENT

The financial environment in which utilities exist has many aspects, and the financial environment faced by one firm is not always the same as that faced by another firm even in the same industry. Similarly, the financial environment varies among power, gas, communications, water, and urban transportation companies. However, there are five financial factors or conditions which are faced by almost all utility firms. These are the existing capital structure, the regulatory structure, the necessity for competitive bidding, the need for financial creditability, and the predominance of institutional investors.

The Existing Capital Structure

Every financial manager must take into account his firm's existing capital structure. Past decisions limit his freedom to make financial decisions in the present. It might be the judgment of the financial manager that it would be most easy and cheap for the firm to raise capital by selling corporate bonds. His decision to sell bonds, however, must be guided by the amount and kinds of existing bonds issued in the past. The manager might well end up selling common stock instead of bonds simply because too many bonds relative to equity have been previously issued. The need to balance the capital structure between various types of securities is always present and at times forces decisions based less on financial efficiency criteria than on conditions inherited from the past.

As a generalization, we can say that the capital structures of most utilities are heavily weighted towards bonds and long-term debt. These are fixed return types of securities, whose owners assume creditor relations with the firm. Large amounts of bonds would be expected from the nature of the industry. The degree of fixed long-term obligations in the capital structure varies among utilities, however. Table 13–3 shows the percentage of each security type in the overall capital structure of a large portion of the utilities industries during a recent year.

Note that the percentage of long-term debt varies from more than 37 per cent for telephone companies to more than 60 per cent for gas transmission firms. Typically, about one half of a utility firm's capitalization is in bonds and long-term debt.[1] The other half of the capital structure generally is in equity-type securities, although the percentage in preferred stock with its fixed return obligation varies from almost zero in telephone companies to almost 10 per cent in electric power companies. Earned surplus or retained earnings make up a substantial part of the capital structure as well.

From the viewpoint of financial management, these ratios have some significance. The market for capital is highly competitive, and the amount owned of one type of

Table 13-3 Capitalization Ratios of Selected Public Utilities, 1968 (Percents)

Security Type	Electric Power	Gas Distribution	Gas Transmission	Telephone
Long-Term Debt	53.8	48.5	60.1	37.3
Preferred Stock	9.6	5.7	7.7	00.2
Common Stock and Premiums	24.1	46.2	21.1	42.4
Earned Surplus	12.5	*	11.1	20.1
Total	100.0	100.0	100.0	100.0

*Included in common stock and premiums.

Source: Power: *Statistics of Privately Owned Electric Utilities of United States,* Federal Power Commission (1968), p. 20; Gas Distribution: *Moody's Public Utility Manual, 1970,* p. a69; Gas Transmission: *Statistics of Interstate Natural Gas Pipeline Companies,* Federal Power Commission (1968), p. 13; Telephone: *Statistics of Communications Common Carriers,* Federal Communications Commission (December 1968), p. 34.

security often affects the standing or market evaluation of another security by the same firm. Overcapitalization was a historical fact in parts of the utility industry. That is, the amount of outstanding securities exceeded the asset value of the properties committed to utility service. Some financial managers have been constrained to make certain decisions based on the fact that past abuses during speculative periods have left certain utilities with undesirable reputations.

The existing capital structure also affects the ability of a utility to weather variations in earnings coming from changes in demand for services. A high ratio of long-term debt may saddle a utility with high fixed charges that must be met to prevent bankruptcy. When earnings drop, during recessions or because of shifts in demand, the firm may be in financial trouble. Since investors try to evaluate risks when committing capital, a firm's capital structure probably affects its ability to sell equity issues. While there is considerable debate on this subject, it is widely held within the utility industry itself that capital structure affects a firm's "cost of capital."[2]

The Regulatory Structure

Very few managerial decisions in the public utility industries are made without consideration of the regulatory structure. Financial decisions are no exception to that rule. Regulation is an ever-present part of the utility financial environment. Financial decisions must be made within the context of regulation and must conform to the existing regulatory structure. Equally important, though often overlooked, is the fact that the financial decisions may cause regulatory action to take place.

Most commissions are empowered to control the capital structure of utility firms. While this power is sometimes not exercised, or is exercised in a purely routine manner, utilities generally must obtain permission in order to issue stocks, sell bonds, and the like. This authority is exercised at both the state and the federal levels. At the state level, for example, forty-two state commissions can regulate security issues or mergers and consolidations, thirty-three can regulate purchases of securities from other utilities, and thirty-one can regulate transactions with affiliates.[3]

At the federal level six laws apply in part to financial transactions. These are the Securities Act, 1933; the Securities Exchange Act, 1934; the Public Utility Holding Company Act, 1935; the Federal Power Act, 1935; the Communications Act, 1934; and the Natural Gas Act, 1938. The first two apply to all corporations, while the last four apply specifically to utilities. Federal jurisdiction is limited, of course, to firms in interstate commerce. Since federal controls are more comprehensive and more uniform than state controls, the tendency is for state controls merely to supplement federal acts.[4]

These financial controls arose partly out of the excesses of the holding company period and partly because other aspects of utility operations can be affected by the capital structure. Much of the concern with other aspects of utility operations turns on the degree of indebtedness assumed by the utility firm.

As noted previously, indebtedness leads to fixed obligations which a utility must meet. In times of shifts or decreases in demand such fixed obligations can become burdensome. Conceivably a firm could request a rate increase in order to cover its fixed obligations; that is, the capital structure is connected with the prices or rates charged. Similarly, if the amount of bonded indebtedness relative to equity affects the risk rating of both the bonds and the common stock, thereby causing their prices in the competitive financial marketplace to increase, the utility's cost of capital will be increased. (Remember that cost of capital is one of the factors given consideration in commission determination of the allowable rate of return.) To preserve the credit standing of a firm, rates and earnings may have to be increased if its debt ratio is high. This whole problem might be avoided by regulatory restraint in the issuance of more bonded indebtedness.

Finally, the debt-to-equity ratio determines the leverage of the equity stock on the one hand and affects control of the company on the other. While control is not the issue it was during the holding company era, a commission may be concerned that equity holdings may become so highly leveraged as to become speculative. This would once more affect the risk factor and the cost of capital.

Regardless of the historical reasons, commission control of capitalization is a fact of life for the regulated industries. While it is generally thought that this control is exercised in the public interest, and as a device to protect customers, investors, and the financial status of the utility itself, substantial analysis in recent years suggests that regulation has led to overinvestment in utilities—the so-called A-J-W effect.[5] But this theory aside, the fact remains that financial decisions are made within the confines of a regulatory structure, and this will continue as long as the public wants to continue regulatory control.

Competitive Bidding

Since large amounts of capital frequently are needed in an expanding utility industry, during earlier days it was not unusual for a utility firm to establish an ongoing business relation with one or more of the nation's large investment banking firms. These specialists in raising capital were in a position to advise the utility about timing of capital issues, methods of raising capital, how the investments market was likely to react to various financial developments within the firm, and the like. Clearly, these investment banking firms were also in a prime position to get the financial business of the utility firm. That is, they would act as underwriters of the securities and handle the financial transactions for a fee.

These types of financial relations between business corporations and investment bankers were common, and the public generally was little concerned. If the investment banker overcharged his customer for the services of raising capital, the corporation suffered. However, in the public utility industries a different situation existed. If an investment banker overcharged a utility for its services, the excess costs were borne by the public in the form of higher rates. Or if an investment banker urged a general business corporation to issue too much debt in order to make business for the banker, the stockholders and bondholders of the corporation might suffer from overcapitalization. But if the same thing took place with a public utility, the effects were felt by the consumer in the form of higher charges.

Some of these things apparently occurred during the excesses of the 1920's and the holding company period. Business relations between utility firms and investment bankers did have some effect on the financial health of the firms and hence upon the prices for services.

As regulation developed and grew, it became necessary to face the problem of how new issues of securities were marketed. Investment banking firms played an important role in the financial operations of utilities. There seems to be some evidence that this role was abused by persuading firms to overcapitalize, or by overcharging for financial services, or by failure of investment bankers to compete with one another for the utilities' business.[6]

State regulation in Massachusetts in 1919 required that utilities secure competitive bids on new issues of electric and gas bonds. The Interstate Commerce Commission required competitive bidding on equipment trust certificates in 1926. However, most state commissions did not require competitive bidding until after the Holding Company Act of 1935 and until the various federal commissions had adopted this device.[7] The turning points in requiring competitive bidding came in 1941, when the Securities and Exchange Commission promulgated its Rule U-50, and the Federal Power Commission required competitive bidding for capital issues on all firms in its jurisdiction.[8]

While arguments are numerous as to the actual effects of required competitive bidding, it is a corporate fact of life. A utility typically must put its capital offerings up for bids by syndicates of investment bankers and accept the highest offer. The investment bankers' "underwriting spread," or difference between the stated value of a bond and the proceedings to a utility, is minimized by having several groups bidding to market the issue. No continuing relation exists between a utility firm and given underwriters. The financial manager of a utility obviously must possess a degree of expertise in money market affairs and must know how and when to present securities for competitive bidding.

Financial Creditability

The imperative need to maintain the financial creditability and reputation of the utility is a further constraint on its financial manager. Over a long period of time a utility establishes an image with investors and in the capital markets. Often that image is one of stability and strength, although sometimes it is one of growth and development. Whatever the image, most financial managers recognize the necessity of maintaining and nurturing it. Occasionally an attempt will be made to change the financial image of a firm, but for the most part it is a matter of maintaining and reinforcing a company's financial reputation.

This reputation may be both an advantage and a disadvantage to a firm. If the image is favorable, a financial manager will have an easier task in raising certain types of new capital. Thus, a reputation for stability may help in selling bonds, whereas a reputation for growth might make equity securities easier to market. Of course, the issuance of a large amount of equity securities by a utility with a stability image might change the opinions of investors, or a large issue of bonds by a growth-type firm might not be easily accomplished. Hence, the image may adversely affect and limit a financial manager's range of choice in a given situation.

More will be said about financial creditability in the discussion of accounting. But for now we will say simply that financial managers of utility firms generally are acutely aware of the financial images of their firms and must keep them in mind when making financial decisions.

Predominance of Institutional Investors

Another factor in the financial environment of utilities is the predominance of institutional investors. While current studies generally are not available, it is agreed that insurance companies, pension funds, mutual funds, trusts, and other institutional investors are large owners of utility stocks and bonds.[9] This follows from the types of securities sought by these institutions and the reputation of utility firms for stability and liberal interest and dividends.[10]

The significance of institutional investors owning utility securities is twofold. First, the financial affairs of utilities are greatly entwined with those of the institutions. The financial health of insurance companies, for example, may well depend on the financial health of utilities, or the availability of industrial pensions for workers in corporations is directly tied to the health of utilities. In a word, a larger public than immediate customers exists which is interested in the operations of utility firms.

Second, institutional investors are typically professionals. Insurance companies, pension funds, trusts, and mutual funds are managed by full-time, well-trained professionals who demand accurate and detailed information before committing the savings of their many customers and beneficiaries to an investment. A utility financial manager must be aware of this degree of expertise and, again, must be aware of the financial reputation of his firm. The opinions of professional money managers can affect the financial reputations of utilities favorably or unfavorably and can make the job of utility financial managers easier or infinitely more difficult.

MANAGERIAL ALTERNATIVES IN FINANCE

Operating within the financial environment of the utility industry, a financial manager is faced with a series of choices as he attempts to solve the capital acquisition problems of a utility. In a very real sense, he has a number of trade-offs and must make at least four decisions. These are the issue decision, the timing decision, the return decision, and the working capital decision. Insofar as the financial environment allows choice in making these decisions, he will always be faced with the incremental process of striving for a proper financial balance.[11]

The Issue Decision

Essentially, a utility can raise capital in five ways. It can issue bonds and other long-term debts, sell preferred stock, sell common stock, borrow at banks and other financial institutions, and retain earnings within the firm. The first three are involved in the issue decision, but the remaining two will affect the choice of the utility financial manager. It should be added that while only a single decision may be necessary relative to which method to use at any given time, the utility will very likely use all five methods of raising capital over the long run.

The most common financial trade-off is between debt and equity. Here the existing capital structure may be the major restraint, as noted before. The other aspects of the financial environment, such as the regulatory structure, competitive bidding, financial creditability, and the predominance of institutional investors also will be important. Debt issues traditionally have been cheaper than equity as far as the cost to the firm is concerned. However, this traditional situation markedly changed during the high interest and tight money situation of the late 1960's.

Once it is determined that at the particular point in time it is desirable to sell equity securities, the further decision between common and preferred stock must be faced. Utilities have generally continued to use preferred stock, and they supply the majority of new preferred stock in today's financial market. There does seem to be a demand for such securities, and with their ever-present and continuing need for capital, utilities have taken advantage of this demand. Preferred stock usually has a fixed return or dividend and in some ways is similar to a mortgage bond or debenture. However, there are tax ramifications for the utility, since interest paid on debt is tax-deductible whereas preferred dividends are not. Also, the preferred stock market is not infinite; thus the decision to sell preferred stock rather than common stock is not an easy one. Moreover, the fixed dividend rate on preferred stock has generally been higher than the dividend rate on common stock in the post-World War II period, reflecting the fact that common stock has the opportunity to share in the growth of a firm with increasing dividends or increasing market value, while the preferred dividend is a fixed amount.

There are many possible preferred stock provisions which can be utilized to make an issue more marketable. Preferred issues usually are cumulative, that is, if preferred dividends are not paid, they accumulate and must be satisfied before common dividends can be paid. Preferred stock convertible into common stock at a given ratio is another usual provision. The effect of conversion privileges is to tie the price of preferred stock to the price of common stock. Hence, if a preferred issue is convertible into two shares of common, the market price per share of the preferred should be very close to twice the price of the common. However, convertible preferred stocks have a "downside" protection in their dividends. That is, an investor can logically expect that the low price of preferred will be set by comparable returns on capital in a decreasing market. Thus, a preferred stock yielding $5 annually would sell in the range of $100 if the general interest rate in the economy was 5 per cent or under. There will be a risk factor which will affect the market price, of course. The upper price ranges on a convertible preferred stock would reflect the price of the common stock and the conversion ratio. In effect, an investor in utility convertible preferred stocks gets the best of both worlds. The effect of cumulative and conversion provisions is to increase the marketability of the preferred stock. This fact is not overlooked by utility financial managers.

If the decision is to raise capital by issuing common stock, a financial manager has several options. He may make a stock offering to existing stockholders. Here, present owners are given an opportunity to subscribe to the new issue in proportion to their present holdings. Usually this is enhanced by setting the subscription price somewhat below the current market price. Clearly, somewhat less money is raised by stock offerings than by selling in the general market. The effect on the market price of the stock also must be considered, as well as conditions in the capital market.

If the decision is made to issue new stock without offering, the possibility of private placement exists. In some instances, large investors such as pension funds or insurance companies will be willing to buy up an entire new issue at a negotiated price. This removes the uncertainty for the utility financial manager but may mean a somewhat smaller dollar return to the firm. Also, this avoids the necessity of competitive bidding, dealing with syndicates of underwriters, and preparing the issue. Both advantages and disadvantages exist.

A further choice may be to raise capital by short-term bank loans or by a policy of increasing retained earnings by maintaining a stable dividend pay-out ratio. While these are not directly issue decisions, they are alternatives or partial trade-offs available to financial managers. Finally, it must be remembered that the financial environment within which the firm finds itself will influence these possible choices.

Timing Decision

Financial markets vary notably over time and reflect opinions of present and future economic conditions. When to introduce new issues is a major decision for utility financial managers. If the market for new bond issues is depressed, the decision may be to consider an alternative type of issue. If possible, a decision to delay until better financial conditions prevail may be made. If most new issues of stocks have been selling well, an acceleration of capital acquisition may be wise. All of these decisions require some judgment as to conditions in financial markets now and in the future; thus financial managers must be informed of continuing financial developments in competitive money markets.

The Securities and Exchange Commission regularly releases data on the registration of new securities. Several publications exist which discuss the relative success or failure of various issues of bonds, preferred stocks, and common stocks. All of these information sources are important to financial managers.

While the possibility of delay for better conditions does theoretically exist, in the practical world of finance such an option may not always be present. The growth of a utility firm can rarely wait for the best market conditions. The refunding problem is a particularly acute one and is usually impossible to delay. Alert financial managers have some idea of future capital needs through projections of growth, known expansion projects, and the like. Naturally they know when bonded indebtedness will have to be refunded. All of these known facts allow a manager to schedule or predict the financial needs of his company. These known capital needs also limit his choices as to timing. Hence, it is often only the incremental or additional project which can be delayed or accelerated according to conditions in the financial market and the timing decision.

Return Decisions and the Cost of Capital

To some extent, the decisions of a utility financial manager affect the rate of return of a utility. While this rate is set by commission action as an allowable return, the figure may often be exceeded or not reached, depending on economic and financial conditions. Here the cost of capital comes into play, and as noted previously, this factor is given weight during commission determinations of allowable rates of return.[12]

Hence, if capital costs are increasing because of higher interest rates on bonds and indebtedness, as they were during the late 1960's, a firm may be forced to seek regulatory relief in higher prices to customers. If the firm can keep its cost of capital down or steady, however, by dint of astute financial management, the necessity to go to regulatory commissions for relief can be delayed. Much expense and effort go into a commission proceeding; thus a firm is usually better off economically if it can operate without the need for frequent commission proceedings. Since the cost of capital is such a large portion of the expense of operating a utility, the success of the financial manager in keeping the cost of capital low is of great importance to his firm, its customers, and its present investors.

The cost of capital may be important financially in another way as well. Once a utility financial manager determines the present cost of capital to the firm and judges the cost of adding capital in the present financial markets, he has a figure which may be used to help rank various alternative expansion projects requiring capital expenditures that could be undertaken. Suppose the cost of capital is 9 per cent and there are five alternative projects which the utility could undertake. Each of the five alternatives can be analyzed, income from each can be projected over the useful life of the project and discounted to the present value of the income flow, and a probable present value income flow from each project can be calculated. This can be compared to the capital cost of the proposed project and to the 9 per cent cost-of-capital figure. Top management now has a device for ranking the various proposals or alternatives.

Of course, there may be a compelling reason why an expansion project yielding under 9 per cent might be undertaken, particularly if the regulatory authorities require it or if an increase in demand makes it mandatory in order to maintain service. Similarly, there may be very good reasons not to choose the project yielding the highest discounted return. But the point is that the cost of capital provides a device for evaluating alternatives and at least allows management to better appreciate what the financial ramifications of decisions will be. It should be added, of course, that cost-of-capital estimates are subject to error and are based on the enlightened judgment of the utility financial manager, just as the projected life of a project and its income flow are also judgments. Even so, a method of evaluation is provided, no matter how rough and inexact.

Finally, the utility manager may be able to affect financial creditability and future capital availability by his decision on returns. Here the dividend pay-out ratio may be of great importance. If substantial earnings are retained in the firm and not paid out in dividends, the financial manager may ease somewhat the burden of frequent capital acquisition. On the other hand, capital markets are quite competitive, and in order to sustain the financial reputation of the firm a liberal percentage of earnings may have to be paid to the stockholders in spite of needs for retained earnings. Once more a return decision is necessary and the financial environment within which the utility finds itself is important.

Working Capital Decisions

A firm must maintain a certain degree of liquidity in order to meet its operational obligations. Payrolls must be met, suppliers must be paid, taxes come due regularly, and interest deadlines cannot be postponed. If financial creditability is to be maintained, dividend deadlines also must be met. Finally, some additional liquid funds must be on hand in order to meet unforeseen contingencies. Therefore, working capital decisions must be made.

Decisions on liquidity will be influenced by the amount of cash flow available to a firm. The method by which assets are depreciated is of considerable importance here. Tax policies of the Internal Revenue Service, local taxing units, and regulatory commissions having jurisdiction are also of some importance in this regard. Funds earned in depreciation accounts are not idle, of course, and provide a prime source of cash flow.

Working capital decisions also turn on the availability of short-term bank loans. If the credit of a firm is good, it may well depend upon its ability to borrow large sums for short terms to meet major contingency needs or major predictable working capital needs such as tax payments and the like. Here the cost of borrowing short-term funds must be balanced against the general cost of capital for the various types of securities the firm might be able to issue in the capital markets. Since both the cost of capital in the capital markets and the interest rate on bank loans vary over time, the financial manager is constantly faced with changing conditions as far as working capital decisions are concerned.[13]

The Incremental Process

It is obvious that the financial manager has a series of interrelated decisions to make on an almost constantly recurring basis. The issue decision, timing decision, return decision, and working capital decision are all variables which affect one another. No one decision can be good or lasting for any length of time, since conditions change over time. Hence, the decision-making process is a constant challenge.

Basically, an incremental process must be adopted to meet this constant decision-making problem. That is, the financial manager must always be striving for the best possible balance of the factors affecting his firm, and he achieves this balance by considering the added or incremental factor. Will a new issue of bonds at this time provide a better or worse capital structure? Existing capital structures must be considered as well as the other financial environmental factors, but the desired level of balance is obtained or partly obtained only with the incremental amount of bonds issued. Will a stock offering to existing stockholders affect financial creditability, ease a working capital problem, affect the rate of return and force the firm to seek regulatory relief, or upset financial managers of institutional funds? Such factors must be weighed, but the decision can only be an incremental one based on the added factor under consideration. The point is that the financial problems of utilities are never solved once and for all, and they present an on-going challenge to financial managers.

CREDIT PROBLEMS

Among the utilities, only urban transit avoids a customer credit problem. Almost all businesses are faced with the problem of extending credit to customers, even though they may not wish to do so. However, the common problem of slow payment may be aggravated in the utilities for several reasons.

First, there is a built-in hostility to monopolistic-type businesses under the prevailing system of economic enterprise in the United States. In the utility field the customer typically has little choice. He must buy power from the electric company, gas from the gas company, and so forth. Hence, some customers may be less than prompt in paying their monthly bills.

Second, use of utility services varies over the year, with the possible exception of urban transit. Hence, high gas bills come during the winter, high water bills during the summer, high power bills during winter or summer, depending on the demand characteristics and the like. Customers rarely appreciate how their use of service adds up over the month, and arguments about overbilling and incorrect meter readings are common. Similarly, the payment of monthly bills slackens markedly during periods of peak use, as higher-than-expected bills put unforeseen pressures on family budgets.[14]

Third, utilities exist in a regulatory environment, and regulators are particularly sensitive to customer complaints. Even though a minority of regulators are elected, all regulators exist in a political climate. Hence, a utility may expect regulatory authorities to be less than sympathetic to various alternatives available to the firm to speed up collection of accounts. Indeed, regulators may exercise a positive disservice to a utility in this problem area by giving credence to customer complaints and causing further delays by forcing meter checks or similar procedures.

At some point, services must be terminated if payment is not forthcoming. A choice, and perhaps the opportunity to build an improved public relations image, also exists for a utility. This matter of "late bills" is sometimes routinized by utilities and is not looked upon as requiring continual decision-making. In such cases, the utility may well be overlooking an opportunity to improve its public image and may become known as a bureaucratic business monopoly without a concern for individuals.

This is not to say that bills should be extended without reason and that this aspect of the financial problem of the utilities is unimportant. Indeed, this is an area of genuine concern for utilities. However, utility management should be alert to the possibility of constructing a public image of being "human" and "understanding" by avoiding routinization of this function and providing trained personnel to look into each individual customer credit problem. The bill collector and the meter man may be prime public relations representatives for the gas, power, and water companies, just as the operator is a prime public relations representative of the telephone company.

ACCOUNTING AND REPORTS

The keeping of accounts and reports involves much more than merely recording numbers in a set of books. In the utilities at least four important functions are served by accounting and reporting. These are (1) internal control, (2) regulation of rates and earnings, (3) taxation, and (4) comparability for investors and investor confidence.

In the early days of utility development the importance of these functions was little appreciated. During the promotional period there may have been actual reason to avoid having an efficient system of accounts and reports, so that some of the activities of the developers were not fully disclosed. Similarly, rate regulation was not highly developed early in the history of the utilities. With the increasing public concern about rate and earnings control, plus the growing professionalization of utility management, the need for accurate and efficient systems of accounting and reporting became self-evident.

THE ACCOUNTING ENVIRONMENT

The accounting manager operates within a set of environmental conditions just as the financial manager operates within a financial environment. While the choices or decision trade-offs are not as great for the accountant as for the financial manager, many of the problems are similar. Six factors must be recognized as affecting accounting decision-making. These are the uniform system of accounts, the overcapitalization problem, cost allocation complexities, internal control needs, tax ramifications, and comparabilty needs.

The Uniform System of Accounts

In order to achieve properly the four functions noted at the beginning of this section the utility accounting system must be uniform. Without uniformity, the comparisons necessary for internal control, rate regulation, taxation purposes, and investor confidence would be impossible.

It should be noted that two types of uniformity are needed in utility accounting.

The first is uniformity in accounting form and method within a given company from one accounting period to another. Comparisons for purposes of internal control and investor confidence require data that are similar from year to year. The second type of uniformity is the similarity of accounts among similar classes of utilities in a given geographic region. Comparisons for rate regulatory purposes, taxation, and investor confidence are impossible if one firm keeps its accounts in one manner and another firm keeps its accounts in another way. This latter type of uniformity is the most familiar one and is stressed by public regulation.

The development of uniform systems of accounts was a slow process.[15] Some state commissions, such as one in Massachusetts, set up uniform systems very early, and uniformity of accounts for railroads generally developed earlier than for utilities.[16] In some instances, the regulated utilities themselves tried to develop uniform accounting systems.[17] However, it was not until 1922, when the National Association of Railroad and Utility Commissioners (N.A.R.U.C.) prescribed a uniform classification of accounts, that many states took action in this area. These accounting rules served as models, and forty states had adopted these classifications by 1925.[18]

Substantial benefits were expected from these rules. But mere publication of orders and requirements rarely produced uniformity. It takes time to adjust accounting systems, and many diverse methods had to be made into one. Similarly, substantial revisions in systems came about during the 1930's because of some of the disclosures made during the investigation of utility holding companies.

At the federal level uniformity of accounts was achieved as federal commissions were established. The Federal Communications Commission adopted a uniform system in 1935. The Federal Power Commission invited the National Association of Railroad and Utility Commissioners to join it in developing a system of accounts which was acceptable to state agencies as well as to the F.P.C. This system was adopted by both groups in 1937.[19] Thus, a uniform system of accounts at both the federal and the state levels exists today, with forty-one states using either the F.P.C. or the N.A.R.U.C. system in electric utilities and forty states using the F.C.C. system for telephone accounting.[20]

Overcapitalization Problems

Since a utility is allowed a rate of return based on its fair value, the account listed as "utility plant" is of major importance. The F.P.C. and N.A.R.U.C. systems of accounts adopted original cost as the basis of calculating utility plant. Original cost has a special meaning in this instance. The balance sheet reflects the cost of the property to the person first devoting it to public service.

Overcapitalization had been a problem during the developmental period of utilities. During the holding company era properties were bought and sold between utilities. Standard accounting practice would be to list these items at cost. However, the prices paid for properties were not always arrived at by "arm's length bargaining" and were often inflated. Rates were frequently based on these inflated property costs.

With the special definition of original cost used in the uniform system, it is the initial cost of the property which goes into the utility plant account. If the price is higher than the original cost, the difference is either amortized over a number of years if the commission having jurisdiction agrees or charged to earned surplus and hence to stockholders. When this system was put into effect by the F.P.C. during the 1930's, it was discovered that $1.6 billion in excess of initial original cost was appearing on utility books.[21]

It is clear that the accounting manager in a utility firm operates under some very special rules regarding capital and the utility plant. In addition to these definitional matters utility accountants are required to keep continuing property records and inventories, costs of construction in progress, abandonment records, and similar items. Most of these requirements try to ensure that overcapitalization does not again become a problem.

Cost Allocation Complexities

Since operating expenses are allowed in calculating rates for services, the proper allocation of costs becomes a problem. Which expenditures should be charged to capital and which should be charged to income? The cost of doing business is one matter, the cost of new investments is another.

In addition, many utilities have operations not connected with their utility business. A regulated company is allowed a return only on property devoted to public use or utility purposes. A utility may have other investments. For example, it may sell appliances or advertising (such as in the telephone book "yellow pages"). All these nonutility items must be accounted for differently than utility items. Further, depreciation cost becomes a complex matter. With various accelerated depreciation plans, accounting for these costs affects the rates charged.

Finally, the allocation of costs among various services and many regulatory jurisdictions is complex. In a utility with two services, such as electric power and gas, the allocation of common and joint costs between the two separate services can affect the rates markedly. In the telephone industry the allocation of costs between interstate and intrastate service has always been bothersome and a point of contention. This is the famous "separations" problem, which is a study in itself.[22] United States Supreme Court Justice Douglas summed up this problem well in stating:

> A separation of properties is merely a step in the determination of costs properly allocable to the various classes of services rendered by a utility. . . . Allocation of costs is not a matter for the slide rule. It involves judgment on a myriad of facts. It has no claim to an exact science.[23]

Internal Control Needs

Most utilities now use computers and various electronic data processing systems for purposes of internal control and information. These needs must be taken into consideration by the accounting manager in two ways. First, the various accounts are the prime inputs into such systems of control. Thus, record-keeping may need to be tailored to fit the system used. Second, the accounting manager must select which information is needed at which level of management for control purposes. Too much information may be worse than not enough. When these systems were first installed, there was a tendency to furnish too much information. Expenses may go up under such circumstances without a commensurate increase in the effectiveness of control. This is a very real choice faced by the accounting manager.

While he must design and maintain a system that is efficient from a data processing viewpoint and that informs management of what it needs to know, the accounting manager must also supply information to regulatory and tax authorities. Electronic data processing has been a useful tool for the accounting function but it has not been without its problems.

Tax Ramifications

As explained in Chapter 7, the tax-paying and tax-collecting function of utilities is of considerable importance and complexity. Depreciation accounting also has many tax, as well as rate, ramifications. Sometimes conflicts between rate regulatory rules and tax commission or Internal Revenue Service rules may arise. Indeed, some utility accounting managers find it necessary to maintain two sets of accounts: one for rate regulatory purposes and one for tax purposes.

Accelerated depreciation accounting, which utilities have been allowed to do under law for some time, may cause complications not met by the usual accountant. Once more, since a utility is a public service and a regulated industry, how costs are handled will affect the rates charged the general public. The constraints of various systems such as "flow-through" or "normalization" of depreciation accounts must be taken into account by the utility accounting manager. Since systems and regulations vary from firm to firm, and from regulatory jurisdiction to jurisdiction, no generalization can be made. However, it is possible that several different systems may have to be in operation concurrently where there is no uniformity between state and federal tax agencies or state and federal regulatory agencies.

Comparability for Investors

A final factor in the utility accounting environment is the absolute need for comparability for purposes of evaluation by investors. As mentioned before, each utility takes on a financial image, created in large part by the periodic accounting reports issued by it. The accounting manager always has the problem of how much information to make available, in how much detail, and how to keep potential investors informed.

REPORTS

The preparation of periodic reports presents a real challenge to both the accounting and the financial managers. Reports for internal control purposes have already been mentioned. Further, compliance with the reporting requirements of state and federal authorities is a constant task. Reports are also required by various local, state, and federal tax jurisdictions within which the utility operates. Generally, a utility has little control of the form of these reports and the type of data required. Even so, timely and correct reporting is one of the important accounting functions.

It is in reports to stockholders and to the investing public that a utility firm may exercise its imagination and create a financial image. Easy to read and informative reports are always appreciated. Often a utility will include a good bit of basic economic data about its service territory and the geographic location in which it operates. In some instances, discussion of local economic and business conditions is helpful. Occasionally, projections of economic trends which will affect the future utility business are undertaken.

In all instances, the managers of a utility have an opportunity to project an image to the utility owners, potential investors, and the public. In a very real sense, quarterly and annual reports present a worthwhile challenge to which the utility ought to devote considerable energy. Not only can the report build a financial image but it can also serve as a public relations vehicle.

SUMMARY

In this chapter we have considered the two important managerial functions of finance and accounting. The capital acquisition problem is a major and recurring one in the utility industry, because of the industry's capital-intensive nature, its amazing long-term growth, and the refunding or revolving nature of much of its capital. All types of securities are used by utilities to raise capital, but in different proportions by different firms. A definite financial environment exists, and decisions in this area are affected by the capital structure, the regulatory structure, the necessity for competitive bidding, the need for financial creditability, and the predominance of institutional investors. Various alternative choices must be made involving the issue decision, the timing decision, the return decision, and the working capital decision. Striving for the proper financial balance in these decisions basically involves an incremental process. Finally, a special set of credit problems presents both a challenge and an opportunity to the financial manager.

In the area of accounting and reports, four functions are served. These are the need for internal control, the regulation of rates and earnings requirements, the tax function, and the function of giving investors confidence and an idea of comparability. A definite accounting environment exists within which decisions must be reached. This involves the uniform system of accounts, the overcapitalization problem, cost allocation complexities, internal control needs, tax ramifications, and comparability needs. Finally, periodic reports must be prepared for various purposes and groups, and the stockholder and public reports offer a great opportunity to enhance the image of the firm.

NOTES

1. This is in sharp contrast to other industries, such as manufacturing, where debt issues rarely make up as much as 30 per cent of the capital structure and more typically represent a considerably smaller portion.

2. There has been long-standing concern with this topic in the specialized area of finance. Much of this stemmed from the pioneering work of Franco Modigliani and Merton H. Miller, "The Cost of Capital, Corporation Finance and the Theory of Investment," *American Economic Review,* vol. 48, no. 3 (June 1958), pp. 261-297, and "Some Estimates of the Cost of Capital in the Electric Utility Industry, 1954–57," *American Economic Review,* vol. 56, no. 3 (June 1966), pp. 333-391. The literature on this subject is so extensive that the idea is now popularly referred to as the "M and M thesis."

   Other views are contained in Alexander Barges, *The Effect of Capital Structure on the Cost of Capital* (Englewood Cliffs, N.J.: Prentice-Hall, 1963); Joseph R. Rose and David Durand, "The Cost of Capital, Corporation Finance and the Theory of Investment: Comment," *American Economic Review,* vol. 49, no. 4 (September 1959), pp. 638-654; and Jean Crochett and Irwin Friend, Myron J. Gordon, Alexander A. Robichek, John G. McDonald, and Robert C. Higgins, "Some Estimates of the Cost of Capital in the Electric Utility Industry, 1954–57: Comment," *American Economic Review,* vol. 57, no. 5 (December 1967), pp. 1258-1288. Many other articles and references to this topic also exist.
3. Federal Power Commission, *State Commission Jurisdiction and Regulation of Electric and Gas Utilities, 1960* (Washington, D.C.: U.S. Government Printing Office, 1960), p. 6.
4. See Paul J. Garfield and Wallace F. Lovejoy, *Public Utility Economics* (Englewood Cliffs, N.J.: Prentice-Hall, 1964), pp. 426–430 and 441–444 for a detailed discussion of federal control of financial practices.
5. See Harvey Averch and L. L. Johnson, "Behavior of the Firm Under Regulatory Constraint," *American Economic Review,* vol. 52, no. 5 (December 1962), pp. 1052–1069; S. H. Wellisz, "Regulation of Natural Gas Pipeline Companies: An Economic Analysis," *Journal of Political Economy,* vol. 71, no. 1 (February 1963), pp. 30–43; F. M. Westfield, "Regulation and Conspiracy," *American Economic Review,* vol. 55, no. 3 (June 1965), pp. 424–443; W. G. Shepherd, "Regulatory Constraints and Public Utility Investment," *Land Economics,* vol. 42, no. 3 (August 1966), pp. 348–354; A. K. Klevorick, "The Graduated Fair Return: A Regulatory Proposal," *American Economic Review,* vol. 56, no. 3 (June 1966), pp. 477–484; Alfred E. Kahn, "The Graduated Fair Return: Comment," *American Economic Review,* vol. 57, no. 1 (March 1968), pp. 170–174; and R. H. Males, "Investment Behavior of a Utility Under Regulatory Constraint," *Public Utilities Fortnightly,* vol. 84, no. 6 (September 11, 1969), pp. 21–26.
6. Irston R. Barnes, *The Economics of Public Utility Regulation* (New York: F. S. Crofts, 1942), pp. 729–739.
7. Emery Troxel, *Economics of Public Utilities* (New York: Rinehart, 1947), p. 152.
8. Harold H. Young, *Forty Years of Public Utility Finance* (Charlottesville, Va.: University Press of Virginia, 1965), pp. 113–114. Actually only twenty-eight states and the District of Columbia require competitive bidding, and the S.E.C. exempts smaller security issues. See U.S. Federal Power Commission publication cited in note 3.
9. During the 1940's, it was estimated, 85 to 90 per cent of all utility bonds were owned by institutional investors. See Eli Winston Clemens, *Economics and Public Utilities* (New York: Appleton-Century-Crofts, 1950), p. 116. Some idea of the current situation is obtained by noting that in 1968 life insurance companies owned more than $17 billion in public utility bonds, which was 10 per cent of their total investment; $2.2 billion in utility preferred stock, about 65 per cent of their total investment in this classification; and $1.2 billion in utility common stock, about 12 per cent of their total investment of this type. See *Life Insurance Fact Book* (New York: Institute of Life Insurance, 1968), pp. 76 and 80–81.
10. For example, the common stock of the American Telephone and Telegraph Company once was commonly referred to as a "widows and orphans" investment, since it was so popular with trusts, pension funds, and insurance companies. A recent survey of forty-nine employee benefit funds showed twenty-two funds holding A.T.T. common stock, and about 12 per cent of the bond holdings of such funds in the utility category. See "Surveys of Pooled Pension Fund Holdings," *Trust and Estates,* vol. 108, no. 6 (June 1969), pp. 92–94.
11. Readers wishing to understand more completely the decision-making processes of financial managers may wish to consult James C. Van Horne, *Financial Management and Policy* (Englewood Cliffs, N.J.: Prentice-Hall, 1968) or J. Fred Weston and Eugene F. Brigham, *Managerial Finance,* 3d ed. (New York: Holt, Rinehart, and Winston, 1969).
12. Calculation of the proper cost of capital for regulatory and management purposes sounds deceptively easy. A weighted average of the costs of the various funds used by a utility in its capital structure is the typical approach. The weights used are the amounts of each factor–

bonds, preferred, and common plus surplus–times their current market value times the percentage of the capital structure existing. It should be emphasized that current market value, not historical costs, is the proper factor in the weighting. Few problems exist with bonds and preferred stock. However, several problems exist with assigning a proper cost to equity. Much debate over what ratio to use as between price-earnings or price-dividends, and how much growth to allow, has occurred in financial and regulatory circles. See Morris Mendelson, "Regulation and Utility Finance," *Land Economics,* vol. 45, no. 2 (May 1969), pp. 288–292.

13. The possibility of leasing capital equipment also exists, although it has not been as highly developed in the public utilities field as in some other types of business enterprises. The reason for this lack of popularity probably stems from the specialized nature of much of the capital of utilities and the fact that tax savings involved may be less important for utilities. While taxes saved by deducting lease payments are important to industry in general, utilities benefit less than other businesses because of the capital-intensive nature of the business and the manner in which taxes are handled for regulatory and tax purposes. For a good discussion of the benefits of leasing, see Joe Braly, "Lease or Buy: A Controversial Ouestion for Public Utilities," *Public Utilities Fortnightly,* vol. 67, no. 11 (May 25, 1961), pp. 721–732.
14. Because of this problem some utilities have instituted programs of uniform monthly bills. In such schemes use of the service for the year is estimated (with previous use data plus a growth factor) for a customer and the projected yearly bill is divided into twelve equal monthly bills.
15. See Jay H. Price, Richard Walker, and Leonard Spacek, "Accounting Uniformity in the Regulated Industries," *Law and Contemporary Problems,* vol. 30, no. 14 (1965), pp. 830–835.
16. Massachusetts specified uniform accounting for railroads in 1876, for gas companies in 1885, and for electric companies in 1887. The Interstate Commerce Commission began work on a nationwide system of uniform accounts for railroads in 1890. See Jay Rhoads Foster and Bernard S. Rodey, Jr., *Public Utility Accounting* (New York: Prentice-Hall, 1957), p. 43.
17. An early gas association did work towards this goal in 1896. See Foster and Rodey, p. 42.
18. See Charles F. Phillips, Jr., *The Economics of Regulation,* rev. ed. (Homewood, Ill.: Richard D. Irwin, 1969), p. 147.
19. See Arthur L. Litke, "Uniform Accounting–Boon or Bane for the Electric Industry?" *Public Utilities Fortnightly,* vol. 76, no. 12 (December 9, 1965), pp. 35–50.
20. Federal Power Commission, *Federal and State Commission Jurisdiction and Regulation, Electric, Gas, and Telephone Utilities, 1967* (Washington, D.C.: U.S. Government Printing Office, 1968), p. 18.
21. Litke, p. 43.
22. For a comprehensive treatment of this problem, see Richard Gabel, *Development of Separations Principles in the Telephone Industry.* M.S.U. Public Utilities Studies (East Lansing, Mich.: Institute of Public Utilities, Michigan State University, 1967), p. 166.
23. *Colorado Interstate Gas Co. v. Federal Power Commission,* 324 U.S. 581, 589 (1945).

ADDITIONAL READINGS

1. Bauer, John, and Nathaniel Gold, *Updating Public Utility Regulation* (Chicago: Public Administration Service, 1966), ch. 10, "Obtaining New Capital Funds," pp. 154–167.
2. Clemens, Eli Winston, *Economics and Public Utilities* (New York: Appleton-Century-Crofts, 1950), ch. 5, "Public Utility Finance," pp. 100–126; ch. 19, "The Regulation of Accounting," pp. 451–463; ch. 20, "Regulation of Securities and Finance," pp. 464–485.
3. Garfield, Paul J., and Wallace F. Lovejoy *Public Utility Economics* (Englewood Cliffs, N.J.: Prentice-Hall, 1964), ch. 19, "Utility Financing and Financial Regulation," pp. 412–433.

4. Glaeser, Martin G., *Public Utilities in American Capitalism* (New York: Macmillan, 1957), ch. 16, "Accounting Methods and Regulation," pp. 254–269; ch. 22, "The Control of Financial Policies," pp. 367–383.
5. Leavenworth, Richard S., *Engineering-Economic Aspects of the Decision-Making Process in Municipal Electric Utilities.* Report EEP–10 (Stanford, Calif.: Institute of Engineering-Economic Systems, Stanford University, 1964), ch. 4, "The Discount Rate," pp. 95–107; ch. 6, "Financing New Plant," pp. 146–154.
6. Phillips, Charles F., Jr., *The Economics of Regulation: Theory and Practice in the Transportation and Public Utility Industries,* rev. ed. (Homewood, Ill.: Richard D. Irwin, 1969), ch. 6, "Accounting and Financing," pp. 143–177.
7. Salmonson, Roland F., ed., *Public Utility Accounting: Models, Mergers and Information Systems.* M.S.U. Public Utilities Studies (East Lansing, Mich.: Institute of Public Utilities, Michigan State University, 1971).
8. Solomon, Ezra, "Alternative Rate of Return Concepts and Their Implication for Utility Regulation," *The Bell Journal of Economics and Management Science,* vol. 1, no. 1 (Spring 1970), pp. 65–81.
9. Tenner, Irving, *Financial Administration of Municipal Utilities* (Chicago: Public Administration Service, 1947), ch. 2, "Financial Policies," pp. 9–15; ch. 4, "Preparing and Controlling the Budget," pp. 31–43; ch. 5, "Debt Administration," pp. 45–61; ch. 7, "Cash and Banking," pp. 77–89.
10. Trebing, Harry M., and R. Hayden Howard, eds., *Rate of Return Under Regulation: New Directions and Perspectives.* M.S.U. Public Utilities Studies (East Lansing, Mich.: Institute of Public Utilities, Michigan State University, 1969). See the following articles in particular: Myron J. Gordon, "Rate of Return on Equity Capital Under Regulation," pp. 65–72; Robert S. Hamada, "The Effect of Leverage and Corporate Taxes on the Shareholders of Regulated Utilities," pp. 73–97; and A. James Meigs, "Capital Flows to Public Utilities and the Structure of the Money and Capital Markets," pp. 33–56.
11. Troxel, Emery, *Economics of Public Utilities* (New York: Rinehart, 1947), ch. 6, "Accounting Control," pp. 115–137; ch. 7, "Regulation of Financing," pp. 138–163.
12. Young, Harold H., *Forty Years of Public Utility Finance* (Charlottesville, Va.: University Press of Virginia, 1965).

14

Utility Pricing Policies and Problems

The pricing of utility services is a key managerial function. Administrative commissions typically do not set prices. Rather, the usual procedure is for an administrative or regulatory commission to ascertain the earnings level or revenue requirements of a utility. The task of translating this level of earnings into specific rates is up to the utility itself, subject to commission scrutiny for possible discrimination and ultimate approval.

Hence, there are two approaches possible to setting rates. One has to do with overall revenue requirements and the other with specific prices, rate structures, and rate schedules. These approaches are interconnected. However, there has been far more controversy over revenue requirements and fair value than over specific rates and rate schedules.

Utility pricing is a special case of general pricing. Generally, prices are determined by supply and demand, but it is what lies behind supply and demand that is important. To understand prices one must understand the determinants, elasticity, and peculiarities of demand, the costs and factor prices of the firm, and any special economic factors of the industry involved. That is, one must understand the peculiar pricing environment.

THE UTILITY PRICING ENVIRONMENT

Utility prices differ in complexity and function from general prices, because of the peculiar economic characteristics surrounding the industry. It should be noted that it is the combination of these characteristics which is unique to utilities, not the existence of any one characteristic. Each of these can be found in industries not considered utilities, but the "bundle" or combination of economic characteristics probably is unique to utilities.

CAPITAL CHARACTERISTICS

Utilities have more dollars invested in capital per dollar of sale than do most other industries. For pricing purposes, this means that utilities have a high level of fixed costs. The dollars invested typically are contractual; thus interest and amortization charges continue regardless of output. This is the typical definition of fixed costs (costs which continue even at zero output).

Not only are utilities capital-intensive, with high fixed costs, but the capital is of a specialized type with little alternative use. Since the capital rarely can be shifted to other undertakings, economists call it "sunk capital." That is, it is sunk into one use and usually into one geographic area as well. Many industries possess types of capital which can be shifted to other uses or other places. But a power generating plant can do little other than generate power, or a gas or water line has but a single function and is literally sunk in the ground, making it immovable.

The importance of sunk cost for utility pricing is that since there is no alternative use for the capital, there will be great pressure on utility managers to use their plants someway or somehow under all circumstances. Since it is only through use of the investment that capital can be recovered, various pricing forms may arise which keep the capital producing yet do not return fully allocated costs. Given the sunk nature of capital in utilities, it is sometimes better to use a plant and recover a part of the costs than not to use it at all.

SERVICE CHARACTERISTICS

It is often said that the service of a utility is essential. Given our type of society and standard of living, this is probably true. While we stop short of calling utility services necessities, and while life could go on without them, life would be a good bit less pleasant without power, gas, water, and telephones. Modern society is based on instant utility service, and if we intend to maintain anything resembling our present way of life, utility services are essential.

This essentiality factor means that some users have little choice and little opportunity to bargain. For the average household, either telephone service is provided or it is not, electricity is used or it is not, water is piped in or it is not. The degree of use can vary, but a customer cannot decide to have 10 per cent power or telephone services one month but not the next. Few customers can furnish their own utility services. While large users, such as industrial customers, can provide their own, most customers use such a small amount that it would be uneconomical to provide their own. For them it is a "to use or not to use" question.

Clearly, this essentiality factor can creep into pricing. For the user with little alternative, a utility can exploit its position as a supplier. Perhaps in the past some utility managers have taken advantage of the essentiality factor. At least some state regulatory boards see their role as one of protecting consumers faced with little choice.

In addition, utilities are faced with the problem of a product which cannot be stored or produced for inventory and brought out to satisfy demand during peak periods. While it is true that sometimes the factors going into utility production, such as natural gas, or water, or coal, can be stored for future use, this does not change the fact that the delivery system or the production system must be designed with instantaneous demand in mind. When you flip a light switch or turn a faucet or pick up the phone, you are demanding utility service. And the utility must be prepared to serve you at that very instant, without delay, and with high quality service. This means that considerable plant and investment must be on hand just in case everyone picks up the phone or flips the light switch at the same time. Hence, excess capacity is almost always present in a utility plant.

However, excess capacity, available to serve if needed, must be paid for. Users must pay for its "readiness to serve." This need for excess capacity creates a pricing problem. How much excess capacity is needed at any one time? Who should be charged for this "readiness to serve" capability? What is a fair way to reflect these pricing problems in rates and not unduly restrict or affect demand?

COST CHARACTERISTICS

Partly because of the high level of fixed costs, and partly because of technology, utilities generally are decreasing cost industries. By using fixed costs more intensively, per-unit costs go down as output increases. With a given unit of plant, the economies of production may be considerable. Further, from a long-run cost viewpoint, utilities also attain lower unit costs as the size of plant increases. The economies of large scale production seem to continue on and on as utilities expand in size. Costs per kilowatt of installed electric capability go down as larger and larger units are installed; a twelve-inch gas line is more than twice as efficient as a six-inch line, and the like.

Knowledge of both of these factors of decreasing per-unit cost (greater utilization of a given plant and economies of large scale production) are not lost on utility managers and regulators. This means that added customers sometimes can be sought at prices lower than those paid by existing customers if such actions will cause unit costs to fall. That is, decreasing costs, combined with the characteristics of large sunk investments, the essentiality of "monopoly" services, and the existence of excess capacity provide a powerful inducement for utilities to discriminate among customers by charging different customers different prices for the same quantities of service.

UTILITY PRICING THEORY

All pricing policies and prices are ultimately based on some type of pricing theory. While the details of pricing theory in general, and even many of the finer points of utility pricing theory, are beyond the scope of this book, the necessary fundamentals are not too difficult to grasp. For our present purposes, this includes some basic knowledge of how the concepts of demand, supply, differential pricing, promotional pricing, and marginal cost pricing influence utility pricing policies and rate schedules. Readers desiring more extensive or specialized background in this area will find an abundance of literature available, ranging from elementary economics textbooks to extremely esoteric treatises, monographs, and journal articles. The figures at the end of this chapter briefly present some of the key theoretical pricing concepts involved.

DEMAND OR CLASS PRICING

If utility management were not restricted by regulation or possible shifts of customers to other means of service, theoretically it could set a separate price for each customer just equal to what the service is worth to him. But in the practical world prices must be administered. Even though utility management could theoretically charge what the traffic would bear, pragmatically it could not go this far simply because the paperwork connected with pricing would be burdensome. Also, managers of utilities are concerned about the long run and about the image of the company. Hence, they cannot maximize in this theoretical sense because of administrative and pragmatic reasons. In addition, of course, utilities are subject to regulatory restraint.

But utility management can and does set up various classes of customers, and it can and does discriminate in the simple sense of charging different prices for the same service. While it may not maximize in the absolute sense, management does maximize in a more limited sense. This is done by "class pricing."

Generally, customers are classified according to their elasticities of demand. Elasticity of demand in reality is a conceptualization of the availability of alternatives. Elasticity measures the responsiveness of quantity purchased to changes in price; an elastic demand is very responsive, an inelastic demand, not very responsive. For example, a 10 per cent price change causes more (if elastic) or less (if inelastic) than a 10 per cent change in the quantity purchased. In effect, some (price elastic) customers can shift to other sources more readily in response to price changes, while some (price inelastic) customers have few alternatives and will not readily shift.

Of course, there may be many subclasses and many rate schedules established. However, in almost all utilities at least three classes are used for pricing. Residential customers generally have the least elastic demand schedules. Their ability to substitute is very small. Commercial customers have more power to substitute. Sometimes they are large enough to combine and supply their own services, such as some shopping centers using gas turbines to produce their own electric power. Considerable amounts of power are used for lighting and display purposes; thus a small change in price may cause a response in service used. Finally, industrial customers are very large users of power. Generally, they demand and receive the lowest prices. Often they are such large users that they can produce their own supply of electricity. Also, substitution can take place. For instance, if electricity is used for heating processes, gas can be substituted. This may be worthwhile if price increases even slightly or if the alternative energy source is much cheaper. Hence, industrial demand is very price elastic and this class receives the lowest price of all.

To summarize, the first step in utility pricing is dividing the market demand into classes based on elasticities. Considerable variations in elasticities exist, with residential classes having the least elastic, commercial classes a more elastic, and industrial classes the most elastic demand. Price schedules reflect these class divisions and elasticities by charging the highest prices for residential consumers, middle prices for commercial classes, and lowest prices for industrial classes of customers. The system of class pricing is made possible by elements of monopoly, a necessary attribute to establishment of classes in the first place, and resale is made difficult in order for the system of class prices to prevail.

SUPPLY AND COSTS

Supply in effect is made up of costs. For utility pricing, the simple classification of costs into fixed and variable costs is useful. Fixed costs are those costs which do not vary with output and which are literally fixed in the short run; that is, those costs which continue even with zero output. Variable costs, on the other hand, increase as output increases (although not necessarily proportionately) and decrease as output decreases. In a utility, fixed costs encompass most of the plant costs, such as interest, amortization, time depreciation, overhead, and administrative costs. Variable costs would involve labor, use depreciation, expendable supplies, fuel inputs, and the like.

Costs can also be divided up (to some degree) among the various customer classes. There is some evidence that it costs a utility less per unit to serve a large user than to serve a small user. While the exact extent of these cost savings depends on each situation, it is clear that a large industrial user must be billed only once, while many small users buying the same amount of service must be billed many times. Economies in other service costs, such as meters, accounting, or repairs and maintenance will be less for one large customer than for many small customers. For various reasons, some differences in costs of serving the various classes exist.

Utility managers know that these service cost differences exist, and they know the difference between fixed and variable costs. (Utilities are faced with a high level of fixed costs, as noted.) Given this situation, management attempts to apply the "contribution concept" to utility pricing.

The contribution concept merely means that each previously established customer class should have a price which makes the greatest total contribution to overall revenue and still serves the customer class. In effect, management attempts to price each class in such a way as to cover the variable costs of serving that class and make the greatest total contribution to overall fixed costs. Variable costs for each class (and in general) are a minimum below which prices cannot go. However, since fixed costs are relatively large and variable costs are relatively small, this minimum often is quite small.

On some customer classes, prices will recover both variable and fixed costs and considerably more. On other classes, prices may recover just variable and fixed costs. Finally, on some classes, prices may recover just variable costs and only a small portion of fixed costs. Even so, the greatest total contribution has been made. If the service sold at a low price had not been sold at all, fixed costs would have continued and would have had to be covered by other customers.

In summary, the second step in utility pricing is to divide costs into variable and fixed costs, and by customer class. Next, each price for each class is set in such a way as to always cover variable costs and make the greatest total contribution possible to fixed costs and still sell the service.

DIFFERENTIAL OR DISCRIMINATORY PRICING

Now both sides of the demand-supply equation can be put together. The result is what is commonly called differential pricing, with economic discrimination. Customers are classified according to elasticities, and each class is charged a price which covers variable costs and makes the greatest total contribution to fixed costs while still serving the customer class. This leads to the highest price for residential, next highest for commercial, and lowest price for industrial classes of customers. Industrial classes may be served at less than total costs, but if excess capacity is available (and it almost always is) and the price covers variable costs and makes some contribution to fixed costs, it is worthwhile to give this class a lower "discriminatory" price.

Actually, the lower price to industrial customers may not be discriminatory in the economic sense. Economic discrimination usually is defined as differences in prices not reflecting differences in costs. It may cost less to serve a large customer. Administrative, billing, and service costs per unit of use may be considerably lower to industrial customers. If it actually costs less for the utility to serve a large customer, equity seems to indicate that he should pay less. A lower price under these conditions does not discriminate against the high-cost class of customer and in favor of the low-cost class of customer; it merely reflects reality.

The existence of a high number of common and joint costs also complicates the matter of economic discrimination. Common costs are those costs which are common to the entire output of the firm, that is, they are difficult to allocate to a single unit of production. This commonality of costs extends to various customer classes as well. A typical example of common costs is the general category called "administrative expenses." It is almost impossible to allocate meaningfully the salary of the president of a firm to given blocks of output. The same can be said for public relations expenses, marketing expenses, and the like. These expenses are common to all units of output.

A separate subgroup of common costs are joint costs, which are not only difficult to allocate but are produced in fixed proportions. The classic example of these costs is in the production of cotton and cottonseed. One cannot be produced without the other, and there is no way to separate the costs of producing either product as a separate entity.

Since the definition of economic discrimination turns on differences in prices not reflecting differences in costs, the existence of common and joint costs inevitably leads to discrimination. That is, if it is impossible to ascertain per unit costs because of these difficulties, the firm always (by definition) discriminates.[1]

Quite apart from the matter of economic discrimination, if a customer class with an elastic demand pays less than the total of the variable and fixed cost of serving it (in effect is given favorable discriminatory rates), all customers may be better off because of this. If excess capacity is available, and given the fact that fixed costs must be met by all customers collectively, if a customer receiving the lower price pays the variable costs of serving him and makes any contribution to fixed costs at all, all customers will have to pay less in fixed costs than if he were not served. All customers gain as long as the favored customers pay their variable costs and make a contribution to fixed costs.

This is one of the hardest concepts for the general public and regulators to understand, because it is based on discrimination and unequal price treatment. It also leads to various types of promotional pricing and to complicated pricing structures which are not easily understood by customers. Of course, it can lead to abuses as well.

However, if properly understood, differential pricing is a benefit to all customers if the lower price covers variable costs and makes some contribution to fixed cost, and if excess capacity exists which would not be used except by offering the lower discriminatory price.

PROMOTIONAL PRICING

Many types of pricing structures are designed to promote demand or stimulate use. The most obvious type of promotional pricing is where a firm intentionally sets its price to some customer class below both fixed and variable costs in the hope that use of the service will build up to the point at which a future net revenue contribution is made. This type of "loss leader" pricing was practiced by some early utilities but today generally is not permitted by regulatory authorities.

It is well to remember, however, that the demand for utility services is not the same over the twenty-four hours of a day, the thirty days of a month, or the twelve months of a year. Utility demand fluctuates over time, and this presents opportunities for promotional pricing.

Certain classes of customers may be given very low rates if they are willing to take service at off-peak hours. Electric water-heating rates which provide for use only during certain periods of the day are an example of this pricing form. An example of a similar pricing form is service to customers on an "interruption" basis. Here the customer gets a very low rate for the service, but it may be interrupted or taken away if needed elsewhere in the utility system. Some natural gas utilities use this pricing form for industries utilizing service during the slack summer months, with possible interruption during the peak winter months.

It would be theoretically possible to set rates in such a way as to vary them during the day, charging customers lower rates during the times that the plant is used at less than full capacity and higher rates during the full-capacity or peak periods. Just as long as the price charged covers the variable costs of the service and makes some contribution to fixed expenses, and as long as excess capacity exists, such pricing forms are economical. These promotional devices are not only economical to the firm but, as noted, they are beneficial to all customers, since many of the costs of service are sunk and little alternative exists.[2]

MARGINAL COST PRICING

Marginal cost pricing is closely akin to promotional pricing. This concept has stirred the interest of theoretical economists for many years. It is based on normative judgments relative to the best allocation of resources in the economy. The concept turns on the idea that price should stimulate use and that a firm should aim at getting the greatest possible economies of scale. Price under such a plan is a consumer rationing device only and theoretically should follow marginal costs of production.[3]

If prices were equal to marginal costs only, more customers could use the service and the best allocation of resources would prevail. In effect, this would "discourage the wasteful use of public utility services while promoting all use that is economically justified in view of the relationship between cost incurred and benefits received."[4]

It should be noted that in a decreasing cost industry, rates based on marginal cost would be too low to cover total costs of production over time. A subsidy would be necessary to make up this difference. Obviously, this lack of revenue to cover total costs limits the application of the concept for privately owned nonsubsidized utility firms. However, marginal cost pricing is an alternative in government-owned utility plants.[5]

MANAGEMENT APPROACHES TO RATE STRUCTURES

The problem of designing meaningful rate structures is difficult. Pricing schedules must be constructed to allow convenient and efficient administration, while at the same time being easily understood by the public and lending themselves to convenient billing and collecting. Management rarely talks in terms of fixed, variable, common, marginal, and incremental costs. The contribution theory, while well known in principle, is usually not conceived in terms of neat graphs and hypothetical textbook discussions of elasticities of demand and class pricing. Yet the task of translating pricing theory into pricing practice is performed typically by the economics and rates department.

Usually, the process of making price or rate schedules involves four steps: defining costs from a managerial viewpoint, distributing costs among customer classes, considering measurement factors with modifications of costs, and designing pricing structures reflective of the first three steps.

MANAGERIAL COST DEFINITIONS

From management's point of view, costs can be broken down into the four categories of customer, operational, demand, and overhead or general expenses.

Most utilities have some costs or expenses directly related to customers. These include such things as meter reading, accounting, billing, collecting accounts, and connecting and disconnecting services. These expenses are found in varying degrees in power, gas, telephone, and water utilities. Local transit utilities are an exception.

Every utility also has some costs directly related to operations. These may be called "operational costs," "output costs," "energy costs," or sometimes "commodity costs." These include such things as salaries of operating personnel, cost of energy or commodity inputs (coal, gas, or nuclear energy for power, the wholesale cost of natural gas for a natural gas distribution utility, and the field gas price for gas transmission companies), maintenance and repair charges related to operating the system, use depreciation, excise taxes or sales taxes–in short, all those costs resulting from the operation of a utility system.

Perhaps the largest costs, and the most difficult to handle for management, are the "demand costs." These are often referred to as "readiness to serve costs," "capacity costs," or "load costs." Generally, these include the cost of a utility plant, its production and distribution system, property taxes, time depreciation and obsolescence, capital charges, return on rate base, charges earned during construction—that is, all costs associated with supplying a utility system ready to serve any demands placed upon it.

The final cost category is overhead or general expenses. Administrative costs, marketing and public relations expenses, supervision costs, costs of purchasing and supply, industrial relations costs, and other similar costs which involve the entire operation are often common, or general in nature, and are thus difficult to assign to a specific phase of the utility business.

COST DISTRIBUTION TO CUSTOMER CLASSES

As noted before, prices charged to various customer classes vary. Part of this variation occurs because each customer class does not require expenditure of equal amounts as far as the utility is concerned. In order to have the rates charged at least partly reflect the costs of servicing each customer, managerial defined costs must be distributed or allocated to various customer classes.

Costs in the first category, customer costs, are allocated according to the number of customers. Each customer requires an account, a connection and ultimately a disconnection, a meter read monthly (or other period), and the like. Costs in the second category, operational costs, vary with the volume of use of the service. They can be allocated on a use basis. Typically, they increase as use increases and decrease as use decreases.

Costs in the third category, demand costs, are the most difficult to allocate. Various customers place different demands on the utility system at different times. Some help in allocation of these costs is gained by understanding some of the technical measurement concepts discussed in the next section. But the point is that some allocation of "readiness to serve" or "capacity" must be made according to the demands or potential demands a customer places on the utility plant.

Costs in the final category, general expenses, are usually common to the entire operation. Therefore, they are arbitrarily allocated in some proportion to all other costs by some convenient accounting method.

MEASUREMENT FACTORS

While practice among utilities varies, most managers recognize four factors or measurements of service which must be considered when establishing a rate or a price. These are peak load, the load factor, the utilization factor, and the diversity factor.

The peak load is the maximum production of the utility system during a stated time period. Sometimes this is referred to as "peak demand." It can be calculated in terms of a day, a month, or a year. Because utility service is nonstorable, the system must be able to meet the peak demand with some level of reserve for contingencies.

Knowledge of peak loads is important for planning and forecasting purposes. If promotional pricing is practiced, knowledge of daily, monthly, and annual peaks is absolutely necessary in order to give lower prices during off-peak periods to stimulate demand. Also, a utility may wish to apply a price penalty against those customers who contribute to the peak period.

The load factor is defined as the average load or use of the facilities expressed as a percentage of the maximum use or peak load during a particular period of time. Load factors may be calculated for any time period or for any group of customers or for any plant, or for an entire utility system. Since the majority of the costs of a utility are fixed and sunk, they will continue regardless of use. Therefore, it is to a utility's advantage to raise its load factor as high as possible. This may be done by pricing, such as promotional pricing, or by marketing efforts. In effect, a high load factor means the utility is getting economies of plant and lower average unit costs.

The third measurement is the utilization factor. The concern here is with reserve capacity. The utilization factor is the peak load as a percentage of system capacity. Reserve capacity is the difference between the utilization factor and 100.[6]

The diversity factor is the final measure of importance. This is the ratio of the sum of the noncoincident peak loads of all the system's customer classes to the system maximum demand. Each customer or class of customers has a different peak period. If they all come at the same time, the diversity factor will be 1. But if the various peak demands come at different times, the diversity factor will be higher. It is clearly economical for a utility to stimulate use by customers whose peak demands come at times other than the system's peak demand in order to utilize its plant more fully. These customers are said to have a high diversity factor.

The higher the diversity factor, the less total system capacity is needed to serve a given customer class. By having many types of customers with many noncoincidental demands, a utility may be able to lower costs in spite of a low load factor. This was one of the factors leading to consolidation of utilities early in their history. However, it should be noted that a customer class cannot at the same time have a high load factor and a high diversity factor.[7]

In summary, these four measurement factors are particularly helpful in allocating demand costs. A customer adding to the peak load causes higher demand costs. A customer adding to the load factor at off-peak periods is valuable because he has lower demand costs. A customer who causes an increase in utilization factor (adding to peak load) is using up excess capacity, and up to a point he is to be encouraged. A customer with a high diversity factor (his peak coming at other than the system peak) is to be encouraged. Understanding these measurement factors as they apply to different customers helps to allocate demand costs and to structure rate forms.

ACTUAL RATE STRUCTURES

During an earlier period utilities had neither effective measuring devices nor appreciation of the economies of size. As various metering or measuring devices were developed, and as it became apparent that decreasing costs were possible with wider use, more sophisticated rate structures evolved. Even so, examples of some historical rate structures still remain in use.

Basically, eight rate structures are noted here. These are (1) flat charges, (2) flat rates, (3) fixture rates, (4) step rates, (5) block rates, (6) demand rates, (7) zone rates, and (8) miscellaneous rates. There are still other rate structures and combinations of structures, but knowledge of these eight gives one a firm foundation in utility rate structures.

The earliest form of rates was simply a *flat charge* for a given time period. Typically, the rate was stated as so much per month, with no attempt to measure use or the various demands that different customers placed on the system. The total charge per month, of course, had to be sufficient to cover all the customer, operating, and demand costs.

The idea of a fixed monthly charge is still found in the concept of the minimum bill, while some utilities continue to use a flat charge. Many local water utilities have a flat monthly charge, and local telephone service is typically based on a flat monthly charge regardless of use or demand on the system. Similarly, many electric companies use a flat charge for street lighting services.

The main criticism of flat charges is that they tend to promote waste. When each customer pays the same amount regardless of use, there is no desire to economize or wisely use the service. This pricing structure can also be criticized for not measuring either use or demand.

With the advent of inexpensive measurement devices, the *flat rate* came into use. Here the charge per unit of use remains the same, regardless of the amount used. Use of the service is taken into consideration, and recognition is given to operative costs. When employed in connection with a minimum bill or minimum charge to collect a portion of customer costs, this rate form may effectively recoup customer and operational costs. (Demand costs must be included as a part of operational costs.) No recognition is given to decreasing costs per unit, to economies of size, or to the measurement factors noted in the previous section.

Some utilities still use this type of rate, often called a "straight-line rate." Some water rates are based on a straight per-gallon use, some off-peak power rates and interruptive gas rates are straight-line, and some long-distance telephone rates and transit rates are flat use rates modified by distance zones.

Fixture rates attempt to measure the demand a customer places on a utility system. These differentials can be used with either flat charges or flat rates. Higher rates are charged where more fixtures or more opportunity for use exists. Examples of fixture rates are found in water rates where the number of faucets are measured, some commercial power rates where candlepower of lighting displays is used as a differential, residential electric rates where the number of appliances is counted, and some commercial telephone rates where the number of phones in an office determines the charge.

Some differential fixture charges are nonproportional and thus reflect economies of use. For example, some electric power rates are for basic service, with a somewhat higher schedule where a range and refrigerator are involved, and with a still higher rate for "all electric service." These schedules are examples of fixture differentials, and rates do not increase in proportion to the number of appliances.

Step rates recognize that use should be stimulated in order to decrease per unit costs and that customers should share in these economies. The per unit charge steps downward as use increases. These rates are rarely used today, because they are regressive and can promote waste.

Block rates are a modification of step rates which overcomes the regressiveness problem. Pricing is on a per-unit basis within blocks of units, with lower per-unit prices in each successive block. When used with a minimum monthly charge, such rate structures partly cover customer costs, give recognition to operational costs, and share economies of better use of the system.

Demand costs are not covered in block rate schedules. They must be recouped by a minimum bill which exceeds customer costs, a high initial block or two blocks, a factor in each block to reflect demand costs, or a combination of these. The exact construction of such a schedule is a matter of managerial judgment and rate expertise.

Block systems are typically used in residential service by power, gas, and water utilities, and they are the rate structure most widely known by utility customers. Where message units are used as a measuring device, block rates also are found in local service telephone rates.

Demand rates are used to reflect the demand costs or "readiness to serve" factor. Essentially, these follow the block concept, with either an added demand or load factor schedule, or with the demand factor built into the block structure. Such rates are used mainly for larger customers, such as the commercial and industrial users.

As an illustrative example, the Hopkinson Demand Rate, developed for industrial electricity consumers as early as the 1890's, is a two-part or two-factor rate using a demand charge. The customer pays a charge for the maximum load he puts on the system. Since the system must be designed to cover this load and must be paid for even though this capacity is used for only a short time, this certainly is reasonable. It should also be noted that the demand charge decreases as demand increases, reflecting both the diversity factor and the economies of use of capital. The "energy charge," while in larger units than the typical block rates for residential customers, reflects operational costs plus economies of large use. A minimum charge also may be included to reflect customer costs.[8]

Zone rates based on distance are common in telephone, telegraph, natural gas pipeline and transit utilities. The zones are variously defined. Telegraph uses a uniform grid overlay system and charges air distance rates between points, long-distance telephone is tapered between zones (increasing at a decreasing rate as distance increases), and gas pipeline and transit rates are based on arbitrarily defined areas. Sometimes demand and use charges are included.

Because almost all prices charged by utilities must be approved by some regulatory commission, numerous rates appear in tariff publications which do not fall neatly into the above categories. These can be called *miscellaneous rates.* They include such things as service charges for connecting and disconnecting customers; charges for special wiring or extensions in power and telephone; charges for longer cords, color phones, or special equipment in telephone; allowances for "all electric" or "all gas" residences, and the like.

In addition, there are many variations of rate forms. Only the ingenuity of utility rate and economics departments limits the various combinations. Rates can be very complex; yet all are designed to recoup customer, operational, demand, and overhead expenses, with modifications to reflect the peak load, the load factor, the utilization factor, and the diversity factor.

SUMMARY: THE ATTRIBUTES OF A "GOOD" RATE

Public utility pricing is extremely complex, although the degree of complexity can range from the elaborate methods sometimes used in pricing electric services to the much more simple methods often used in pricing street transit or water systems. Whatever methods are used, attention must be given to the differing elasticities of customer demands, to various categories of costs both from the economic and the managerial viewpoints, and to political and legal implications of rate structures and levels.

Ideally, a "good" rate or rate structure should meet several criteria. Among other things, it should be reasonable and not unduly discriminatory. It should provide a relatively stable cash inflow to the firm, while enabling the firm to maintain its financial integrity. It should reflect economies of use and of scale and share these economies with consumers, without waste or misallocation of economic resources. It should be convenient for the customer to pay and convenient and inexpensive for the firm to collect. And from a public relations viewpoint, it should be easy for a customer to understand the basis upon which he is charged.

Needless to say, not all rates meet all these criteria.

Appendix: Theoretical Pricing Concepts

Figure 14–1 shows seven separate hypothetical supply curves cutting a hypothetical electric power demand curve. In a competitive market the price would be established by the equilibrium of supply and demand for the industry as a whole, at P_1, with each firm furnishing a small portion of the supply. But the typical utility case involves only a single firm in a market; that is, the firm is the industry.

In this situation some customers are willing to pay P_7, others P_6, and so on downwards to P_1. However, because of the single price, no one pays more than P_1; all customers willing to pay more receive a "consumers' surplus," whose total is represented by the shaded area $P_1P_7S_7S_1$. The utility's revenue is measured by the area $OP_1S_1Q_1$.

In the absence of regulation or other restrictions, a "discriminating monopolist" could set "value of service" prices for each individual customer, thus taking away all consumers' surplus and increasing firm revenues to $OP_7S_7S_1Q_1$. Since this is not possible or feasible in the real world, though, the utility may settle for recovering only a portion of this surplus by engaging in class pricing.

Figure 14–2 shows three supply curves, representing three separate customer classes (S_3, residential; S_2, commercial; S_1, industrial), cutting the demand curve. By charging each class separate prices, P_3, P_2, and P_1, the utility increases its revenues to the amount represented by the hatched area; it does not, however, appropriate all of the consumers' surplus.

Figure 14–1 Value of Service Pricing

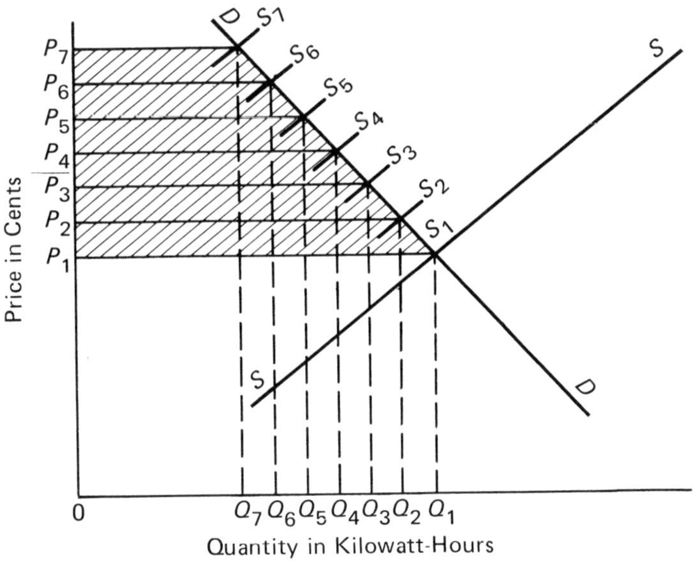

Figure 14–2 General Class Pricing

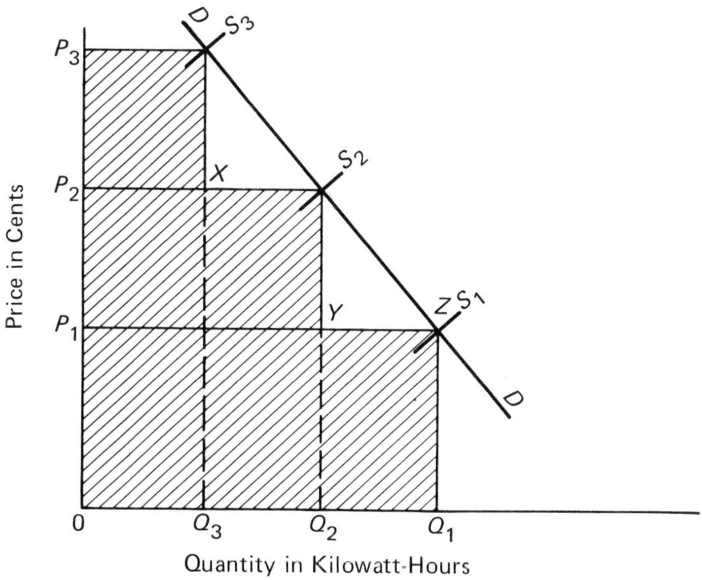

Figure 14-3 more realistically shows separate demand schedules, with differing degrees of elasticity (D_3, or residential, least elastic; D_1, industrial, most elastic), cutting the three supply schedules. Separate equilibrium prices for each class, established at quite different levels, are designed to obtain the optimum revenue contribution and the greatest possible amount of consumers' surplus from each class. Clearly, customers buying at lower prices (such as P_1)must not be allowed to resell to those with less elastic demands and higher prices (as P_3).

Figure 14-3 Class Pricing with Different Demand Elasticities

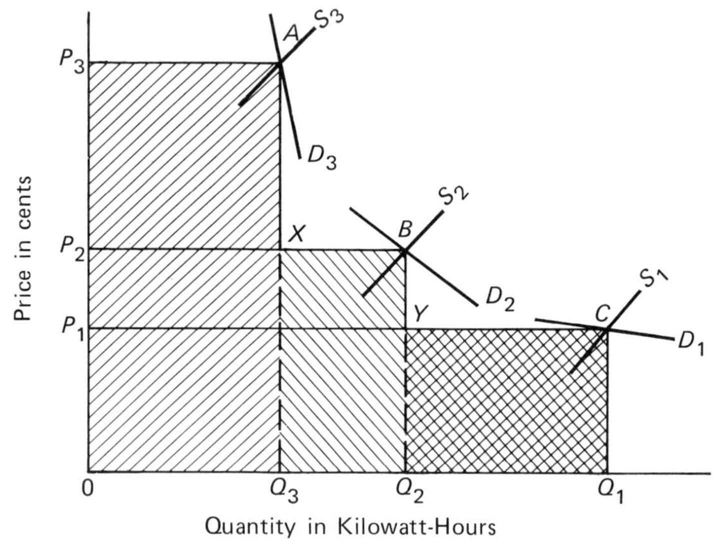

Figure 14-4 shows the effects of marginal cost pricing under conditions of a U-shaped average total cost curve (note that marginal revenue, fixed cost, and variable cost curves are omitted for simplicity).

A nonregulated firm might price at *OR* and sell quantity *OX*, receiving excess profits of *RMTC*. Under regulation (and assuming that ATC includes a fair rate of return on a fair value) price probably would be set at *OB*, resulting in sales of *OY*. Marginal cost pricing, however, would decrease the price to *OA* and increase the quantity sold to *OZ*. Although society's consumption would be increased (from *Y* to *Z*), the firm would be operating at a loss—this could not continue indefinitely.

Figure 14-4 Marginal Cost Pricing

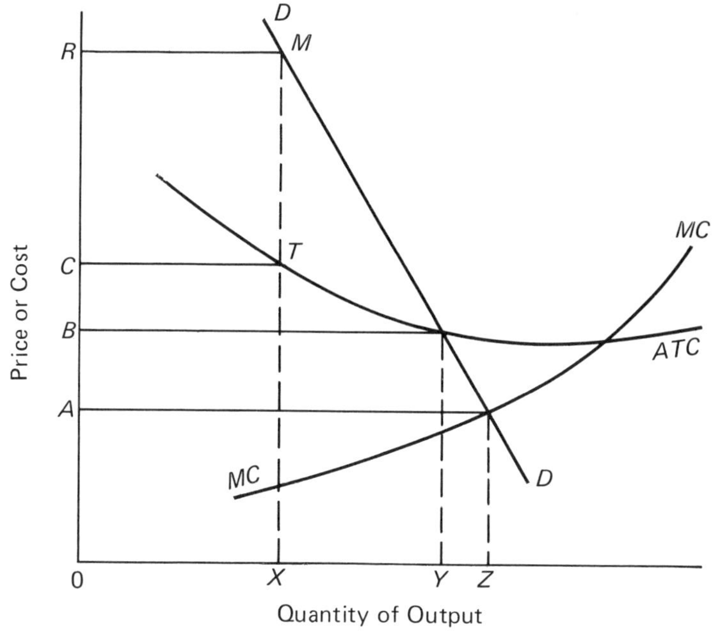

NOTES

1. The literature on common and joint costs and their effect on regulated prices is widespread. The joint cost effect was first noted by F. W. Taussig, "A Contribution to the Theory of Railroad Rates," *Quarterly Journal of Economics,* vol. 5 (July 1891), pp. 443–445. It was further refined in a famous series of comments by A. C. Pigou and Taussig, "Railway Rates and Joint Costs," *Quarterly Journal of Economics,* vol. 27 (February & June 1913), pp. 378–381, 535–538, 687–694; and was conclusively discussed by Donald H. Wallace, "Joint and Overhead Costs and Railway Rate Policy," *Quarterly Journal of Economics,* vol. 48 (August 1934), pp. 583–619.
2. The theory and mechanics of such peak load pricing can be found in Ralph Kirby Davidson, *Price Discrimination in Selling Gas and Electricity* (Baltimore: Johns Hopkins Press, 1955); and in Marcel Boiteux, "Peak-Load Pricing," in James R. Nelson, ed., *Marginal Cost Pricing in Practice* (Englewood Cliffs, N.J.: Prentice-Hall, 1964), pp. 59–89. S. C. Littlechild provides a good review of the literature in "Peak-Load Pricing of Telephone Calls," *The Bell Journal of Economics and Management Science,* vol. 1, no. 2 (Autumn 1970), pp. 199–210. Also see P. O. Steiner, "Peak Loads and Efficient Pricing," *Quarterly Journal of Economics,* vol. 71, no. 4 (November 1957), pp. 585–610; Jack Hirshleifer, "Comment," *Quarterly Journal of Economics,* vol. 72, no. 3 (August 1958), pp. 451–462; James S. Buchanan and Andre Gabor, "Comment," *Quarterly Journal of Economics,* vol. 80, no. 3 (August 1966), pp. 463–471; P. O. Steiner, "Peak-Load Pricing Revisited," in Harry M. Trebing, ed., *Essays on Public Utility Pricing and Regulation.* M.S.U. Public Utilities Studies (East Lansing, Mich.: Michigan State University, 1971), pp. 3–21, with "Comment" by Ralph Turvey, pp. 23–30; Oliver E. Williamson, "Peak-

Load Pricing and Optional Capacity Under Indivisibility Constraints," *American Economic Review,* vol. 56, no. 4 (September 1966), pp. 810–827; Ralph Turvey, "Peak Load Pricing," *Journal of Political Economy,* vol. 76, no. 1 (January-February 1968), pp. 101–113; and Israel Pressman, "A Mathematical Formulation of the Peak-Load Pricing Problem," *The Bell Journal of Economics and Management Science,* vol. 1, no. 2 (Autumn 1970), pp. 304–326.

3. James C. Bonbright, "Two Partly Conflicting Standards of Reasonable Public Utility Rates," *American Economic Review,* vol. 47, no. 2 (May 1957), p. 388.
4. James C. Bonbright, *Principles of Public Utility Rates* (New York: Columbia University Press, 1961), p. 292.
5. The literature on marginal cost pricing is immense. A good discussion of the theory and its ramifications can be found in Charles F. Phillips, Jr., *The Economics of Regulation,* rev. ed. (Homewood, Ill.: Richard D. Irwin, 1969), pp. 387–399. See also Harold Hotelling, "The General Welfare in Relation to Problems of Taxation and Railway and Utility Rates," *Econometrica,* vol. 6, no. 3 (July 1938), pp. 242–269; R. H. Coase, "The Marginal Cost Controversy," *Economica,* vol. 13, no. 3 (August 1946), pp. 169–182; R. H. Coase, "The Theory of Public Utility Pricing and Its Application," *The Bell Journal of Economics and Management Science,* vol. 1, no. 1 (Spring 1970), pp. 113–128; Emery Troxel, "I. Incremental Cost Determination of Utility Prices," *Journal of Land and Public Utility Economics,* vol. 18, no. 4 (November 1942), pp. 458–467; Emery Troxel, "II. Limitations of the Incremental Cost Patterns of Pricing," *Ibid.,* vol. 19, no. 1 (February 1943), pp. 27–39; Emery Troxel, "III. Incremental Cost Control Under Public Ownership," *Ibid.,* vol. 19, no. 3 (August 1943), pp. 292–299; Dudley Pegrum, "Incremental Cost Pricing: A Comment," *Ibid.,* vol. 20, no. 1 (February 1944), pp. 58–60; Emery Troxel, "Incremental Cost Pricing: A Further Comment," *Ibid.,* vol. 20, no. 1 (February 1944), pp. 60–63; Eli W. Clemens, "Incremental Cost Pricing and Discriminatory Pricing," *Ibid.,* vol. 21, no. 1 (February 1945), pp. 68–71; Bonbright (cited in note 4), pp. 386–406; William Vickery, "Some Objections of Marginal Cost Pricing," *Journal of Political Economy,* vol. 56, no. 3 (June 1948), p. 218; William Vickery, "Some Implications of Marginal Cost Pricing," *American Economic Review,* vol. 45, no. 2 (May 1955), pp. 605–620; Robert W. Harbeson, "A Critique of Marginal Cost Pricing," *Land Economics,* vol. 31, no. 1 (February 1955), pp. 54–74; Eli W. Clemens, "Marginal Cost Pricing: A Comparison of French and American Industrial Power Rates," *Land Economics,* vol. 40, no. 4 (November 1964), pp. 389–404; James R. Nelson (cited in note 2), pp. 59–89; William G. Shepherd, "Marginal Cost Pricing in American Utilities," *Southern Economic Journal,* vol. 31, no. 1 (July 1966), pp. 58–70; Haskell P. Wald, "The Theory of Marginal Cost Pricing and Utility Rates," *Public Utilities Fortnightly,* vol. 79, no. 13 (June 22, 1967), p. 15; and Hans E. Nissel, "Incremental Cost Pricing and the U.S. Utility Rates," *Public Utilities Fortnightly,* vol. 84, no. 4 (August 14, 1969), pp. 19–29. The whole matter is reviewed and updated in Harry M. Trebing, ed., *Essays on Public Utility Pricing and Regulation,* ch. 2, pp. 69–210, with discussions by F. S. Walters, M. Z. Kafoglis, P. Lhermitte, P. Caille, E. W. Clemens, J. R. Nelson, W. J. Baumol, A. M. Frogatt, and W. H. Melody.
6. Reserve capacity may be shared where the unit is homogeneous, as in electric power. Two neighboring utilities may interconnect or pool their reserve capacity to the benefit of both. This is particularly worthwhile if they happen to be located in different time zones so that the peak load periods do not coincide.
7. See Eli W. Clemens, *Economics and Public Utilities* (New York: Appleton-Century-Crofts, 1950), p. 284.
8. The technicalities of complex rate structures are beyond the scope of this book. Other well-known rate schedules include the Wright Demand Rate and the Doherty Three-Part Rate. Good brief discussions of these schedules are found in Paul J. Garfield and Wallace F. Lovejoy, *Public Utility Economics* (Englewood Cliffs, N.J.: Prentice-Hall, 1964), pp. 156–158. Also see Phillips, *The Economics of Regulation,* rev. ed., pp. 349–352.

ADDITIONAL READINGS

1. Barnes, Irston R., *The Economics of Public Utility Regulation* (New York: Appleton-Century-Crofts, 1942), ch. 10, "Utility Pricing Policies," pp. 319–369.

2. Bonbright, James C., *Principles of Public Utility Rates* (New York: Columbia University Press, 1961), ch. 16, "Criteria of a Sound Rate Structure," pp. 287–316; ch. 17, "Marginal Costs, Short Run and Long Run," pp. 317–336; ch. 18, "Fully Distributed Costs," pp. 337–368; ch. 19, "The Philosophy of Marginal-Cost Pricing," pp. 386–406.
3. Caywood, Russell E., *Electric Utility Rate Economics* (New York: McGraw-Hill, 1962).
4. Clemens, Eli Winston, *Economics and Public Utilities* (New York: Appleton-Century-Crofts, 1950), ch. 11, "The Theory of Public Utility Rate Making," pp. 247–273; ch. 12, "Electric Utilities and Their Rates," pp. 274–293; ch. 13, "Gas Utilities and Their Rates," pp. 294–319; ch. 14, "Water, Telephone, and Urban Transit Utilities and Their Rates," pp. 320–344; ch. 15, "Rate-Making Techniques: The Institutional Background of Price Fixing," pp. 345–369.
5. Davidson, Ralph Kirby, *Price Discrimination in Selling Gas and Electricity* (Baltimore: Johns Hopkins Press, 1955).
6. Garfield, Paul J., and Wallace F. Lovejoy, *Public Utility Economics* (Englewood Cliffs, N.J.: Prentice-Hall, 1964), ch. 10, "Pricing Policies," pp. 134–188; ch. 11, "Pricing Policies (Continued)," pp. 184–248.
7. Glaeser, Martin G., *Public Utilities in American Capitalism* (New York: Macmillan, 1957), ch. 24, "The Economics of Regulated Monopoly Price," pp. 403–418; ch. 25, "Cost Analysis in Its Relation to Selling Policies," pp. 419–436.
8. Nelson, James R., ed., *Marginal Cost Pricing in Practice* (Englewood Cliffs, N.J.: Prentice-Hall, 1964). See the following chapters in particular: Gabriel Dessus, "The General Principles of Rate Fixing in Public Utilities," ch. 2, pp. 31–49; Marcel Boiteux, "Marginal Cost Pricing," ch. 3, pp. 51–58; Marcel Boiteux, "Peak-Load Pricing," ch. 4, pp. 59–89.
9. Phillips, Charles F., Jr., *The Economics of Regulation,* rev. ed. (Homewood, Ill.: Richard D. Irwin, 1969), ch. 10, "The Rate Structure," pp. 303–345; ch. 11, "The Rate Structure (Continued)," pp. 346–400.
10. Trebing, Harry M., ed., *Essays on Public Utility Pricing and Regulation.* M.S.U. Public Utilities Studies (East Lansing, Mich.: Institute of Public Utilities, Michigan State University, 1971), ch. 2 (various authors), "Applied Pricing Practices and Problems," pp. 69–210.
11. Troxel, Emery, *Economics of Public Utilities* (New York: Rinehart, 1947), ch. 20, "A Proposal: Marginal Cost Pricing," pp. 441–463; ch. 25, "Managerial Control of Prices," pp. 549–569; ch. 26, "Pricing for Buyer Classes," pp. 570–593; ch. 27, "Pricing Forms," pp. 594–618; ch. 28, "More Discriminatory Pricing," pp. 619–644; ch. 30, "Pricing of Municipal Services," pp. 666–686; ch. 34, "Prices of Regional-Project Service," pp. 762–784.
12. Wilcox, Clair, *Public Policies Toward Business,* 4th ed. (Homewood, Ill.: Richard D. Irwin, 1971), ch. 14, "The Rate Structure," pp. 321–343.

15

Utility Public Relations

A wit once described public relations as the art of treating members of the public as if they are not your relations. More seriously, public relations have been defined as "building and holding good will," "doing good and getting credit for it," "winning the respect of one's community," and "putting one's best foot forward." A more comprehensive definition might say that public relations for a firm or an industry consists of attempting to win or retain public support for its activities by means of an informational program carried out by specialists using the techniques of social science and communications.

Although the specialized public relations man and the public relations department are relative newcomers, public relations itself has been around since the beginning of time. Cleopatra practiced public relations with Julius Caesar and Mark Antony, as did the Queen of Sheba with Solomon. All individuals and organizations, whether or not they are conscious of it, are constantly making favorable or unfavorable impressions on others. No person or organization has a choice of impressing or not impressing the public. The only choice is whether such impressions are to be haphazard or planned, conscious or unconscious.

Public relations, unfortunately, is sometimes confused with advertising, publicity, promotion, or propaganda. These terms are not synonymous. Advertising is the purchasing of space or time to influence actions. Publicity is communications in action and normally obtains space or time without purchasing it. Promotion is the commercial application of advertising or publicity, or both, while propaganda is political application.[1] Public relations makes use of publicity but is much broader in concept. Public relations includes the overall conduct of an organization plus the telling of its story. Publicity is the act of telling.

THE NEED FOR GOOD PUBLIC RELATIONS

Utility firms frequently have exclusive rights to the sale of their particular product in a given market area. This has led many people to think of utilities as monopolies. Although any competent utility executive can easily refute the charge of monopoly, at least to his own satisfaction, utilities sometimes act as "take it or leave it" monopolists in neglecting their cultivation of public understanding and sympathy. Historically, the neglect or misuse of public relations probably has resulted in far greater costs to the utility industry than would have been required for the maintenance of an adequate public relations program.

The Granger movement, which during the period following the Civil War led to the establishment of state regulatory commissions, and eventually to the Interstate Commerce Commission, grew out of the discontent of midwestern farmers with railroads and related businesses. This is an outstanding example of what can happen when public relations are neglected. Legal and administrative precedents established by the Grangers, coupled with lack of foresight and indifference on the part of some utility managements, ultimately led to a snowballing of regulation. The Public Utility Holding Company Act, the Natural Gas Act, the Federal Power Commission, the Federal Communications Commission, the Securities Exchange Commission, and various other federal and state regulatory laws and agencies, as well as the public ownership movement, have been influenced by the public's belief that it has needed protection from the abuses of privately owned utilities. Sound industry and firm public relations, in all likelihood, would have prevented or mitigated much of this deluge.

In recent years public utilities, like other businesses, have become increasingly aware that the doing of good deeds is not enough. The public must be told and convinced that good deeds are being done. A firm or an industry does not necessarily get the favor of the public merely by deserving it—although this usually is a prerequisite. In an age acclimated to regulation and public ownership in the utility field, privately owned utilities must present their case through well-organized and consciously planned public relations programs if they are to survive and prosper. When it is time for franchises to be renewed or rates to be raised, or when debates are raging over public versus private ownership, it is not sufficient that privately owned utilities do a good job. The community and voting public must be persuaded that a good job is being done. Upon being asked why his firm spent so much effort on public relations activities, one public utility executive replied, "To stay in business."

STRATEGY AND TACTICS OF PUBLIC RELATIONS: THE SIX P'S

A sound public relations program must be based upon what might be labeled the "Six P's of Public Relations." These are Philosophy, Policy, Performance, Publics, Planning, and Publicity. Although this nomenclature has a hackneyed ring, it summarizes the key elements of the problem.[2]

PHILOSOPHY, POLICY, AND PERFORMANCE

No public relations program can be better than the organization it represents. The first essential of a successful program, therefore, is a philosophy of management which is acceptable to the public at large. The day of the "public be damned" tycoon has passed, if it ever existed. Modern society expects its businesses to be good citizens as well as efficient producers. Good business citizenship requires integrity, fair play, and devotion to public service from management. This philosophy does not require neglect of stockholder interests, of course, but it does require that consideration be given to the interests of other groups, such as consumers, suppliers, employees, and the community at large.

The finest management philosophy is worthless unless it is placed into operation. This involves the second and third P's, that is, the establishment of company policies consistent with the managerial philosophy of good citizenship and actual day-to-day performance in line with established policies. The road from philosophy to performance is not always easy. The best-intentioned management is ineffectual unless its intentions are translated into policy, and the best policies are worthless unless the men on the firing line are sold on the policies and actually perform in accordance with them.

PUBLICS

The "general public" is too vague a concept for use in public relations work. Actually, every industry or firm has many publics, all with somewhat different interests and reached through different appeals and different channels of communication. The publics of utilities may be classified broadly as internal, associated, and external. Internal publics include company management officials, employees, and stockholders. Associated publics are made up of suppliers, creditors, securities dealers, customers, and even competitors. External publics include the community, government, the academic world, and various special groups with differing and often shifting viewpoints.

Successful public relations requires a rifle rather than a shotgun approach, and the rifle must be aimed. Each specific public must be approached in the manner most likely to influence it in the desired direction. Content and media suitable for influencing a stockholder might be of little interest to an employee or a customer, and vice versa. The considerable overlap between various publics must be recognized, of course. This is especially important in the utilities field, where an employee, for example, may also be a stockholder and a customer as well as a member of the community and a participant in government.

The overlapping of publics presents difficulties and challenges for a public relations program. An employee is interested in high wages, employment stability, recognition, and pleasant working conditions, while a customer is interested in good service at low rates and a stockholder in profits. Public relations directors, even in nonutility industries, have to proceed carefully in order not to antagonize one public while trying to win another, and in utility industries, where the overlapping of publics is unusually significant, this problem becomes far more complicated. On the other hand, the overlapping of publics in the utilities field provides an excellent opportunity for a public relations program to create cross-fertilization among different publics; that is, by winning the good will of an individual employee, for example, a firm also may win the good will of a consumer, an investor, and a voter. And good will, wherever created, has a snowballing effect through an individual's contact with other members of the community.

PLANNING

Careful planning is essential for successful public relations. Every sensible businessman formally or informally plans his producing, selling, financing, and similar operations. Public relations planning is equally important. Even though a business may be strong from the viewpoints of philosophy, policy, and performance, and may know its various publics, uncoordinated press releases or incautious words or actions may undermine its position in the eyes of its publics. People tend to remember the bad things much longer than the good, and inconsistency or carelessness in public communications is evidence of the worst kind of public relations.

A primary function of planning is to give direction to the public relations program. No organization has unlimited resources, and dollars spent for public relations must be channeled into programs where the returns are greatest. The hiring of public relations personnel because it is "the thing to do" is a needless, if not immoral or illegal, waste of consumers' or stockholders' money. And a purposeless program is as undesirable as no program at all. A purposeful public relations program establishes its objectives, determines how these objectives can best be met, and evaluates the effects of its operations.

Objectives of a sound public relations program may be both general and specific. General objectives may include the "selling" of our competitive free enterprise system, one's own industry, and one's own firm to the organization's various publics. Specific objectives may embrace a variety of topics, depending upon an organization's particular surroundings, problems, and ambitions. Specifically, for example, a utility firm may wish to show that it is a good company to work for or invest in, that its rates are reasonable, that it does not pollute the physical environment, that it is interested in community development, or that it is better suited to meet consumer needs than would be true of a publicly owned installation.

Whatever objectives an organization sets for its public relations program should be attainable and thoroughly understood by all personnel engaged in direct public relations work. Also, planning should be designed to head off potential future problems before they actually develop. Expensive emergency advertising and crash programs seldom are as effective as the traditional ounce of prevention.

In military terms, the charting of objectives consistent with the organization's philosophy and policies might be called the strategy of public relations and the selection of methods for carrying out objectives its tactics. Selection includes both a choice of tools (written words, spoken words, pictures, or combinations of these) and of media (books, pamphlets, general circulation magazines, newspapers, trade journals, house organs, annual stockholder reports, letters, press conferences and interviews, public speeches, radio and television appearances or advertising, telephone contacts, direct personal contacts, films and film slides, billboards, car ad cards, and the like).

Selection also includes choosing an originating point for the public relations program. So-called institutional advertising, that is, attempts to bolster our free enterprise system or to win friends for an entire industry, frequently is best handled by a group of companies operating through a trade association. On the other hand, a large and far-flung utility firm may by itself successfully undertake regional or even national programs of an institutional type.

At the individual firm level choices have to be made between a centralized public relations program originating from and carried out by the head office, a decentralized program, or some combination of these alternatives. Experience seems to have demonstrated that "grass roots" public relations adapted to local conditions generally is better, both from the viewpoints of cost and of effectiveness, than are handouts from the "big city." Some types of activities, of course, require central direction or performance, but this does not have to be too obvious in most situations.

The tools and media needed for the most effective presentation will vary with the different publics and with the nature of a firm's objectives, just as should the content of the material presented. This variation requires considerable research into the reading, viewing, and listening habits of the different groups as well as into their ideas and beliefs (or the lack thereof) on particular matters of interest to the firm or industry.

Public relations personnel must remember, too, that they have no captive audiences and that the effectiveness of their presentations depends upon whether or not these are interesting to the public at which they are aimed as well as upon their informational and persuasive content. Publishing pamphlets which no one reads, or attempts to convert people who already are converted, for example, is an unnecessary waste of resources which largely can be prevented by adequate research.

The evaluation of public relations effectiveness is as important a function of planning as is choosing the proper tools and media. The best planners sometimes make mistakes, and individuals and groups frequently change their viewpoints on particular problems. In order to insure that the right kind of material is reaching the right public and having the desired effect, continuous research is essential. The job of the public relations man does not end when a story is printed in a newspaper. He must follow up by finding out who read the story and what reaction it inspired. A variety of established techniques is adaptable to this kind of research.

PUBLICITY

The sixth P, publicity, is the operational aspect of public relations. Many otherwise excellent programs founder at this stage. Publicity is a technical job, requiring specialists. These specialists must make a great many day-to-day decisions concerning what is to be released, to whom it is to be directed, and when and how it is to be communicated. They must have an extensive knowledge of media and an acquaintance with those people controlling access to media as well as an understanding of the habits and psychology of the various publics.

Not all publicity is good publicity, and the success of a program is not measured by the quantity of materials released (or even by the quantity which actually reaches its intended audience, which may be quite different). Successful publicity consists of bringing sufficient material consistent with an organization's public relations objectives to the attention of the proper publics at the most appropriate time. This does not mean that unfavorable news, for example, should be suppressed rigorously, even if that were possible. It does mean, however, that the organization's viewpoint should always be presented, even in apparently unfavorable situations. Publicity activities rightly are concerned primarily with presenting an organization in the best light—the "other side" usually will be found ably presenting its own case.

MISUSE OF PUBLIC RELATIONS: LOSING FRIENDS AND ALIENATING PEOPLE

Although public relations activities are essential for any firm or industry, and particularly important for those subject to public regulation, or even public competition or public ownership, the whole area of public relations work often is questioned, doubted, or criticized by influential segments of the general public. Unfortunately, because of dubious past practices by inept or unethical practitioners, much of this criticism has been justified.

Organized public relations programs on a large scale apparently started in the public utilities industries, led particularly by the electric utilities, shortly after World War I. These programs were designed mainly to combat public ownership; defend existing earnings levels, capital structures, and holding company organizations; weaken regulation; and perhaps promote securities sales. The emphasis was essentially negative rather than positive; that is, it was against public regulatory and ownership trends, rather than for the virtues and efficiencies of less-regulated private ownership.[3]

The moral and legal rights of a privately owned utility to present its viewpoints on matters of public policy which directly affect its operations or its very existence cannot be seriously questioned. Such presentations, though, differ from advertising or promotional efforts designed simply to increase sales or to improve a firm's or an industry's general image in that they are much more directly for the benefit of the utility (that is, its investors or managers) than for the benefit of consumers. As such, a good argument can be made that their expenses should be borne by investors, in the form of nonallowable operating expenses and thus lower profits, rather than by consumers in the form of allowable operating expenses and higher rates.

Regulatory commissions, however, during the 1920's and since, sometimes have been lax in allowing operating expenditures which are properly chargeable to investors rather than consumers. In all fairness, it is difficult to draw a line between proper public relations activities and "improper propaganda." With inadequate staffs and unsure legal grounds, it is not surprising that some commissions have been lenient. Nor is it surprising that some utilities have taken advantage of this leniency.

Particularly during the 1920's and early 1930's many utility firms individually and through formal and informal trade association or community interest groups engaged in a form of public relations activities, largely at consumer expense, that would not conform to the ethical standards of most people today (or even then, had these practices been widely known). Heavy-handed and often successful attempts were made to penetrate schools and colleges by pamphlets and speakers, to censor and to subsidize textbook authors and publishers, and to influence editorial writers through the distribution of commercial advertising revenues or even cruder methods. Even worse, it was not generally known that utility firms were engaged in these and similar activities and were actually responsible for many supposedly objective and nonbiased studies and statements supporting the utility viewpoint until the United States Congress called for and eventually released a lengthy study of the matter by the Federal Power Commission.[4]

The reaction against utility public relations practices, and other practices, of the 1920's was such that even legitimate public relations activities were handicapped for some time. Eventually, however, forgetting more than learning, some firms and associations apparently began sponsoring a more sophisticated dissemination of the same kind of information and opinion, this time through substantial contributions to so-called patriotic (or right wing) organizations which tend to equate patriotism largely with unregulated private capitalism.[5] Many such organizations, apparently well financed, became very vocal following World War II.

It is clear that good public relations programs are essential for privately owned, regulated utility firms. It is equally clear that at times some firms and organizations have extended the public relations concept to include what many, even those otherwise friendly to these utilities, consider repugnant propaganda and that this sometimes has been done in a covert manner and at consumer expense. Any public relations program conceivably can backfire against its originators, but regulated firms and industries are particularly vulnerable in this respect. Public relations activities of regulated firms, like Caesar's wife, should always be above suspicion.

RELATIONS WITH REGULATORY AUTHORITIES

It is essential, of course, for public utility firms to maintain the best possible relations with those local, state, or federal agencies responsible for their regulation. The sayings about the difficulties of fighting city hall, or the attraction of flies with honey rather than vinegar, are meaningful.

Utilities must conduct their relations with the regulatory authority "public" on a high ethical plane and with considerable circumspection. Expensive entertainment of commissioners or commission staffs, or other favors, should be carefully avoided. Some individuals are influenced by such blandishments, just as some are susceptible to outright bribery, but a friend obtained by such methods cannot be considered dependable. Also, such dealings are hard to conceal from the public eye and, when exposed or even suspected, will severely tarnish the image built up by a firm over years of otherwise good public relations work. Thus, aside from the significant moral or legal implications, it simply is poor business to attempt to unduly influence the decisions of public officials by treading a path of borderline ethics.

Also, commissions should not be subjected to direct political pressures through lobbying or legislative influence, nor should their decisions be challenged in the courts simply as a nuisance gesture. Continual battling between the regulated and the regulators, whether openly or underground, is costly on at least three counts. It is expensive to the firm, it antagonizes the regulators, and it hurts the firm's public image.

This does not mean that a regulatory decision should not be challenged in the courts if it is significant to the company's operations or profits and if there appear to be good legal grounds for challenge. It means, rather, that legal challenges should not be routine or designed merely to keep a firm's attorneys busy. Automatic challenges may force a commission to give careful consideration to its procedures and orders, but both in the short run and in the long run the legal odds tend to favor the commission. Even though a small victory may be obtained in a particular case, the ultimate effect of the loss of commission good will may much more than offset the gains. Utility management should not appeal over trifles. Instead, it should at least weigh the certain disadvantages of slightly lower returns for a few years against the possible disadvantages of costly litigation, where overall costs may be much higher than mere legal expenses.

Similarly, there can be no objection to a utility company's attempts, within the recognized legal and ethical framework of public and legislative relations, to influence legislation which bears directly on its interests. All businesses and individuals have this right. This is quite different, however, from attempts to bring political pressure, through influential legislators or government administrative officers, on regulatory commissions handling particular cases under existing laws. Although pressure tactics may sometimes cause even conscientious nonpolitical regulators to yield somewhat, such practices are not likely to be forgotten quickly.

Aside from the foregoing negative approaches, there are several positive avenues toward good regulatory relations. Most important, a firm must have a good public image—that is, good relations with its various other publics—as a prerequisite for good commission relations. Regulators represent consumers and inevitably reflect consumer attitudes to some extent. Thus, no matter how sympathetic regulatory personnel may be as individuals toward a firm's problems, they are constrained in action if the general or consuming public is hostile to the company.

In addition, it is desirable that a utility maintain continued contact, on an informational basis, with commissioners and appropriate commission staff personnel. Regulators should have an opportunity to keep abreast of a firm's cost and revenue developments, which may necessitate rate or operational changes, as they occur. Ample advance warning is more effective than surprise requests. Further, it should be understood that rate increase requests are not a process of horse-trading. Those firms that ask only for what they need and clearly document their needs by well-prepared cases (exhibits and witnesses) are more likely to be respected than are those which ask for much more than they really expect to receive.

In brief review, good regulatory relations consists of making the regulators' task as easy as possible. This is done by maintaining a good public image, by continuous professional contact, by the submission of complete information as necessary for commission use, and, above all, by attempting to avoid embarrassing or harassing commissions by "scoring points" against them.

ORGANIZATION FOR ADMINISTERING PUBLIC RELATIONS

Utility public relations directors, whatever their titles, are found at various managerial levels and in several functional or divisional areas in different firms. Often, for example, the official directly in charge of public relations activities will also head the advertising, marketing, or personnel program. Sometimes, too, public relations is treated as a full-time activity at the vice-presidential or similar level. This is not different from the situation in other industries.

There is no one best organizational position for public relations, applicable to all companies under all circumstances. A firm's peculiar problems, historical organization characteristics, and management personalities and capabilities influence the internal structure of its organization. As long as the public relations functions are performed adequately, the particular titles used and the position assigned in the management hierarchy are mere details. Certain general requirements must be met, however, before a program can operate at its best.

Public relations activities should be directed by someone with sufficient managerial status to obtain coordination of effort at all levels in the firm. If not one of top management, this person must have the sympathy, backing, and ear of the highest company officials. A common organizational weakness, which ranks alongside the lack of clearly defined objectives or long-run planning, inadequate financing, and professional incompetence as a cause of ineffective public relations, is the existence of barriers between top management and the specialists hired to carry out public relations on a day-to-day basis. Everything cannot be left entirely in the hands of the experts.

Close communication between public relations managers and other high management officials is essential for at least two reasons. First, public relations personnel, in order to operate successfully, must at all times be abreast of a firm's basic philosophies, policies, and aspirations. These result largely from the thinking of top management. Second, public relations personnel, by the very nature of their jobs, should be better attuned to trends in public thinking and opinion than are operating executives further removed from the man on the street. Public relations, therefore, provides a channel by which management itself can be kept informed of trends and developments in popular thought. In other words, the public relations department should be viewed not only as a transmitter of facts and ideas to the firm's various publics but also as a transmitter from public to management.

A firm's most influential contacts with its publics, perhaps, are in its day-to-day service operations. Most persons judge a firm by personal experience rather than by reading or hearing about it. Those closest to a problem, or to a customer with problems, usually can best handle the situation. No expensive publicity campaign can offset the poor impression made by a grouchy meter reader, an insolent accounting clerk, or an unpleasant voice greeting a customer calling in about a service failure. Employees, from the office boy up, should understand the importance of presenting a good image to the customers who make their employment possible. Good employee relations, then, designed to make employees feel that they too are a real part of the company, are a vital ingredient in good public relations. As one executive has remarked, employees are really on the company's side when they begin to refer to the firm as "we" instead of "they."

Basically, of course, the chief executive officer of any organization must function as its top public relations man. This responsibility cannot be evaded by delegation of authority to others, even though operational details must be delegated to specialists.

SUMMARY

Good public relations are desirable for any business and are particularly essential for the success of regulated public utilities. Each utility firm has a variety of publics with different interests, approachable by different media and responsive to different appeals. The day-to-day handling of public relations, therefore, is best left to specialists.

Every company, by its own actual conduct, ultimately influences its public image. Even Madison Avenue cannot for long sell a wolf in sheep's clothing. The basic ingredient in public relations is an integrity of operations in which management can take pride and of which the community approves. A good operation may require selling, but a bad one is defeated from the beginning.

Although a firm may utilize several people in full-time public relations work, everyone connected with the firm is continually helping to shape its image. Every employee, therefore, should be aware of the fact that public relations is a part of the functions of everyone, from office boy to president.

NOTES

1. The line between public relations and propaganda is very thin. It is generally accepted that expenditures for public relations purposes by privately owned regulated utility firms are legitimate operating costs, while propaganda expenditures are not. Actually, most people appear to label public relations activities of which they do not approve as propaganda.
2. We do not purport to give here a detailed discussion of the general principles and practices of public relations or even a detailed description of utility practices. There is an abundant literature in this field. The "Additional Readings" at the end of this chapter contain a typical selection of materials that we feel are worthwhile reading for those particularly interested in pursuing this topic beyond our brief presentation.
3. Although the difference between a positive and a negative approach is subtle, to be for something is almost always more effective than to be against something. Successful politicians are quite aware of this.
4. A summary of these findings as related to public relations practices, highly critical of utility firms and associations, was authored by Ernest Gruening, former newspaperman, later Governor of Alaska and United States Senator from that state, in 1931. This book was reissued thirty-

three years later, slightly updated, under the title *The Public Pays: A Study of Power Propaganda* (New York: Vanguard Press, 1964). Although written with a definite viewpoint, this book should be read by every utility public relations man or executive concerned in any way with public relations. It provides some excellent examples of how public relations should not be conducted.

5. Again, a United States Senator, Lee Metcalf, and his aide, Vic Reinemer, attacked utility practices in a book, *Overcharge* (New York: David McKay Co., 1967). This detailed and well-documented account of electric utility activities and the permissive role of regulatory commissions is even more damning in the context of the 1960's environment than was Gruening's account of the earlier period.

ADDITIONAL READINGS

1. Anderson, R. Harold, "Motivating Employees to Customer Relations Activity," *Public Utilities Fortnightly,* vol. 78, no. 12 (December 8, 1966), pp. 24–31.
2. Barnes, Irston R., *The Economics of Public Utility Regulation* (New York: F. S. Crofts, 1942), pp. 782–815.
3. Campbell, Thomas C., Jr., "Public Attitudes Toward Utilities," *Public Utilities Fortnightly,* vol. 57, no. 4 (February 16, 1956), pp. 230–235.
4. Combatalade, E. A., "Public Relations Start at Home," *Public Utilities Fortnightly,* vol. 57, no. 3 (February 2, 1956), pp. 161–168.
5. Gruening, Ernest, *The Public Pays: A Study of Power Propaganda* (New York: Vanguard Press, 1964), pp. xlviii, 273.
6. Hennessy, Bernard C., *Public Opinion* (Belmont, Calif.: Wadsworth Publishing Co., 1965), part III, "The Environment of Opinion," pp. 153–246.
7. Herrman, Walter J., "The Public Relations Department in a Rate Case," *Public Utilities Fortnightly,* vol. 69, no. 7 (March 29, 1962), pp. 446–453.
8. Jones, Eliot, and Truman C. Bigham, *Principles of Public Utilities* (New York: Macmillan, 1931), ch. 14, "Public Relations," pp. 670–713.
9. Karn, Dan E., "Utility Public Relations Practices," *Public Utilities Fortnightly,* vol. 57, no. 2 (January 19, 1956), pp. 80–87.
10. Kekst, Gershon, "Special Audience Communication: Public Relations Cornerstone," *Public Utilities Fortnightly,* vol. 75, no. 12 (June 10, 1965), pp. 19–23.
11. Metcalf, Lee, and Vic Reinemer, *Overcharge* (New York: David McKay Co., 1967), part III, "How It Stays There: The Generation, Transmission, and Distribution of Propaganda," pp. 92–226.
12. Rincliffe, R. G., "Human Relations in the Utility Business," *Public Utilities Fortnightly,* vol. 57, no. 1 (January 5, 1956), pp. 25–31.
13. Rukeyser, Merryle Stanley, "The Art of Producing Good Will," *Public Utilities Fortnightly,* vol. 78, no. 9 (October 27, 1966), pp. 32–40.
14. Simon, Raymond, ed., *Perspectives in Public Relations* (Norman, Okla.: University of Oklahoma Press, 1966), ch. 4, "Managing and Organizing for Public Relations," pp. 106–136.
15. Welch, Francis X., *Preparing for the Utility Rate Case* (Washington, D.C.: Public Utilities Reports, 1954), ch. 2, "Public Relations and the Rate Case," pp. 18–37.

16. Winsborough, Robb M., "Public Relations Build a Better Regulatory Climate," *Public Utilities Fortnightly,* vol. 57, no. 10 (May 10, 1956), pp. 649–654, and no. 11 (May 24, 1956), pp. 732–738.

17. Wright, Theon, and Henry S. Evans, *Public Relations and the Line Manager* (New York: American Management Association, 1964), part I, "Principles of Planning and Control," pp. 21–98.

16

Utility Forecasting and Planning

Every business decision is based upon some kind of forecast, explicit or implicit, and every action taken is an attempt to carry out some plan. There is really no choice as to whether or not an organization, or an individual for that matter, should engage in forecasting and planning. These activities are a major and continuous part of everyday existence. The only choice is whether or not forecasting and planning will be organized or unorganized, formal or informal, conscious or unconscious.

Business forecasting is simply an attempt to determine, within some range of probable accuracy, what the situation confronting a business will be at some future time. Planning, then, is an attempt to adjust current operations to meet the forecasted future situation. As indicated in Chapter 11, forecasting, planning, and associated activities rank high among top management responsibilities.

In practice, most forecasting activities and many of the details of planning are staff functions. Top management, both at the formulative and administrative levels, however, must be closely involved with forecasting and planning. The need for these activities must be understood, human and other resources for carrying them out must be provided and supervised, objectives and guidelines must be established, results must be reviewed, and indicated necessary actions must be initiated and followed through.

FORECASTING AND PLANNING NEEDS AND OBJECTIVES

In public utilities, as in other businesses, good forecasting and planning lead to more efficient utilization of resources. Ideally, a firm should strive to use its facilities at their optimum levels. Excess capacity, either from underselling or overbuilding, should be minimized. (Some "planned overcapacity," of course, may be legally required as a safety margin.) Overselling, leading to customer (and perhaps regulatory authority) dissatisfaction or to operations beyond the optimum cost level or even to the necessity for unduly rapid expansion programs, should be avoided. Planned orderly growth, based on reliable forecasts, almost always is much less expensive to a firm than are crash construction or expansion programs made necessary by underestimation of demand or by the postponement of staged additions to capacity.

The legal and economic characteristics of public utility enterprises make reliable forecasting and good planning even more essential in this industry than in nonregulated industries. A public utility's legal duty of service means that it must be prepared to render service whenever service is demanded. Nonregulated firms, however much they may desire to serve all demands, have no legal obligations to do so.

Further, a fairly long time is usually required for a utility to bring new productive capacity into existence. For example, it may take as long as seven to ten years to get conventional hydroelectric or steam power generating facilities into operation, while nuclear generated power may require an even longer period. Most types of businesses are not faced with such a long time lag between conception and operation.

Typically, also, because of earnings regulation, utility firms are unable to build up substantial excess reserve funds for construction of new capacity. Instead, they must rely more on the capital market. This may create particularly difficult forecasting and planning problems, especially during periods of changing capital markets and construction and equipment costs. Those responsible for planning new capacity must always recognize that its installation costs may change significantly between the time a decision for expansion is made and the time when it must be paid for.

The financial aspect always dominates in forecasting and planning, because relations between anticipated receipts and proposed expenditures are always involved. The amount available for spending is always limited; thus a choice must be made to maximize some specific goal. It is generally assumed that a nonregulated company tries, in some way and by some definition, to maximize its profits. A publicly owned enterprise, on the other hand, may be interested primarily in maximizing or expanding its services. A privately owned regulated utility falls somewhere between these two extremes. It must have adequate profits, but its profits are limited to some extent by regulation. Consequently, its proposed expenditures for additions or betterments are likely to be designed for a combination of satisfactory (not maximum) profits and more or better services.

In summary, utility firms have all the needs of other types of firms for adequate forecasting and planning, plus special needs and problems arising out of the peculiar characteristics of utilities. Their first need, of course, is for good forecasting. Certainly, adequate planning does not automatically result from good forecasting, but without good forecasting it is unattainable.

PROBLEMS AND TECHNIQUES OF FORECASTING

Forecasting has been called both a science and an art. Practically speaking, it may be considered a combination of both, because it typically employs some methods of the scientist and some insights of the artist. It is practiced by specially trained personnel, via several generally recognized methodologies, and is described in a considerable body of literature. Certainly, though, the choosing of relevant variables, the choice between alternative methodologies, and the practical interpretation of the results of applying some methodology to some data are more in the realm of the artist than of the scientist.[1]

Ideally, even the beginning young forecaster should be well grounded in economic theory, quantitative techniques, and the capabilities of electronic computers, and he should be blessed with a good imagination and an inquiring disposition. As soon as possible, he should become well acquainted with the internal workings and external environment of his firm and industry. But no matter how thorough his education, a forecaster should not be expected to assume a major leadership role in conducting and interpreting a crucial forecast until he develops the required skills and intuitions that come only from experience in lesser roles. To borrow a military analogy, an effective fighting force cannot be developed on the drill fields alone. In forecasting, there is no substitute for blooding the troops.

KINDS OF FORECASTS

Forecasts may be classified either as short-run or long-run. A short-run forecast, which may extend for a few weeks up to a few years into the future, contemplates operations mainly within the limits of existing facilities. A long-run forecast, which may deal with a period of from five to twenty or more years, envisions a time within which a firm's resources and facilities may be considerably expanded, altered, or shifted into other endeavors.

Since they deal with and are limited by the resources currently in hand or clearly in sight, short-run forecasts and the plans based on them are much more detailed and inflexible than are long-run forecasts and plans. But they also give management a fairly quick feedback on the reliability and effectiveness of its forecasting and planning. This may tend to dampen the optimism of short-run forecasters and planners. It is usually easier to explain an underestimate of sales to a management when a firm's facilities are operating at or near capacity, for example, than to explain an overestimate when the firm has substantial excess capacity.

Long-run forecasts, on the other hand, are intended to lay out general routes rather than specific paths. Such forecasts, and the plans resulting from them, must necessarily be updated, revised, and extended constantly as the passage of time brings newer and better information and changes in the firm's external and internal environments.

Both long-run and short-run forecasts of numerous aspects of a firm's activities must be made. One department of a firm, for example, may be concerned primarily with future financing needs, another with construction needs, and still others with personnel requirements. The basic or key forecast, though, almost always is the forecast of demand for the firm's services. All other forecasts, wherever they may occur in the firm and for whatever purpose, ultimately must be based upon anticipated or potential sales.

FORECASTING TECHNIQUES

Unfortunately, there are no exotic trade secrets in forecasting. Mainly the ingredients are a lot of hard, detailed, and careful work, plus substantial elements of judgment. Various manipulative techniques may be used in blending these components, however.

Methods may range from the one extreme of simply extending a curve which has been fitted to past trends, or simply polling consumers or sales people, to the other extreme of elaborate econometric or computer simulation models. There is no one best manipulative technique suitable for all occasions. The technique should vary with, among other things, the importance of the forecast, how soon it is needed, the resources available for preparing the forecast, the amount and kinds of data available, and often with the backgrounds and preferences of the forecasters.

Whatever the type of data manipulation chosen, the forecaster must select what appear to him to be relevant independent variables from the universe of available data. Further, he must assume that the relations between these variables, including prices, technology, and consumer preferences, and the variable which he is attempting to predict remain relatively stable over the future time period concerned. This does not mean that variables and the relations between them are not expected to change. Rather, it means that changes are not expected to be unusually great or erratic and that they will follow determinant patterns.

Usually, the most important variables in determining the demands for established utility services are population and income. Thus, in a marketing forecast it is quite common to relate expected changes in these variables to anticipated company sales, based on the past experiences of the company itself or of similar firms in similar circumstances. Also, particularly in a long-run forecast, it is quite common to start from a general or overall projection and work down to the specific region served by the individual firm.

For example, in a population estimate for ten years in the future, a forecaster might start with a Census Bureau projection of total national population. This would then be proportioned down into his own area, based on comparisons of past relations between national and area populations. The resulting figure would be modified by any other specific information available concerning prospective new local industries, shifts in patterns of economic activities, or population movement trends. Some of this modifying information might be available within the utility firm itself, while other information might be obtainable from other utilities, chambers of commerce, planning boards, developmental agencies, banks and other financial institutions, real estate agencies, or similar bodies.

Finally, for marketing purposes, it might be important to determine the characteristics and life styles of the projected population. That is, sales might vary between urban and rural populations, industrial and white-collar workers, young and old people, low- and middle-income families, and the like. Here, in arriving at a forecasted total sales figure, the forecaster's knowledge of the consumption habits of those who purchase his firm's services is crucial.[2]

Perhaps the most universal and the most violated rule in forecasting is the rule that simplicity is a virtue. The smallest number of variables and the least complex manipulative technique which will accomplish the desired objective of the forecast are always preferable. This saves time and money and is easier to comprehend by those who must make planning decisions based on the forecast.

Unfortunately, forecasters, like military commanders, are prone to overkill.

Whether from Parkinson's Law of work expanding to fill the available time or from the feeling that a forecast is a work of art and an end in itself, many forecasters tend to prefer elaborate models over simple ones. (It is entirely natural that a highly trained technical person will prefer to use his technical abilities to the fullest, whether this is necessary or not. An electric utility management official once told one of the authors that if he did not keep an eye on his engineers they would gold-plate the transformers.)

Sometimes a sophisticated model is necessary to produce a forecast sufficiently reliable for management decision-making. At other times, a simple straight line extension of past trends on a sheet of graph paper may suffice. The essential point is that both management and forecasters should understand that a forecast is only a piece of information (and usually only one of several pieces) to be used as a basis for decisions. The particular forecast's importance in the overall picture, therefore, depends upon the importance of the decisions to be made and upon the importance of other available pieces of pertinent information.

If management actually communicates its real forecasting needs to its forecasting staff, it is possible, and even likely, that better utilization will be made of forecasting resources and talents. That is, less effort will be spent on less important forecasts, thus freeing more time and resources for more sophisticated and more crucial work. The result should be forecasts more suitable for decision-making, with less expenditure of resources.

FORECASTING ACCURACY

Despite the best efforts of forecasters and the desires of management, it should never be expected that a particular forecast will be completely accurate. A forecast, as an abstraction from reality, necessarily includes unresolvable uncertainties, which can only be expressed in terms of probabilities.

Management, desiring the best possible information for a crucial decision, may not be completely happy with a forecaster who hedges his conclusion by a statement that the probabilities are nine out of ten that his predicted outcome will transpire within a range of plus or minus 10 per cent. The forecaster probably is not completely happy with such a statement either, but it may be the most positive assurance that his science and art will permit under the circumstances.

The degree of forecasting accuracy depends upon the variables chosen, the data collected, and the manipulative technique used. It is never possible to identify, much less use, all pertinent variables affecting future conditions. Nor is it possible to collect all pertinent data concerning the relatively few variables chosen for use—and even the data collected will have varying and often unknown degrees of relevance and reliability. Furthermore, no manipulative technique, no matter how sophisticated, can accurately depict all possible interrelations among several variables. The deficiencies of science, in other words, must be supplemented by the skill, judgment, and experience of art, but art itself is imprecise by nature.

Generally, the longer the time period covered in a forecast, the more will uncertainties, changing trends, and unforeseen developments intervene. Even though some errors will tend to cancel each other out, others will pyramid. Thus, the range of probable error tends to be greater, the longer the time period involved. This is why long-run forecasts, and even short-run forecasts to some extent, must be constantly re-evaluated and revised.

Forecasting accuracy is not always improved by introducing more variables and collecting more data. This is particularly true for many kinds of relatively short-run forecasts, where a limited amount of data concerning a few key indicators sometimes may be as useful as great masses of expensively acquired data which require complex manipulations. This proposition might be equally valid in long-run situations if the relative weights of key variables did not change. Unfortunately, however, they do change. Consequently, over the long term, there is some merit to the idea of safety in numbers.

Sometimes forecasting accuracy can be improved at an additional expense, sometimes not. Forecasters often spend relatively too much effort in collecting data and too little effort in analyzing them. But even if improved accuracy can be achieved at additional cost, a decision must be made between the costs involved in obtaining more accuracy and the costs of errors. One may be traded off against the other. The costs of forecasting errors depend upon the importance of the decisions made as a result of the forecast, the weight given probable forecast errors in making these decisions, and the possibilities and probable costs of taking corrective actions when these errors are later discovered.

Even if it were possible to achieve near perfection in forecasts, it usually would not be economically worthwhile to do so. Perfection is not a prerequisite for success in our imperfect world. Most successful decisions are made with far from perfect knowledge.

Despite the many inherent weaknesses and limitations of attempts to peer into the future, however, and without any possibility of attaining perfection, it still remains true that forecasting of some kind forms the basis for all business planning and decisions. It follows, therefore, that within reasonable limits, as determined by its needs and resources, every business organization should attempt to obtain the best possible forecasts.

Good forecasting, first of all, requires good forecasters. Such individuals probably are partly made and partly born. Forecasters certainly are in limited supply. It is the worst kind of false economy to assume that because a young man has been successful in some phase of a firm's activities and can be promoted to a forecasting position at a salary a couple of thousand dollars a year lower than one required to hire a competent forecaster from outside the firm, that the young employee should be transformed into a forecaster. Unfortunately, this frequently happens, and usually the results are not good.

Having acquired good forecasters, management should keep them informed of its needs, both as to the types and uses of required forecasts, and the maximum permissible range of probable errors in particular situations. The forecasters, of course, should be given adequate time and resources to do what is expected of them. And finally, some postaudit review system should be established to evaluate forecasting performance and to insure that corrective actions be taken against consistent poor performance.

This being done, management should not expect miracles, but it should expect and should receive forecasts upon which it can rely as being generally adequate for its decision-making and planning needs.

THE INTEGRATION OF FORECASTING AND PLANNING

Basically, forecasting is concerned primarily with demand and planning with supply. That is, the forecaster attempts to say what the demand for the firm's output will be at some future time, within the limitations of specified assumptions. The planner, on the other hand, lays out the most appropriate sequence of steps to meet this demand, also subject to specified limitations such as the firm's overall goals and policies and its internal and external environments. Finally, administrative or tactical management tries to carry out this sequence of steps.

Although forecasting is the basis of planning, and a plan cannot be better than its supporting forecast, the forecast does not predetermine the plan. Forecasters usually are not planners. The two functions are quite different. A forecast can best be viewed as a desirable central point, toward which roads—that is, alternative plans—of varying types of construction can be built from many directions.

Short-run plans, based on short-run forecasts and constrained by currently existing resources or budgetary allocations, may involve only such matters as changes in marketing emphasis or personnel assignments. These and similar matters normally are routinely handled at the administrative level of management, and often at levels considerably below top management.

Forecasts indicating the desirability of major changes or the acquisition of substantial new resources, however, as is typical of many long-run forecasts, must receive the attention of top management, often formulative as well as administrative management. For example, a forecast showing that the demand for a firm's services may double within ten years may point out the necessity (if this demand is going to be met) of major new construction projects. This, in turn, may require the raising of new funds on the capital market, the recruitment and training of new operating personnel for the new plant facilities, and perhaps changes in pricing policies. Changes in the firm's established goals and policies may even be required.

The task of planning in such a case is to spell out in detail just what is required and in what order the various required actions should follow each other. Various alternative actions and sequences, with cost estimates for each, must be prepared. Finally, management adopts and sets into motion one of the various possible plans, hopefully one which is sufficiently flexible for a change in direction if following conditions or information indicate that this is desirable.

Most of the details of such plans, of course, are developed by staff personnel of assorted backgrounds and qualifications, like engineers, accountants, or attorneys. This diversified staff, however, must be coordinated and supervised from one source, and it must work closely with many of the firm's operating divisions or departments. And, at the very least, there must be constant and close communication between the coordinating supervisor and top management.

MANAGEMENT'S PLANNING FUNCTIONS

Management's first function in connection with major planning is to decide whether or not, on the basis of forecasts and other available information, any additional planning should be undertaken. If specific further planning is approved, its objectives must be spelled out and general guidelines established for its performance. Necessary resources must be made available, of course, and a date must be set for completion. Then, while the planning staff is at work, some effective system of two-way communications should be maintained between staff planners and management.

When major plans, or alternative plans, are completed, management exercises its functions of choosing, rejecting, modifying, or adopting. Then, necessary administrative orders must be issued, and whatever other actions that are necessary must be started, to translate the adopted plan into an action program.

Even then, however, the planning process does not come to a halt, especially if any significant length of time is involved between plan and operations. Both management and staff planners will want to keep close watch on developments inside and outside the organization to see if unforeseen circumstances or changing environmental conditions call for modifications in the original plan and proposed actions based on it. Most plans and programs are flexible enough to permit adjustments, and few actually become operational without some modifications.

PASSIVE AND ACTIVE PLANNING

Some planning may be called "passive." That is, a firm may simply attempt to be ready to meet the forecasted demands for its product as these demands become effective; in other words, the major concern is with having the right facilities at the right place at the right time. This, of course, may involve such activities as raising additional capital, constructing new facilities, and hiring and training personnel. But it is essentially an adjustment of the firm to the prospective future market rather than an attempt to modify or influence the market itself in any significant manner.

On the other hand, some planning is "active," because it includes serious efforts devoted to influencing the firm's future market. This active planning may be designed to obtain greater use of facilities, to balance load factors, to expand the existing market among present customers, to attract new customers, or for a variety of other similar purposes. Instead of accepting the future as a given factor to which the firm must adapt, active planning is dynamic in that it consciously tries to shape the future market as well as the future capabilities of the firm.

Commonly used devices in active planning include expansion and growth facilitation based on such marketing techniques as promotional rates, new types of services, the advertising or promotion of products which increase the consumption of utility services, and the like (see Chapter 12 for more complete discussion of some of these techniques). In addition, utility firms often work diligently at attracting new industries into their service areas. Such new industries may consume utility services in their production processes and also may attract additional people into the area or contribute to higher employment and income levels or increased community economic stability. All these things, of course, create more demands for utility services.

The division between passive and active planning is usually not as clear as the foregoing discussion might imply, nor is one necessarily preferable to the other. All utility firms engage in both types of planning, and most major specific plans involve elements of both. The predominant nature of a plan is, or should be, determined by the nature of its objectives.

SUMMARY

All economic activities, private or public, are based on some type of forecast and conducted according to some plan, implicit or explicit. Utility firms, because of their peculiar environmental constraints, have particularly strong needs for good forecasting and planning.

Consequently, most utility firms devote considerable efforts to short-run and long-run forecasting and to passive and active planning. Although there are exceptions, it appears that some of the country's most reliable business forecasting and most careful business planning is found among our communications and energy-supplying utility organizations.

The details of forecasting and planning are primarily staff activities that utilize a variety of specialized talents. Top management, however, should be closely involved with these functions from beginning to end—and usually is in the best managed and most successful organizations. One of general management's most important responsibilities is to make decisions designed to solve the problems and take advantage of the opportunities of the future. Forecasting sheds light on the nature of these future problems and opportunities, and planning provides orderly and efficient methods of meeting them.

NOTES

1. A good, concise, and practical introduction to general business forecasting problems, techniques, and basic data sources is given in William F. Butler and Robert A. Kavesh, eds., *How Business Economists Forecast* (Englewood Cliffs, N.J.: Prentice-Hall, 1966), part I.
2. Excellent brief discussions of concepts, methods, and data sources for marketing research, not especially oriented toward utilities but generally applicable for short-run marketing forecasts, are found in Paul E. Green and Donald S. Tull, *Research for Marketing Decisions* (Englewood Cliffs, N.J.: Prentice-Hall, 1970), ch. 16, and E. Jerome McCarthy, *Basic Marketing: A Managerial Approach,* 4th ed. (Homewood, Ill.: Richard D. Irwin, 1971), ch. 5.

ADDITIONAL READINGS

1. Butler, William F., and Robert A. Kavesh, eds., *How Business Economists Forecast* (Englewood Cliffs, N.J.: Prentice-Hall, 1966), part I, "Major Approaches to Business Forecasting," pp. 1–133.
2. Dauten, Carl A., and Lloyd Valentine, *Business Cycles and Forecasting,* 3d ed. (Cincinnati: South-Western Publishing Co., 1968), part VII, "Forecasting Sales," pp. 513–560.
3. Green, Paul E., and Donald S. Tull, *Research for Marketing Decisions,* 2d ed. (Englewood Cliffs, N.J.: Prentice-Hall, 1970), ch. 16, "Forecasting in Marketing Research," pp. 543–569.
4. Jarmon, W. R., "Forecasting and Budgeting for a Medium-Sized Telephone Company," *Public Utilities Fortnightly,* vol. 81, no. 8 (April 11, 1968), pp. 43–46.
5. McCarthy, E. Jerome, *Basic Marketing: A Managerial Approach,* 4th ed. (Homewood, Ill.: Richard D. Irwin, 1971), ch. 5, "Forecasting Market Opportunities," pp. 115–134.
6. Salin, J. A., "The Computer as a Utility Management Tool," *Public Utilities Fortnightly,* vol. 79, no. 12 (June 8, 1967), pp. 31–39.
7. Shubin, John A., *Managerial and Industrial Economics* (New York: Ronald Press, 1961), part IV, "Forecasting and Long-Term Business Planning," pp. 355–499.
8. Wood, Allen J., "Planning of Large Systems," *Public Utilities Fortnightly,* vol. 81, no. 1 (January 4, 1968), pp. 16–26.

Part Four

Public Ownership of Utilities

17

The Environment of Public Ownership

Most organized governments, at all levels, in most places, and during most historic times, have been keenly interested in and actually involved in various kinds of economic activity. The tradition and practice of government "intervention" in economic affairs has been unbroken from the early governments of Mesopotamia, Egypt, Greece, and Rome, through the Middle Ages and the early national states, and to the present time. The laissez faire tenets of Adam Smith and his followers have been much more discussed than applied, even in the free enterprise strongholds of the English-speaking world.[1]

Government intervention, in the United States as elsewhere, has been rationalized on many grounds, including national defense, the need to combat unemployment, revenue needs for other government activities, failures or inadequacies of private operations, private abuses, resource conservation, or on the ideological grounds of "social welfare" or the "governmental nature of the undertaking." Often, too, a particular intervention has been incidental to some related government project. Regardless of the rationale, government intervention is expressed in the forms of promotion and subsidy, taxation, regulation, and ownership. This chapter, and those immediately following, are concerned with the last-named form of government activity in the utility industries.

Public ownership of utilities, by our definition, includes ownership at the federal, state, county, or municipal levels as well as public utility districts (whatever they may be called), which often cut across state internal political subdivisions, and nonprofit cooperatives. That is, it includes any organization providing utility services except the privately owned, profit-making organizations (the so-called "investor-owned utilities," or I.O.U.'s).[2]

Despite the often-heard charges of "creeping (or leaping) socialism," it must be emphasized that the provision of utility services in the United States, like that of most other goods and services, is predominantly under private control. Even in the electric utility field, where the private-versus-public arguments have been, and are, most fierce, less than one fourth of power produced is from publicly owned facilities. (Of this publicly produced power, about three fifths is from federal facilities, with the remainder about equally divided between municipal production and production from all other public sources, like states, public utility districts, and cooperatives.)[3]

The ownership situation is quite different in most of the rest of the world. Outside the United States, for various reasons, some ideological and some not, a large portion of utility services are publicly supplied. Contrary to our practice, in the world as a whole privately owned utilities are exceptional rather than commonplace.

In order to understand the economic impact, problems, and likely future trends of our somewhat unique blend of private and public ownership of utility facilities, and to evaluate properly the often emotional arguments of advocates for more public or more private ownership, it is necessary to understand something of the legal and historical environment and the climate of public opinion in which our system developed and exists. The remainder of this chapter will explore these topics. Following chapters in this part will deal more specifically with the issues and problems of public ownership.

THE LEGAL BASIS FOR PUBLIC OWNERSHIP

It is a well-established legal principle that public funds can be used only for public purposes.[4] Since the provision of utility services by a public agency does involve the use of public funds, then, early legal challenges to public ownership of utility facilities revolved around the determination of what may be considered a public purpose. Most of these early cases and decisions were at the state rather than the federal level (that is, they involved municipalities, which are state creations), and in general they supported the proposition that the provision of utility services is a public purpose in the eyes of the law.

For example, an 1892 United States Supreme Court decision upheld a municipality's right to establish its own gas utility despite the protest of a privately owned firm which had been supplying the city's gas needs for many years.[5] In 1903 a similar set of circumstances brought a similar ruling in an electric utility case.[6] The following year saw a similar decision in a water utility case.[7]

Later decisions upheld the rights of cities to maintain and operate public fuel yards[8] and gasoline service stations.[9] In 1934 it was held that a city-owned utility, even though it was competing with a privately owned firm which paid gross revenue taxes to the city, was not required to conduct its business at a profit.[10] Also, a state's right to establish an industrial commission, authorized to engage in utility, milling, manufacturing, and warehousing operations and a number of other activities, has been upheld.[11]

From these and similar decisions it can be seen that the sovereign powers of states (see Chapter 3) in matters of ownership, as in regulatory matters, are interpreted broadly. A state, or its properly authorized political subdivisions, unless restricted by its own constitution, can engage in whatever kinds of economic activities, including public ownership, that its legislature finds appropriate. Only a few state constitutions place many limits on state or local utility ownership.

Federal ownership of utilities did not become an important legal issue until the 1930's. At that time it was found that the federal government is no more hampered by constitutional restraints than are most state and local governments. Although the United States Constitution is a permissive rather than a limiting document (see Chapter 3) and does not specifically say that utility ownership is permitted, such powers as those over navigable waters and interstate commerce, the power to tax and spend for the general welfare, and the elastic clause have been interpreted to include the right of public ownership. Private utility legal attacks on federal ownership were repulsed decisively in several leading cases regarding the operations of the Tennessee Valley Authority.

First, in a suit to prevent government acquisition of transmission lines for sale of power from Wilson Dam, the Supreme Court held that the water utilized and the power generated belong to the federal government, that the government has a right to sell its own property, and that it thus has the right to acquire the facilities necessary for such roles.[12] Next, the right of a federal agency to purchase municipal revenue bonds issued to finance electric plants and distribution systems was upheld.[13] Later, in a suit to prevent Tennessee Valley Authority competition with private firms holding franchises in certain geographic areas, the Court ruled that a nonexclusive franchise does not confer a private monopoly.[14] Finally, it was held that even the sovereign power of a state could not prevent federal construction and ownership of electric utility facilities in connection with a navigation and flood control project within a state's boundaries.[15] For practical purposes, the legal battle against federal ownership was over.

In summary, then, the extent of public ownership of utilities at both state (including local) and federal levels is generally limited only by public opinion as expressed through legislative bodies, and not by constitutions and courts. This explains a great deal of the public relations (or propaganda) activities of those privately owned utilities susceptible to public ownership or public competition.

THE HISTORICAL DEVELOPMENT OF PUBLIC OWNERSHIP

It is logical that one should ask why public ownership of utilities has grown to its present level in a country where private ownership of economic facilities is an accepted way of life. In answer to this question, several erroneous or incomplete ideas have been disseminated.

"EXPLANATIONS" OF PUBLIC OWNERSHIP

One explanation, which might be called the conspiracy answer, is that public ownership of utilities is the entering wedge of a vast Marxist-inspired plot. It is alleged that when enough essential services are controlled by the conspirators, they will be able to disrupt the economy sufficiently to allow a revolutionary takeover of the economy. Or alternatively, the precedents established by public ownership of utilities will weaken the resistance of private investors in other industries and condition the minds of the general public to an acceptance of government ownership, thus facilitating a gradual evolution into socialism or communism. This "explanation" would not be worthy of mention in a serious discussion if it were not so vociferously expounded by several small but apparently well-financed groups with access to communications media in all parts of the country. Despite the lack of any sound evidence whatsoever, these groups do make themselves heard.

Another group, without necessarily believing in any widespread conspiracy, or without arguing that a majority of our elective officials or voters are against private enterprise as such, maintain that public ownership is an inevitable outgrowth of "big government." The more authority a government has, the more it reaches for, they say. This argument implies that since "big government" is a relatively new phenomenon in this country, public ownership also is a relatively new development. Only by weakening government authority, "getting government out of business," can utility businesses be saved for private ownership. One obvious fallacy in this argument is its emphasis on public ownership as a recent development.

A third group, largely composed of scholars and neutral observers rather than propagandists or utility affiliated individuals, takes the position that public ownership has come about because of inadequacies or failures of competition and regulation and consequent monopoly abuses perpetuated by privately owned firms. This position, although based on elements of fact insofar as inadequacies or abuses of private ownership have contributed to public ownership in some instances, is not completely valid. Many other instances of public ownership could be cited where no private abuses have been alleged.

Finally, there are those who attempt to explain public ownership of utilities by rather abstract references to the "public nature" or "essentiality" of the services performed, or even by reference to "social welfare." Answers of this type are actually more in the nature of ideological justifications than explanations, however, and are often presented in conjunction with the "inadequacies and abuses" explanation.

An observer from another country, of course, might equally well ask why utility services in the United States are supplied principally by private ownership, in marked contrast to most of the rest of the world. Again, the answer is not obvious. We could reply that for some reasons, which economists, sociologists, and political scientists have never explained in a completely satisfactory manner, most of our people have felt that government should not provide services which can be provided better, or just as well, by private enterprise.

If this somewhat unsatisfactory philosophical explanation is accepted, we could further point out that when the major inventions were created upon which the technologies of our major utilities are based (telegraph, telephone, electric light bulb, for example), private capital and investor willingness to risk it in new undertakings were available. (This is quite different from the situation in many countries, past and present.) In addition, government funds, especially in view of the prevailing free enterprise tradition, were not readily available for massive new undertakings. Government, even though able and willing to encourage, promote, facilitate, and sometimes subsidize, was inclined generally to avoid outright ownership of utilities.

Also, the development of regulation which protected consumers from private ownership abuses, or which led consumers to believe that they were adequately protected, no doubt greatly reduced popular demands for public ownership. Regulation has been regarded as a workable substitute for public ownership in many quarters. Although it is not completely consistent with a laissez faire philosophy, it is more closely related to the principles of free enterprise than is actual public ownership of production facilities. Ironically, some of those who protest against regulation might have even more reason to protest if regulation had not been instituted!

The laissez faire or free enterprise tradition must be accepted with significant reservations, however. Although we have generally supported the idea that free enterprise should do what it can do at least as well as, or as inexpensively as, public enterprise, we have been highly critical in our interpretation of what is meant by "as well as." Where our professed ideology has conflicted with our pocketbooks and consumer aspirations, ideology has generally lost. This is quite apparent from a review of our history. Public ownership is not new. It has grown up concurrently with private ownership and has been adopted for a variety of reasons.

WATER, GAS, STREET TRANSIT, AND COMMUNICATIONS

Municipal ownership of water facilities has a long history in this country as well as abroad. Several of our municipal water systems date back to the Revolutionary War era or earlier. Today a great majority of our cities of more than 5,000 population, including most major cities, operate municipal water facilities. Also, about one half of our cities operate sewage treatment plants.

Privately owned water systems as a percentage of all water utility facilities declined steadily throughout the nineteenth century, an era of generally great expansion in private enterprise. During this period the private percentage dropped from more than 90 per cent to less than 50 per cent of communities served, despite the rapid growth of new communities. Apparently, the decline in the relative percentage of the population served was much greater.[16] Private capital, having more attractive investment alternatives, has been for a long time very reluctant to enter the water utilities field. Consequently, there is very little current public-versus-private-ownership controversy in this area.

During the last century, when manufactured gas became important for lighting, many municipalities constructed their own plants and distribution facilities. With the coming of electric lighting, changing technology, and the increasing importance of natural gas, however, most municipalities disposed of their gas operations. Today the gas utility field is dominated by private concerns, with little ownership controversy.

The ownership of street transportation facilities is fairly well mixed. Some municipal transit facilities date back to the nineteenth century, but much more public ownership has been brought about recently by the inability of private firms to maintain profitable operations.

The automobile, the five-day work week and longer vacations, and the advent of television, among other factors, have decreased street transportation facility patronage. Fewer riders have meant higher costs per customer, higher rates, less adequate service, and consequently still fewer riders. As a result, many communities have been forced into the street transportation business against their wishes, and in other cities private operations are continued only through subsidies of various kinds. City-operated street transit in general has been no more of a financial success than private transit, but city operations do not have to show a profit; many are supported by public funds derived from other sources.

Contrary to the European and world pattern, there has been very little public demand for, and activity toward, public ownership of communications utilities in this country.[17] There have been, of course, suggestions for public ownership of the telephone, telegraph, and even radio and television communications systems, and more recently in connection with communications satellites, but these suggestions have not been as seriously considered as suggestions for public ownership in most other utility fields. Almost the only exceptions are local telephone cooperatives, many organized some time ago in isolated rural areas which could not obtain private services but some of more recent vintage, and a remaining handful of municipally owned telephone plants (plus some publicly owned radio and television stations affiliated with educational institutions).

ELECTRIC UTILITIES

The electric utility industry has been for many decades, and still is, the center of the public-versus-private-ownership controversy. At first, this controversy was related to municipal ownership. More recently, it has expanded in scope.

Municipal

From the electric utility industry's beginnings in the late 1800's up to the early 1920's there was a definite trend toward municipal ownership. In many instances, this public ownership came about because private electric services were not available except at very high prices, or even at any price. Many communities were faced with a practical choice between public ownership or no electricity for many years into the future. During the 1920's, though, partly because of better organization and more integration in the private sector of the industry and partly, perhaps, because of expensive and aggressive public relations and propaganda campaigns by privately owned utilities, the trend toward public ownership was reversed for a time.

During the 1930's the trend again turned in favor of municipal electric ownership. Several factors contributed to this. The development of diesel technology made small-scale municipal generating operations more efficient than formerly; enthusiastic free enterprise diesel equipment salesmen thus contributed to public ownership in many communities. Low-priced federal power, combined with "preference clauses" favoring public purchasers, greatly stimulated municipal ownership in some areas. Federal government loans to cooperative associations and other public bodies were of considerable importance. Also, there was a strong popular reaction against the abuses of electric utilities during and following the 1920's, as revealed by various holding company difficulties and congressional investigations. Finally, during the depression era of the early and middle 1930's private firms often were unable or unwilling to expand their services in small communities.

Today almost 2,000 municipalities in this country sell electricity (over 1,000 fewer than at the early 1920's peak). Most of these communities, however, are fairly small, and only a very few are of major size. Also, less than one half of these cities actually produce their own electric power; instead, they buy for resale from other public or private producers. Municipal production amounts only to about 5 per cent of the country's total electric generation. Or, stated in another way, private power production is about fifteen times as great as municipal production.

State

Only a few states, as distinct from their internal political subdivisions, have taken an active part in utility ownership, even in the electric field.[18] The New York State Power Authority was created in 1931, primarily to handle power produced from the St. Lawrence River Project (which went into operation in 1958). It also produces power from the Niagara River. A South Carolina Public Service Authority, created in 1934, was intended to handle power from the Santee-Cooper Project and on a smaller scale perform somewhat the same functions as performed by the T.V.A. in the Tennessee Valley. Both Texas and Oklahoma have public agencies, established during the 1930's, to build and operate power dams.

It is in the politically "conservative" state of Nebraska, however, that public ownership of electric utilities has reached its ultimate peak. That state, in 1939, created a Consumers Public Power District, which rapidly acquired existing private facilities. By 1946 all electric power distribution in the state was under public ownership.

Apparently, most state governments during recent years have felt that any consumer desires for public ownership of electric utility facilities can be satisfied adequately by municipal, public utility district, or cooperative ownership. The authorization for utility districts to issue revenue bonds, and sometimes general obligation bonds (tax-supported), and the availability of federal loans for cooperatives, plus preferences in buying federal power, led to a rapid expansion in the number of both these forms of organization after the mid-1930's. There are now around 1,000 public utility districts or cooperatives in the country, with a combined electric power production approximately equivalent to the total municipal production—that is, about 5 per cent of all electric output.[19] Like municipally owned facilities, though, many of these organizations depend entirely or in part on power purchased from other public or private producers.

Federal

The federal government has been in the electric power business since the early 1900's. The Reclamation Act of 1906, elaborating upon an act of four years earlier, stated:

> . . . Whenever a development of power is necessary for the irrigation of lands under any project undertaken . . . or an opportunity is afforded for the development of power under any such project, the Secretary of the Interior is authorized to lease . . . giving preference for municipal purposes, any surplus power. . . . (34 Stat. 117)

This act, which continued to be the basis of federal power policy for twenty-two years, contains the first mention of the preference clause favoring public purchasers. Under this statute and following amendments the sale of electric power was only incidental to the major purposes of irrigation, reclamation, and conservation. Power not needed in the operation of the major project itself was sold on the best terms possible. Power surpluses were small, and there was little public-versus-private-power controversy.

The Boulder Canyon Project Act of 1928, authorizing the construction of Hoover Dam for irrigation, domestic water supplies, and electric power generation, first put the federal government in the power business on a large scale. This act provided

> . . . delivery at the switchboard to states, municipal corporations, political sub-divisions, and private corporations of electrical energy generated . . . upon charges that will provide revenue, which, in addition to other revenue . . . will . . . cover all expenses of operation and maintenance. . . . (45 Stat. 1057)

Even the Boulder Canyon Project did not arouse much controversy over public versus private ownership. Although the amount of power involved was substantial, the dam was primarily for purposes other than supplying power, and electricity sales actually were to be at price levels designed to subsidize water users.

It was the Tennessee Valley Authority, organized as a government corporation rather than as a Department of Interior agency in 1933, that aroused private electric utilities to the dangers of federal encroachment into their domain and touched off a series of legal battles.[20] The T.V.A., in addition to its power features, included strong elements of regional development within its economically stagnant geographic territory, with considerable emphasis upon better land use, reforestation, and the creation of additional employment. A substantial part of its costs were allocated to flood control and navigation improvement. Also, it involved a "yardstick" concept, by which the performance, costs, and rates of private electric utilities supposedly could be measured. Its original installation, at Muscle Shoals on the Tennessee River, utilized a dam which the federal government had started to construct for nitrate production during World War I and which had been a white elephant and a source of continued controversy since then.

In total, the T.V.A. was a vast and complex social experiment. The nation was in the grip of its worst depression. It was the hope of the Roosevelt Administration and Congress that in addition to increasing employment in the region and indirectly throughout the nation, the experiment would provide an example and guideline for similar regional developments elsewhere in this country and abroad. Thus, the electric power aspects of the project were somewhat de-emphasized in the legislative history and announced purpose of the act. But it was clear, then as now, that power production was one of the primary goals.

At that time, in the country as a whole, only about two thirds of the population, and only a little more than 10 per cent of the farms, were receiving electric services. Many rural areas were completely unserved and without prospects for service.[21] National average rates, in current dollars, for equivalent consumption were at least 30 per cent higher than at present. In real terms (that is, after adjustment for changes in the purchasing power of money), this means that average electricity prices then were at least three times higher than today's prices.[22] Further, the average customer at that time consumed only about one eighth as much electricity as today's average customer.

Later federal hydroelectric undertakings, such as those in the Columbia River Valley, did not utilize a separate corporate form of organization and did not attempt overall regional development on the same scale as in the Tennessee Valley. Although these projects continued the emphasis on such purposes as irrigation, navigation, flood control, and related uses, many of them placed equal or greater emphasis on electric power production.

For example, in the Bonneville Power Administration Act of 1937, the administrator (under Interior Department jurisdiction) was instructed to dispose of power ". . . in order to encourage the widest possible use of all electric energy that can be generated and marketed and to provide reasonable outlets therefor and to prevent the monopolization thereof by limited groups. . . ." Also, the administrator was directed to ". . . at all times . . . give preference and priority to public bodies and co-operatives" (50 Stat. 731).

Although the legal right of the federal government to engage in the electric utility business was settled during the 1930's, whether or not the government "ought" to do this remains controversial. There were particularly keen controversies regarding T.V.A. building of steam generation plants, and in connection with the government's role in atomic power production after World War II. These battles were and are fought in the arena of public opinion and in legislative halls, however, rather than in the courts.

In retrospect, it is possible to identify differing federal electric power policies during the various presidential administrations of this century. It is true that the President can only propose. Policy decisions and appropriations are controlled by Congress. But strong or popular Presidents are able to influence Congress.

From the time of Theodore Roosevelt to that of Franklin Roosevelt the production and disposal of electric power was considered only incidental to other and more important purposes of federal projects. The Franklin Roosevelt and Truman administrations, however, envisioned the federal government in the power business on a large scale. Prices were not established for profit but for maximum consumption and regional development. Sales were pushed by installing high-capacity facilities and charging low rates, with the expectation that demands would grow to the potential supply level. Transmission lines and supplemental steam plants were acquired or built, and preference clauses and various other aids were given to publicly owned systems.

The Eisenhower administration advocated quite different policies. Private utilities received sympathy and more tangible benefits. Funds for new federal construction and expansion were restricted in some instances, giving rise to some now-famous controversies. Also, a "partnership plan," contemplating joint federal, state, local, and private utility cooperation was formulated. Federal power development was not reversed, but it was slowed at least temporarily.

The Kennedy, Johnson, and Nixon administrations appear to fit somewhere between the Roosevelt-Truman administrations on the one hand and the Eisenhower administration on the other. Perhaps this is to be expected. The major battles have been fought and the major issues decided. By the 1960's the federal role was seen as one of administering previously established policies rather than instituting new policies.

CONCLUSIONS CONCERNING PUBLIC OWNERSHIP

A review of the history of public ownership of utilities in this country makes it clear that public ownership is not new, not a direct effect of any recent growth of "big government," not the result of a sinister Communist conspiracy, and not primarily inspired by ideological factors. Expediency rather than philosophy has been behind most public operations. This has been especially true at the local levels.

Many communities have "socialized" their public utilities for the same reasons that they have "socialized" their police and fire departments, schools, and streets. Rural communities have organized utility districts and cooperatives to provide services otherwise not available. Small towns have developed electric, street transit, and water services because such development would not have been profitable, at least without prohibitive rates, under private ownership. Some of these operations have not been profitable for municipalities, of course, but a government agency does not necessarily have to make profits to remain in business. Still other cities have engaged in public ownership because of financial breakdowns of private operators, or because of real or imagined abuses or exploitation by private firms. Public ownership in these and similar instances perhaps may be viewed by the general public as the lesser of two evils.

At the federal level, public ownership was brought about initially for a variety of reasons. A considerable amount was incidental to other government operations, such as irrigation, navigation, and flood control. National defense fathered the original Muscle Shoals dam, which later formed a nucleus for the T.V.A. Defense also was responsible for federal activity in the atomic energy field and, to some extent at least, for steam generation plants to supplement hydroelectric generation. The large river valley development projects can be attributed partly to attempts to stimulate employment and business activity during a period of severe economic depression, partly to a desire to raise substandard regional incomes, partly to the wish to attain maximum utilization of a great natural resource, and partly to the fact that costs and risks in such undertakings were so high that private enterprise could not, or would not, undertake such massive programs.

It would not be entirely correct to say that philosophies of "public ownership for its own sake," or "public ownership due to the nature of the business" have played absolutely no part in actual public ownership decisions. Even at the federal level, however, where ideological influences probably have been of most importance, the influence of philosophical attitudes appears to have been very small as compared to the influence of more pragmatic arguments in support of public ownership.

ARGUMENTS FOR AND AGAINST PUBLIC OWNERSHIP

Public ownership of utilities, like any other public ownership, may be debated both on ideological and nonideological grounds. Ideological arguments usually do not convince anyone of the rightness or wrongness of his position, however, and, as noted, have been of little actual importance in controversies over public versus private ownership. We feel, therefore, that understanding and discussion of pragmatic issues are of considerably more importance than debate of abstract ideology.

We feel, also, that our own position should be made clear at the outset, as should the positions of all who engage in such discussions. Although we consider ourselves supporters of free enterprise in the context of our national tradition, we also recognize the right of a democratic society to restrict free enterprise within limits. In short, philosophically we are neither for nor against public (or private) ownership of utilities as such. Rather, as economists, we are for efficiency in resource allocation and use regardless of where it is found, as long as our society has the freedom to change existing policies or institute new policies as it sees fit. We must acknowledge, too, our opinion that in most circumstances in most industries in this country private enterprise has been more efficient than public enterprise; but there are exceptions.

Briefly, supporters of public ownership, aside from ideology, maintain that this permits lower prices to consumers. This is attributable to generally lower rate bases; lower executive salaries; lower financing costs (that is, lower interest rates because of public or tax-backed loans and lower underwriting costs); less advertising, taxation, and public relations expenses; and no costs for regulation or profits. Also, it is sometimes maintained that public ownership stimulates better labor-management relations and provides a yardstick against which "reasonable" private utility rates and services can be measured.

Advocates of private ownership counter by arguing that public management, with its lower executive salaries, may be inferior; that low financing costs may lead to uneconomic overexpansion and consequent resource misallocation; that advertising promotes better utilization of facilities; that labor-management relations are not demonstrably improved under public ownership; and that dissatisfied consumers have less recourse against publicly owned than against regulated privately owned utilities (some public operations are subject to state commission regulation similar to that applicable to private firms, but not many).

Further, private ownership supporters argue that the yardstick concept and lower public costs and rates in general are unrealistic because public systems do not pay taxes or may even be subsidized by taxation. Some public systems, though, do make substantial equivalent payments in lieu of taxes, while others contribute to general public funds and thus enable taxes to be lower than they otherwise would be. Some, of course, do not make such payments or contributions, and certainly in some cases lower rates are offset by correspondingly higher taxes.

Private ownership proponents often allege, also, that public ownership leads to political rather than to economic decisions and that inefficient personnel may be employed and inefficiencies in operation ignored or hidden. These allegations are no doubt true in some instances. So far as political rather than economic decisions are concerned, though, if they are designed to carry out the real wishes of the public, there are few grounds for condemnation. Also, inefficiencies can be covered up both in public and private operations. There is no evidence that private industry has a monopoly of honesty, integrity, and ability, any more than that government has a monopoly of blundering bureaucracy. Actually, the overall record of public management seems to compare favorably (at least) with that of private management.

Unfortunately for those who like black and white answers, these are not easily formulated. In terms of comparative efficiency, which is the economic (nonideological) criterion for judging private versus public ownership, a wealth of statistics supporting both private and public groups can be found. This is because no two operations are exactly comparable, and no single operation is completely comparable with itself over time. Often, for example, private ownership supporters compare small (high-cost) city operations with large (low-cost) private systems. Or public power advocates compare rates in areas served by federal hydroelectric generation with rates charged by private steam generation systems elsewhere.

Although the evidence is not and can never be conclusive enough for broad generalizations applicable to all situations, it appears that if operations roughly similar in nature and size are compared, costs are not greatly different between public and private systems. In the electric utility field, for example, municipalities generally appear to have higher power generation and transmission costs, while private firms have higher sales, collection, and administrative expenses—remember, though, that many municipally owned utilities do not generate their own power.

Without deliberate fence-straddling, the authors can only conclude that from a strictly economic (that is, nonideological) viewpoint private ownership is more efficient and thus more desirable in some situations and public ownership in others. Each case must be considered individually on its own merits.

But even if we can determine which form of ownership is likely to be most efficient in a particular situation, this does not necessarily mean that the decision to go public or go private will be based on this determination. In the past, as probably in the future, other considerations have been more important. Actually, cost comparisons have been and are used more as ammunition for supporting previously established viewpoints than as grounds for decision-making.

The current flames of controversy in the public-versus-private-ownership dispute are kept alive mainly by two groups. On one side are the private electric utility firms, obviously and legitimately interested, with modest support from some conservative business and academic people and vociferous support from a small group of extreme "right-wing" individuals and organizations following the conspiracy approach and deploring almost all government actions taken during the twentieth century. On the other side is an equally dogmatic but more poorly financed group that appears to follow a "public ownership at all costs" philosophy. This latter group, although making wide use (or misuse) of "comparative" statistics, as do their opponents, apparently is motivated as much by ideology as are some of the "right-wingers." In between is the great body of the nonideological, pragmatic, general consuming public, confused, bored, or antagonized, perhaps little influenced by widely conflicting claims, primarily desiring reasonable (and lower) rates and adequate (and better) services.

The private utility campaigns against public ownership use a combination of statistical comparisons and ideology. In our opinion, the ideological emphasis is at best ineffective, at worst self-defeating. To combat public ownership most effectively, which certainly is a legal right and perhaps a moral responsibility of management to its stockholders, it would appear that positive rather than negative public relations programs would be more useful. That is, the "antisocialism" approach should be abandoned and the "efficiency" approach emphasized.

Most Americans, even those favoring public over private ownership of some utilities, are not socialists, probably resent being told that they are socialists or the unconscious dupes of socialists, and do not continually vote for socialist candidates. Such claims are likely to destroy more good will than they create. Instead of irritating potential friends by ideological name-calling and emotionalism, it appears that privately owned utilities could more appropriately concentrate on doing a better job than their publicly owned rivals (if, wherever, and whenever possible) and then on demonstrating to the general public that they can do and are doing a better job.

A 1967 publication alleged, with documentation, that many private electric utilities have been contributing substantially to nonprofit (tax-exempt) "front" organizations attacking the motives and patriotism of those supporting or accepting public ownership.[23] Further, it was alleged that most of these contributions, with the acceptance if not outright permission of regulatory authorities, were charged as operating expenses and thus passed along to consumers.

Certainly, anyone has a right to contribute to any legal cause. It is doubtful, though, that a privately owned regulated utility has any right to expect that its consumers finance campaigns against public ownership; if stockholders wish to do this, that is their own affair. It would appear that these allegations, if false, would provide grounds for libel suits. On the other hand, if true, they constitute grounds for severe moral if not legal condemnation of the utility managements concerned, and they represent grave dereliction of duty on the part of some regulators.

SUMMARY

In contrast to most of the rest of the world, the provision of utility services in the United States is largely a private responsibility under public regulation. Even in this country, though, there are varying degrees of public ownership in the several utility fields. Legal rights for public ownership are firmly established, but controversy over private versus public ownership has been widespread.

Our public ownership is not new and is not primarily due to ideological motivations. Rather, it has grown up alongside private ownership, although the public-private balance has fluctuated at times, and it has been adopted for a variety of pragmatic reasons.

Regardless of which political party is in power, it does not seem likely that any significant absolute decrease in public ownership of utilities can be expected in the foreseeable future. Political factors or public opinion may influence to a considerable extent the relative shares of future new markets going to public and to private organizations, however. It appears, then, that the most effective managerial policy for private firms wishing to maintain their present share of existing markets and to obtain an increasing share of future markets is to influence public opinion in a positive manner. Such firms should not expect consumers to finance their campaigns against public ownership, however, and should be wary of ideological appeals.

NOTES

1. A brief survey of the role of governments in economic affairs generally, from the earliest times to the present, can be found in Lester S. Levy and Roy J. Sampson, *American Economic Development* (Boston: Allyn & Bacon, 1962), chs. 21–24.
2. "Public ownership" often is defined elsewhere to exclude nonprofit cooperatives, on the grounds that the sellers are selling to themselves at cost. By this reasoning, however, it might be equally logical to exclude many other publicly owned operations.
3. The relative shares of electric energy sold consumers by these various sources is somewhat different, as many public and private organizations buy from each other for resale. The federal government sells little power directly to final consumers.
4. For examples, see *Loan Association v. Topeka,* 87 U.S. 655 (1873), and *Fallbrook Irrigation District v. Bradley,* 164 U.S. 112 (1896).
5. *Hamilton Gas Co. v. Hamilton City,* 146 U.S. 258 (1892).
6. *City of Joplin v. Southwest Missouri Light Co.,* 191 U.S. 150 (1903).
7. *Helena Water Works Co. v. Helena,* 195 U.S. 383 (1904).
8. *Jones v. City of Portland,* 245 U.S. 217 (1917).
9. *Standard Oil Co. v. City of Lincoln,* 275 U.S. 504 (1927).
10. *Puget Sound Power and Light Co. v. Seattle,* 291 U.S. 619 (1934).
11. *Green v. Frazier,* 253 U.S. 233 (1920).
12. *Ashwander v. TVA,* 297 U.S. 288 (1936).
13. *Alabama Power Co. v. Ickes,* 302 U.S. 464 (1938).
14. *Tennessee Electric Power Co. v. TVA,* 306 U.S. 118 (1939).
15. *Oklahoma v. Atkinson Co.,* 313 U.S. 508 (1941). This was not a Tennessee Valley Authority case.
16. Based upon discussion and statistics found in Eliot Jones and Truman C. Bigham, *Principles of Public Utilities* (New York: Macmillan, 1931), pp. 723–726.
17. It is possible that the existence of the postal service as a competitive method of message transmission dampened demands for nationalization of wire services during earlier days.
18. There is a long history, of course, of active state involvement and ownership in transportation and closely related fields. Also, North Dakota's right to engage in a variety of economic undertakings, including utility services, was upheld in *Green v. Frazier,* cited in note 11.
19. This includes the production of state-owned projects.
20. See the cases cited in notes 12, 13, and 14.
21. In the Tennessee Valley area less than 4 per cent of the farms received electric services. Within twenty years after the beginning of T.V.A. almost 90 per cent of the region's farms were electrified, and per capita electric consumption in the region was almost twice the national average and at lower than national average rates.
22. Based on calculations by the authors. These figures are not intended to be completely precise but only to show the general magnitude of change. Calculated results could vary, depending upon the specific dates, data, and deflaters used. The authors believe these figures are very conservative.
23. Lee Metcalf and Vic Reinemer, *Overcharge* (New York: David McKay Co., 1967). See

especially Chapters 14, 17, and 18. This publication implies that the utility firms concerned have used "right-wing fronts" to fight their battles. In reality, though, it may be even more correct to say that the "fronts" have "used" the utilities.

ADDITIONAL READINGS

1. Barnes, Irston R., *The Economics of Public Utility Regulation* (New York: F. S. Crofts, 1942), ch. 24, "Public Ownership," pp. 816–887.
2. Clemens, Eli Winston, *Economics and Public Utilities* (New York: Appleton-Century-Crofts, 1950), ch. 23, "Municipal Public Ownership of Utilities," pp. 548–579.
3. De Luccia, Robert, "A Look at the New Federal Power Policy," *Public Utilities Fortnightly,* vol. 53, no. 12 (June 10, 1954), pp. 745–755.
4. Fite, Gilbert C., and Jim E. Reese, *An Economic History of the United States,* 2d ed. (Boston: Houghton Mifflin, 1965), ch. 31, "The New Deal: A Further Look," pp. 613–631.
5. Glaeser, Martin G., *Public Utilities in American Capitalism* (New York: Macmillan, 1957), ch. 26, "The Development of Public and Cooperative Ownership," pp. 439–454.
6. Jones, Eliot, and Truman C. Bigham, *Principles of Public Utilities* (New York: Macmillan, 1931), ch. 15, "Public Ownership," pp. 714–784.
7. Manning, Ernest C., "Should Government Operate Utility Services?" *Public Utilities Fortnightly,* vol. 71, no. 7 (March 28, 1963), pp. 28–34.
8. Metcalf, Lee, and Vic Reinemer, *Overcharge* (New York: David McKay Co., 1967), ch. 14, "Get the Government Out of Government," pp. 179–191; ch. 17, "How to Find Reds Under Every Bed," pp. 201–209; ch. 18, "Book Reviews for the Birchers," pp. 210–220.
9. Sporn, Philip, "Observations on Private Versus Public Power," *Public Utilities Fortnightly,* vol. 53, no. 12 (June 10, 1954), pp. 717–733.
10. Thompson, C. Woody, and Wendell R. Smith, *Public Utility Economics* (New York: McGraw-Hill, 1941), ch. 28, "Public Ownership of Utility Services," pp. 598–635.
11. Trachsel, Herman H., *Public Utility Regulation* (Chicago: Richard D. Irwin, 1947), ch. 21, "Rural Electrification," pp. 415–439.
12. Troxel, Emery, *Economics of Public Utilities* (New York: Rinehart, 1947), ch. 29, "Municipal Utility Systems," pp. 645–665.
13. Vennard, Edwin, *Government in the Power Business* (New York: McGraw-Hill, 1968), pp. x, 352.
14. Wilcox, Clair, *Public Policies Toward Business,* 4th ed. (Homewood, Ill.: Richard D. Irwin, 1971), ch. 21, "Fields of Public Enterprise," pp. 481–503; ch. 22, "Public Power Projects," pp. 504–530.

18

Managing Publicly Owned Utilities

Chapter 11 points out some of the major differences between the institutional environments of nonregulated and of regulated businesses and discusses the managerial implications of these differences. There is an equally great gulf between the institutional environments of private businesses (even the regulated ones) and publicly owned organizations. These differences affect the functions and activities of formulative and administrative management in public enterprises.[1]

It may be true that "management is management" in some general sense, but management does not operate in a vacuum. Institutional environments clearly do influence managerial processes significantly and even play a selection role in determining what kinds of people attain management ranks. Public management differs from private management, in utilities as elsewhere.

Public ownership takes several forms, and its organizations vary greatly in size. The federal government uses both the government corporation (like the Tennessee Valley Authority) and special agencies within traditional departments of government (like the Bonneville Power Administration, within the Interior Department). State ownership may take such forms as the Nebraska Public Power System or the New York State Power Authority.

At the local level a large number of municipalities provide electricity, water, street transit, and sometimes other utility services either directly through a municipal department or through some form of separate semiautonomous organization. In addition, various sizes and kinds of utility or service districts or nonprofit cooperatives frequently provide utility services in designated areas established without any particular regard for internal state political subdivision boundaries.

With this wide variety of organizational forms, sizes, and institutional environments, one would expect to find a variety of managerial goals, constraints, and policies among publicly owned utilities. Observation indicates that this is true. But observation also indicates some common managerial threads amidst all this variety as well as some common managerial differences from the privately owned utilities.

GOALS

Despite such statements as may be found in enabling legislation, charters, or public pronouncements by officials, it is very difficult to pin down specifically or to generalize upon the real goals of most publicly owned utilities. Perhaps these goals vary to some extent from utility to utility and from time to time. One commonly stated goal, for example, however it may be worded, is "to give the public the fullest and best service which the utility is capable of rendering at the lowest possible cost." But what does this mean?

If fullest service means the most service, it is not always consistent with the best service or the lowest cost. Does fullest service refer only to utility services, or does it imply something in connection with conservation, preservation of the ecological system, opportunities for minority groups, land use planning, community employment stability or growth, and the whole gamut of similar activities which may be lumped together conveniently under the descriptive heading of "social welfare"? If the utility does concern itself greatly with these broader social problems, how does this affect the quality and costs of its utility services? And are operating revenues expected to cover all costs? Clearly, such a general statement of goals can be interpreted in many ways.

As political creations of the general public, publicly owned and managed organizations must shape their goals toward the voting public's wants.[2] But what are these wants? How are they determined? To what extent can management itself shape these wants? How far can management deviate from apparent public wants without endangering its own tenure or the organization's continued existence?

Insofar as utility services are concerned, it appears to be almost always safe to assume that the public wants the most for the least and prefers to have it now. That is, the public likes abundant and high-quality services at low prices and is generally not too concerned about any indirect or direct subsidies necessary to achieve this.

The costs of subsidies, shared by all taxpayers, are not perceived by most individuals in the same way as is an increase in the monthly utility bill. Also, most members of the public, in their capacities as consumers of utility services, are not very interested in trading off immediate and certain short-run benefits for potentially greater long-run benefits. The concept of possible resource misallocation due to subsidization does not excite the general public nearly as much as it excites some economists. Experienced politicians and public managers are well aware of these public viewpoints and usually act accordingly—or else, they soon become ex-politicians and ex-managers.

It probably is more fruitful to observe what publicly owned utilities actually do than to attempt to speculate about vaguely stated goals which often may be inconsistent or variable. There is little doubt that the great majority of public managers view themselves as peculiarly charged with the trusteeship of public resources for the benefit of the present and future generations. But aside from this (which, of course, is not completely unique to public managers), what are their constraints and what policies do they follow? That is, does the practice of public management actually differ from that of private management? If so, how?

In the broad social sense the function of every legitimate business undertaking, whether publicly or privately owned, is to serve society. In order to perform this function, among other things, the undertaking must be able to attract and retain sufficient capital for its necessary operations. The privately owned business attracts and retains capital through the expectation of profits by investors, whereas the publicly owned enterprise does not necessarily have to make profits at all. If necessary, it can operate indefinitely at a break-even level, or even at a loss if it is tax-supported. This suggests one major difference between public and private management. Their major constraints are different.[3]

CONSTRAINTS

As indicated in Chapter 11, the major constraints faced by managers of privately owned regulated utilities are, in order of importance, (1) the necessity for making a profit, (2) special utility regulatory laws, (3) general laws applicable to all businesses, and (4) public opinion. This order of constraints is probably reversed in the case of publicly owned utilities.

There is no compelling reason for a publicly owned enterprise to make profit a paramount goal. Some do attempt to make a profit, of course, and it might even be argued that a profit goal is a desirable yardstick for measuring managerial efficiency and for the allocation of capital resources in public undertakings. But the facts are that profits are not necessary for the survival of the undertaking and that public management is usually not judged by a profit standard.

Most publicly owned utilities are not subject to the special regulatory laws applicable to privately owned utilities.[4] Instead, they are subject only to their own enabling legislation and charters, which generally are not too restrictive. They are, of course, subject to the same general laws of business conduct which apply to all businesses, nonregulated and regulated, private and public.

Publicly owned enterprises exist only because the public at large (if it thinks about them at all) thinks they are doing a better job (or at least as good a job) as a privately owned business would do. That is, they live or die on the basis of public opinion. Despite this, however, it is usually not essential that a publicly owned utility engage in as much defensive public relations activity as may be desirable for a privately owned utility. There have not been many recent instances, or even serious threats, of take-overs of publicly owned utilities by private business, and the public operation normally has little to fear from regulation.

This is not to say that publicly owned utilities do not concern themselves with public relations. Rather, it means that public relations activities are designed for somewhat different purposes. Those dealing with public funds are expected to render periodic public accounts of their stewardship. Also, being primarily political creations, they cannot avoid using some political influence and political connections. Like privately owned enterprises, they are likely to emphasize the good (that is, what voters want to hear) and minimize the bad.

The formulative management of a publicly owned enterprise is elected by political votes rather than by economic votes. This being so, that level of management where strategy is made is likely to be less self-perpetuating and to have a greater rate of turnover of personnel than is found in privately owned utilities. Also, with formulators closely attuned to political winds and frequently thinking of their own political futures, strategy is likely to be influenced often by election returns. In addition, in order to achieve personal or general political goals formulators often attempt to control tactics, which properly belong to the area of administrative management.

Administrative managers, on the other hand, are generally appointed because of their technical competence (although having "pull" with the political in-group is no handicap, other things being equal). They are not expected to, and usually do not, become deeply involved in the political currents which play an important role in determining strategy. They are most likely to remain strictly tacticians and must be prepared to adapt to a variety of frequently changing strategies.

The managerial experience gap between formulators and administrators is typically much greater, and may potentially lead to greater problems of communication, in publicly owned than in privately owned utilities. A corporate board of directors is typically made up entirely or largely of people with long and varied past experience in some form of administrative management. The "directors" of a publicly owned enterprise, though, necessarily acquire their positions through political processes. This means that because of their differing backgrounds and interests, they frequently do not and cannot have the managerial experience and viewpoints usually found on corporate boards.

Although formulative managers of public enterprises are subject to voter control in about the same way that corporate directors are subject to stockholder control, public enterprises are not usually judged on the same basis as private enterprises. Further, inasmuch as the performance of publicly owned utilities is usually only one of the many standards by which elected officials are judged—and usually far from the most important standard—and inasmuch as most officials like to be reelected or elected to other offices, it is sometimes possible for these officials to use their utility management roles to win favor with voters. This may not contribute either to economic efficiency or to the happiness of those administrators who are strongly imbued with economic efficiency ideals.

POLICIES

Even with the best of intentions, and entirely without political motivations, formulative managers of publicly owned enterprises often establish policies quite different from those of private firms. They simply view their responsibilities differently.

PRICING

Public organizations are much less likely to base their pricing policies on costs of service (however these may be derived and calculated) than are private firms. Their marketing concepts are not determined primarily by profit-and-loss considerations. For example, growth in the volume of sales is frequently sought by publicly owned utilities, both by expanding services to include new areas and customers and by increased sales to present customers, even though this expansion may not bring in revenues sufficient to cover its costs. Prices of break-even services may not be increased when costs increase. Similarly, free or less-than-cost services are often provided to various public agencies such as fire departments, school systems, or the like. Or some publicly owned utilities which do have revenues in excess of costs turn over these excesses to their parent governments in order that taxes may be kept lower than they otherwise would be.

These kinds of marketing and pricing activities, in effect, amount to a subsidy paid by some users of services to other users, or even to nonusers. That is, the publicly owned utility in such cases is engaged in the separate government functions of taxation and income redistribution. Whether or not these are legitimate functions of publicly owned utilities is highly debatable. Some believe that utilities should only provide utility services, while others feel that a public undertaking should be much broader in scope than a private undertaking.

PLANNING

Many large publicly owned utilities, and even some of the quite small ones, engage in extensive long-range regional or community planning.[5] Publicly owned enterprises, though, often are more handicapped and less flexible than are privately owned firms in such planning. Long-range active planning is expensive and does not promise an immediate payoff. Also, formulative managers may be changed by political elections. Consequently, long-range planning may be given a low priority by some formulative managers who are more concerned with practical politics.

In addition, surpluses beyond operations needs of publicly owned utilities are often minimized by pricing or profit-limiting policies, or are drained away by income redistribution processes. Thus, they simply cannot afford to undertake desirable long-range planning.

It is true that some of our very best long-range regional and community growth forecasting and planning has come from publicly owned utilities. But this appears to be the exception rather than the rule. All too often, long-run social and economic benefits are sacrificed for short-run political gain.

MANAGEMENT DEVELOPMENT

Consistent policies designed to select and develop future top managers in an orderly manner are notably lacking in most publicly owned utilities. Formulative management is attained by political processes over which the utility organization has little or no control, and even the appointment of top administrators may often be politically influenced.

This method of managerial selection has both advantages and disadvantages. On the one hand, it ensures that the general public, who "owns" the utility, retains control over its management. Presumably, therefore, goals and policies will be consistent with what the public wants. On the other hand, this is likely to lead to a considerable amount of management by amateurs. The opportunities for competent and experienced lower-level managers to work their way up through the ranks to the highest management levels are definitely limited. In effect, this may result in some trade-offs of economic efficiency for public responsiveness. Whether this is good or bad depends on one's personal value judgments.

In fairness to the many highly competent persons who have dedicated their careers to management at various levels in publicly owned utilities, many of whom could earn considerably higher material rewards and personal prestige in private firms, it must be pointed out that the overall record of public management compares favorably with that of private management. Many publicly owned utilities do not make profits, or even operate at substantial losses. But this usually is a reflection of public expectations and public goals rather than an indication of managerial incompetence. One may legitimately argue about the desirability of given public goals without condemning the public managers charged with attaining these goals.

We have seen no evidence to indicate that the opportunity for public service is likely to attract less competent people than is the opportunity for private gain, although the basic motivations of the people attracted by these differing opportunities may be somewhat different. Fortunately (we think), in our society public service is considered by many to be highly rewarding personally even if not overly lucrative financially.

SUMMARY

Public ownership of utilities occurs in an assortment of levels, forms, sizes, and institutional environments. This means that managerial goals, constraints, and policies may vary considerably in detail among these utilities and may even vary over time in a particular organization. But despite these variations, there are basic managerial differences between publicly owned utilities as a class and privately owned utilities.

Publicly owned enterprises generally are not subject to the severe discipline of the profit-and-loss statement and usually are not closely controlled by regulatory agencies. Their institutional environments are much more political and much less economic in nature than are those of privately owned undertakings.

This does not imply that public management is of lower quality or more lax or less efficient than private management. Rather, it simply means that the performances of public and of private managers are judged, at least in part, by different constituents and by different criteria. Differing goals and constraints lead to differing policies and require different actions. What might be judged good management in a public undertaking might be considered poor management in a private firm, and vice versa.

In many instances, for various reasons, the public has deliberately chosen to have some kinds of its desired utility services rendered by public rather than by private ownership. Such a choice, in itself, indicates that the public expects performance in some way different from that obtainable from a private firm. Thus, it is not surprising, and not a basis for condemnation, that publicly owned utilities have different operational goals and standards than do privately owned firms.

All businesses exist to serve the public, and as long as the public is adequately informed and has freedom to make changes that it deems desirable, we cannot say that a politically controlled organization is any less preferable than an economically controlled one.

NOTES

1. It may be worthwhile for readers to review Chapter 11 briefly at this point.
2. Strictly speaking, public utility districts and various kinds of nonprofit cooperatives must respond to their customer memberships rather than to the general voting public. Membership voting in such nonprofit organizations, though, is on a "one member, one vote" basis rather than on a basis of economic power (that is, shares held) as in a private corporation. Thus, even in these particular types of publicly owned organizations, procedures are more likely to be politically determined than economically determined.
3. Long-continued substantial deficits may (or may not) lead to changes in the top management of a publicly owned utility, but deficits alone are not likely to cause the demise of the utility itself if its services are wanted and are reasonably adequate.
4. Some kinds of publicly owned utilities in some jurisdictions *are* regulated by the same authorities that regulate privately owned utilities, but this is not common.
5. Compare with Chapter 16.

ADDITIONAL READINGS

1. Bauer, John, and Peter Costello, *Public Organization of Electric Power* (New York: Harper, 1949), ch. 11, "Public Standards and Techniques," pp. 197–224.
2. Firth, Robert E., *Public Power in Nebraska* (Lincoln, Nebr.: University of Nebraska Press, 1962), ch. 11, "Management and Organization of the Districts," pp. 233–253.
3. Sampson, Roy J., "Public Ownership Constraints on Utility Management," *Journal of the American Water Works Association,* vol. 61, no. 10 (October 1969), pp. 495–498.
4. Tenner, Irving, *Financial Administration of Municipal Utilities* (Chicago: Public Administration Service, 1947).

Note: Also see "Additional Readings" For Chapters 11 and 20.

19

Issues in Public Ownership

As noted in Chapter 17, public ownership varies considerably by specific type of utility, and several patterns of public ownership exist. In some areas public ownership is relatively unimportant and noncontroversial. Natural gas is an example. In other areas ownership patterns are important but noncontroversial. Water utilities and telephone service illustrate this pattern. Finally, a third pattern exists where ownership is both important and controversial. Historically, electric power and transit services provide examples of this. In these utilities a considerable portion of service is provided by publicly owned enterprises, and there has been considerable controversy over the ownership pattern. (In the face of declining markets and other woes, the controversy over ownership of transit facilities recently has come down to the point of having publicly owned transit or having no transit at all. Therefore, the ownership controversy has been most keen in the electric power field during the last thirty or forty years.)

There are several government levels or organization patterns of public ownership. The federal government is involved in many ways; to a small degree various states are also involved; cities and municipalities are involved; and finally, others, such as rural electrification and rural telephone cooperatives, power districts, conservation districts, electric districts, and public utility districts (P.U.D.'s) are also involved. It should be noted that all of these government levels are not involved in the same way. That is, some publicly owned electric utilities, for example, primarily produce and transmit power, while others primarily distribute, and still others engage in all three of these functions.

As the public-versus-private-ownership controversy is greatest and the public ownership issues most clear-cut in the electric utility field, this field will be used as the major example for discussing public ownership issues in this chapter. The same general types of issues arise, in varying degrees, in connection with other types of public ownership, of course.

Although issues may be classified in various ways, perhaps the key issues concern the proper role of public ownership at the various government levels, pricing policies, and questions of expansion.

THE "PROPER" ROLE OF PUBLIC OWNERSHIP

Although a little less than one fourth of this country's electric power is produced from publicly owned facilities, the concentration is much heavier (almost two thirds) in the hydroelectric field. Consequently, there is a very close connection between hydroelectric power production and various government water projects involving irrigation, navigation, reclamation, or flood control. Today there is fairly general agreement that public power production at the multipurpose water projects is in the public interest. There is some disagreement, though, concerning how this power should be distributed and marketed.

There are at least nine possible ways to dispose of electric power from a multipurpose water project. First, a government agency can build the water project and sell the falling water to private firms, who invest in generators and transmission lines to produce and market the power. Second, the government agency can sell the falling water to another government agency, a state or municipality, who owns the generators and transmission lines. Third, the government agency can build the generation capacity and lease these facilities to private firms, who provide their own transmission and distribution facilities. Fourth, government-owned generation facilities can be leased to other governments, who would provide their own facilities for transmission and distribution.

As a fifth option, the government agency can invest in generating facilities but sell the power to private firms, who transmit it. Sixth, the government agency can produce power but sell it to other governments for transmission. Seventh, the government agency can produce power and build transmission lines to sell to private firms at or near the market, who in turn distribute the power to consumers. Eighth, the government agency can produce and transmit but sell to other government agencies for distribution to consumers.

Finally, the government agency can completely enter the power business by building the project, owning the transmission system, and distributing power to the ultimate consumers. All of these options except the last one are found in some form or another at various federal projects. In all instances, the federal government has remained the supplier or wholesaler of public power, leaving to others the distribution and retailing of power.

THE FEDERAL ROLE

The ownership issue at the federal level turns on the twin points of the preference clause and transmission policy. (We have noted in Chapter 17 that the preference clause can be found in almost all statutes establishing federal water and power projects.) There has been some misunderstanding that the preference clause gives a price preference, but this is not the case. The preference clause merely means that the preferred agencies have the first choice of buying federal power. Privately owned power firms have often purchased large blocks of federal power and have benefited from public investment.[1] However, publicly owned systems have had preference and have been served with federal power first. While it was quite controversial for many years,[2] the preference clause issue appears to have become a settled matter within the last twenty years.

The issue of federally provided transmission lines continues to be controversial and continues to be solved on a project-by-project and appropriation-by-appropriation basis. Historically, the struggle over private versus public power was fought more often over this issue than any other. In a few instances, Congress failed to appropriate funds for transmission lines, thus leaving federal projects literally "captives" of the private power firms authorized to serve in the territories of particular projects.[3] More typically, Congress has appropriated money for federal transmission to bring public power to other government users under the preference clause, with any excess going to privately owned utilities.[4] Indeed, federally owned transmission lines became the backbone of the combination public-private power pool in the Pacific Northwest and elsewhere. In an era of coordination and interconnection federal transmission lines have benefited both private and public enterprises.[5]

With the passage of time, the issue of the proper federal role has become less important. Recently Congress has seemed somewhat reluctant to commit massive federal funds to multiple-purpose water projects; other social problems seem to have a higher priority. Also, the most fruitful projects have already been developed. These two factors probably will make the issue of the federal ownership role less important in the future.

THE STATE ROLE

Over time, several state governments have become involved in publicly owned power. Some of these installations bear the name of the state, such as the New York State Power Authority, Arizona Power Authority, or Alaska Power Administration, while others carry the name of the river involved, such as the Grand River Dam Authority and the Brazos River Authority. In most instances, these state agencies are involved in either the distribution of power generated at federal projects or in operating state-financed water projects.

In some instances, such as at Hoover Dam, the enabling federal legislation gave preference to the adjacent states, thus causing state government to enter the power distribution business in order to benefit from the project. In other instances, the growth of state government in the power business was a specific issue entangled with the breakdown of state regulation, the holding company excesses of an earlier age, the development of water projects, and the growth of municipal systems and rural electrification cooperation.[6] At any rate, state governments have not generally become involved in the power business, and where involvement has occurred it has typically been in response to a specific development or problem.[7]

THE MUNICIPAL ROLE

In contrast to state governments, cities have often become involved in the distribution and sometimes the production of electric power. Some sizable cities, such as Seattle and Los Angeles, own their own power systems; however, the municipal power movement is generally confined to smaller cities.

The question of the proper role of municipal electric ownership is likely to be a political issue. Much discussion of it usually relates to the quality of service by the existing organization and the degree of protection existing state regulation provides to consumers.

There are four obstacles which arise in municipal ownership, aside from charter limitations.[8] Damages and severance charges will probably have to be paid to an existing private firm. The extent of these is an obstacle. Second, the municipal boundary limits may not constitute an efficient unit of distribution or production; thus prices may not be as low as anticipated, and those living outside the city boundary but closely associated with the city may face a worse situation. Third, financing problems may arise. Public funds must be available to pay for seizure or severance, and on-going capital investment will be necessary. The question of willingness of property owners to bond for a municipal operation is a very real one. Finally, where alternative sources of power supply are not available, assuming a city restricts its role only to distribution (as the majority of them do), the city may become a captive customer of the private utility which previously owned its distribution system. Apparently, the obstacles to municipal electric ownership are great enough so that few cities today decide to embark on this route. The number of municipal power enterprises has declined from a high of 3,084 cities in 1923 to less than 2,000 at the present time.

COOPERATIVES AND OTHER AGENCIES

Government ownership has bloomed in rural areas. This movement is based on two factors: lack of service by existing utilities and sponsorship by the federal government. Only about 10 per cent of the nation's farms were served with electricity as late as the middle 1930's. Regulated utilities generally did not find it profitable to serve rural areas, where customer density typically was light, investment per customer high, and consumption low. The utilities were too busy developing their business in urban areas and had too many other places to use capital at a greater advantage. In time, no doubt, the rural areas of the nation would have been served by regulated utilities, but government sponsorship greatly accelerated rural electrification.

The story of this movement is quite remarkable. In the twenty years after the passage of the Rural Electrification Act (Norris-Rayburn Act) in 1936, rural electrification grew from 10 per cent to almost 94 per cent in 1955, and it has since surpassed 98 per cent of all farms. Beginning in 1949 the basic act was amended to include telephone cooperatives, and now over 75 per cent of farms have telephone service. The story of this broad-based social provision of utility service is indeed amazing.[9]

This tremendous growth was principally accomplished with the cooperative type of organization and with federal loans plus the preference clause and transmission line policy mentioned before. Literally, the federal government became, in many instances, the wholesale supplier of power and, at the same time, the bankers who helped finance the cooperative development. President Franklin D. Roosevelt established the Rural Electrification Administration in 1935 in the Department of Agriculture by executive order, and enabling legislation followed the next year. Basically, since 1935 the federal government has extended $6.4 billion in long-term (thirty-five-year) loans at low interest rates (2 per cent) to 1,100 borrowers, who serve 5.8 million customers in forty-six states.[10]

Many of these R.E.A. cooperatives are distributors of power. Both the federal government and privately owned utilities serve as their wholesalers. In some instances, however, cooperatives generate their own power, individually or in the form of associations of several distribution cooperatives banded together to provide generation and transmission facilities for the entire group.

Along with this R.E.A. movement, and sometimes considered part of it, has been the P.U.D. development. In some states, notably the Pacific Northwest, county-wide cooperative units have been allowed. These hybrid government agencies include both rural and urban areas and are established only after a vote of the citizens in a county. Generally, these districts possess the power to tax and to borrow on the general credit of the district, and they may be authorized to undertake the provision of several services in addition to power. Regionally, these public units are of considerable importance.

Besides calling attention to the role of the federal government, these cooperative units and their operations generate some controversy. While it is generally argued that cooperatives have a positive role to play, there are some objections to the manner in which this role is carried out. These will be discussed further in the following chapter.

PRICING POLICIES

Once the "proper" ownership role of a unit of government has been established, the problem of what price policy should be followed becomes an issue. Basically, a government production unit has several options it can follow in pricing.

As one option, a price can be established at a level roughly comparable to adjacent privately owned and regulated utilities. At such a price level, income will be earned which would be called profit in a regulated firm. This "profit," or gross income as it is sometimes called, can be used to offset a portion of the costs of some other service or to provide some other public service outright. A type of cross-subsidization is involved here, in which consumers provide revenue to support other undertakings by way of power rates, telephone rates, or the like. If there is general agreement as to the desirability of the subsidized service, or if all consumers share according to their contribution by way of utility bills, little controversy arises. These conditions are not always fulfilled, however, and this type of pricing policy may become a controversial issue.

A second option is to establish a price level which covers all costs. This "price-at-cost" option can be deceptively simple. It clearly turns on a determination of the costs of supplying the service, a factor which may be harder to determine than it would seem. But even if costs can be determined, one might argue that it is marginal costs which may be of most importance in power pricing as well as in economics in general. Marginal costs are even more difficult to assign. Further, there will be a problem of providing financial reserves and providing for future growth. The price-at-cost idea is very difficult to put into practice, even though it is easy to expound.

A third option is to set prices to promote the widest possible use. That is, the pricing system may be used to allow the most people to benefit the greatest possible amount from the publicly owned enterprise. Once more, this is a pleasant philosophy but most difficult to practice and may require the public undertaking to be subsidized from other revenue sources.

In practice, all of these options have been used. Congress has not always been clear and has specified "widest possible use" as a criterion in a number of instances. It has also provided that power rates should cover costs or be consistent with "sound business principles," which assumes the recouping of costs. Finally, it has provided that power revenues will specifically subsidize water charges.

States and municipalities vary, but it is common for them to follow the first option, that is, to assist other services. Cooperatives generally follow a combination of lowest possible rates consistent with covering costs and following "sound business principles." But as long as options exist and enabling legislation is not clear, pricing policies will be an issue.

COST ALLOCATION

Cost allocation is implicit in almost any pricing policy. Where multiple purposes are involved, as in federal water projects, a considerable portion of the total cost is common or joint in nature.[11] That is, many physical facilities serve several functions jointly. To be sure, many parts of the project are specific, like power generators, flood control gates, navigation locks, and the like. The costs of these can be properly and correctly allocated to the specific services involved. But much of the cost is common or jointly caused by all of the various purposes or functions. An example of this is the dam itself. It is difficult to allocate or assign this common or joint cost to a specific function or service of the project.

When services are marketed or sold, the allocation of the costs to each function can become an important issue. All functions of a multipurpose project are not marketable. Society itself stands the cost of flood control, navigation, and recreation. Irrigation water and power are marketable functions, and the amount of the total costs assigned to these functions will obviously affect the price at which they must be sold under all but the third option noted in the previous section. Even here, there will be interest in the degree of subsidization necessary to attain widest possible use; thus cost allocations will continue to be an important issue.

Various methods of cost allocation on multipurpose projects have been suggested, without a great deal of agreement.[12] The federal government tends to use the "alternative cost occasioned" approach, whereby an estimate is made of the cost of a single-purpose project for each function and the proportion each function occasions or causes to the sum of these alternative cost estimates establishes the specific cost allocation factor. Judgment is involved in any formula, and in actual practice, costs sometimes have been allocated after the prices have been established and after the project has been in operation for some time.[13]

COMPARISON AND COMPETITION

Comparisons between enterprises with different ownership patterns producing the same service are inevitable. Many things can be compared, but it is principally the rates to the consumer which are discussed. Pricing policy and cost allocation issues tend to come to a head in public-versus-private-ownership rate comparisons.

But the issue goes deeper than mere comparison. Because rates may be lower for governmentally produced power, regardless of whether it is federal, state, municipal, or cooperative, the suggestion of competition naturally follows. The idea of publicly owned plants, whose rates would be used as a yardstick for comparison of the performance of privately owned plants, has a long history. Originally, the yardstick concept was given popularity by President Franklin D. Roosevelt as a type of monopoly control and as an answer to the inefficiencies of regulation. Later, the concept was used to justify the expansion of federal power. Some still hold to the concept,[14] which has been called "institutional competition."[15]

Comparisons of power-producing units are very difficult. Thus, in its unrefined state, the yardstick comparison has little economic validity. There is a difference in the amount of taxes paid by private as compared to public enterprises. The costs and sources of capital vary considerably, with the public enterprises typically having access to capital at much lower costs. The cost allocation issue can often distort any comparison. Differences in the size of production units and the economies of scale can cause differences in rates not attributable to ownership patterns. Finally, a series of miscellaneous differences, such as the time when development took place (much government power was installed during the 1930's depression or at an earlier time), labor costs of each, and the like, is involved.

Even though the yardstick concept compares unlike things, apples compared to oranges, as it were, some scholars feel that adequate adjustments for the differences can be made and that comparisons can yield valid data for policy purposes.[16] Although they may not be valid economically, it is quite probable that comparisons will continue to be made.

PUBLIC OWNERSHIP EXPANSION

Another issue in public ownership is whether or how far public enterprise should expand. The desire to grow and expand is not limited to privately owned enterprises. In addition to the built-in preference for growth, the managers of publicly owned enterprises like them to grow in order to attain economic and technical operating efficiencies. At the federal level there has been a great deal of controversy over this expansion issue. Both production expansion and market expansion have been involved.

Some of this expansion may be inherent in a water project. That is, the amount of water flowing in a river will vary during the year. Once a multipurpose dam has been built, it is easy to demonstrate that it could be more efficiently operated and produce power more cheaply (as well as better serve its other purposes) if an upriver dam were available to "even the flow" seasonally. This upriver project will probably be multipurpose also, since it is generally agreed that, wherever possible, falling water should be utilized to produce power as well as for other functions like irrigation, flood control, navigation, and recreation and that resources should not be wasted.

Hence, an attempt to "even the flow" at a downstream dam leads to a justification for further dams above the second project, and so on up the river basin. On the grounds of more efficient production and complete use of committed resources, one federal dam has led to another until today almost all available damsites on the Tennessee River system and the Columbia River system have been developed.

But the expansion issue goes further than regulating river flows. Once customers are developed or served by a federal water project under the preference clause, a vested interest in the source of supply is created. Cooperatives and municipal users are interested in a firm and constant supply of wholesale power. The federal agency involved typically is interested in supplying a firm load.[17] This has led to power production by steam generation by the T.V.A. and to proposals to do the same on other projects. With the exception of the T.V.A., the federal government has avoided entering the steam-generated power business directly, and the so-called "partnership concept," first begun in the Eisenhower administration, has prevailed. Less controversy over this issue exists now than formerly.

The market expansion side of the issue also draws less controversy than previously. Initially, the federal government was quite militant in using the preference clause, transmission line policy, and R.E.A. funds to set up R.E.A. cooperative customers for its power projects. With the passage of time, most potential R.E.A. distributors have been developed. Also the partnership concept has blunted this movement. Finally, lack of funds for R.E.A.'s has also made market expansion less of an issue.

SOCIAL INVESTMENT CRITERIA

As the economy expanded greatly during the 1950's and 1960's, questions arose as to the desirability of further social investment in the publicly owned utilities and the processes by which this investment is undertaken. These questions concerned more than just political or economic philosophy; they also concerned the economic use of a scarce resource, capital.

Beginning in the late 1950's studies of the social investment process began to suggest that public capital should not be used for social investment unless the return from that use was at least equal to the return that could be gained if the same capital were used privately.[18] That is, if a dollar invested in the private sector could earn 8 per cent, the same level of earnings should prevail on a dollar invested in the public sector in order to have economically efficient use of scarce capital. Ownership should not cloud the issue of efficient capital allocation. Under such a criterion, many multipurpose federal water projects might be judged uneconomic, and the process of social investment in these types of undertakings could be questioned.

While it is undoubtedly valid economically to compare the return from social investment to the return from private investment, there is a great deal of difficulty in applying the concept. Benefits from social investment are very difficult to measure and, in some cases, even to identify and estimate. Government planners have probably overestimated benefits in the past, because of social philosophy and a desire to build more water projects. Costs of social capital typically have been very low, not always in fact, but by congressional statute.[19] There is considerable question about the determination of the exact costs of private capital as well. Exact comparisons between private and public investment are most hazardous, and rather heroic assumptions must be made.

This is not to say that this issue is unimportant. Indeed, it is very important that capital should return a benefit in social investment equivalent to what it would return privately. Mere change of ownership does not cancel the necessity for economic comparison and analysis. These recent studies make their greatest contribution in pointing out the need for careful evaluation. However, in an uncertain world with tremendous difficulties of exact measurement and with decision-making being political rather than economic, practical application of the concepts is quite another matter.

SUMMARY

While other issues have been involved from time to time, the issues of the proper ownership role of various government units, price policy, and expansion have been the most prominent. Many of these issues have been partly or temporarily solved by political action.

This political action has involved many groups. Some issues have been resolved by legislative statutes in the form of enabling laws; some have been resolved by legislative appropriation of funds or the lack thereof; some have been resolved by administrative rulings (such as the partnership concept); some have been resolved by votes of the electorate, such as the decision to "go public" by a municipality in struggling with the issue of its proper role; some issues remain basically unresolved. But regardless of the status of these issues, the operational problems remain. Some of these will be considered in the following chapter.

NOTES

1. See Martin T. Farris, "Theoretical Price Implications of the Preference Clause in Public Water Policy," *Papers and Proceedings, Western Farm Economic Association,* 31st Annual Meeting, Pullman, Washington, August 1958, pp. 121–126.
2. A good general discussion of the arguments for and against the preference clause is found in Albert W. Stone, ed., *Is A Preference Clause Among Distributors of Federal Power Justified?*

Montana State University Studies in Law (Missoula, Mont.: Montana State University Press, 1957).

3. See Gus Norwood, "The Consumers' Stake in the Preference Clause," in Stone, p. 15, for the example of Canyon Ferry Dam in Montana, where the lack of transmission lines forced the federal government to sell 99 per cent of the electric output at 2.50 mills per kilowatt-hour to the adjacent privately owned utility. Norwood estimates revenue losses of $626,800 in 1955 because preference customers could not be served.
4. The issue of duplication of private transmission facilities with federal lines has been a most difficult one. By and large, outright duplication is not allowed, and the so-called Keating Amendment has prevented any occurrence of duplication. However, in some instances preference customers have literally been the captives of the privately owned transmission lines. See Lee Metcalf and Vic Reinemer, *Overcharge* (New York: David Mckay Co., 1967), pp. 242–252.
5. During the mid-1960's new rules for the use of public lands as rights-of-way for private electric transmission lines caused some concern. The rules allowed federal agencies the right to use "surplus capacity" in privately owned lines where public lands were involved. Privately owned firms looked upon this as a further move to "nationalize the power industry," but their alarm seems unfounded. See Charles F. Phillips, Jr., *The Economics of Regulation,* rev. ed. (Homewood, Ill.: Richard D. Irwin, 1969), pp. 584–585.
6. See Robert E. Firth, *Public Power in Nebraska: A Report on State Ownership* (Lincoln, Nebr.: University of Nebraska Press, 1962) for an interesting discussion of these multiple forces. The New York State Power Authority's early years (from 1931, when it was authorized at the urging of Franklin D. Roosevelt, then Governor of New York) may also reflect some of these forces.
7. A survey of state involvement is contained in Edwin Vennard, *Government in the Power Business* (New York: McGraw-Hill, 1968), pp. 51–82.
8. Some of these obstacles and various devices to overcome them are discussed in Martin G. Glaeser, *Public Utilities in American Capitalism* (New York: Macmillan, 1957), pp. 443–445.
9. Two popular discussions of this growth are found in Marquis Childs, *The Farmer Takes a Hand* (Garden City, N.Y.: Doubleday, 1952); and Clyde T. Ellis, *A Giant Step* (New York: Random House, 1966).
10. Phillips, p. 576.
11. Theoretically there is a difference between common costs, which are common to many functions or undertakings, and joint costs, which arise only where a fixity of proportions in production exists. However, traditionally analysts concerned with cost allocation in water projects have used the term "joint costs" in discussing this problem. This probably originated with Martin G. Glaeser, "Those Joint TVA Costs," *Public Utilities Fortnightly,* vol. 24, no. 5 (August 31, 1939), pp. 259–269.
12. See Clair Wilcox, *Public Policies Toward Business*, 4th ed. (Homewood, Ill.: Richard D. Irwin, 1971), pp. 514–516, for a discussion of this.
13. Emery Troxel, "A Critique of Public Power Policies: Discussion," *American Economic Review,* vol. 47, no. 2 (May 1957), pp. 403–405.
14. See Metcalf and Reinemer, ch. 21, "Competition," pp. 237–252.
15. Walter Adams and Horace M. Gray, *Monopoly in America* (New York: Macmillan, 1955), pp. 70–72. Also see Phillips, pp. 716–717, for a discussion of the difficulties arising in the concept.
16. James E. Bonbright, "Rate Making Policies of Federal Power Projects," *American Economic Review,* vol. 36, no. 2 (May 1946), p. 430.
17. In the past there has been considerable controversy over whether the federal government has "utility responsibility" at its projects, that is, whether it is committed to supply all needs of preference customers on a "firm" basis now and in the future. See "Interpretation and Clarification of Power Policy Directives Issued by the Department of Interior," *Hearings on Power Policy Before the Committee on Interior and Insular Affairs,* House of Representatives, 83d Congress, 1st Session (December 29, 1953; January 4 and 5, 1954).
18. There is a considerable body of literature on this point. For examples, see Roland W. McKean, *Efficiency in Government Through Systems Analysis* (New York: Wiley, 1958); Otto Eckstein, *Water-Resource Development: The Economics of Project Evaluation* (Cambridge, Mass.:

Harvard University Press, 1958); John V. Krutilla and Otto Eckstein, *Multiple Purpose River Development: Studies in Applied Economic Analysis* (Baltimore: Johns Hopkins Press, 1958); Jack Hirshleifer, James C. DeHaven, and Jerome W. Milliman, *Water Supply: Economics, Technology and Policy* (Chicago: University of Chicago Press, 1960); and Robert Haveman, *Water Resource Investment and the Public Interest* (Nashville, Tenn.: Vanderbilt University Press, 1965).

19. In justifying social investment, the "interest charge" used on the cost side has typically been the "imbedded cost of the federal debt." This figure is typically under 4 per cent, since much of the federal debt was issued years ago during a low-interest period and because of the federal tax exemption on such borrowings.

ADDITIONAL READINGS

1. Bauer, John, and Peter Costello, *Public Organization of Electric Power* (New York: Harper, 1949).
2. Childs, Marquis, *The Farmer Takes a Hand: The Electric Power Revolution in Rural America* (Garden City, N.Y.: Doubleday, 1952).
3. Ellis, Clyde T., *A Giant Step* (New York: Random House, 1966).
4. Firth, Robert E., *Public Power in Nebraska: A Report on State Ownership* (Lincoln, Nebr.: University of Nebraska Press, 1962).
5. Metcalf, Lee, and Vic Reinemer, *Overcharge* (New York: David McKay Co., 1967).
6. Phillips, Charles F., Jr., *The Economics of Regulation,* rev. ed. (Homewood, Ill.: Richard D. Irwin, 1969), pp. 574–585.
7. Smith, Lincoln, *The Power Policy of Maine* (Berkeley, Calif.: University of California Press, 1951).
8. Vennard, Edwin, *Government in the Power Business* (New York: McGraw-Hill, 1968).
9. Wilcox, Clair, *Public Policies Toward Business,* 4th ed. (Homewood, Ill.: Richard D. Irwin, 1971), ch. 22, "Public Power Projects," pp. 504–530.
10. Zank, Elmer E., and Henry H. Bakken, *Light and Power: Rates and Cost of Serving in Wisconsin R.E.A. Cooperatives* (Madison, Wis.: University of Wisconsin Press, 1959).

20

Problems of Public Ownership

The problems of public ownership primarily involve the operation and management of public enterprises. To some degree, the problems of management in general are the same for public as they are for private enterprises. But as pointed out in Chapter 18, the environment of public ownership imposes different goals, constraints, and policies on publicly owned enterprises. These differences are most readily illustrated by considering the five major problems of capital acquisition and use, rate-making, taxation and accountability, interrelation among enterprises, and developmental questions.

PROBLEMS OF CAPITAL ACQUISITION AND USE

Capital is a scarce resource for all enterprises. Public enterprises have the same problems of capital sources and effective utilization of capital as do private enterprises, although the constraints and environments differ.

SOURCES OF CAPITAL

The source of capital varies according to the level of public enterprise involved. Very few federal enterprises can borrow on their own credit; rather, they must make their needs annually known before Congress (typically, congressional committees) and compete with all other possible applications for capital at the federal level.[1]

Social programs at the federal level enjoy varying degrees of popularity with the passage of time. A good example of this variation over time is found in agricultural programs. During the period from the mid-1920's to the mid-1950's Congress generally was willing to finance multiple and diverse agricultural programs. Although they can be considered as separate social programs, rural electrification, rural telephone service, and multipurpose water projects were closely tied to agricultural programs. Since that time, agriculture has suffered in relative popularity as urban problems have become more pressing. The result has been that considerably smaller amounts of capital than requested have been made available by Congress for rural power and telephone service, water projects, and the like. Development of multipurpose federal water projects has slowed considerably, and many cooperatives serving rural areas have been hard-pressed for capital for expansion and replacement.[2]

Municipalities, public utility districts, and some other government units do not depend on the federal government for capital. But these units also face capital problems, which arise from the need for additional authority to borrow, the state of capital markets during recent times, and the constraints imposed by the financial image of the government unit.

The people served by a government unit must be willing to legally pledge the property and the credit of the unit in order to borrow. Agreeing upon this is not easy. Most commonly, revenue bonds are used, and a portion of the revenue from the service involved is pledged for repayment of the loan. Not only does this impose a limitation but it also means that perhaps some of the free or subsidized services provided by the publicly owned utility must be foregone. Agreement on this move sometimes may prove difficult to get. Where the taxing power exists, this, too, is typically limited to a set amount of the valuation of the property contained in the government unit. A privately owned utility does not depend on the willingness of its customers to accept further indebtedness; a publicly owned utility does.

Further, the state of financial markets during recent years has created capital problems. For years, tax-free local government securities enjoyed great popularity and a ready market. But in the tight money market of the late 1960's higher and higher interest rates had to be paid even by public enterprises. Many government enterprises found that their costs of capital were doubling or tripling. Also, financial markets did not seem as willing to absorb tax-free securities as they had once been. Traditional corporate borrowings were yielding unusually high returns. Many investors preferred to receive 9 per cent on a high-rated corporate utility bond, representing a mortgage on considerable valuable physical property, to 7 per cent on a revenue bond pledging a portion of the utility income of some little-known electric district or city—even with a tax advantage.

Finally, a government unit earns a financial reputation just as a corporate unit does. To a considerable degree, the financial image of a government borrower is based on its past history and political image. Publicly owned utility enterprises suffer with or benefit from the actions of the government borrower in past years and its use of funds on unrelated government undertakings. These actions may be little connected to the utility enterprise, but they will affect the market evaluation nevertheless.

If a municipality has missed an interest payment on street improvement bonds, it will affect the financial marketplace image of its electric power revenue bonds, even though there is little connection between the municipal power operation and the paving of streets. Or if a municipality overextended itself in an expansion of a sewerage system in the 1920's and had financial difficulty, it will affect the ability of a municipal power enterprise to borrow in the 1970's.

UTILIZATION OF CAPITAL

Even if capital is available, the problem of proper utilization still exists. Here again, public enterprises experience more difficulty than private businesses. In a privately owned utility some ranking of priority in the use of capital can be attained by estimating future returns from projects and comparing these to the cost of capital. Some type of similar procedure is necessary in publicly owned enterprises.

In a public enterprise, the ranking of projects is difficult. First, profit as such is rarely the goal, and the usual profit-oriented procedure may be unsuitable. The goals of the operation may be to provide widest use of the service at lowest price to the consumers. A profit-oriented ranking of projects will be only partly helpful in this case. Second, the cost of capital used may not be a true figure. Third, monetary returns from investment increments may be impossible to determine if free services are supplied or if all services are not sold. Finally, exact numerical comparisons are most difficult to make.[3]

Most people would agree that a publicly owned utility should not use capital in an "inefficient" manner. However, measuring efficiency without the profit criterion is not easy. In summary, this utilization difficulty, plus constraints on the sources of capital, impose unique and often troublesome problems on the managers of public enterprise. Management of capital is always a problem for utilities; it is doubly so for publicly owned utilities.

RATE-MAKING

Once a general pricing policy has been established, no matter how vague, the added problem of implementing this policy in actual rates remains. For privately owned utilities, regulatory commissions typically approve rate schedules drawn up by the utilities, but this is not usually so for publicly owned organizations. Rather, it is assumed that since the users in effect own the enterprise, no device to guard their economic interests is necessary. (Rates of public enterprises are state-regulated in some states, especially in situations where municipally owned organizations sell to users outside municipalities.) The process of rate-making in public enterprise is generally oriented more toward social goals than toward profit-making.

Socially oriented rate-making may take many forms and reflect various philosophies and concepts. For instance, marginal cost pricing (discussed in Chapter 14) may be used. Prices could be set to reflect only the marginal cost of service to each class of user, thus stimulating use at a rather low price which would include no "profit."[4] Obviously, this will depend on having a pricing policy of widest possible use at lowest possible price. It would also depend on the public enterprise not being forced to subsidize another service.

Many types of innovational rate forms could be used in public enterprises. Rates at the same level for a large geographic area and possessing no factor to offset transmission costs have been used,[5] as have rates based on use of power for a year rather than for an hour.[6] Seasonal variations in rates are another possibility, as are many other variations, all based on the marginal cost pricing idea.

In practice, most publicly owned utility enterprises have followed the lead of privately owned utilities. Block rate systems are common, and customers are classified into groups, with different charges for each group. The danger of discrimination exists, because generally there is no regulation. Some observers feel that public power rates have been unduly low in some categories in order to attract industrial users. Certainly the tendency to give very low industrial rates exists. Differences in elasticities of demand for power among customers exist regardless of the ownership pattern of the supplier. Further, attraction of industry with low power rates fits into the concepts of regional economic development or the widest possible use at the lowest possible price.

TAXATION AND ACCOUNTABILITY

Public enterprises do not collect and pay taxes as do privately owned utilities. On the other hand, it is common for "in lieu of tax" payments to be made by public enterprises to other agencies of government. The most widely known of these "in lieu" plans is in the T.V.A. area, where an attempt was made to offset the tax loss suffered by local governments when the T.V.A. took over the utility plants of private firms.

The amount of these in lieu payments varies, and one important problem is, What is an equitable payment? In some instances, in lieu taxes are a stated percentage of revenues; in others, attempts are made to render these payments equivalent to privately owned utility taxes. Sometimes, no in lieu payments are made, but free services are rendered instead. Regardless of how much is paid and the method of calculation, it is likely that no "in lieu of taxes" plan will satisfy all citizens or all political subdivisions. No level of government ever feels that it has too much money allocated to it.

While citizens in general make a choice in these instances between supporting public undertakings by way of their tax bills or having a hidden tax in their utility bills, there is a tendency to compartmentalize thinking on public enterprises. We know of instances in which increases in school taxes were blamed upon failure of in lieu payments to reach anticipated levels. The tax exemption of public enterprise is not without its problems.

Accountability is also a problem. Accounting is usually designed to inform shareholders, bondholders, and regulatory commissions about the details of private utility operations during the past accounting period. For public enterprises, however, accountability is more socially oriented. Concern is for the degree of use and the price to consumers.

Depending on the goals established, perhaps more concern should be shown over how many other services are subsidized or over how much profit is shown in public enterprises. However, our thinking is greatly conditioned by the more prevalent free market system, and it is common for the public to be concerned over the management practices of a public enterprise unless some profit or net revenue is registered yearly. Further, it is quite difficult to show degree of use, lower consumer prices, or even degree of subsidization of other services by using traditional accounting methods of income statements and balance sheets. Accounting in public enterprises presents a real challenge to those charged with this function.

INTERRELATIONS AMONG ENTERPRISES

As previously noted, many publicly owned enterprises depend upon privately owned corporations to supply a portion of their services or to act as wholesalers. For example, rural telephone cooperatives must depend upon A.T.T. for long-distance service, and many municipal power operations and rural cooperatives depend on privately owned groups for a supply of power at wholesale. Historically, different ownership philosophies have caused strong feelings, which have sometimes affected these interrelations. From an operational point of view, it is not always easy for a privately owned utility to give good services at low rates to what it considers its competitor. R.E.A.'s have often justified their requests for more capital for their own power plants on the basis of lack of a reliable and cheap wholesale source of power. Also, one rationalization for many federal water projects and transmission lines has been the difficulties met by publicly owned enterprises in securing good power sources at wholesale.

In some areas the relations between the privately owned power wholesaler and publicly owned power distributors have been good; in other areas the extension of the public power fight to these relations has led to strong government reaction. In a very real sense, some private power companies have done a great deal to extend public ownership by failing to cooperate as wholesalers—thus making a case for more public power.

In recent times considerably more cooperation between public and private owners has taken place. It has not been unusual for publicly owned power producers to be included in regional power pools with privately owned producers. In addition, in some large and complex projects, joint ventures have been undertaken by a combination of public and private owners.[7] Indeed, as was suggested in Chapter 1, the extent of this cooperation, regardless of ownership philosophy, has been so great that we now find ourselves in a new era of cooperation.

Equally important are the interrelations among public enterprises. Problems exist both between different levels of government and at the same level. With the federal government acting as banker as well as wholesale supplier to many cooperatives and municipal systems, supervision and some degree of control are natural. For example, the Rural Electrification Administration has not only acted as spokesman for cooperatives but has also imposed various degrees of controls on these groups. T.V.A. has exercised control in its area also. All of the cooperatives and municipalities have not always agreed with these controls, supervision, and restrictions. In some areas disagreements have been greater than in others. The managers of publicly owned enterprises have had to deal with supervision by other government units, and while this has not been the same as the supervision by regulatory commissions of the privately owned utilities, constraints do exist, regardless of ownership patterns.

Finally, the interrelations among publicly owned enterprises have presented both opportunities and problems. Many public power enterprises are interconnected and operate cooperatively. The so-called G & T movement (Generation and Transmission Cooperative) is a good illustration of these interrelations. In a number of instances R.E.A. loans have been made available for super-cooperatives, or cooperative associations of distributors who have found it necessary or desirable to build their own generation and transmission facilities. The opportunity to join such associations, and the desirability of assuring an alternative source of wholesale supply, plus cost and other ramifications, present real problems as well as opportunities for many publicly owned enterprise managers.[8]

DEVELOPMENTAL PROBLEMS

Expansion and development of public enterprises are sometimes questioned as not being proper public goals, and this was discussed in the preceding chapter. But when they are undertaken, there are also operational problems, which concern the use of funds, the reliability of power sources, and territorial integrity.

USE OF FUNDS

In the continuing struggle between private and public ownership, the spotlight of public attention was focused on the management and use of R.E.A. loans during the 1960's. The original R.E.A. act restricted this type of public ownership to rural areas and small towns under 1,500 population. It is quite apparent that service to rural customers was the object. Some well-located R.E.A.'s, though, found themselves serving populations well in excess of the original limit and also serving industrial and commercial customers. From the point of view of the managers of these cooperatives, this can solve as well as create problems. Urban areas are generally more profitable to serve, and industrial customers present very desirable demand characteristics.

Further, the original act empowered cooperatives to lend funds to their customers for "improvements," generally at an interest rate of 4 per cent. These loans were originally intended to assist farmers with their wiring and plumbing expenses so that power could be utilized. However, given the above-noted desirability of nonfarm customers, some R.E.A.'s used this authority to assist industrial customers. For example, some cooperatives made loans to such undertakings as ski resorts and gravel-crushing firms. This problem of how to utilize R.E.A. funds to best serve customers and still stay within the proper role of the organization has been quite vexing to managers of these cooperatives.

RELIABLE POWER SOURCES

Again and again, publicly owned power groups have had to face the problem of securing a reliable source of wholesale power for their operations. This is the basis of the G & T movement mentioned before, and the repeated rationale for the need for more federal power projects. This problem is the same for R.E.A.'s as for municipalities and other agencies. Long-term purchase contracts must be negotiated, and favorable treatment by suppliers, both private and public, must be assured in order to guarantee expansion and development of public enterprises.

As suggested, some privately owned firms may have inadvertently done more to further the public ownership movement by their power supplier relations than by any other single undertaking. Fortunately, it appears that in recent times publicly owned enterprises have come to be regarded as an important and needed part of the total picture rather than as temporary and hated competitors. Nevertheless, the managements of publicly owned enterprises will probably continue to face the problem of sources of supply.

TERRITORIAL INTEGRITY

Another developmental problem is, What geographic area should be served? As noted, most publicly owned enterprises are not regulated by commissions. While this may seem to be an advantage, it also may be a disadvantage. A commission recognizes a given service territory; thus, through commission action or by franchises from local governments, one firm serves a given area. No such advantage exists for public enterprises. On some occasions, privately owned power enterprises have moved into areas served by R.E.A.'s. The publicly owned enterprises, therefore, do not always feel secure and generally desire territorial integrity.

Further, the R.E.A.'s maintain that they need territorial integrity in order to facilitate borrowing of capital in the private market. As noted, sources of capital seem to be the most pressing current problem of cooperatives. In the 1970's the original thirty-five-year loans are being repaid and new capital is needed for re-equipment and expansion. This is taking place at a time that Congress is less than willing to continue to act as "banker." From the point of view of the cooperatives' management, regulation by a state commission and assurances of territorial integrity might greatly facilitate borrowing.[9] Many cooperatives are actively seeking state commission regulation!

SUMMARY

Public ownership is not without operational and managerial problems, and public policy has not solved all of these. These problems concern capital sources and utilization, rate-making, taxation and accountability, interrelations among public and private enterprises, and developmental questions. Many of these affect the future of public enterprises and present a continuing challenge to the management of public enterprises. Public policy may assist in solving some issues in the future, but by and large, managerial problems will persist. Fortunately, public ownership is less controversial than it has been in the past, and public enterprise is increasingly recognized as an integral part of the utility industry. This recognition will probably do more to solve the problems of public ownership than any other single factor.

NOTES

1. The T.V.A. now has the power to issue revenue bonds, although for many years it depended soley on annual congressional appropriations of capital.
2. During the late 1960's Congress appropriated funds for less than half the total loan applications from R.E.A. cooperatives. David A. Hamil, "Financing Remains Critical Issue for R.E.A. Program," *Public Utilities Fortnightly*, vol. 85, no. 12 (June 4, 1970), pp. 44–47.
3. R. S. Leavenworth, *Engineering-Economic Aspects of the Decision-Making Process in Municipal Electric Utilities.* Report EEP-10 (Stanford, Calif.: Institute of Engineering-Economic Systems, Stanford University, 1964), pp. 95–145.
4. While most government undertakings are priced to cover operational costs only, T.V.A. pays a portion of its revenues from both power and nonpower services to the United States Treasury. This repayment schedule is designed ultimately to return the public capital invested. Similarly, most multiple-purpose water projects repay the cost of power and some irrigation capital investments on a fifty-year schedule and at an artificially low rate of interest. While these payments are considered loan amortizations to the federal treasury, they also could be considered "profits." It is difficult to define the term "profit" when talking about public enterprises.
5. The Bonneville Power Administration felt that the pricing policy authorized by Congress required a uniform charge over the geographic area it served. Hence, initially a charge of $17.50 per kilowatt-year was made to all areas more than thirty miles from the dam site.
6. The kilowatt-year concept in the Pacific Northwest probably came about because of a desire to stimulate use and a fear that such a large block of power could not be disposed of by conventional pricing. Charles McKinley, *Uncle Sam in the Pacific Northwest,* (Berkeley, Calif.: University of California Press, 1952), p. 167.
7. Many examples could be cited. One is the development of several hydroelectric projects on the Columbia River by P.U.D.'s, where privately owned utilities guaranteed to take a certain percentage of the power, thus assuring marketability of revenue bonds. Another example is the undertaking of WEST (Western Energy Supply and Transmission Association) in building high-power complexes. WEST has both privately and publicly owned members. A third example is the Southwest-Northwest Intertie project, where a combination of privately owned and publicly owned power enterprises and the federal government is providing a regional interchange of power and long-distance extra-high-voltage transmission lines.
8. It has been suggested that G & T's have been undertaken even when privately owned facilities were available (see Phillips, p. 578); also that some G & T costs may have been unduly high (see Charles E. Olson, "Inefficiency and Subsidy–A Conflict in Public Policy?" *Public Utilities Fortnightly,* vol. 81, no. 12 (June 6, 1968), p. 38, and Olson, *Cost Considerations* . . ., pp. 55–68). But G & T's have defenders, like Norman M. Clapp, "REA's Power Supply Program," *Public Utilities Fortnightly,* vol. 81, no. 12 (June 6, 1968), pp. 24–32, and Metcalf and Reinemer, pp. 237–252. The Phillips, Olson, and Metcalf-Reinemer books are fully cited in "Additional Readings" at the end of this chapter.
9. See Hamil (cited in note 2).

ADDITIONAL READINGS

1. Bauer, John, and Peter Costello, *Public Organization of Electric Power* (New York: Harper, 1949).
2. Hanson, A. H., *La Gestion des Services Publics par les Autorités Locales,* vol. I (Pays-Bas, La Haye: Martinus Nijhoff pour L'Union Internationale des Villes et Pouvoirs Locaux, 1966).
3. Leavenworth, Richard S., *Engineering-Economic Aspects of the Decision-Making Process in Municipal Electric Utilities.* Report EEP-10 (Stanford, Calif.: Institute of Engineering-Economic Systems, Stanford University, 1964).

4. Metcalf, Lee, and Vic Reinemer, *Overcharge* (New York: David McKay Co., 1967).
5. Olson, Charles E., *Cost Considerations for Efficient Electric Supply.* M.S.U. Public Utilities Studies (East Lansing, Mich.: Institute of Public Utilities, Michigan State University, 1970), ch. 5, "Performance in an Era of Changing Technology," pp. 55–68; ch. 34, "Pricing of Regional-Project Services," pp. 762–785.
6. Phillips, Charles F., Jr., *The Economics of Regulation,* rev. ed. (Homewood, Ill.: Richard D. Irwin, 1969), pp. 574–585.
7. Tenner, Irving, *Financial Administration of Municipal Utilities* (Chicago: Public Administration Service, 1947).
8. Troxel, Emery, *Economics of Public Utilities* (New York: Rinehart, 1947), ch. 30, "Pricing of Municipal Services," pp. 666–686.

Part Five

Current Problems and the Future

21

Utility Growth and Technological Change

No industry likes to stand still or decline, and the utilities are no exception. In general, there has been a great deal of recent concern over the growth of the economy. Many studies of economic growth have been undertaken, a distinct theory of economic growth has been developed, and specific courses in economic growth are available at most large universities.

But all sectors or parts of the economy do not grow equally. Since our interest is in utilities, it is proper to ask, How have the utilities fared? To understand growth in utilities, one must understand the causes of growth in general as well as the causes of growth in utilities in particular. Further, some idea of how growth is measured would be helpful. Finally, some consideration should be given to the problems of growth and to the positive or negative effects of utility regulation.

A comprehensive study of the growth of individual utilities is beyond the scope of this book. However, some discussion of utility growth, its measurement, causes, and problems can be undertaken. This discussion concerns two general topics: growth, technology, and productivity; and problems of growth and technology.

GROWTH, TECHNOLOGY, AND PRODUCTIVITY

What causes economic growth in general? This question is at the heart of the relatively new science of economic growth. Economic development undoubtedly flows from a combination of many factors, but in general, four factors seem to be very important determinants. These are natural resource availability, labor inputs, capital, and the proper system or set of institutions to stimulate growth. These same four factors are important for the growth of an individual utility, although at a somewhat different level.

An abundance of natural resources is important to economic growth. Scholars have stressed particularly the supply of iron ore resources and energy resources, especially coal. Even so, natural resources alone do not make growth. Some countries have these key resources and yet have not grown; other countries which do not possess these resources have grown in spite of this shortcoming. Clearly, more than physical resources is necessary.

An added dimension to growth is human labor. Growth is caused and directed by people. The results of economic growth are purchased or used by people. But warm bodies are not enough. Labor inputs must be trained, must have various degrees of skill, and, above all, must be motivated or stimulated. The fruits of economic activity must be distributed in such a manner as to create a market for further production. The study of the role of human resources, or human capital as it is sometimes called is a most interesting one.

Many observers of growth stress the third factor, capital. Economic growth may well depend upon the provision for and the use of capital. It is difficult to estimate how much of a society's income must flow into capital forms before economic growth takes place, but there is no doubt that a considerable amount of capital resources are necessary for economic growth. Further, capital takes many forms. The usual forms of factories, tools, equipment, and inventory must be supplemented with what is commonly called "social overhead capital." It is in this regard that utilities are pivotal as determinants of economic growth. Before growth can be undertaken, a society must have adequate energy sources, a good communications system, and an efficient and widespread transportation network.

The final factor is that a system or set of institutional arrangements that stimulates growth must prevail. This system must provide incentives for risk-taking, allow profits, stimulate savings and capital accumulation, and reward effort. Further, to sustain growth the system must reward development of new ideas and new ways to do things. In short, it must provide for innovation and technological advancement.

Just as a nation must have resources, labor, capital, and the proper system within which to operate, an individual utility must possess these, but at a different level. Physical inputs of supplies and resources are necessary; trained, skilled, and well-motivated human resources are important; a great deal of physical capital of a very specialized nature is mandatory; and the proper institutional system, stimulating innovation and technology while rewarding risk and providing incentives, must prevail. When these factors exist, and if the utilities' services are needed and desired, the industry will grow and develop.

THE RECORD OF UTILITY GROWTH

In the domestic economy, what is the record regarding utility growth and development? In order to answer this question some measurement of utility growth is necessary. There are at least three ways to measure utility growth: physical measurement, comparative measurement, and service measurement. Each has its limitations, but each tells something about utility growth.

Physical Measurement

Even physical measurement of utility growth is difficult to obtain and to analyze. It is typical for data to be presented in terms of individual sectors of the utility group, such as power, natural gas, and telephone. Good measures of growth do not always exist, as statistics are collected with specific goals in mind, such as revenue, profits, employment, and the like. Adjustments are always necessary because of population growth, changes in the character of the service, and other factors.

However, the physical record of utility growth has been outstanding. Production of both electric power and natural gas has more than doubled each ten years for many decades, as has the number of telephones in service.[1] Analysis of these data leads to the general conclusion that these utilities have been expanding 7 to 8 per cent per year on the average. Naturally, all components or parts are not growing at the same rate. For example, Shepherd indicates that power production in general increased 8.2 per cent yearly between 1950 and 1964 but that the publicly owned segment increased at 10.5 per cent yearly, while the privately owned sector increased at 7.7 per cent yearly; and that the number of phones in the Bell system grew at a yearly rate of 7.5 per cent from 1956 to 1963, while the phones installed in independent systems grew at 11 per cent for the same period.[2]

In a massive study of productivity undertaken by the National Bureau of Economic Research, indexes were calculated for changes in the economy from 1869 to 1953. Considering 1929 as 100, the 1953 index of physical output for power was 491, for natural gas 562, and for telephones 226.[3] For comparison purposes, the private domestic economy's physical output had an index of 203. While scholars may not agree as to the proper measure and what the data mean, there is little doubt that the utilities have a remarkable record of growth.

Comparative Measurement

A slightly more sophisticated approach is to measure growth against that of other countries. By this measurement, the average American utility customer uses many times more power, natural gas, and telephone service than the average customer in other nations.

Another comparative measurement technique is to consider growth of utility services over time as compared to growth of the entire economy shown by the Gross National Product. Since the GNP grew at the rate of 3.6 per cent per year between 1950 and 1964, the previously noted growth rates of power production (8.2 per cent) and telephones in service (7.5 per cent and 11 per cent) indicate that the utilities are growing faster than the GNP. Comparisons with foreign countries are possible here also, and Shepherd has found that in Britain and the United States electricity growth has been nearly three times as rapid as the real GNP in each country, whereas in Germany and Italy, power output is only slightly faster than GNP.[4]

Per capita electricity output and per capita telephones in service can also be compared by country. These generally show the same trend, with the United States having one of the highest outputs per capita. Even though these data must be used with great care, they do confirm the general impression of wide use and rapid growth of utility services in the United States.

Service Measurement

One of the great difficulties in analyzing growth through time is that the services offered have changed. The telephone service offered in 1940 is not the same service as in 1970. Electric power delivered in 1970 has somewhat different characteristics than power in 1940; at least it is delivered in a different fashion and produced differently. Natural gas service is more reliable and has more optional sources of supply.

Exact measurement of service levels probably is impossible. Also, change does not always mean progress, and just rendering the service in a different manner does not always mean that it is better. Even so, representatives of the utilities are fond of pointing out the progress of the past decades.

For instance, telephone service today includes limited picture-phone service, microwave transmission, underground distribution, satellite and long-lasting cable connections to other continents, electronic switching, and new commercial services like TELPAK and WATS. None of these was widely available in 1940.

Natural gas may come from underground storage during peak periods, be regulated in its flow by computers, or be partly made up of gas previously liquefied and transported across oceans from foreign countries by ship. Electricity is produced in atomic plants, often transmitted by direct current or extra-high-voltage lines, sometimes firmed up by pump-back projects, and more and more frequently delivered by underground systems.

Many of these signs of progress relate mainly to efficiency and cost savings devices. This is reflected in rates, and if one equates these technological developments to progress, it is possible to say that service is much better today and charges are the same, or nearly the same, as they were in 1940.

It is hard to overemphasize the price record of the utilities. This record is outstanding. Charges for services have remained remarkably stable or have increased very little during the past three decades. Utility prices have increased far less than overall prices in the economy. Undoubtedly, a great deal of this remarkable price record is due to technological advances and managerial efficiencies. Whether such a record can be maintained in the future is an open question. The past record certainly presents a challenge, and utility management and regulators may have a difficult time making the future equal the past in this regard.

CAUSES CONTRIBUTING TO UTILITY GROWTH

What has produced this record of utility growth? In a very general way, there are two contributing causes. On the one hand, there is the demand factor, made up of population, income, the state of economic health of the whole economy, the desire to increase individual standards of living, and the like. On the other hand, there is the supply factor, made up of plant and equipment, devices available to use the service, the price of the services, the manner in which the service is promoted, the technology of producing the service, the productivity of suppliers, and the like. Complete analysis of all of these factors is not possible here, but some general discussion of each category may prove helpful.

Demand

The fact that our economy in general has been a growing one has helped utilities greatly. Given the essential nature of the services performed, increased population alone would assure increased demand for utility services. The income factor cannot be overlooked. Studies have shown that expenditures for utility services increase more rapidly than incomes increase, at least up to a certain level. As incomes rise, more people use telephone services, and increased power use and gas sales are also related to income increases.[5] Much of this growth can be attributed to the constant striving for a higher standard of living.

The general economic health of the nation will affect the rate of growth in utility services. During periods of decreasing rates of economic growth, utilities experience decreasing growth rates; during periods of increasing rates of economic growth, utility growth rates increase. But apparently the desire for a higher standard of living plus availability of labor-saving devices and stable or slowly increasing prices have caused the use of power, gas, and telephone to grow faster than the general economy.

Supply

On the supply side, utility growth has come from tremendous capital inputs plus better use of people and great advances in technology. The record amounts of capital invested in new and expanding plants and equipment have been noted elsewhere, as has the capital-intensive nature of much of the utility industry.

But aggregate capital alone is not enough to bring about such growth. Technology is also involved. This term refers both to the inventing of new devices and pieces of capital and to the slow and constant upgrading of the existing plant as replacement occurs and as utilities learn to do their jobs better. Many of the increases in the quality of service can be traced to technological advances. In a capital-intensive industry technology is of prime importance.

In order to have an expanding and growing market utilities and equipment suppliers have introduced and promoted more and more devices to use services. All of these lead to a growing market. When these supply factors are coupled with stable or slowly rising prices and increased income and demand in the economy, the result is substantial growth.

Productivity Measurement

One favorite way to measure change in output is to relate it to inputs, such as man-hours worked. The result is often called "productivity measurement." With such an impressive growth record, how productive have utilities been? The answer to this reflects in a rough way the use of capital, the increases due to technology, and the better use of labor and resource inputs.

On the productivity score, utilities come off very well. National Bureau of Economic Research studies show utilities overall increasing in productivity from 1899 to 1953 at the rate of 5.5 per cent per year, as compared to 2 per cent for all manufacturing and 1.7 per cent for the economy as a whole. The study concerns itself with changes in output per labor input and adjusts for capital inputs to arrive at a total productivity index. The same method is used for various components of the economy and by decades over time. In all decades and in all utility sectors industry productivity has been higher than in the overall economy.[6]

While such long-term time series measurements must be used with great care, and while they may reflect numerous unknown factors[7] and include some questionable assumptions,[8] the productivity record of the utilities seems very impressive.

PROBLEMS OF GROWTH AND TECHNOLOGY

In spite of the relatively good record of utilities in economic growth, increased productivity, and apparent technological advance, questions can be posed about the problems of growth and technology. Has the rate of growth been as great as it could have been? Have new technology and innovations been introduced as rapidly as could be expected? Do utilities aggressively undertake research and development to come up with new technology and new and better ways of handling problems? Is the institutional environment such that firms are stimulated to develop technology and promote growth?

All of these questions imply that there exists some comparable standard against which one can measure utility growth and technological advance. If the questions concerned the unregulated sector of the economy, one measure could be comparable profits. Assuming some degree of effective competition in the sale of the product and competition for the use of inputs, the firm that shows the greater productivity has the higher profits. Industries or firms that fail to take advantage of technological change and innovation do not reap the rewards that more aggressive firms gain. The latter are often stimulated by the marketplace to undertake risk, expend money in research and development, expand technological knowledge, and search for more inventive and better ways to produce. The system of the open market and the institutional arrangements of capitalism provide this spur to progress and act in the form of Adam Smith's famous "invisible hand" to encourage economic progress.

But we are not dealing with the traditional competitive marketplace in the utility sector. No such built-in invisible hand is present. Instead, reliance must be placed on the visible hand of regulatory authorities. The rewarding of technological progressiveness with higher earnings is up to regulators, who in turn find themselves constrained to allow only "fair" profits and "reasonable" rates. The competition of the marketplace may be difficult when entry is restricted and a single-firm service area prevails. In a very real way, the problem of growth and technology in the regulated service industries is concerned with the effectiveness of the institutions and system of regulation.

Two questions can be asked here: What is the effect of rate and earnings regulation on utility growth and technological advance? What is the effect of the industry market structure of regulated monopoly on utility growth and technological advance?

THE EFFECTS OF RATE AND EARNINGS REGULATION

As noted, in the relatively competitive sector of the economy the firm that innovates and expands technological knowledge by discovering a "better way" is rewarded with profits. If regulation is effective and really works as it should, a utility firm would have any extra profits coming from technology and innovation taken away by the regulatory process. There may be a bias built into regulation which penalizes, or at least frustrates, the desire to apply technology or to innovate.[9]

As noted in Chapter 10, there may be "disincentives" in the regulatory system. Can a commission which is charged with protecting the public interest by determining fair and equitable earnings and rates legitimately allow some incremental return to the innovative and technologically advanced firm while denying an incentive return to the laggard firm? If no incentive is available, how can we reasonably expect firms to strive for efficiency? No definitive answer to these questions exists, although some suggestions have been made concerning the process of regulation.[10]

Some observers are not overly concerned with the alleged lack of incentive and suggest that the A-J-W effect and regulatory lag provide built-in incentives.[11] The A-J-W effect, discussed in Chapter 10, would stimulate overinvestment in capital if it really works. Assuming that utilities would choose more technologically efficient capital, this stimulation might ensure some degree of growth and innovation. Indeed, some observers have gone so far as to suggest that the rate of return should decline after a certain level in order to partially offset this A-J-W effect.[12]

Regulatory lag also has been discussed previously. The idea here is that the process of regulation is so slow that a firm making a technological change or adopting an efficient innovation can depend upon reaping the rewards from it for some time. Some observers have gone so far as to suggest that as an explicit incentive to efficiency, rates should be subject to review only at periodic intervals, such as every three years. In this manner, firms could count on retaining the benefits of technology and innovation.[13]

It is a fact that, in general, utility firms themselves do not undertake a great deal of research and development. The major exception is the Bell Laboratories branch of the American Telephone & Telegraph Company. In this instance, research and development has led to technological advances with applications in many areas other than utilities.[14] It is worth noting that this branch is not regulated.

Some utility firms have entered into research and development programs cooperatively, such as the cooperative efforts of groups of utilities and the federal government in early experiments with atomic power. Some firms attempt to solve local operating problems with research and development efforts. But by and large, utilities depend upon their equipment suppliers to carry on research and development and to discover and apply new technology. It is possible to suggest that since the rewards of the risk of technological innovations are denied regulated utilities but are available to equipment suppliers, this underemphasis on research and development is primarily the fault of the regulatory system.

THE EFFECTS OF MARKET STRUCTURE

Traditional economic theory says that a monopolist generally will not be stimulated to innovate and adopt new technology because no competitive spur exists. If new technological advances do come along, theory says, the monopolist may withhold introduction of innovations or at least space out new innovations so as to maximize his return on past capital investments.

Some observers feel that such actions have taken place where monopoly in the utilities is involved. The examples most often cited have to do with A.T.T. and the introduction of microwave technology, and with its desire to preserve "systems integrity" to the exclusion of various telecommunication attachments not manufactured by its subsidiary Western Electric.[15] It is true that these technological advances did seem long in being introduced, but it is impossible to determine exactly how soon such innovations would have been introduced in a competitive market. Evidence of withholding or spacing the introduction of technological innovations must of necessity be purely circumstantial.

Almost the opposite factor can also be cited. There seems to be evidence that local monopoly may have a degree of inefficiency not because it is a monopoly but because it is too small to gain economies of large-scale production. The bulk-power industry is cited here, and estimates of lost economies because the industry is organized into too many small and uncoordinated production units run from between 4 and 10 per cent of wholesale price. The suggestion is made that mergers should be allowed so that the approximately one hundred major bulk-power suppliers could be reorganized into twenty to thirty highly efficient suppliers of power.[16]

Finally, it has been frequently pointed out that the monopoly concept upon which regulatory philosophy is based has been outdated and made obsolete by technology. Technology leads to more competition, both within a given utility sector and between utility sectors.[17] This latter form of competition may be especially important where various sources of energy are concerned.[18] Indeed, it has been suggested that the idea of the antitrust philosophy of promoting competition, and the tendency for utilities to be exposed to competition because of advances in technology, are both in conflict with the philosophy of regulated monopoly.[19]

Technology does seem to be spurring more competition on an interindustry basis. The prior competition between electricity and natural gas for cooking and water-heating has broadened to include the very important and growing air-conditioning market. Other competitive uses of natural gas seem possible in the future, such as small power production units for commercial users. New applications of energy in many unique forms and new applications of energy in competition with one another may be just around the corner.[20] The validity of regulation based on the assumption of a market structure of monopoly may well be questioned in the future because of technological changes.

SUMMARY

The growth of the utility sector has been remarkable; by almost any measure, its record has been outstanding. A good portion of this growth has been due to an expanding market and the human desire to attain a higher standard of living. An equally important factor has been the constant history of capital reinvestment by utilities. In this regard, technological change has been a positive factor, allowing increased expansion in conjunction with relatively stable prices.

But there are many problems associated with utility growth and with stimulating technological advance. Most of these are concerned with the system of institutional arrangements under which utilities operate. The "invisible hand" of the marketplace is not allowed to stimulate technology fully. Thus, numerous questions can be raised concerning the effects of the regulatory environment on the pivotal factor of technological development. No simple answers to these questions are available. The matter is one for continued study and analysis.

NOTES

1. Federal Power Commission and Federal Communications Commission data.
2. William G. Shepherd, "Utility Growth and Profits Under Regulation," in William G. Shepherd and Thomas G. Gies, eds., *Utility Regulation: New Directions in Theory and Policy* (New York: Random House, 1966), pp. 6, 8, and 9.
3. John W. Kendrick, *Productivity Trends in the United States.* A Study by the National Bureau of Economic Research, New York (Princeton, N.J.: Princeton University Press, 1961), Table H-IV, pp. 586–587; Table H-VI, pp. 590–591; and Table H-IX, pp. 596–597.
4. Shepherd, p. 6.
5. See Paul W. McCracken, *Economic Progress and the Utility Industry.* Michigan Business Paper No. 38 (Ann Arbor, Mich.: Graduate School of Business Administration, University of Michigan, 1964) for some interesting analysis of these points.
6. Kendrick.
7. Shepherd suggests that in power, increasing use by consumers, increasing size of plant, rising load factors, and "pure" technological improvement have joined to cause these rapid productivity gains (pp. 14–15).
8. William H. Dodge, "Productivity Measures and Performance Evaluation," in Harry M. Trebing, ed., *Performance Under Regulation.* M.S.U. Public Utilities Studies (East Lansing, Mich.: Institute of Public Utilities, Michigan State University, 1968), pp. 20–32; and Yoram Barzel, "Productivity in the Electric Power Industry, 1929–1955," *The Review of Economics and Statistics,* vol. 45, no. 4 (November 1963), pp. 395–408.
9. For interesting discussions of this problem, see Shepherd; and James R. Nelson, "Pricing and Resource Allocation in the Public Utility Sector," in Shepherd and Gies, pp. 58–87.
10. Trebing suggests some modification along the line of the sliding scale system attempted in a few places in the 1920–1940 period: Harry M. Trebing, "Toward an Incentive System of Regulation," *Public Utilities Fortnightly,* vol. 72, no. 2 (July 18, 1963) pp. 22–37. Another suggestion for an incentive over and above a fair return, called a "plus factor for efficiency and risk taking," is contained in Martin T. Farris, "A Critical Appraisal of the Traditional Approach to Regulation of Public Service Industries and a Suggested Alternative," in Burton A. Kolb and Otis Lipstreu, eds., *New Concepts and Current Issues in Public Utility Regulation,* (Denver: Peerless Publishing Co., 1963), pp. 199–200.
11. Both of these factors are discussed in William M. Capron, ed., *Technological Change in Regulated Industries* (Washington, D.C.: Brookings Institution, 1971), ch. 1, "Introduction," pp. 1–12.
12. A. K. Klevorick, "The Graduated Rate of Return," *American Economic Review,* vol. 56, no. 3 (June 1966), pp. 477–484.
13. William J. Baumol, "Reasonable Rules for Rate Regulation: Plausible Policies for an Imperfect World," in Almarin Phillips and Oliver E. Williamson, eds., *Prices: Issues in Theory, Practice and Public Policy* (Philadelphia: University of Pennsylvania Press, 1967).

14. M. D. Fagen, ed., *Impact: A Compilation of Bell System Innovations in Science and Engineering Which Have Helped Create New Industries and New Products* (New York: Bell Laboratories, 1971).

15. William G. Shepherd, "The Competitive Margin in Communications," in Capron, pp. 86–122.

16. William R. Hughes, "Scale Frontiers in Electric Power," in Capron, pp. 44–85; and Charles E. Olson, *Cost Considerations for Efficient Electric Supply.* M.S.U. Public Utilities Studies (East Lansing, Mich.: Institute of Public Utilities, Michigan State University, 1970).

17. Charles F. Phillips, Jr., "Growth, Technology and Competition in Regulation," *Public Utilities Fortnightly,* vol. 81, no. 9 (April 25, 1968); and James W. McKie, "Regulation and the Free Market: The Problem of Boundaries," *The Bell Journal of Economics and Management Science,* vol. 1, no. 1 (Spring 1970), pp. 6–26.

18. Irwin M. Stelzer and Bruce C. Netschert, "Hot War in the Energy Industry," *Harvard Business Review,* vol. 45, no. 6 (November-December 1967), pp. 14–26, 190–192.

19. Charles F. Phillips, Jr., "Increasing Conflict Between Regulation and Antitrust," *Public Utilities Fortnightly,* vol. 87, no. 1 (January 7, 1971), pp. 29–38.

20. Bruce C. Netschert, "The Technology of Energy Use in the Year 2000," *Public Utilities Fortnightly,* vol. 83, no. 8 (April 10, 1969), pp. 19–25.

ADDITIONAL READINGS

1. Capron, William M., ed., *Technological Change in Regulated Industries* (Washington, D.C.: Brookings Institution, 1971). See the following chapters in particular: William M. Capron, "Introduction," ch. 1, pp. 1–12; William R. Hughes, "Scale Frontiers in Electric Power," ch. 3, pp. 44–85; William G. Shepherd, "The Competitive Margin in Communications," ch. 4, pp. 86–122; William M. Capron and Roger G. Noll, "Summary and Conclusions," ch. 7, pp. 197–226.

2. Fagen, M. D., ed., *Impact: A Compilation of Bell System Innovations in Science and Engineering Which Have Helped Create New Industries and New Products* (New York: Bell Laboratories, 1971).

3. Garfield, Paul J., and Wallace F. Lovejoy, *Public Utility Economics* (Englewood Cliffs, N.J.: Prentice-Hall, 1964), ch. 21, "Technology and Public Utilities," pp. 470–486.

4. McCracken, Paul W., *Economic Progress and the Utility Industry.* Michigan Business Paper No. 38 (Ann Arbor, Mich.: Graduate School of Business Administration, University of Michigan, 1964).

5. Netschert, Bruce C., "The Technology of Energy Use in the Year 2000," *Public Utilities Fortnightly,* vol. 83, no. 8 (April 10, 1969), pp. 19–25.

6. Phillips, Charles F., Jr., "Growth, Technology and Competition in Regulation," *Public Utilities Fortnightly,* vol. 81, no. 9 (April 25, 1968), pp. 34–41.

7. Phillips, Charles F. Jr., "Increasing Conflict Between Regulation and Antitrust," *Public Utilities Fortnightly,* vol. 87, no. 1 (January 7, 1971), pp. 29–38.

8. Olson, Charles E., *Cost Considerations for Efficient Electric Supply.* M.S.U. Public Utilities Studies (East Lansing, Mich.: Institute of Public Utilities, Michigan State University, 1970), ch. 5, "Performance in an Era of Changing Technology," pp. 55–68.

9. Shepherd, William G., and Thomas G. Gies, eds., *Utility Regulation: New Directions*

in Theory and Policy (New York: Random House, 1966). See in particular William G. Shepherd, "Utility Growth and Profits Under Regulation," ch. 1, pp. 3–57.

10. Trebing, Harry M., ed., *Performance Under Regulation.* M.S.U. Public Utilities Studies (East Lansing, Mich.: Institute of Public Utilities, Michigan State University, 1968). See the following articles in particular: William Iulo, "Problems in the Definition and Measurement of Superior Performance," pp. 3–19; William H. Dodge, "Productivity Measures and Performance Evaluation," pp. 20–32; William G. Shepherd, "Comment," pp. 33–35.

22

Ecological and Social Problems of Utilities

One of the basic facts of economics is that all benefits have accompanying costs. Another economic fact is that the effects of change, which may bring about both benefits and costs, are not shared equally by all groups or individuals. Some benefit a great deal from economic progress, but do not pay much more for their benefits than do others who benefit considerably less. This is particularly true where a portion of the costs involved are "social costs."[1]

Some kinds of social costs are a direct result of specific economic activity and change (pollution, for example). Other kinds (inadequate educational opportunities, crime, minority group discrimination, poverty, and the like) are not as directly attributable to any specific economic undertaking but rather have grown out of general public attitudes or "the system" as a whole. Still others (urban traffic congestion, central city decay) may be attributable both to specific economic operations and to society at large.

The responsibilities of business for preventing or correcting various kinds of social costs or social problems have been debated acrimoniously for generations. Some have argued that businesses best serve society by operating as efficiently as possible; that is, that the classical "invisible hand" works best for society in a "profit-maximizing" context. Others have maintained that businesses have much broader public service functions which make them responsible for "curing" many of the long-standing ills of our industrial society.

These two polar positions are so well known that further argument on either side is likely to shed little new light. During recent years, however, an intermediate position has come into prominence. This position is that, at the very least, an economic enterprise or an industry should be responsible for its own social costs and that its practices should not further contribute to the many social problems which may be mainly an outgrowth of past and present public attitudes. It should be noted, too, that this position does not distinguish between private firms, nonregulated or regulated, and publicly owned enterprises.

This relatively new midground viewpoint appears to have strong general public support and does not appear to be a passing fad. It already has caused considerable problems for many utilities, both private and public, and promises to cause many more during the coming generation.[2]

UTILITY-CAUSED ECOLOGICAL PROBLEMS: THE ELECTRIC UTILITY INDUSTRY

Only a few years ago the electric utility industry was praised (and self-praised) as a model of rapid growth, efficiency, and cleanliness. But during the upsurge of the movement to improve our physical environment, during the late 1960's and early 1970's, this industry became one of the most severely criticized of the utilities. Other utilities were criticized also, but the electric industry's problems and prospects illustrate clearly many of the problems faced by most other kinds of utilities.

To place the electric utility industry's problems in proper perspective we must realize that the public has grown accustomed to, and expects, a large quantity and a wide variety of high-quality electric services at reasonable rates. Even small deteriorations in services or small rate increases normally bring large public outcries and complaints to regulatory authorities (or criticisms of public officials if the utility concerned is publicly owned). Further, the consumption of electric services in this country has been doubling each decade for some time now, and even conservative estimates predict continued rapid growth in demand for electricity during the next generation. But all of the current practical methods of producing electricity on a large scale have been attacked on ecological grounds.

At present, and for the immediately foreseeable future, there are only three principal ways of producing large volumes of electricity: water power, fossil fuels, and nuclear fission. Each of these has ecological and other weaknesses.

HYDRO POWER

Perhaps hydroelectric generation has been the least controversial method from an ecological standpoint. But many areas of the country are remote from usable bodies of flowing water, and even in those areas well blessed with flowing streams all of the choice (and many not-so-choice) hydroelectric sites are already in use. Both in the Tennessee Valley and the Pacific Northwest, most additional capacity for some time has come from nonwater sources.

In addition, groups concerned with protecting our physical environment point out many ecological disadvantages of hydroelectric dams. Natural stream flows and water temperatures are changed. Nitrogen supersaturation of water occurs below high dams. Some species of fish life and other wildlife are wiped out or are adversely affected. Historic and scenic spots, and sometimes valuable agricultural lands, are covered with water. Local climates may be affected. All in all, given the small number and poor quality of remaining unused hydroelectric sites, and taking into account ecological criticisms, we cannot expect to obtain any substantial future amount of our electricity needs from water power.

FOSSIL FUEL GENERATION

Fossil fuels (coal, oil, natural gas), although they are nonrenewable resources with absolutely fixed supplies, could power steam generators for electricity production for many generations. New supplies no doubt will be found, and better techniques for utilizing lower-quality fuels will be developed. But the fact remains that we have, and will continue to have, an economic scarcity of fossil fuels. Exploration and exploitation of new supplies, the development of new utilization methods, and the use of low-quality fuels are costly. But overcoming the pollution problems inherent in the use of fossil fuels may prove to be even more costly.

Present-day steam generation of electricity by fossil fuel powered generators discharges large quantities of noxious or unpleasant gases and solid materials into the atmosphere. These discharges (mixed with less harmful or less unpleasant materials) are very visible. A few decades ago most communities looked upon belching smokestacks as signs of progress. Today many of the same communities will not tolerate such plants or will endure them only under vociferous protest. The "good economic citizen" of previous decades is now an outcast. His product is wanted, but not his production facilities.

One proposed solution to the problem of pollution caused by fossil fueled generating plants is to locate them away from population centers. But where? It is difficult to find a place where some group will not complain of excessive pollution, and certainly not all existing steam plants can be moved away from population centers. Even if isolation of such plants were possible, the same amount of pollution would be discharged into the earth's atmosphere. Furthermore, the costs of transmitting electricity from remote areas to consuming areas would be very high. Clearly, except in rare cases, isolation of fossil fuel plants is not a practical solution.

Proper use of certain kinds of technological processes (filtering, scrubbing, and the like) can considerably reduce both the gaseous and solid emissions of fossil fuels. This technology still is in the experimental or developmental stage, however. None of it is perfect, and all of it is costly. Future plants can and will be built with relatively efficient pollution control devices and processes—at least efficient as compared to present controls—but it will be very expensive, and in some cases perhaps impossible, to convert the existing older plants to these processes. In any case, such devices seem to be the best present hope for reducing this source of air pollution.

NUCLEAR POWER

For some two decades after World War II, the "peaceful atom" generally was regarded as the future hope of our energy-short world and the heir-apparent of cruder methods of producing electricity. There were a few doubters, of course, particularly on the grounds of costs and safety. But most people apparently trusted scientists, engineers, and the United States Atomic Energy Commission (A.E.C.) to solve all the problems of nuclear fission and thus make possible an abundance of low-cost electric energy whenever and wherever needed.

Today that dream has paled. The A.E.C.'s safety standards have been fiercely attacked, by both ecological groups and reputable scientists. Although no serious nuclear fission accidents have occurred, many people do not feel safe near a nuclear fission plant. It does not seem likely that many such plants will be built near densely inhabited places, where demands for electricity are greatest. This means that power transmission costs will be increased.

In addition, it is now generally recognized that nuclear fission plants do pollute, even though their pollution is not as readily visible as that of fossil fuel plants. Under normal operating conditions some low-level radiation is given off. The effects of this, both on the present population and on future generations (through possible genetic changes), are disputed. Even scientists disagree about this. Some maintain that no dangers exist, others believe that significant dangers exist, while some admit the possibility of some dangers but argue that the potential gains more than offset the potential risks. Laymen cannot be blamed for having doubts.

Recent findings show that low-level radioactivity frequently becomes highly concentrated as it passes upward through the food chain. For example, minute water animals become slightly radioactive. They are eaten in large numbers by small fish, who become even more radioactive. The small fish, in turn, are eaten by larger fish, who eventually become too poisonous to be used as food by man. The full extent and possible dangers of these biological processes are not yet known, but many biologists fear their consequences.

There is also the very real problem of disposing of radioactive wastes. These materials, some of them deadly, must be transported to permanent central storage spaces. However elaborate the precautions, there is always the possibility of an accident during transportation. Further, once stored, some of these materials will remain deadly for hundreds or even thousands of years.

What happens if earthquakes or other natural phenomena, or perhaps inadequate containers, allow these materials to escape five years, fifty years, or five hundred years from now? Will they leak into soil, air, and underground water, thus poisoning large areas and large numbers of unsuspecting people? How can we guarantee that these radioactive cemeteries will be forever maintained? What will such perpetual maintenance cost, and who will pay for it? At our present stage of knowledge, will large-scale production of low-cost electricity by nuclear fission leave our descendants, for untold generations, a heritage of horror? These and similar questions must be answered soon.

Some of the by-products of nuclear fission plants are more readily apparent to laymen. Cooling towers and pools may create or add to fog conditions near plants. The discharge of warm water into streams may raise stream temperatures enough to harm some kinds of fish life or otherwise upset delicate ecological balances. These are not serious long-run problems—at least they can be handled or minimized (at a cost)—but they cannot be neglected in the overall picture.

It is clear that our romance with the atom is over. Some nuclear fission generating plants have been in use for several years, others are under construction, and many, in various parts of the country, are being planned. Almost everyone agrees that a sizable part of the nation's electricity supplies during the coming generation will come from nuclear fission sources. But a large, vocal, and growing number of people are insisting on ecological safeguards which will increase production costs considerably above former target levels.

OTHER PRODUCTION METHODS

There are various other methods of producing electricity on a small scale. These include such exotic devices and techniques as solar batteries, chemical fuel cells, ocean tides, and geothermal sources. These techniques, though, are still experimental. Some or all of these methods eventually may furnish substantial amounts of electricity, without pollution, at least in some areas. But no immediate breakthroughs are visible on the horizon.

Considerable experimental work is being done to develop a nuclear fusion process for producing electricity (that is, using the hydrogen bomb technique rather than the atomic bomb technique used in nuclear fission). But the fusion process of producing electricity still is beyond the reach of science, even in experimental laboratories. Scientists close to this problem predict that fusion may be controllable under practical commercial conditions by the end of the century. These predictions, of course, are only educated guesses—the process may be developed much sooner, much later, or never.

The nuclear fusion process supposedly will be free of the radiation hazards of the fission process. Also, an almost limitless supply of readily available fuel is at hand for nuclear fusion, contrary to the situation with fission. Thus, if and when nuclear fusion is perfected, mankind may for the first time have an abundance of pollution-free and relatively low-cost electric energy at its disposal.

Meantime, it appears that our rapidly increasing demands for electric energy for a good many years into the future must be met from fossil fuel and nuclear fission sources. This inevitably will be accompanied by some pollution. But it appears that society's interest in the ecology will remain sufficiently strong so that pollution minimizing devices and techniques will be used. This will make the production and transmission costs of electricity higher than they would be if present processes were to be continued. Actually, we will be trading off some of the benefits of lower-cost electricity for the benefits of a less polluted physical environment. This is a legitimate social choice.

OTHER UTILITY ECOLOGICAL PROBLEMS

The kinds of ecological problems discussed in the previous sections at best affect our comfort and at worst affect our health or perhaps even our continued existence as a species. In addition, though, various kinds of private and publicly owned utilities, like other businesses, are criticized for still other kinds of practices or omissions related to our physical environment.

Visual pollution, for example, is almost as offensive to some people as the more harmful air or water pollution. This includes such things as poles, overhead wires and cables, and unsightly and unscreened buildings or service facilities. These installations do not actually harm anyone physically, but they do detract from the beauty of an area. Utilities are finding that the public's aesthetic tastes cannot be ignored. More and more communities, for example, are requiring that cables and wires be placed underground and that towers, substations, and the like be adequately and pleasingly camouflaged.[3] This, of course, increases the costs of providing utility services.

There is even a strong and growing feeling among portions of the public that some utilities have a positive duty to provide some kinds of public recreational facilities. For example, boating, picnicking, or camping facilities may be expected from hydroelectric utilities or city water utilities in conjunction with their reservoirs. These kinds of facilities are not as expensive as some of the other kinds of ecological demands, and the pressures for them are not as strong as other pressures, but they must be taken into account by utility managers.

Since utilities do not have the resources to do everything that everyone wishes to protect or improve the ecological environment, priorities must be established. Clearly, it would seem, matters affecting the public's safety, health, and comfort, in that order, should come first, followed by those things related to the public's aesthetic tastes. But none of these things can be measured and ranked precisely. Reasonable people may, and do, disagree upon the relative extent of the harmfulness of various kinds of pollution and upon the desirability of various kinds of beautification or recreational facilities. Public officials and private managers responsible for allocating utility expenditures must exercise good judgment, but they must also remain closely in touch with public preferences.

It seems clear, too, that it is less costly to prevent ecological problems than to correct them after they occur. In view of the widespread public interest in protecting our physical environment, it is unlikely that future utility installations will be built which do not conform to higher ecological standards than those prevailing in the past. Improving past installations to meet current or future standards, though, is another matter. Utility plants typically have long lives, and it is very expensive to modify them significantly after their original construction.

Realistically, this means that perhaps all that can be expected of utilities is that they do not cause further deterioration in our physical environment and that gradually, as old facilities are phased out and replaced by new, ecological improvements will occur. Nor can we expect this process to be inexpensive. Utility managers will be severely tested in raising and allocating the funds necessary to meet society's demands for abundant and high-quality utility services at reasonable rates.

PUBLIC UTILITIES AND GENERAL SOCIAL GOALS

As pointed out before, the responsibilities of business in solving general social problems—that is, those problems which adversely affect society as a whole but which cannot be attributed to any particular undertaking or industry—still are debatable, especially in the case of utility undertakings.

On the one hand, utilities have been singled out as bearing particular social responsibilities. Many utilities are publicly owned. If privately owned, they operate in an institutional environment differing from that of other private businesses. They usually have some special privileges but also many special social responsibilities.

On the other hand, it can be pointed out that society has particularly charged utilities with providing adequate utility services at reasonable prices. This being so, it may be argued that anything interfering with this special charge conflicts with long-established social goals for utilities. The question, then, becomes whether or not the public wants the newer social goals to override the older goals. Unfortunately, it appears that the public wants both goals, even though they conflict.

There is no doubt that a substantial portion of the public expects utilities, like other private businesses and publicly owned economic organizations, to aid materially in correcting many perceived social problems. These problems include racial and sexual employment discrimination, inadequate educational opportunities, hard-core unemployment, poverty, slum housing conditions, central city decay, and the like.

Further, there is no doubt that the ultimate solutions demanded for most of these kinds of problems will be economic solutions; that is, to the extent that they are to be "solved," they will be solved by business or business-type organizations. It is clear, also, that significant programs to alleviate many of these general social problems will increase production costs.

This creates problems for utilities. Many of the same people who expect businesses to bear a major portion of the costs of solving general social problems, along with others, protest vigorously when utility rates are increased or when services deteriorate. Utility managers are caught between the Scylla of social reform expenditures and the Charybdis of regulatory constraints. Extreme skill in navigation is essential. If costs rise significantly without corresponding rate increases, services will deteriorate. But the same public which demands cost increases may insist, through regulatory officials, that rates not be increased and that service quantity and quality be maintained.

In summary, nonutility enterprises can respond more easily to legal and public opinion pressures for costly social reform programs than can utilities. Any necessary price adjustments or service adjustments of nonregulated firms are limited only by demand and competitive market forces (and competitors generally will be facing the same kinds of situations). But utilities have to consider, in addition, the time-consuming and uncertain regulatory process if privately owned, or the uncertainties of political control if publicly owned.

PAYING FOR ECOLOGICAL AND SOCIAL BENEFITS

During the past few years several federal laws and numerous state, regional, and local laws, each with various kinds of authorities and often with overlapping jurisdictions, have been enacted to combat or prevent pollution. In some cases, at least forty different kinds of permits are required to construct an electric utility generating plant. The sheer volume of paperwork and other required formalities alone in such a project is costly both in time and money. Installation and operational requirements to meet legal minimums are even more costly. In addition, public pressures often insist on pollution standards higher than the legally required minimums.

Also, during the past several years a number of federal and state laws, court decisions, and less direct but nonetheless strong pressures, have made business enterprises, including privately owned and publicly owned utilities, into instruments of social reform. This is particularly true in hiring and other personnel matters. Sometimes a portion of the costs involved in such projects (for example, training programs for the hard-core unemployed) are borne by government agencies using general tax revenues. In other situations, all of the costs fall upon the enterprise involved.

It would be difficult to argue that economic enterprises, including utilities, should not bear the costs of preventing socially undesirable pollution which they otherwise would cause. There are wide differences of opinion, of course, concerning how much pollution is tolerable or how much should be paid to prevent a certain amount of pollution. This is simply a trade-off problem, and the decisions will be made by the general public rather than by utility management.

It is incumbent upon utility management, though, to inform the public fully concerning the various choices—that is, What are the monetary costs involved in meeting various levels of antipollution standards? An informed public, no doubt, will make better decisions than an uninformed and highly emotional public.

It is more difficult to argue convincingly that utilities, as an industry group, should be expected to expend large sums in attempts to correct social injustices which they, as an industry, did not create. This, in effect, is a form of taxation and income redistribution, borne by a particular group (utility stockholders or consumers of utility services, or both) rather than borne by society as a whole. Such a burden on a particular group is completely unrelated to causes of the problem, benefits received from its solution, and the ability to pay. In other words, it upsets most of the principles commonly associated with "good" taxation.

Nevertheless, just as in the pollution situation, it is a fact that utilities have been and will be required to meet the costs of certain kinds of legally imposed social welfare standards, particularly in personnel matters. Also, just as in the pollution matter, there are and will be pressures for actions and costs even above the legally required standards. Again, this is a choice of society which the utilities cannot avoid and should not attempt to evade. But again, society should be well informed concerning the alternatives and the effects of various kinds of choices.

Given the fact that utilities in the future will have to spend considerably more on pollution prevention and the correction of social injustices than they have in the past, the question arises as to who will actually pay these costs.

Initially, in the case of privately owned utilities, until regulators allow such expenditures to be reflected in increased rates, these additional costs will be paid by stockholders in the form of lower profits. (Taxpayers in general would bear the costs in the case of publicly owned utilities.) But this cannot be expected to endure for long. Since the profits of regulated utilities are supposedly already limited to the amounts necessary for providing adequate services, the final results are clear: Lower profits ultimately will lead to a deterioration in services. Conversely, the maintenance of profits in the face of higher costs will require higher utility rates.

Thus, in the long run, in most cases, it is clear that the additional utility costs of ecological protection and social reform will be paid by the consumers of utility services, through fewer services or higher rates, or both. The general public should be made aware of this. Then, to the extent that the public wants such protection and reform, regulatory authorities should conform promptly in services and rate adjustment complaints and petitions. The piper must be paid. There is no other way.

SUMMARY

During the past few years vocal portions of the general public have demanded protection of the physical environment and the solution of long-standing general social problems. Many of these demands have already been enacted into law, at all government levels, and it is likely that many more such enactments will be made. These laws and public pressures are rapidly altering the institutional environments and increasing the costs of both private and publicly owned utilities—and the end is not in sight.

The economic problems created for utilities by this changing institutional environment cannot be ignored or escaped. The public, rightly, is the master. But the public is interested in results and is not concerned with solving the economic problems created in attaining results. The solving of economic problems is a managerial function.

The development and utilization of advanced science and technology, in addition to ecological benefits, also may aid utility management in reducing the magnitude of its economic problems. But this cannot be a complete answer. Even the most efficient use of new scientific and technological innovations, plus the research and experimentation required for producing these innovations, will be costly. Management, to do its job effectively, must succeed in closing the present communications gap between utilities on the one side and the general public (including utility customers) and regulatory authorities on the other.

The general public and the regulators must be convinced of the truth that there can be no gains without costs and that all costs cannot be borne by nebulous "fat cat" utility stockholders; that is, the public must pay for what it wants. This will not be an easy task, but it must be accomplished. Then utilities, like other organizations, must comply with informed public decisions. This is the American way.

The public may make mistakes, but an informed public is less likely to make mistakes than an uninformed one. Our American way certainly does not prevent economic mistakes, but it has advantages which most of us feel far more than compensate for its disadvantages.

NOTES

1. The term "social costs," as used here, refers to the harmful effects upon the public at large or upon some substantial portion of the public because of malfunctions in the physical or institutional environments.
2. The literature in the area of business responsibility for ecological and social reform is becoming voluminous. A highly selected, readily accessible, but very small sample, with particular

reference to utilities, is listed in the "Additional Readings" for this chapter. These citations are suggestions only and do not purport to give broad coverage of what is available in the field.

3. Maryland, in 1971, became the first state to require that all electric and telephone lines for new houses, apartments, and mobile homes be installed underground.

ADDITIONAL READINGS

1. Bjornson, Bjorn, "The Challenge of Environmental Changes," *Public Utilities Fortnightly,* vol. 86, no. 4 (August 13, 1970), pp. 13–18.
2. Committee for Economic Development, *Social Responsibilities of Business Corporations* (New York: Research and Policy Committee, Committee for Economic Development, 1971), pp. 7–74.
3. Cook, Franklin H., "Does a Public Utility Have a Public Responsibility?" *Public Utilities Fortnightly,* vol. 82, no. 2 (July 18, 1968), pp. 30–33.
4. Davenport, John, "Industry Starts the Big Cleanup," *Fortune,* vol. 81, no. 2 (February 1970), pp. 114–117 and 174–178.
5. Hartman, R. M., "Environmental Reports and New Power Plant Schedules," *Public Utilities Fortnightly,* vol. 88, no. 2 (July 22, 1971), pp. 13–22.
6. Holcomb, Robert H., "Power Generation: The Next Thirty Years," *Science,* vol. 167, no. 3915 (January 9, 1970), pp. 159–160.
7. Hughes, William R., and Franklin M. Fisher, "Would Increasing Residential Electric Rates Help Preserve Environmental Quality?" *Public Utilities Fortnightly,* vol. 87, no. 7 (April 1, 1971), pp. 3–12.
8. Journey, Drexel D., "Beautification, Recreation, and the Utilities," *Public Utilities Fortnightly,* vol. 80, no. 5 (August 31, 1967), pp. 27–30.
9. Kavanagh, Preston B., "The New Environmental Ball Game," *Public Utilities Fortnightly,* vol. 86, no. 6 (September 10, 1970), pp. 25–30.
10. Monaghan, John R., "1970's–The Decade of the Environment," *Public Utilities Fortnightly,* vol. 85, no. 3 (January 29, 1970), pp. 36–39.
11. Samuels, Warren J., "Public Utilities and Social Problems," *Public Utilities Fortnightly,* vol. 84, no. 3 (July 31, 1969), pp. 15–21.
12. Slesinger, Reuben E., "Regulatory Adaptation to Environmental Changes," *Public Utilities Fortnightly,* vol. 82, no. 5 (August 29, 1968), pp. 19–28.
13. Trebing, Harry M., ed., *Essays on Public Utility Pricing and Regulation.* M.S.U. Public Utilities Studies (East Lansing, Mich.: Institute of Public Utilities, Michigan State University, 1971), particularly Warren J. Samuels, "Externalities, Rate Structure, and the Theory of Public Utility Regulation," pp. 357–403, with "Comments" by Joel B. Dirlam and John F. Roberts, Jr.
14. U. S. Congress. Joint Committee on Atomic Energy. *Environmental Effects of Producing Electric Power,* Part 1 and Part 2, vols. I and II. Hearings Before the Joint Committee on Atomic Energy, 91st Congress, 1st Session (October 28–31 and November 4–7, 1969) and 2d Session (January 27–29 and February 24–26, 1970).
15. Ways, Max, "How to Think About the Environment," *Fortune,* vol. 81, no. 2 (February 1970), pp. 98–101 and 159–166.

23

The Road Ahead

Public utilities, as we know them today in our society, are largely outgrowths of urbanization and specialization. As people have congregated into densely populated areas, and as they have become more interdependent economically, they have relied more and more upon specialists to produce the utility services which each household produced for itself in a simpler age. As technology has advanced, utility services have become mass-produced, as have automobiles, shoes, and most other items of everyday use. This trend toward urban concentration, economic specialization and interdependence, and mass production using an advanced technology continues in full swing.

The history of public utility regulation, management, and ownership in this country is filled with the evolution of ideas and concepts, struggles to develop, regulatory and ownership controversy, technological advance, and maturing management principles. All of this has led to our present generally high levels of utility performance and our current high public expectations of service.

In spite of our accomplishments, however, many questions remain. What of the future? In particular, What is likely to develop in the important areas of utility growth, management and ownership, regulation, and technology during the coming generation?

We have no infallible crystal ball. We do have opinions, though, based upon our considerable studies of past developments and present trends. Based upon these opinions, and certainly with full realization of their limitations, we are willing to set forth some of our speculative views on the immediate future.

FUTURE UTILITY GROWTH

We can see no significant decrease in the growth of the utility services. Rather, it is highly probable that more and more uses for electric power, natural gas, and telecommunication services will be found. It is possible that natural gas use may tend more toward chemical conversions. Natural gas is now a raw material for many types of plastics and synthetics. It is conceivable that it will be used more extensively as an industrial input and less extensively as a fuel. This may be particularly accelerated if the price of natural gas is allowed to rise.

Ecological and aesthetic issues will be "solved" during the next several years. This current problem will diminish in importance as social cost considerations become an accepted part of utility planning. This development may mean that certain applications, such as the use of liquefied natural gas as fuel for vehicles, will become common to combat the automobile air pollution problem and that nuclear power production will become common to combat the air pollution of power production. Distribution systems routinely will be placed underground, and visual pollution will slowly cease as old lines are replaced. It may even be possible for power transmission systems to go underground, and present microwave techniques and future communication satellites may signal the end of the telephone pole.

Progress and growth in water utilities and street transit will be much slower; indeed, transit may continue to decline. In electric power, natural gas, and telecommunications utilities, future growth will seriously challenge the ingenuity of management and cause many short-term problems, but these will be regularly solved after experimentation and perhaps some controversy.

FUTURE UTILITY MANAGEMENT AND OWNERSHIP

Utility management, both private and public, will evidence more "social responsibility" and "corporate statesmanship." The public service philosophy will continue to grow and manifest itself in more enlightened managerial decisions. We suggest that the major future problem of management will concern finance; that is, how to raise the tremendous amounts of capital necessary to meet the growth of demand for services.

One obvious prediction for management is the increased use of computers and electronic data processing. In this area, utilities have not progressed as far as some other sectors of the economy and a good bit of catching up is necessary. It is conceivable that all meters for electricity, gas, and water will be read electronically and that all billing may be done automatically by computers. Much of the technology for this already exists.

Utility management education perhaps will put less emphasis on engineering and more emphasis on liberal arts, business administration, and economics. The role of the utility engineer will remain important, of course, but we suggest that the top decision-makers of the future will require a somewhat more general background of education and experience.

While controversy in some geographic areas will continue, by and large the ownership issue will be of less importance. The cooperative stage already has signaled more acceptance of a mixed ownership in utilities, with active cooperation between ownership types. We suggest that there will be little increase in public ownership, but that the mixed-ownership system will remain a permanent utility characteristic. Active and cooperative acceptance of public ownership, plus reform and modifications in regulation, will make this issue of little importance in the future.

FUTURE UTILITY REGULATION

We suggest that the utilities will continue to be regulated. That is not to say that future regulation will be exactly like the present. Indeed, we foresee considerable modification and reform of regulation, but not its abolition.

More cooperation between utility ownership patterns, more social responsibility on the part of management, the tremendous problem of serving future growth in demand, plus technological advances, all lead us to see a continuation of regulation but in a modified form. It is probable that more competition will be allowed between utility firms, at least in certain areas. We can foresee, for instance, the time when the American Telephone & Telegraph Company operates in two markets; one regulated and one unregulated and competitive. The regulated market might well be the basic residential service area, while the competitive area might well be the microwave communications market between cities or the industrial communications market. So, too, with electric power and natural gas. In some areas, such as industrial and commercial markets, competition may well be allowed and fostered. In the basic residential market area, though, regulation will continue.

There probably will continue to be basic questioning of the institutional framework of regulation. Some modifications to promote efficiency may be devised. Certain regulatory devices, some of which are based on a past era (such as the stringent control of intercorporate relations), may be abandoned. The questioning and reexamination of regulatory institutions is a worthwhile undertaking and should be encouraged. Certainly, technological advances will call for continuing reexamination of regulation.

FUTURE UTILITY TECHNOLOGY

We are not engineers or physical scientists; thus our crystal ball becomes very cloudy at this point. However, as social scientists and observers of the utility scene, we continue to have faith in technological advance and suggest that perhaps the biggest changes of all will come in future technology. The exact nature of these changes is hazy at best, but the effects may be tremendous.

Changes in fuel technology undoubtedly will come. Without question, nuclear fission will play an increasing role in supplying future power requirements. Ecological considerations of air pollution are presently accelerating this trend, and the Atomic Energy Commission estimates that by 1980 some 30 to 35 per cent of domestic electric capacity (120 to 170 million kilowatts) will come from nuclear fission. The problems of thermal pollution and disposition of radioactive wastes remain. However, we anticipate these will either be solved or will push development into one of the other fuel applications.

Experimentation with fast breeder reactors is presently being accelerated. The big advantage of this is the conservation of natural energy resources and the reduction of radioactive wastes. Both liquid metal-cooled and gas-cooled fast breeder reactors are possible. Both applications hold prospect for recovery of up to 75 per cent of the energy contained in naturally occurring uranium, as compared to the use of less than 1 per cent in present applications. Instead of radioactive wastes, the reactor creates more fuel for additional use.

Fusion reactors could go a long way toward solving the thermal pollution problem as well as preserving natural resources. This process generates energy by joining rather than by splitting atomic nuclei. Deuterium and tritium, isotopes of hydrogen, which are used as fuel, are in abundant supply and occur in water. It is estimated that one gallon of seawater could yield enough deuterium to provide energy equivalent to the combustion of three hundred gallons of gasoline. Theoretically, the thermal discharge would be from 50 to 75 per cent lower than present nuclear fission plants.

Other techniques also may be possible. Magnetohydrodynamics, or MHD, could be used as a supplemental source of power. This process creates electric current by passing hot, ionized gas or liquid metal through a magnetic field. Thermionic generation, utilizing a phenomenon discovered by Thomas A. Edison in 1878, is a possibility. By heating metal sufficiently, electrons boil off as the point is reached where the metal acquires enough energy to overcome retarding forces at its surface, and direct current electricity is produced. Thermoelectric generation using the Seebeck principle, discovered a century ago, products low voltages of direct current when heat is applied to two joined dissimilar conductors.

Fuel cells may come into wider use. These battery-like devices use a continuous flow of gas as a fuel to provide a chemical reaction which induces low-voltage direct current. The best-known application of this technology was in United States space missions, where fuel cells had platinum electrodes and hydrogen was the fuel which reacted with oxygen to produce electricity and water as by-products.

In some areas geothermal generation is a possiblilty. Natural steam or hot water entrapped below the surface of the earth's crust is released by drilling and piped into generating facilities. The development of deep drilling techniques may make this energy source available in many areas. Geothermal power is currently produced in several parts of Europe and in California from natural geysers. Solar energy may also be used in some areas in the future. Tidal power, developed in France, might come into limited use if some technological problems can be solved and if the price of power rises enough.

In natural gas technology the possibility exists of gasification and liquefaction of our abundant coal supply. Existing supplies of coal in the United States are sufficient to supply energy for the next two hundred to four hundred years. During gasification or liquefaction, sulfur and other pollutants are removed, making the resulting fuel highly desirable from an ecological viewpoint. Use of nuclear explosions to increase gas-well capacity and to create underground gas supplies in present low-yielding gas areas has already taken place on an experimental basis in "Operation Gasbuggy."

Natural gas is also being liquefied and transported over long distances. Improvements in cryogenic technology in order to hold liquefied natural gas, or LNG, at low temperatures will mean that sources such as North Africa, Venezuela, Arabia, and

Indonesia may become regular large-scale suppliers of the United States market. Since LNG occupies such a small volume as compared to natural gas, it is possible that long-distance overland pipelines might adopt this technique.

Cryogenic technology also may be applied to electric power transmission. By use of low temperatures, transmission losses are drastically curtailed. But perhaps the most promising advantage of low-temperature power transmission is the fact that electron resistance is greatly lowered and power transmission consequently may go underground. The Edison Electric Institute has estimated that one third of the total power requirements of New York City could be supplied through a single cryogenic cable inside a pipe of 18-inch diameter.

In communications, picture phones are already in experimental use, more powerful microwave systems have proved technically feasible, and a whole series of communication satellites may be just around the corner. More sophisticated data processing communication systems, with automatic systems using present computer technology, are possible. The use of the laser beam for communications is already proved and soon may be widely used.

Many other technological wonders lie within the realm of possibility and even probability. The limiting factor in most cases is not science or technology but economics. Tremendous amounts of capital are necessary to institute most new technologies, and the economic and management question of whether or not an innovative technology will pay must determine whether or not it is used.

And thus we end our cloudy glimpse into the future on a note that has been emphasized constantly from the beginning of this book: economics is the key to the study and understanding, and to the actual development, of public utilities.

Index of Names

Index of Cases

Index of Subjects

UNIVERSITY OF BRISTOL LIBRARY
W.M.L.

BCDEFGHIJ–H–79876543

74 16606